Creative Resources for the Anti-Bias Classroom

Creative Resources for the Anti-Bias Classroom

by

Nadia Saderman Hall

Delmar Publishers

I(T)P® an International Thomson Publishing company

Albany • Bonn • Boston • Cincinnati • Detroit • London • Madrid
Melbourne • Mexico City • New York • Pacific Grove • Paris • San Francisco
Singapore • Tokyo • Toronto • Washington

NOTICE TO THE READER

Publisher does not warrant or guarantee any of the products described herein or perform any independent analysis in connection with any of the product information contained herein. Publisher does not assume, and expressly disclaims, any obligation to obtain and include information other than that provided to it by the manufacturer.

The reader is expressly warned to consider and adopt all safety precautions that might be indicated by the activities herein and to avoid all potential hazards. By following the instructions contained herein, the reader willingly assumes all risks in connection with such instructions.

The publisher makes no representation or warranties of any kind, including but not limited to, the warranties of fitness for particular purpose or merchantability, nor are any such representations implied with respect to the material set forth herein, and the publisher takes no responsibility with respect to such material. The publisher shall not be liable for any special, consequential, or exemplary damages resulting, in whole or part, from the readers' use of, or reliance upon, this material.

Cover design: Publisher's Studio

Delmar Staff
Publisher: William Brottmiller
Administrative Editor: Jay Whitney
Associate Editor: Erin O'Connor Traylor
Project Editor: Karen Leet
Production Coordinator: Sandra Woods
Art and Design Coordinator: Carol Keohane
Editorial Assistant: Mara Berman

Printed in the United States of America

For more information, contact:

Delmar Publishers
3 Columbia Circle, Box 15015
Albany, New York 12212-5015

International Thomson Publishing—
Europe
Berkshire House
168-173 High Holborn
London, WC1V 7AA
England

Thomas Nelson Australia
102 Dodds Street
South Melbourne 3205
Victoria, Australia

Nelson Canada
1120 Birchmount Road
Scarborough, Ontario
Canada, M1K 5G4

International Thomson Editores
Campos Eliseos 385, Piso 7
Col Polanco
11560 Mexico D F Mexico

International Thomson Publishing
GmbH
Kongiswinterer Strasse 418
53227 Bonn
Germany

International Thomson Publishing—
Asia
60 Albert Street
#15-01 Albert Complex
Singapore 189969

International Thomson Publishing—
Japan
Hirakawacho Kyowa Building, 3F
2-2-1 Hirakawacho
Chiyoda-ku, Tokyo 102
Japan

1 2 3 4 5 6 7 8 9 10 XXX 03 02 01 00 99 98

Library of Congress Cataloging-in-Publication Data

Hall, Nadia Saderman.
Creative resources for the anti-bias classroom / by Nadia Saderman Hall
p. cm.
Includes bibliographical references and index.
ISBN 0-8273-8015-1
1. Early childhood education—Curricula. 2. Early childhood education—Activity programs. 3. Education, Elementary—Curricula. 4. Education, Elementary—Activity programs. 5. Curriculum planning. 6. Toleration—Study and teaching. 7. Social interaction—Study and teaching. I. Title.
LB1139.4.H35 1998
372.19—dc21 97-38958
CIP

To my parents and Michael,
and my children, Becka and Alec,
Roots and Blossoms.

Table of Contents

Preface

This book was written in response to the need of child care and educational communities for a resource book dedicated to anti-bias programming. While there are many excellent resources for preschool and elementary school children, no single text exists that covers the entire age range from infancy to age 11. The author acknowledges the serious deficit inherent to this hands-on "cookbook" approach to planning. To offset this weakness, *Creative Resources for the Anti-Bias Classroom:*

1. offers experiences that are developmentally grounded and respond to the wide differences in the developmental continuum of children's learning and growing; and
2. asks students and teachers to evaluate the purpose of these experiences and how their children are developing in relation to the larger issue of anti-bias education.

It is also the author's assumption that students using this text have been exposed to child development courses and curriculum/methodology theories.

The fundamental goal of this text is to provide a balance of activities that demonstrate how all aspects of curriculum planning can be infused with the anti-bias approach. Books have been selected as the primary vehicle to construct curriculum webs and to design many of the anti-bias activities. The author believes that books are pivotal in designing integrated programs while promoting literacy skills from the earliest age possible. The wealth of children's literature today dealing with such topics as interracial families, same-sex families, homeless families, refugee and immigrant families, families with special needs children, etc., is an untapped source of ideas that needs to be explored with children. To ignore these books would be an abrogation of our responsibility as teachers, which is to assist children to view their physical and social world through the prism of human diversity.

The activities in this book have been designed to make the *extraordinary* feel *ordinary* over the course of a young child's life. The activities reflect a progression from simple exposure to the different facets of diversity to working through meaningful and relevant experiences that foster a deeper understanding of human similarities and differences. Practitioners should monitor responses to activities that are meant to sensitize children's awareness of differences as indicators for future program planning.

As with any activity resource book, the author encourages flexibility and personal creativity to ensure that your individual and group needs are met. To keep the anti-bias spirit alive and flourishing in your classroom, the appendix includes reproducible forms to track needs and resources specific to your group and community.

Finally, a note about political correctness. I have discovered that the terms for various groups in today's society differ considerably between Canada and the United States. Terms are not interchangeable and some have very different implications; therefore some compromises have been made. The terms *Native Americans* and *Canadians* have been selected over *Indians.* Children with special needs are commonly referred to as physically or cognitively challenged. I find this term limiting because it focuses only on the child's physical disability and does not acknowledge other strengths. For this reason the term *differently abled* has been chosen, which I feel is more positive. It has been applied in instances where children are asked to think about or experience what it might be like to be nonverbal, have visual or hearing impairments, or have difficulty with motor planning and organization. I hope readers take no offense and remember that the guiding spirit of this book is inclusion.

About the Author

Nadia Saderman Hall began her professional career as an infant therapist in a home intervention program. Her love of infants led her to create and codirect the Infant-Parent Learning Program, which assisted new parents to understand developmental issues. Her primary focus in curriculum design and program development has always been infant mental health. As the manager of early childhood training programs at the Canadian Mothercraft Society, she developed a post-diploma specialization in Infancy for Early Childhood Education (ECE) practitioners. In collaboration with Native Child and Family Services, Toronto, she created culturally specific child protection training to support children and families in the city's native community. The Anti-Bias Post-Diploma course was developed with her former co-author Valerie Rhomberg in response to her participation on Metro Toronto's Anti-Racist Education in Child Care Committee. With Ministry of Citizenship funding, she coordinated and wrote an ECE vocational language course for foreign-trained early childhood practitioners that assisted immigrant women to complete equivalency teaching requirements. *The Affective Curriculum: Teaching the Anti-Bias Approach to Young Children,* the first text on this subject co-authored with Valerie Rhomberg, was written in response to the ECE community's request for more in-depth examination of anti-bias education and the implications for program design.

Ms. Saderman Hall has taught curriculum and child development courses for over 12 years and delivered many workshops and addresses all over Canada, the United States, and New Zealand. Her recent year abroad in New Zealand, with extensive travel throughout Southeast Asia, has enriched her understanding of human diversity.

Nadia holds an M.A. from the University of Toronto; an M.Ed. from the Ontario Institute of Education, University of Toronto; a Teacher's Certificate, Primary Specialist, and Diploma of Child Study from the University of Toronto.

Acknowledgments

A book of this nature requires continuous creative nourishment. There are many special colleagues, friends, and family members who nourished the spirit and encouraged the weary mind during this process.

This book would have never been written without the inspiration and fundamental ideas of the first text, *The Affective Curriculum: Teaching the Anti-Bias Approach to Young Children,* written with Valerie Rhomberg. Val convinced me there were more ideas and resources to share and gave generously of her time by photographing the many examples of anti-bias materials and children at play.

Val Rhomberg, Wendy Weidman, Debbie Mckenna, Ofelia Nema, and Carol Stephenson were invaluable during the initial brainstorming sessions. Val suggested several of the children's books with webbing and activity ideas. Ofelia contributed innovative games and materials that are beautifully designed and capture the spirit of the anti-bias approach. A number of her creations are rendered in the book's photographs. I am grateful to Carol's encouragement to stretch the thinking abilities of primary and junior school-age children. She offered key ideas which inspired the direction of the school-age chapter. Both Debbie's and Wendy's ideas for infant and toddler activities are very much appreciated.

Carol Goldman was indispensable. As always she opened her heart and mind to give me insight into the needs of children who do not communicate verbally. Her staff at Zareinu, especially Cynthia Moylan, shared generously with materials and ideas.

In New Zealand, Ruth Eckford came to the rescue and generously provided the use of her computer.

I am very grateful to Tracey Neidhardt whose talent and ability to translate my ideas into beautiful illustrations rounded out an important dimension of the book.

Thank you to Rudy Rhomberg for all his technical assistance in formatting all the webs and charts, and to Val for inputting all the information. A special thank you goes to the wonderful children and staff at Montrose and Kensington child care centers for the joy of photographing them.

My mother, Lydia, was there for me as always at the crunch, giving of herself, alternately as an editor and a source of inspiration.

Reviewer List
Sheila E. Abramowitz, Orange County Community College, Middletown, NY
Nancy Benz, South Plains College, Lubbock, TX
Jann James, Ed.D., Armstrong Atlantic State University, Savannah, GA
Judith H. Reitsch, Ph.D., Eastern Washington University, Cheney, WA
Delia Robinson Richards, Ed.D., Prince George's Community College, Largo, MD

Foreword

Early Childhood Anti-Bias education is in its toddlerhood. During the eighties, a number of theorists and practitioners such as Louise Derman-Sparks, Carol Brunson Phillips, Patricia Ramsey, and Gyda Chud laid the theoretical foundation. They conceptualized a contextually and developmentally appropriate anti-bias curriculum. In the nineties, Nadia Saderman Hall, Valeria Rhomberg, Julie Bisson, and myself were a few of the new voices added to the choir. I think we attempted to translate some of the theory to teachers and parents, and to share practical ideas for implementing anti-bias education in the early childhood classroom.

So often, people try to pit one curriculum book against the other. I've had teachers say to me, "Oh we use *Roots and Wings* rather than the *Anti-Bias Curriculum.*" And I've had college instructors ask me, "What do you think of the *Affective Curriculum?*" First of all, let me say that I think Nadia and Valerie's first book, the *Affective Curriculum* is great. Second, anti-bias work is not a competition. We need all of the voices at the table. Each of the authors I've mentioned bring a unique, original, and valid perspective to the development and implementation of anti-bias education. While there are some differences in our approaches, there is a great deal of continuity. It is very exciting that there is so much give and take between anti-bias educators in the Commonwealth nations and the United States. I think it's a testimony to each person's commitment to the well-being of children, families, and communities.

To the credit of the leaders in our field, we have managed to "get the word out" about the development of children's identity, the development of prejudice in children, and the impact bias has on children's development. Today, many teachers, administrators, and parents are well aware of the importance of addressing identity and diversity through their curriculum. I refer to the anti-bias movement as a "toddler" because we have a solid foundation, we have a clear set of goals. For the past few years, it seems as though we've been a bit stuck in trying to figure out how to put the goals into practice on a daily basis. Resources like the *Affective Curriculum* gave us many activity ideas. But it has been painfully evident that teachers desperately wanted and needed more. As a college instructor and trainer, the questions I hear the most are, "How do we implement anti-bias education on a daily basis?" "Where can I get activity ideas? Don't you have any other activity books?"

It's exciting to realize that as a field we are moving forward. In terms of Erikson's stages of development, we are showing signs of initiative. Like the preschooler says, "Hey, I've got a good idea." We have a new generation of anti-bias curriculum books that will be gifts in the hands of teachers who are ready to take that next step. *Anti-Bias Resources* will help all of us take the next step. I am so grateful to Nadia for providing activities across the age span. It's wonderful to have a resource that includes infant, toddler, preschool, and school-age activities all in one place. As a teacher with mostly preschool experience, it is so helpful for me to see the whole picture, to gain an understanding of what the possibilities are with infants, toddlers, and school-age children. I can only imagine that *Anti-Bias Resources* will be helpful to preservice as well as seasoned teachers, family child care providers and classroom teachers, parents and administrators.

It takes a lot of courage to write an anti-bias resource book. There is the fear of attacks from people at all points on the political spectrum. There is also the fear that readers will misinterpret and misuse the activities provided. Nadia has taken the risk to share her best thinking and her best practice with us. Before implementing any activity, we must have in our minds a clear picture of ourselves, our children, our families, and our communities. We must be able to answer questions like, Who are our children? What are their abilities? What are their wants and needs? What do our parents want for their children? What are the issues in our community? What are our hopes and dreams for our community? Once we understand our context, we are ready to receive *Anti-Bias Resources* with open arms.

Stacey York
Author of *Roots & Wings: Affirming Culture in Early Childhood Programs*
Redleaf Press

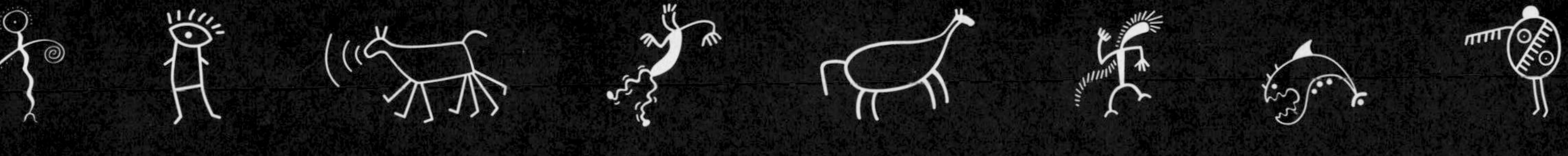

UNIT 1

Introduction

"Children and teachers require learning environments that allow them to hypothesize, investigate, experiment, and construct new understandings of themselves and others with whom they work."

Rebecca New (1994)

"Teachers need time to reflect on themselves with the same intensity and vigor that is given to the study of others. . . . In order to accommodate to new ideas, new values, and new practices, teachers must restructure their own personal knowledge systems and clarify realities obscured by their own personal blind spots."

Barbara Bowman and Frances Stott (1994)

The anti-bias classroom is rooted in the singular belief that children will grow up to be flexible, accepting, open-minded, and nonjudgmental adults if they can live, learn, and play with the rich diversity of the human experience. This approach to education, which spans the development of children from infancy to adolescence, has a clear continuum between its short-term and long-term goals.

Key Developmental Goals and Anti-Bias Goals

In the short term, children will develop an understanding of people—their needs, desires, beliefs, and actions, both in the past and the present. It is through the exploration of everyone's basic necessities of life that children will learn that there are many different ways to meet these needs and that there is no one right way to do things. Having children listen to, share, and discuss the commonalities and differences in their families and ways of life will allow them to affirm and respect, rather than deny and devalue, the diversity that exists in the world.

The long-term goal relates to learning and upholding values of equity, inclusion, and social justice. Once children can view differences in a positive manner, the next logical step is for them to show concern for the welfare of others who are being deprived or treated unfairly because of those differences. The short-term objectives become long-term actions: personal as well as collective responsibility and commitment to work toward making the world a better place for everyone.

Children's ability to be at ease with and to appreciate the differences among themselves and their wider social networks melds with the best practices of early childhood education. Intrinsic to these best practices is the nurturance of key developmental goals that are anti-bias in spirit.

Key Developmental Goals

The development of a strong self-identity and sense of well-being. Emotional well-being is contingent upon whether children's emotional needs for security and dependency are met *responsively,* and whether their bids for self-initiated and self-directed actions are supported. If this happens, children receive the message that they are valued and respected as individuals. If children receive negative feedback about how they look (race, appearance), how they behave (gender, culture), and how they demonstrate competence (ability, age), then it will be extremely difficult for them to feel positive about anyone else.

Respect for oneself and others. When children are acknowledged as unique individuals with similarities and differences in family composition, ethno-racial background, appearance, language, abilities, and life experiences, they learn to respect themselves and others.

Cooperation and conflict negotiation. Pro-social skills, particularly when used to foster respect for differences and challenge stereotyping, are essential to build in the classroom.

Capacity for empathy and standing up for the rights of others. Once children understand how it feels to be different, they become empowered to take action against prejudicial comments and behaviors. Research has documented that the capacity for empathy has its roots in infancy. Young babies respond to the distress of others by crying. Toddlers, who are becoming aware that they are a separate self, actively demonstrate soothing behaviors. Preschoolers who have been "emotionally coached" by their families since infancy have a good grasp of feelings; they are more adept at recognizing causes, reading physical cues, and handling emotional situations. The capacity for more advanced states of empathy coincides with the easing of the egocentrism that dominates the preoperational child's thought processes. By this stage children can sense that distress may be caused by external circumstances—poverty, family problems, forms of injustice, etc. Thus, proactivism can begin with the 9-year-old child. (For a more in-depth discussion on the development of empathy see Goleman, 1995.)

The use of the anti-bias approach with children fits into the complementary framework proposed by Abraham Maslow. Maslow's paradigm outlines a clear progression originating with the necessity of physiological well-being, security, trust, and acceptance as the scaffolding for feeling a sense of belonging, upon which competency, achievement, and a realization of one's potential can be built. The parallel points along this humanistic axis are:

1. basic human needs for physiological and psychological safety, all of which can be met in different ways;
2. the formation of an individual's self-identity and esteem which evolves within the security of a family; and
3. growing awareness and acceptance of the commonalities and distinctiveness in people's lives.

The path toward self-actualization has many indicators. The values of creativity, acceptance of self and others, the pleasure and satisfaction gained from establishing relationships with others, and above all, respecting the uniqueness of each child (Maslow, 1954) echo the fundamental goals of the anti-bias approach.

Major goals for an anti-bias classroom have been identified by many leading advocates of this philosophy (see Derman-Sparks, 1989, 1992; Ramsey, 1987; Stonehouse, 1991). Chud (1993) proposes the following:

1. To promote positive self-concepts, high self-esteem, critical thinking skills, and social relationships based upon respect, sensitivity, empathy, and shared understandings.
2. To offer children a range of opportunities, skills, and strategies to recognize and respond to unfair or unjust attitudes and behaviors that are rooted in racism, sexism, ageism, classism [sic], homophobia, or handicapism.

These goals are closely linked to developmental capabilities and can only be mastered once certain developmental milestones have been achieved.

Developmental Milestones in the Anti-Bias Framework

Positive self-concepts can only occur after a child is able to:

- recognize the self as separate and autonomous;
- recognize individual physical characteristics and those of others;
- recognize and achieve gender and racial constancy;
- recognize the self in relation to one's family—racial identity, language, customs, and behaviors;
- recognize the self in relation to a larger group—peer, ethnic, racial, and class; and
- recognize the self in relation to larger social networks, such as the community, city, and country.

Shared understandings can only occur when a child has the ability to see another's point of view.

Critical thinking skills can only occur once children have the capacity to:

- understand class inclusion;
- see a whole and its parts separately;

- compare events and people in both positive and negative terms; and
- solve problems on an abstract level.

Confronting injustice or discriminatory behaviors can only happen when children:

- are able to express their ideas and feelings; and
- have reached the stage where they can plan, organize, and carry out actions based on a strongly held value or opinion.

Key Anti-Bias Goals

Anti-bias skills are derived from the major goals and can be grouped into four major categories. These skills are also sequenced developmentally to assist educators in promoting anti-bias attitudes at appropriate stages of development. (Adapted from York, 1992.)

Positive Self-Concept/Esteem—Affective Skill Building:

- fosters positive self-concept and sense of self
- labels feelings and emotions
- helps others
- demonstrates pride in accomplishment
- understands relation to one's family
- tries new experiences
- works cooperatively
- able to be a group member
- copes with change
- demonstrates empathy

Mutual Respect:

- respects other cultures, races, and beliefs
- values self and the uniqueness of others
- respects gender and ability equity
- sees different points of view
- examines alternatives
- is open-minded

Understanding Similarities and Differences—Active Observing and Listening

- identifies similarities and differences
- listens to others
- constructs relationships and draws conclusions
- notices fair and unfair behavior
- solves problems
- gathers information
- demonstrates an inquiring attitude
- makes inferences

Proactivism

- makes choices
- avoids name-calling and teasing
- participates in group action
- challenges stereotypes
- takes action against unfair situations or comments

These anti-bias skills can flow from any of the 10 identified areas classified as *sources* of bias:

Areas of Bias

1. *Ability* refers to one's physical, mental, or emotional capabilities. Children more commonly notice physical disabilities.
2. *Age* relates to the state of being young or old. Again children appear more aware of what constitutes an "old" person.
3. *Appearance* describes one's height, size (fat, skinny), and any disfiguring conditions such as scars or distinctive markings.
4. *Belief* constitutes an acceptance or a strongly held conviction. Beliefs can include those in institutionalized religions, animism, spiritualism, and atheism, as well as political convictions.
5. *Class* (socioeconomic status) refers to distinctions based on social and economic values. Among the more common elements that determine a person's class are occupation, educational background, type of housing, clothing, and transportation directing one's lifestyle.
6. *Culture* is a way of life shared by members of the same group; individuals can belong to different cultures within the family, ethnic group, and society. Culture generally includes language, religious beliefs, celebrations, customs, and ways of thinking that reflect how one acts toward others. Group members feel a sense of security because of the many things they hold in common.
7. *Family composition* refers to family structure, including the number and relations of its members and their assigned roles.
8. *Gender* designates one as male or female. Children commonly perceive the issue of roles as associated with being male or female.
9. *Race* identifies groups of people who share a common origin and physical characteristics such as skin color, hair, facial appearance, and body structure. Many different ethnic groups are included in each race.
10. *Sexuality* indicates one's sexual preference and orientation. Issues of sexuality can refer to family composition (gay or lesbian couples) and homophobia.

Application of Anti-Bias Skills in Curriculum Planning

Although the anti-bias approach is fundamentally affective in its orientation, it lends itself naturally and effectively to the thinking skills promoted during the primary and middle elementary school years. Such *mathematical* skills as observation, discrimination, classification, comparison, critical thinking, and problem solving can be continuously challenged when exploring similarities and differences among people. Other skills such as hypothesizing, predicting, questioning, analyzing, and synthesizing can be successfully exercised within both the *science* and *social studies* areas as children investigate the nature of the human experience over historical time as well as physical space. Children can explore social *values* from within the immediacy of a family's culture as well as working through issues and influences in the ever widening circles of child care/school, the neighborhood and community, the city, the country, and ultimately the global dimension. Classrooms can engage in projects within the community, affording students the opportunity to plan, organize, participate, and take responsibility for activities that are designed to make life better for others.

The breadth and open-endedness of *language arts* experiences make them a powerful tool for the anti-bias educator. It is within the language and communication scope of the curriculum that children have the opportunity to listen, interpret, reflect, record, and communicate feelings about the issues of diversity and equity on a daily basis.

An anti-bias classroom can flourish regardless of the educational setting. The process, however, takes time and can only be implemented within the developmental capacities of children. For this reason, the anti-bias approach is best begun in infancy. During this stage of development, everyone and everything is a source of curiosity and for exploratory behaviors. Infants and toddlers will benefit from exposure to different scents, languages, textures, patterns, and music. Interacting with materials that reflect inclusiveness—multiracial dolls, puzzles, books, or dramatic play props that are bias free in terms of gender, race, ability, and age—will enable very young children to obtain a degree of familiarity and comfort with a number of areas of diversity.

Continued exposure to and exploration of the many facets of diversity will enhance the preschooler's ability to cope with the familiar and the not-so-familiar, while concurrently working on safely exploring one's own identity. By the end of the primary years (5–8 years), children who are instilled with an attitude of inquiry and openness to new experiences, who are able to confidently compare their own abilities and physical characteristics with others, and who are shedding the constraints of egocentric thinking will be most likely to demonstrate empathy for and be nonjudgmental about people who are different.

The final step in the progression can be attained by the end of the elementary school years (9–11 years). Encouraging the ability to challenge stereotypes, speak up against discriminatory statements, and take action on behalf of inequities should be a vital aspect of the integrated curriculum.

Educators of very young and school-aged children are more than aware of the complexity of their work and know that no ready-made scripts can formulate lifelong attitudes about people. The intent of this book is to demonstrate how any area of development or learning outcome can be enriched by the anti-bias perspective. The anti-bias approach is not an add-on; it is a way of learning that permeates every element of the curriculum for all children, i.e., interactions and modeling, family involvement, community relationship, staffing, routines, and the physical environment. It requires a commitment on the part of the educator to become more knowledgeable, to incorporate this knowledge and be aware of how any opportunity can be seized to sensitize children to diversity and most importantly, to develop within children positive attitudes about these differences.

This publication is not intended to be a theoretical text or a "cookbook." A recipe approach rarely responds to varying developmental needs and does not provide room for spontaneity and flexibility. Instead, this text is a resource of inclusionary experiences that are developmentally grounded and where necessary, includes theoretical discussions. The proposed activities support the developmental progression of anti-bias skills using approaches that are age appropriate for the differing age groups. A summary of the anti-bias skills being practiced with every age group is presented at the beginning of each unit. Activities are organized according to curriculum area—sensory, math, language, gross motor, etc.—and within each grouping, from youngest to oldest. These curriculum areas change to reflect the different skills and needs of infants/toddlers, the preschool-kindergarten group and elementary school students. In the preschool unit, only the activities designated as *socio-emotional* are assigned additional curriculum areas.

To assist educators in their developmental planning, each unit offers a web of both developmental and anti-bias skills specific to that age group. An overview with key developmental information highlights the major pedagogical issues particular to that age. Teachers and students of the preschool-kindergarten age group are encouraged to study activities both at the toddler and primary grade levels, because many of the experiences can be adapted either up or down for children ranging in age from 3 to 6 years. A sample parent letter has been included for the infant, preschool-kindergarten, and elementary school age groups to encourage family support and involvement in this approach to teaching and learning.

All of the activities follow a clear format that includes the following elements.

Age. Suggested age range for whom the activity would be developmentally appropriate.

Curriculum Area. A designated curriculum focus for the elementary school child and a developmental area for the early childhood years (0–5 years).

Curriculum Objectives. These objectives reflect the primary skills to be practiced and support the indicated curriculum or developmental area; sometimes objectives from other areas are included.

Anti-Bias Area. Indicates one or several areas of diversity to be explored in this activity.

Anti-Bias Skills. The skills identified are within the developmental capabilities of the specified age group and indicate in what ways children can benefit in their interactions with diversity. These skills will not be measurable immediately, but are cumulative and require continuous practice.

Materials. Provides a list of required resources and in some instances, a brief description of how to prepare innovative, noncommercial materials. It is the materials that dictate how the different areas of bias are supported.

Approach. This element identifies the most appropriate method to take with the activity and is contingent upon the children's developmental capabilities. Among the choices are incorporation, personalization, modified personalization, and extension.

Incorporation simply requires including an item or some aspect that reflects one or more areas of bias into the experience. Incorporation can range from pictures (depicting family composition, age, race, appearance, belief, gender), to skin-toned paints, paper, crayons, nylon stockings, and felt (representing race), to utensils, spices, music, or fabrics from different cultures, to real or miniature adaptive equipment (such as braille books, hearing aid, leg braces, asthma mask) for children to explore varying abilities. Visual images are particularly powerful and pictures from magazines, newspapers, discarded library books, discounted photo-essay books, and cards can be utilized to make countless language and math games. For older children, collect photos that will spark a discussion and present images that challenge stereotypical thinking.

Personalization involves a real person, reflecting a particular area of diversity, visiting and interacting with the children. Visitors can be from the childrens' families or the community. The purpose of this approach is to enable children to interact directly with someone whom society has designated as "different" in order to have their assumptions or stereotypical perceptions dispelled.

Modified Personalization occurs when the children themselves participate in the activity. In this approach, children can learn from one another how they and their families are similar and different. It is also possible to have children experience firsthand how it feels to be treated differently and what kinds of emotions that treatment engenders.

Extension occurs when an activity is expanded into another area of diversity through the use of divergent questioning or having the children explore different actions. This approach offers the child another perspective and stimulates critical thinking and problem solving.

Facilitation. This section offers detailed strategies on how to implement the activity. In many cases, questions and/or responses to children's comments are provided. These serve as guidelines to assist the children to think critically about the issue and to support positive interactions. In other activities, factual research and/or developmental information has been integrated for more effective implementation.

Expansion. Some activities can be the basis for further exploration. Where natural follow-ups do occur they are included.

Community Resource. Some activities are followed by suggestions for resources (both human and inanimate) that will strengthen the experience for the children.

Finally, a list of picture or reference books, and where appropriate, songs/finger plays, are supplied at the end of every chapter to supplement the teacher's preparations. These resources are cross-referenced with the appropriate activity.

The author took advantage of a number of outstanding children's books on the market today as sources for activity planning. Seven exemplary books were webbed and activities designed for the elementary age child. Many other books were used as vehicles to explore feelings, ideas, and values related to the different areas of bias.

The appendix contains two convenient annotated listings of children's literature that readers are encouraged to share with their children. The selected books exemplify the best attempts to present the daily situations of play, work, and living that occur in families from different ethno-racial and religious backgrounds, economic levels, family structures, and areas of ability. In this way children are exposed to and can discuss how the major life themes are handled by people of all skin colors, by those who speak different languages, by those who have different physical, mental and emotional abilities, and by those whose family structures include biracial, same-sex, extended, or blended family members.

A matrix and a variety of charts have been designed to assist teachers in planning and evaluating both the physical environment and the curriculum as they work toward the goal of building anti-bias skills. The appendix includes a reproducible anti-bias matrix and environmental support chart, as well as a blank form for organizing literature resources. A community resources form will help educators organize their own personal files of local and regional resources.

All 300 activities have been sequenced in a Developmental Overview Chart. Activity titles from the different age groups are coded and provide a visual display of how the developmental progression of the anti-bias skills of positive self-concept/esteem, mutual respect, understanding similarities and differences, empathy, and proactivism unfolds.

ANTI-BIAS AREA ABBREVIATIONS

AB:	**Ability**	**FC:**	**Family Composition**
AG:	**Age**	**GEN:**	**Gender**
AP:	**Appearance**	**R:**	**Race**
BEL:	**Belief**	**SX:**	**Sexuality**
CLS:	**Class**	**ALL:**	**All Anti-Bias Areas**
CUL:	**Culture**		

ANTI-BIAS IMPLEMENTATION APPROACHES SYNOPSIS CHART

AGE	ACTIVITY	INCORPORATION	PERSONALIZATION	EXTENSION
Infant/Toddler				
Anti-Bias Areas				
Preschool-Kindergarten				
Anti-Bias Areas				
Elementary				
Anti-Bias Areas				

ANTI-BIAS IMPLEMENTATION APPROACHES SYNOPSIS CHART

AGE	ACTIVITY	INCORPORATION	PERSONALIZATION	EXTENSION
Infant/Toddler	Water Play	1. Add cultural containers, spices that may be unfamiliar to children. 2. Laminated picture of a child/children of different racial backgrounds playing with water, taped to water play container.	1. Invite senior citizen to join the children and interact during water play. 2. The senior could be a grandparent of one of the children.	NOT APPLICABLE FOR THIS AGE GROUP
Anti-Bias Areas		**CUL R**	**AG FC**	
Preschool-Kindergarten	Facial Sort	Collect pictures of people of different races, ages, and appearances, and sort the following: 1. EYES (with/without glasses) 2. TEETH (with/without braces) 3. NOSES (diff. sizes, shapes, colors) 4. CHEEKS (wrinkled, smooth) 5. FACES (with/without scars, birthmarks)	Invite one of the following to play the game with the children: 1. Male 2. Someone who is blind 3. Grandfather	1. How do you think someone who is blind can tell which one of the pictures has a nose, eyes, etc.... on it? 2. Does anyone know the word for eye, nose, cheek, etc.... in another language?
Anti-Bias Areas		**AB AP AP/R AG AP**	**GEN AB AG/FC**	**AB CUL**
Elementary	Obstacle Course	Children use various aids/equipment to navigate an obstacle course on the floor: 1. crutches 2. flippers 3. snowshoes	Invite one of the following as a guest to interact with the children: 1. Person with Seeing Eye dog 2. Person of Asian origin 3. Person who is very tall/short	1. Do you think grandparents could do what you just did? 2. Who else do you think would enjoy hopping, skipping?
Anti-Bias Areas		**AB CUL CUL**	**AB R AP**	**AG ALL**

Teacher Supports: The Physical Environment

It is important that children handle materials and play with equipment on an ongoing basis to acquire the degree of familiarity, comfort, and understanding that is necessary in the anti-bias approach. Anything less leads to artificial and tokenistic experiences. It is also critical that materials accurately portray contemporary lifestyles and cultural traditions. For example, Native Americans no longer live in teepees, and the Inuit or Aleuts of the Arctic do not live in igloos. Teachers need to be mindful in identifying historical and contemporary facts.

Many of the materials cited in the activities have to be bought and collected, so teachers need to acquire a new mind-set, becoming scavengers and pack rats, frequenting garage sales and secondhand shops. The mandate is to always be on the look out for ways to incorporate anti-bias materials into existing stock and to create new teaching resources. The following list of materials comprises essential resources for the anti-bias classroom. Many of the staple items are given by generic names, while others are specific to educational supply companies.

Home/Dramatic Play Center

- Variety of bags and baskets for fake food and shopping
- Multiracial dolls and dolls with adaptive equipment for a range of disabilities (Lakeshore/Wintergreen has an extensive and accurate selection)
- Eating utensils from different cultures: Chinese soup spoons, chopsticks, tin, wooden, and plastic bowls, dishes, cups, ladles
- Cooking utensils from different countries: saucepans, kettles, steamers, strainers, wok, garlic press, tortilla press, grater, tea balls, fry pan, eggbeater, whisk, etc.; most utensils can do double duty for sand and water play (Hispanic and Asian cooking sets may be purchased from Constructive Playthings if items are unavailable in your community)
- Cushions, pillows, mats, small area rugs, placemats from different cultures with traditional colors, patterns, and designs
- Variety of infant carriers: snuggly, cradleboard, cloth wrap, stroller, basket, etc.
- Variety of bedding for dolls: woven blanket, cradle, hammock, futon
- Food containers, boxes, tins representing items from different cultures with labels in different languages, gourds and coconut shells
- Clothing, shoes, hats, scarves, belts that represent both everyday wear and holiday dress from a variety of different countries
- Duplo World People® include figures representing three generations and multiethnic backgrounds (Kaplan, 17-31831)

Visual Images

- Photographs, pictures, posters that portray adults and children from a wide range of ethnoracial backgrounds, ages, gender, and abilities participating in everyday activities
- Pictures of homes and buildings from different countries
- Pictures of modes of transportation in different parts of the world
- Art forms: paintings, sculpture, dancing, musical instruments, and theater
- Rural and urban life scenes

- Toys and play materials from around the world
- Families reflecting different composition, involved in typical routines
- Books that celebrate the ordinary using children from different backgrounds, abilities, gender, and appearance
- Books that are dual track, using English and other languages, braille, and Signed English
- Artifacts such as wall hangings, beadwork, enamel ware, woodwork, and pottery that exemplify distinctive cultural colors, patterns, and textures
- Signs printed in different languages, braille, and Signed English for key areas, displays, and information bulletin boards
- Borders or trimmers that have either children's photographs or illustrations of children reflecting areas of diversity (Trend Inc. or Denison available through educational supply stores or catalogs)
- Clear self-stick covering paper as an alternative to laminating your pictures
- "Everybody's Beautiful" people cutouts (Kaplan, 17-31369)
- Children with special needs puzzles include images of children who are physically challenged, visually and hearing impaired (Constructive Playthings)
- Nonsexist, multiethnic career puzzles
- Wooden stand up families and differently challenged children block figures (Constructive Playthings, GC-101, 103, 104, 109 and 120)

Arts

- Cassettes of multiethnic songs and dances
- Musical instruments from different cultures
- Finger plays, chants, dances, and songs taught in a variety of languages that reflect the diversity of the staff, children and families, and greater community
- People-colored crayons
- People-colored construction paper (PACON, SC7—PE658, Lakeshore)
- People-colored tempera paints
- People-colored felt markers
- People-colored felt for flannel board stories; Family Flannel sets (Constructive Playthings LFF series) can be mixed in order to portray a variety of family compositions
- Make-a-Face sheets (RY-928, Lakeshore) in skin tones
- People shapes (LC-169, Lakeshore)
- People sponges, Active Kid sponges (Kaplan, 17-33774); Hand sponge sets (Constructive Playthings)
- People-shaped cookie cutters (look for hand and foot cookie cutters as well)
- Playdough made from people-colored paints, Multicultural Dough (Kaplan, 17-31823)
- Clay
- Puppets
- Essential oils, extracts, and scents that are used in different cultures for food preparation or perfume; add to sensory play materials
- Fabrics and materials that reflect traditional textures, designs, and colors of different cultures

Food

- Snacks and meals that reflect menus from different cultures
- Eating utensils and dishes that represent diverse cultures to serve food

Nature

- Shells, sand, and stones from different areas of the world
- Plants and pictures of those that grow in desert, tropical, temperate, marshy, and tundra regions
- Herbs that are used in food preparation across the world
- Spice smelly jars

Places to Scrounge for Anti-Bias Materials

- Parents and family members
- Multiethnic community resource centers
- Secondhand stores; thrift shops
- Markets
- Travel agencies for posters, brochures
- Airline magazines
- Consulates and embassies
- Third World craft stores
- Museum gift stores
- Friends who travel abroad
- UNICEF calendars and diaries
- Garage sales for used books, *National Geographic* and *Equinox* magazines
- Discarded library books
- Discounted photo-essay books
- Postcards
- Government departments that deal with Native and Northern affairs in Canada, and international development

ANTI-BIAS ENVIRONMENTAL SUPPORT CHART

List materials available to children in each area.

AGE	DRAMATIC PLAY	ENVIRONMENT/ SCIENCE	LANGUAGE ARTS	MATH/ MANIPULATIVE	SENSORY	CREATIVE	LARGE MOTOR EQUIPMENT	ANTI-BIAS SKILL
MONDAY								
Anti-Bias Area								
TUESDAY								
Anti-Bias Area								
WEDNESDAY								
Anti-Bias Area								
THURSDAY								
Anti-Bias Area								
FRIDAY								
Anti-Bias Area								

ANTI-BIAS ENVIRONMENTAL SUPPORT CHART

List materials available to children in each area.

AGE	DRAMATIC PLAY	ENVIRONMENT/ SCIENCE	LANGUAGE ARTS	MATH/ MANIPULATIVE	SENSORY	CREATIVE	LARGE MOTOR EQUIPMENT	ANTI-BIAS SKILL
MONDAY ***Infants***	–Boxes (various languages)	Not applicable	–Board books of baby routines –Mirror	–Family puzzles –Nesting cans	–Maracas & other shakers –Water	–Skin-toned paint	–Crawl boxes (with pictures)	–Exposure to diversity –Sense of self in relation to family
Anti-Bias Area	**CUL**		**R GEN**	**GEN FC AG R**	**CUL**	**R**	**AG R GEN**	
TUESDAY ***Toddlers***	–Bags	Not applicable	–Felt pieces (people)	–Laundry scoops –Building spools	–Skin-toned goop –Sand –Shells	–Braille placemats	–Stuffed skin-toned nylons (act as balls)	–Strengthen self-identity –Beginning to notice similarities/ differences
Anti-Bias Area	**CUL**		**R GEN FC**	**R CUL GEN AG**	**CUL R AB**	**AB**	**R**	
WEDNESDAY ***Preschool-Kindergarten***	–Dolls (multi-racial, gender specific) –Cradle board, snuggly, stroller, cloth wrap	–Concave, convex, and regular mirrors	–Shoes from various countries (sandals, thongs, clogs, ballet slippers)	–Paint chips (various colors, skin tones) –Occupation puzzles	–Playdough (skin-toned and other) –Surgical gloves –Cookie cutter (people-shaped and with one leg)	–Skin-toned markers, crayons –Paper –Felt –Glue	–Crutches –Snowshoes –Flippers	–Awareness of differences –Trying new experiences
Anti-Bias Area	**CUL GEN**	**AP**	**GEN AG CUL**	**R GEN**	**R AB**	**R CUL**	**AB CUL**	
THURSDAY ***Elementary/ Primary***	–Child-sized wheelchair –White cane –Communication boards	–Assortment of occupational tools –Tree stumps	–Disability awareness kit –Books –Photos –Card games –Taped stories, songs (various languages)	–Attribute blocks –Classification items: –People –Money –Stamps –Coins	–Braille cards –Texture cards –Wood blocks	–People puppets –Felt –Glue	–Balls –Ropes –Hoops	–Ability to examine alernatives
Anti-Bias Area	**AB**	**GEN**	**AB CUL R**	**AG R GEN CUL**	**AB CUL**	**AG R GEN AB**	**GEN AB**	
FRIDAY ***Elementary/ Junior***	Not applicable	–Plants –Herbs –Pots –Spices –Magnifying glass	–Photos –Tape Recorder –Books –Kalimba, native drums –Maps –Travel brochures –Posters	–Dice –Board games –Tangrams –Tessellations	Not applicable	–Looms –Needles –Thread –Fabric –Mosaic tiles –Metal work –Wood –Feathers –Beads	–Scooter boards –Hollow blocks	–Ability to participate in group action
Anti-Bias Area		**CUL**	**GEN R CUL**	**R CUL GEN**		**CUL AB**	**GEN AB**	

The Social Environment: Guidelines for Teacher Interactions

Teacher awareness and sensitivity toward each area of bias is crucial to successfully implementing the anti-bias approach. Every interaction sends a strong message of inclusion or exclusion. Ongoing, honest self-evaluations and objective observations of children's interactions will assist the educator in reaching the goal of an inclusionary classroom atmosphere. Some fundamental points to remember when offering an anti-bias perspective:

- Know your own biases and hesitations; being aware of them will prevent you from inadvertently transferring these attitudes to the children.
- Ensure that your words, facial expressions, and body language all send messages of being at ease and comfortable with the familiar as well as the unfamiliar.
- Model inclusive behaviors.

Interactions with Infants and Toddlers

Gonzalez-Mena (1993) argues a strong case that "teaching anti-bias to infants has very little to do with what you hang on the walls, what play activities you plan or whether you celebrate holidays . . . It has everything to do with the agreement you make with each parent about the way to take care of each baby—feed, diaper, hold, talk to, and interact with their babies."

Creating an anti-bias environment for infants and toddlers hinges on the kind of relationship a teacher makes with each child and family. When working with very young children, caregivers need to remember that every type of verbal and nonverbal communication conveys an attitude of acceptance and respect or discomfort with and intolerance toward the individual child. The correlation is clear as children internalize these responses; the accumulation of such messages has a significant impact on the fragile and evolving sense of self.

Caregivers must become aware of how their own personal values and attitudes can interfere with the creation of an environment that makes each child feel valued and special. The following list of questions requires honest self-reflection. The behaviors identified are fundamental in building relationships with infants and toddlers. Examine if the child's gender, ethno-racial background, appearance, family structure, or physical ability influences your behavior either positively or negatively.

- Do you hold and cuddle children equally? Do you use less physical contact with some?
- Do you smile at certain children more than others?
- Do you have a special look for certain children? If yes, what is the reason?
- Do you maintain eye contact with all children? If not, what is the reason (e.g., deference to cross-cultural communication styles)?
- Do you engage in social interaction games—tickle songs, finger plays, etc.—with all children with the same level of enthusiasm and spontaneity?
- Do you support curiosity and self-initiated exploration equally?
- Do you speak with certain families with more enthusiasm and purpose than others?
- Do you solicit developmental information from families equally?
- Do you make detailed observations of each child in your care?
- Do you extend and enrich interactions to build language development equally?
- Is your style of interaction more directive (giving commands and instructions) to some while more questioning and coaching to others? Do you intervene more with some while supporting independence of others?

- Do you individualize the routines of feeding, toileting, and dressing? Can you identify the ways this happens?
- If you disagree with a family over child-rearing issues how does that affect your relationship with the child?
- Do you attempt to negotiate or work out a compromise, or does your conflict consume your energies?
- Are you aware of each child's temperament characteristics?
- Do you support each child's style of relating?
- Do you respect parental preference for eating practices (dietary needs)? toilet training practices? sleep routines? use of a pacifier or bottle?
- Do you recognize signs of stress in each individual child?
- Do you demonstrate that each family is valued by incorporating cultural differences—languages, foods, clothing, music, etc.—into your program?
- Does each child see himself and family members reflected in daily experiences and the physical environment?
- Identify the ways that you demonstrate respect for the diversity of your children and families.

Interactions with Preschool and Elementary School Children

- Set clear guidelines around what kind of behavior is not acceptable, e.g., name-calling, etc.
- Intervene immediately when you hear exclusionary comments.
- Voice your own feelings of discomfort around the exclusion.
- Help children to problem solve around what was unfair.
- Offer thought-provoking comments to expand their thinking and encourage action-taking strategies.
- Make sure your language is free of stereotypes and hidden biases.
- Never ignore discriminatory slurs or behaviors. Challenge assumptions and misconceptions by providing correct information and fostering attitudes of empathy. (For more in-depth discussion on the implications of teacher interactions refer to Derman-Sparks, et al., 1980; Derman-Sparks, 1989.)

In summary, active listening, observing of children's interactions, and being in touch with how personal attitudes and values affect the classroom environment are critical components of anti-bias education. Teachers must put aside emotions of anxiety, embarrassment, or discomfort when dealing with the issues of human diversity. Instead, they must be prepared to ask questions and be open to learning from colleagues and families. Children deserve no less from their mentors.

UNIT 2

Anti-Bias Activities for Infants

"The challenge for the teacher is to treat each child as an individual, to seek differences, and to be equitable. If you treat everyone the same, you are not making use of each child's uniqueness."

Meg Robinson, 1992

Developmental areas are inextricably interconnected during the infancy period. Infants will thrive if their physical needs are met; however, those needs are intimately dependent upon their state of emotional well-being. Development cannot be compartmentalized; instead, caregivers must be attuned to how nurturing one area of development affects the growth of others. Key requirements for quality care and education happen when:

- Adults respond to infants' sounds of distress and pleasure sensitively and consistently.
- Infants feel secure and trust that an adult will meet their needs responsively and promptly.
- Infants' bids for self-initiated actions are supported.
- Adults respect infants' individual temperaments.
- Adults encourage and expand infants' verbal and nonverbal communication.
- Adults provide an environment that is psychologically and physically safe to explore.
- Adults are sensitive observers and can support emerging developmental skills.
- Adults respect infants as active participants in an interaction, and establish relationships based on reciprocity; this entails sensitive cue reading and the ability to let infants take control of their exploratory needs.
- Adults create an atmosphere of acceptance and value each aspect of the infant's being.
- Adults acknowledge infants' pain over separation with family and provide individualized coping strategies.
- The day is spent in warm, intimate, social caregiving routines; flexibility is demonstrated by following the rhythms of the individual infants.
- Adults acknowledge infants' vulnerability and extreme dependence on others for well-being.
- Adults praise and show encouragement for developmental accomplishments.
- Adults view infants within the context of their families, understanding and appreciating the cultural values and attitudes that accompany them.
- Adults appreciate and support the variety of individual differences in development.
- Continuity and consistency between home and child care are maintained.

Web for Infants
Anti-Bias and Developmental Skills

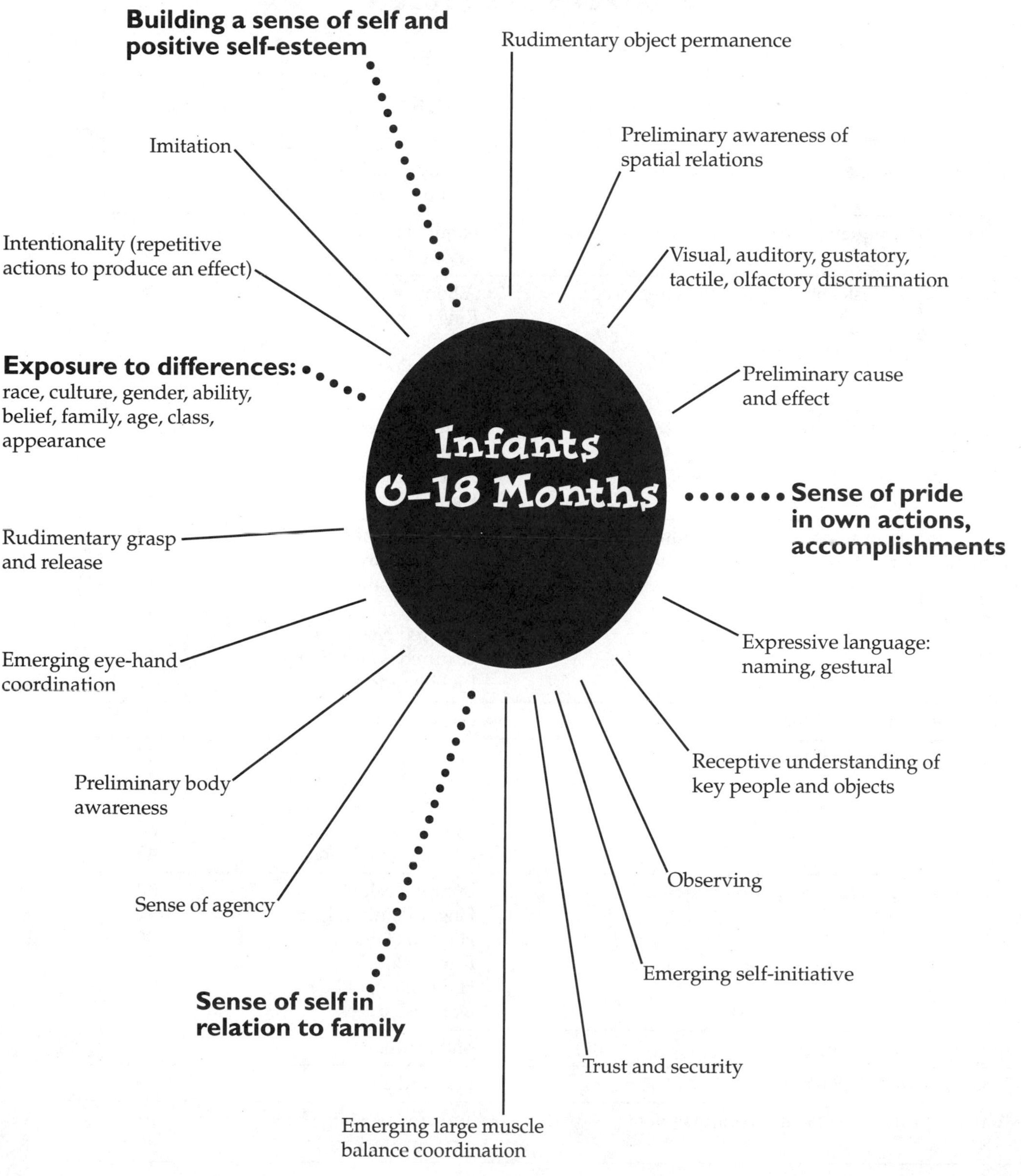

Summary of Anti-Bias Skills Infant Activities

Anti-Bias Skills	Activity Title	Page Number
To promote a sense of self in relation to family.	Family Lullabies	24
	Family Hide-and-Seek	25
To value the uniqueness of self and others' families.	Family Hide-and-Seek	25
	Diving Pool	44
To promote self-esteem and positive self-concept.	A Book of Me	26
	Ring Game	32
	Mobile Mania	33
	Diving Pool	44
	Stickers on You and Me	45
To promote a sense of family belonging.	Family Lullabies	24
	Family Hide-and-Seek	25
	A Book of Me	26
	Family Puzzle	38
To expose infants to patterns and textures from different cultures.	Textured Snake	27
	Scrubbie Play	29
	Basket Nesting	34
	Tongue Pull	37
	Textured Nesting Cans	37
	Textured Sound Shakers	40
	Ribbons and Bows	41
To expose infants to different smells.	Feely Smelly Cubes	28
To expose infants to different skin tones.	Hand/Foot Water Play	30
	Finger Painting Pictures	31
	Lids and Tops	35
	Family Puzzle	38
	Bouncing Balloons	43
To expose infants to areas of diversity.	Bumpy Feelings	30
	Finger Painting Pictures	31
	Hidden Hankies	36
	Family Puzzle	38
	Hide and Find Box	39
	Drum Madness	42
To foster a sense of agency.	Mobile Mania	33
To label feelings and emotions.	Lids and Tops	35
To foster pride in personal accomplishments.	Textured Nesting Cans	37
	Tin Can Stacking	43

Letter to Families of Infants/Toddlers

Dear Families,

We are attempting to familiarize the children with various aspects of diversity in all of our program areas. Our goal is to help children feel really comfortable with any and all differences they may encounter in our "global" village throughout their lives.

To reach this goal we are asking for your help. Since exposure to concrete items is the best way for young children to learn and to begin to understand the many similarities and differences that exist in life, we are asking for contributions of the following items:

- fabrics of various patterns, textures, and colors
- outgrown leg/arm braces; old glasses and crutches
- written materials in various scripts, e.g., Persian, Hebrew, Greek, Japanese, etc.
- songs and dance music from different countries
- child-sized wheelchair
- dolls of various skin colors
- cooking utensils
- various traditional clothing such as a sari, kilt, or kimono

This is just a short list and any other items that you feel may be useful will be most welcome.

We hope you take this wonderful opportunity to enrich the quality of our center. Please spread the word among your friends and acquaintances as well. We are looking forward to your contributions, big or small, and to working together with you!

Sincerely,

Family Lullabies

Age

3–18 months

Curriculum Area

Socio-emotional

Curriculum Objectives

To establish a sense of family belonging; to foster strong self-esteem.

Anti-Bias Areas

Family Composition, Culture

Anti-Bias Skill

To promote a sense of self in relation to family.

Materials

Tape recorder and blank tapes

Approach

Modified Personalization

Facilitation

Distribute tapes to family members of each child in your care. Ask them to record favorite lullabies or family songs in their own language. Play the tape to the infants on an individual basis or as a small group. Make sure you can identify the voices in order to label family members for individual infants. Learn the lullabies and sing them to the infants. This will strengthen the infants' sense of security as they hear sounds that are familiar and reassuring.

Expansion

Collect lullabies in other languages.

Community Resources

Local library for musical tapes of lullabies.

Ethnic lullabies are available on tape from ARTS Inc. Redleaf Press has the following titles available on cassette: *Globalullabies*, by Freyda; *Celtic Lullaby*, by Margie Butler; and *A Child's World of Lullabies: Multicultural Songs for Quiet Times*, by Hap Palmer.

Family Hide-and-Seek

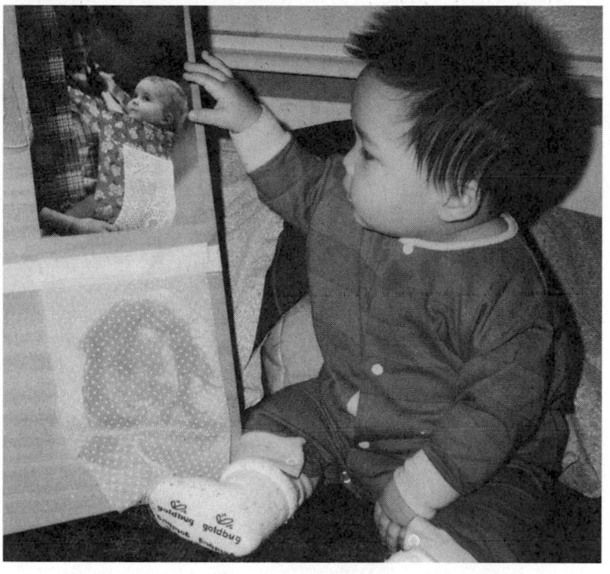

Finding familiar faces makes me feel secure.

Age

6–18 months

Curriculum Area

Socio-emotional

Curriculum Objectives

To establish a sense of family belonging; to foster strong self-esteem.

Anti-Bias Areas

Race, Culture, Family Composition

Anti-Bias Skills

To promote a sense of self in relation to family; to value the uniqueness of one's own family and others' families.

Materials

Individual photos of the children with their families mounted on a large wooden or bristol board. Cover the pictures either from the top or from the left side with thin velcro and different types of materials, i.e., crinkly cellophane, burlap, velvet, gauze, or mesh.

Approach

Incorporation

Facilitation

Help the infant to practice object permanence by engaging each child to lift and find a picture of herself and her family. Label the people in the photo, describe what she looks like, what she is doing: "Who is behind this? It's Sean. What's Sean doing? He's holding a baby doll. Nice hugs. Who's under here? It's Kisha and her dad. Kisha is smiling."

Encourage trial-and-error experimentation as the infant discovers double screens, or screens that need lifting from bottom up and right to left.

Expansion

Laminate pictures of children of different racial or cultural backgrounds, gender or ability, playing, eating, socializing with their families and tape them to the floor. Comment on the content casually as the infant explores them while crawling or stepping over them.

A Book of Me

Age

6–18 months

Curriculum Area

Socio-emotional

Curriculum Objectives

To build strong self-identity; to support attachment relationships.

Anti-Bias Areas

Culture, Gender

Anti-Bias Skills

To promote self-esteem and a sense of family belonging.

Materials

Small, individualized photo albums with pictures of the children taken during play and routine times, as well as photos supplied by the families.

Approaches

Modified Personalization and Incorporation

Facilitation

The formation of a strong self-concept evolves over a long period of time. Infants gradually learn that they are separate beings. It is during this process that they discover they can make things happen.

Chronicle each infant's developmental progress by photographing key routines and play interactions. Create a photo record by filling small hand-sized albums for each child. Replace the photos every six months with new ones.

Use any opportunity to sit and look at the individual albums. Label and discuss what the infant is doing, what object and with whom he is playing, and the emotions demonstrated in the photos. It is important that each child feels affirmed and valued. Support any verbal attempts to label people, objects, and self.

Textured Snake

Age
3–10 months

Curriculum Area
Sensory

Curriculum Objectives
To stimulate tactile, visual, and auditory sensory pleasure; to develop eye-hand coordination.

Anti-Bias Area
Culture

There are so many different things to explore in this toy.

Anti-Bias Skill
To expose infants to patterns and textures from different cultures.

Materials
Scraps of fabrics with distinctive patterns and surfaces: brocade, fringed suede, corduroy, velvet, fake fur, terrycloth, braided cotton, etc.; thread; large wooden beads and buttons; wire; split peas; and cellophane wrap and cotton batting.

Stuff some of the fabric pieces with such noise-producing materials as dried beans or cellophane wrap, and the rest with cotton batting. Attach buttons securely to the head and secure a small arrow-shaped piece of fabric for the tongue. Stitch each segment together in a line, alternating noisy and quiet sections. Stitch wire threaded with three wooden beads tightly into final segment. Always be vigilant in your supervision when toys have small pieces.

Approach
Incorporation

Facilitation
Infants derive great pleasure from visually inspecting and physically examining new toys. Finger dexterity and eye-hand coordination evolve with practice at this stage of development.

Place the snake in front of the infant and encourage manipulation of the different materials. Exploration can happen while babies are on their stomachs or sitting upright with or without support. Model poking, squeezing, pulling, and moving the beads. Support similar motor manipulation by the infants. Label and describe simply what the infant sees, feels, hears, and does.

Feely Smelly Cubes

This smells nice but feels scratchy.

Age

6–12 months

Curriculum Area

Sensory

Curriculum Objective

To stimulate tactile, olfactory, auditory, and visual exploration.

Anti-Bias Area

Culture

Anti-Bias Skill

To expose infants to different smells.

Materials

Twenty-four 5-inch green, orange, yellow, and blue scouring pads; thick needle; yarn; ground ginger, vanilla extract, and cinnamon; small bell; and a handful of hard chickpeas.

Sew six pads together (color design is optional) and enclose a bell in one cube, chickpeas in another, and a different sachet in each of the other cubes.

Approach

Incorporation

Facilitation

Put out the cubes for the infants to explore. The size will require two-handed manipulation for rotating, squeezing, shaking, mouthing, and visually inspecting them. Label the infants' experiences—what they smell, hear, feel, and see, especially contrasts in sound and smell. Model smelling the cube: "Mmm, this smells like ginger. Try this one. It smells like vanilla. It's a bit scratchy, isn't it? Shake, shake. Listen to the bell. This one sounds different."

Store cubes separately in plastic bags from other blocks as the spices are very aromatic.

Scrubbie Play

Age

6–12 months

Curriculum Area

Sensory

Curriculum Objective

To stimulate tactile and visual exploration and discrimination.

Anti-Bias Area

Culture

Anti-Bias Skill

To expose infants to patterns and textures from different cultures.

Materials

Green, yellow, blue, and red scrubbers; red, blue, yellow, and green plastic and wooden napkin rings; and elastic.

Thread the elastic through alternating scrubbers and napkin rings. Tie ends together to form a tight ring. Make the texture and color pattern interesting.

Approach

Incorporation

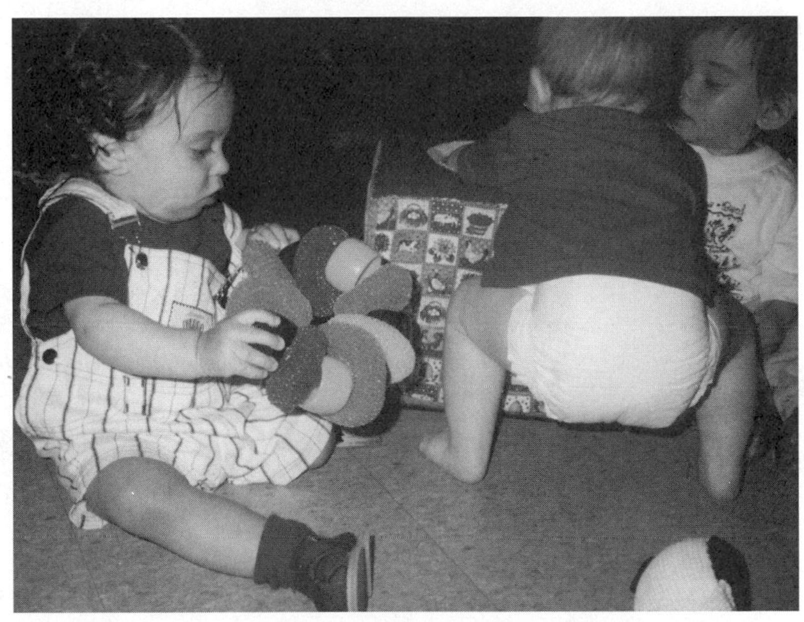

I can feel smooth and rough at the same time.

Facilitation

Infants gradually build an understanding of how objects are similar and different through continuous physical manipulation. By allowing infants to hold, mouth, poke, twist, and run their fingers over the strung objects, they may notice that not all blue objects are the same shape or feel the same. The textures are sufficiently distinctive yet equally pleasurable to encourage exploration. Providing simple labels for texture and color will lend verbal support to the children's physical observations. Ongoing opportunities to experience sensory discrimination at this stage lay the foundation for noticing more refined differences and similarities in people, places, and things that occurs later on in a child's development.

Hand/Foot Water Play

Age
9–18 months

Curriculum Area
Sensory

Curriculum Objectives
To provide tactile, visual, and olfactory stimulation; to promote self-initiative.

Anti-Bias Areas
Race, Culture

Anti-Bias Skill
To expose infants to different skin tones.

Materials
Large and small sponges, shaped like hands and feet, in skin tones and primary colors; water in a deep, see-through container; and a spice such as cumin, ginger, etc.

Approach
Incorporation

Facilitation
Place sponges in the water and add spice. Encourage the infants to manipulate and squeeze the sponges. Comment on the color, texture, and size of the sponges. As the infants bring the sponges up to their mouths, point out the smell. Build the children's sense of body awareness by labeling all actions and making connections between their hands/feet with the sponges: "That's the big foot, there's the little hand. Look, the sponge fell on Alec's foot. All wet."

Bumpy Feelings

Age
9–18 months

Curriculum Area
Sensory

Curriculum Objectives
To promote tactile, auditory, and visual exploration, and independent manipulation of the index finger.

Anti-Bias Areas
Race, Ability, Age

Anti-Bias Skill
To expose infants to areas of diversity.

Materials
Pictures depicting children and adults of different ages, races, and cultures; bubble wrap; and masking tape.

Approach
Incorporation

Facilitation
Place pictures on floor and cover with bubble wrap paper. Hold bubble wrap in place with masking tape. Encourage infants to explore the bubble wrap paper either with their large muscles by crawling, walking, jumping, or with their small muscles by poking, patting, picking, or banging. Facilitate popping the bubble wrap to stimulate auditory pleasure. Show your enthusiasm when they create the sounds either accidentally or intentionally. Make sure the bubble wrap is wide and long enough for two to three infants to participate simultaneously. Remove socks for additional sensory exploration.

Once the novelty has worn off, focus their attention to the pictures underneath. Label the people and their emotions or actions simply: "Look, I see a mommy with glasses, just like Sarina's mommy. Oh, in this corner I see a grandfather playing ball. Do you like playing ball with grandpa?"

Finger Painting Pictures

Age

12–18 months

Curriculum Area

Sensory

Curriculum Objectives

To facilitate visual, tactile, and olfactory exploration; to develop object permanence and eye-hand coordination.

Anti-Bias Areas

Race, Age, Culture, Gender, Ability

Anti-Bias Skills

To expose infants to areas of diversity and different skin tones.

Materials

Pictures of children and adults of different ages, cultures, races, genders, and abilities, mounted on picture board and covered in clear contact paper; masking tape to adhere the board to the table; and three or four different flesh-tone colors of finger paint.

Make sure the picture boards are a reasonable size to support the infants' sweeping arm movements.

Approach

Incorporation

Facilitation

Set out a picture board in front of the infants; place a small amount of finger paint on it. Encourage the infants to poke, pat, and smear the paint using either fingers or an open palm. Model actions if necessary, and point out how the pictures become covered or uncovered with the swipe of a finger or hand. By commenting on the pictures as they become visible, you are providing receptive and expressive language opportunities. Turn the activity into a hide-and-seek game: "Where's the girl with the ball? Let's find her. Here she is. Now Victor find her."

Infants will enjoy the sensory experience of squeezing and moving their hands through the soft texture of the paint. Allow them to enjoy this tactile experience without forcing the underlying cognitive benefits.

Ring Game

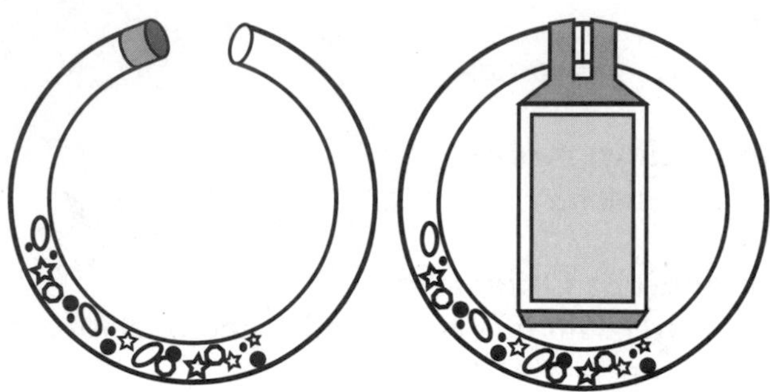

I can find myself and others by a flick of a wrist.

Age
4–10 months

Curriculum Area
Cognitive

Curriculum Objectives
To strengthen cause and effect, intentionality, and observation.

Anti-Bias Areas
Race, Gender

Anti-Bias Skills
To promote self-esteem and positive self-concept.

Materials
Plastic tubing, ¼ inch in diameter; water and glycerine; small beads; corks to plug the tubing; cloth tape and string; plastic mirror; and cardboard and picture.

Tightly cork one end of the plastic tube. Add water, glycerine, and beads. Gently form tube into a ring and insert other end of the plastic tubing onto the protruding portion of cork. Tightly wrap cloth tape around the sealed portion of tube to secure. Cut a piece of sturdy cardboard into a rectangular shape that will fit into the center of the ring. Paste picture of an infant/young child on the cardboard and cover with clear contact paper. On the reverse side glue a plastic mirror of equal size to the cardboard. Use wide cloth tape to cover the perimeter of the cardboard, ensuring that the mirror is completely framed. Attach the cardboard to the ring by threading strong string at the top and bottom and securing the ends to the ring. Wrap cloth tape around the stringed areas of the cardboard to reinforce the toy.

Approaches
Incorporation and Modified Personalization

Facilitation
This activity allows infants to discover all kinds of effects as they explore the ring's properties. Very young infants will manage to grasp the ring and mouth it before focusing on either the picture or their reflection in the mirror. Gently turn the ring to the left or right to produce movement in the tubing. Focus their gaze on this action by saying, "Look at the beads swimming up. Here they come down."

Older infants will independently observe how the slightest action on their part will cause the beads to move through the water. The mirror and picture provide another source for building self-identity. Simple comments on what the infant is doing and seeing will encourage further observation and manipulation of this toy.

Community Resource
Plastic tubing and corks are available at hardware stores or home supply outlets.

Mobile Mania

I can make it turn and watch the faces change.

Age

4–10 months

Curriculum Area

Cognitive

Curriculum Objectives

To help infants recognize facial expressions; to encourage infants to repeat pleasurable actions, and help them see that they can cause objects to move.

Anti-Bias Area

Race

Anti-Bias Skills

To promote self-esteem and positive self-concept; to foster a sense of agency.

Materials

Pop bottle; small colored pompoms; bells; glue; Nerf® ball; mesh netting; elastic; and two pictures, one with a person smiling and the other with a person showing sadness (people of different racial backgrounds).

Partially fill the bottle with pompoms and bells. Paste pictures on either side of the Nerf® ball. Cut a small hole in the bottom of the ball and glue it to the top of the bottle. Encase the ball in mesh net, and knot and tie elastic string to the top.

Approach

Incorporation

Facilitation

Infants need opportunities to practice the skill of reaching and grasping for suspended things, because initially they are not adept at judging distance and accurately targeting an object. This mobile is large enough to guarantee success with accidental swipes, and produces pleasant sounds and movement of the pompoms for additional sensory pleasure.

After the infants master the eye-hand coordination necessary for this game, remove the elastic and roll it on the floor in order to practice a different set of motor skills. Focus the infants' attention on the faces and the emotions represented. Label the happy and sad faces, as well as the sounds and sights that result from their actions. Make the connection that the infant is the source of these sensory pleasures: "What a good hit. You made the happy face spin. Listen to the bells. You are making a lovely sound. Hit it again. Oh, look, here is the sad face."

Basket Nesting

How will these baskets fit together?

Age

8–15 months

Curriculum Area

Cognitive

Curriculum Objectives

To explore size and spatial relations; to increase problem solving through trial and error.

Anti-Bias Area

Culture

Anti-Bias Skill

To expose infants to patterns and textures from different cultures.

Materials

Collection of baskets from different cultures

Approach

Incorporation

Facilitation

Put out baskets for infants to explore. Allow them to visually inspect and manipulate the materials. Comment on the different shapes, sizes, and/or colors of the baskets as the infants play with them.

Demonstrate how to put a smaller basket inside a larger one, and encourage the infants to try. To facilitate this, only put out similarly shaped baskets at first. Verbally prompt the children by saying, "Look, I'm hiding the little basket inside the big basket."

Nesting materials according to size gradation teaches children sequencing and ordering. For infants this task should be practiced with materials that have wide openings to allow for easy insertion and retrieval.

Community Resource

Local markets or shops that carry crafts from Asia or Africa.

Lids and Tops

Age

8–18 months

Curriculum Area

Cognitive

Curriculum Objectives

To practice aim, targeting, and release; to explore spatial relations and cause and effect.

Anti-Bias Area

Race

Anti-Bias Skills

To label feelings and emotions; to expose infants to different skin tones.

Materials

Thin orange juice lids; smaller and thicker tops from juice bottles; large, plastic see-through container; lid with a slit cut in the shape of a smile or a frown that is large enough for the other lids/tops to pass through; stickers with happy or sad faces on colored backgrounds of different skin tones; and skin-toned markers.

Approach

Incorporation

Facilitation

Infants need practice filling and dumping objects. Initially, the tops and lids will be novel enough only to sustain interest in examining and manipulating them. Label the emotions on the sticker faces as they are dropped and picked up. Offer the container without the lid to younger infants, and drop a few tops inside to create a noise. Shake the container to produce more sound and draw their attention to the lids making those sounds. Encourage the infants to imitate your actions. Show them how to turn the container upside down and shake the lids out again.

For the older infants, snap on the lid with the happy face slot and direct the children to try pushing the tops through the opening. Observe how they explore spatial relations, and support their attempts at removing the cover in order to retrieve the lids. See if they can find the lid with the happy or sad face when you request it. For infants who are visually discriminating, see if they can put the happy face stickers in the container with the happy smile slot, and the sad face stickers in the corresponding container.

Hidden Hankies

How does it come out?

Age
12–18 months

Curriculum Area
Cognitive

Curriculum Objectives
To strengthen object permanence, intentionality, and eye-hand coordination.

Anti-Bias Areas
Culture, Race, Gender, Age

Anti-Bias Skill
To expose infants to areas of diversity.

Materials
L'eggs® pantyhose containers or other egg-shaped plastic containers that twist apart; colorfully designed handkerchiefs; pictures of people or children representing different ages, genders, cultures, and racial backgrounds.

Secure pictures to the top or bottom portions of the eggs with clear contact paper. Hide handkerchiefs inside the eggs.

Approach
Incorporation

Facilitation
Infants never tire of hide-and-find games. Give infants the plastic eggs to explore; encourage all types of motor experimentation. Model either pulling apart or twisting actions so the infant can discover the "treasure" inside. Encourage children to imitate these hand motions and express surprise each time they find a handkerchief. The game will initially require your facilitation to enclose the handkerchief into the container, but with repeated practice the infant will be able to master the three-step process of pulling the egg apart, stuffing the handkerchief inside, and putting the container back together. Label the picture on the egg as the infant reaches for the different containers: "There is a girl on this egg. What's inside?"

Tongue Pull

Age
12–18 months

Curriculum Area
Cognitive

Curriculum Objectives
To strengthen object permanence, eye-hand coordination, and pulling and grasping; to encourage imitation.

Anti-Bias Area
Culture

Anti-Bias Skill
To expose infants to patterns and textures from different cultures.

Materials
One small tie; square pillow; and a variety of culturally distinctive scarves.

Decorate a pillow as a face with a happy smile. The smile should have a slit wide enough to pull the scarves through; leave the top of the pillow partially open to retract the scarves. Knot all of the scarves together with the tie attached to one end. Stuff the scarves into the pillow with the tie protruding from the smile.

Approach
Incorporation

Facilitation
Pull on the tongue (tie) to produce an ongoing flow of scarves. Encourage the infants to imitate your actions. Label their actions as well as the changing colors, patterns, and textures of the scarves. Play peek-a-boo with the scarves as they emerge from the hole. Make the tongue disappear slowly and then quickly by pulling them back through from the top. Share the infant's excitement as new colors appear and when you make the tongue disappear: "You're pulling the scarf. It's a big, red scarf. Pull more—look, another scarf is coming out. This scarf is silky and smooth. Keep pulling."

Expansion
Add a scent, such as rose or clove, to a few of the scarves. Repeat the activity and focus the infant's attention on the smell.

Textured Nesting Cans

Age
12–18 months

Curriculum Area
Cognitive

Curriculum Objectives
To stimulate visual and tactile exploration; to understand spatial relations through motoric trial and error.

Anti-Bias Area
Culture

Anti-Bias Skills
To foster pride in personal accomplishments; to expose infants to patterns and textures from different cultures.

Materials
Seven cans of descending size; coverings; cloth tape and glue.

Cover cans with fabrics, sandpaper, burlap, silk, leather, contact paper, flannel, fur; glue. Ensure the rims of the cans are covered with cloth tape for additional safety.

Approach
Incorporation

Facilitation
Allow the infants to explore the various textures. Label the sensations as they manipulate the cans: "This can is smooth. This one is bumpy."

Put the cans in ascending order in a row in front of the infants. Demonstrate putting a small can into a larger one, and encourage the children to try. Turn the cans over and let the children stack cans on top of one another. Praise all efforts as infants learn about the dimensions of space and size.

Family Puzzle

Age
12–18 months

Curriculum Area
Cognitive

Curriculum Objectives
To heighten visual discrimination; to strengthen grasp, release, and targeting.

Anti-Bias Areas
Race, Family Composition, Age

Anti-Bias Skills
To promote a sense of family belonging; to expose infants to different skin tones and to areas of diversity.

Materials
Photos of children's families, both nuclear and extended, mounted on bristol board and laminated. Glue small wooden knob to top of each puzzle piece, and create a board from a shoebox with matching shaped holes to allow for the photo pieces to be inset. Change the shape contours of the photos for added visual discrimination for the older infants.

Approach
Incorporation

Facilitation
Place two photos in front of the infant. Allow the child time to visually inspect them, and provide language labeling related to what the child is seeing. Point out and name key figures in the photos, and describe simply what they are doing. For the first few times, select photos of the child's family. This activity should be repeated with each individual child. Guide the photo puzzle piece to the appropriate opening and demonstrate how the piece fits in. Encourage the infant to experiment and problem solve the spatial challenge. For older infants who are familiar with their family puzzle pieces, mix up the photos so that children can identify other children and their families while placing them in the puzzle board.

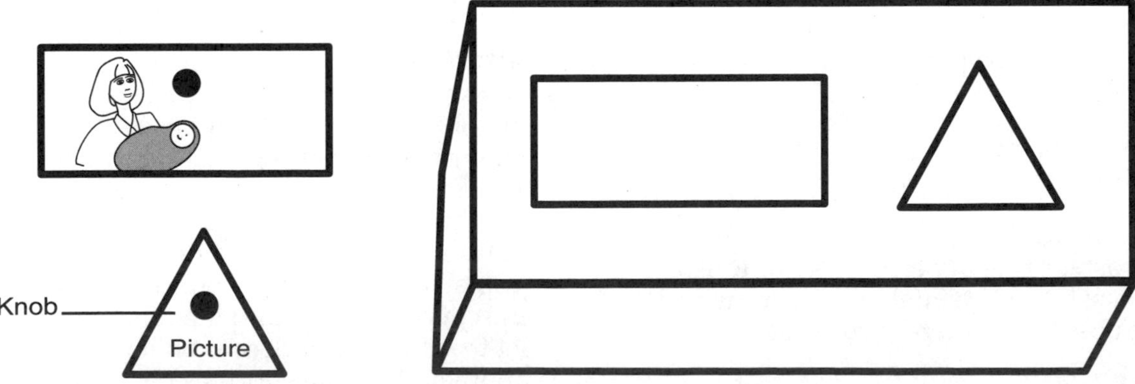

I can make this picture fit the hole.

Hide and Find Box

Age

8–18 months

Curriculum Area

Cognitive

Curriculum Objectives

To strengthen object permanence; cause and effect; and intentionality.

Anti-Bias Areas

Race, Ability, Age, Gender

Anti-Bias Skill

To expose infants to areas of diversity.

Materials

Box with holes on top and on side at bottom, used as a secret entrance; anti-bias pictures, mounted and laminated; velcro; fabrics in a variety of textures, colors, and level of transparency, used as pockets or screens; and small manipulative objects that are varied in sound and shape.

Approach

Incorporation

Facilitation

Present the box full of toys and photos in pockets to a small group of two to three infants. Support all exploratory play by the infants, such as shaking, squeezing, banging, throwing, and pulling out and pushing objects into the pockets. Comment on the children's actions, and encourage them to repeat either accidental or intentional behaviors of object permanence and spatial relations exploration. Hide the pictures in the pockets and encourage infants to find and hide them. Point out and label the people in the photos, as well as their actions and emotions.

What will I find next?

Textured Sound Shakers

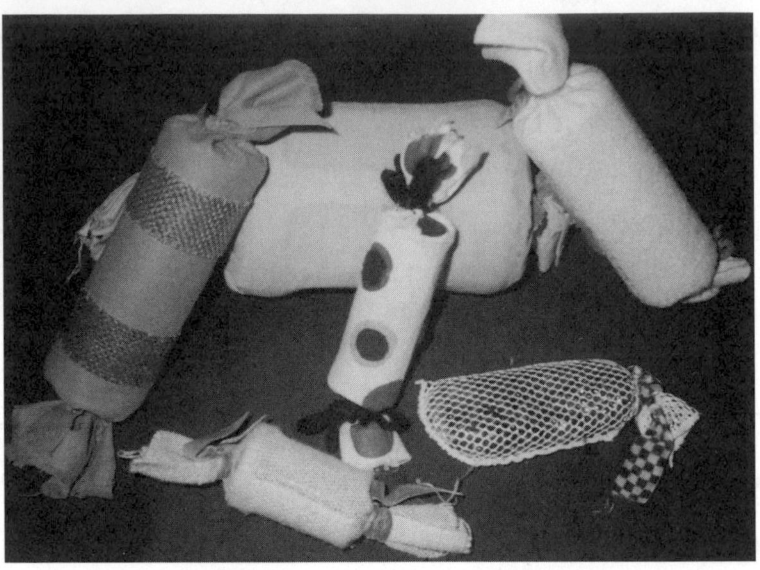

Squeeze me, throw me, shake me, smell me.

Age

4–12 months

Curriculum Area

Motor

Curriculum Objectives

To strengthen eye-hand coordination, and grasping and shaking skills; to encourage intentionality to produce sounds.

Anti-Bias Area

Culture

Anti-Bias Skill

To expose infants to patterns and textures from different cultures.

Materials

Plastic containers; distinctively patterned material from different cultures; a variety of noise-producing objects; glue; and ribbon.

Collect a variety of plastic containers that have screw-on tops and differ in size and shape. Cover the containers with material scraps, and fill with noise-making items such as small stones, sand, shells from nuts, nuts and bolts, etc., in order to produce sounds that differ in volume and pitch. Glue the tops to ensure added safety. The easiest way to cover the shakers is to roll the containers in a rectangular swatch of material and tie both ends with interesting ribbons.

Approach

Incorporation

Facilitation

Infants need many opportunities to learn how to grasp objects and soon after, practice shaking them. Pleasure is derived immediately upon producing a sound, so these shakers will naturally reinforce the children's experimentation. Encourage infants to explore the range of sounds by imitating their movements with the collection of shakers. Label simply what the infant sees, hears, and does: "Shake, shake. What a loud sound Gleny's made. Shake, shake. This green one makes a soft sound."

These early practice sessions teach infants that they can be the source of producing an interesting sound or event, and lay the foundation for creating a sense of personal agency.

Ribbons and Bows

Age

6–12 months

Curriculum Area

Motor

Curriculum Objectives

To improve goal-directed reaching and voluntary release; tactile, visual, and auditory discrimination; and large muscle balance.

Anti-Bias Area

Culture

Anti-Bias Skill

To expose infants to patterns and textures from different cultures.

Materials

Tie a variety of ribbons reflecting different weaving patterns, designs, and textures onto a rail. (A pull-up bar mounted into a wall, preferably in front of a mirror, to encourage pulling-to-stand and cruising behaviors is essential in an infant room.) Securely attach small bells to a few selected ribbons.

Approach

Incorporation

Facilitation

Encourage the infants to reach and grab the ribbons. By hanging the ribbons of different lengths, the infants will have to adjust their goal-directed reaching appropriately. Support their curiosity and surprise when they discover the ribbons that jingle by labeling the bell. Describe the ribbons and the infant's actions simply: "Is the ribbon soft? It's tickling your cheek. Here's a lovely ribbon. Pull it."

This activity will strengthen the upper and lower torso as infants learn how to balance themselves while reaching up for objects. Support infants who are not yet steady sitters. Encourage those who are demonstrating emerging pulling-to-stand behaviors.

Drum Madness

Age

6–18 months

Curriculum Area

Motor

Curriculum Objectives

To encourage crawling after a rolling object; to teach infants that they can cause movement.

Anti-Bias Areas

Race, Gender, Appearance

Anti-Bias Skill

To expose infants to areas of diversity.

Materials

Large plastic container with lid (12-inch diameter, 20-inch height); cardboard; textured and clear contact paper; pictures of children playing, representing diversity in race, gender, and appearance; glue; acorns, chestnuts, and gravel.

Cut a piece of cardboard to fit the diameter of the container. Fill two-thirds of the container with gravel, and then insert and glue the cardboard inset; fill the top section with the nuts. Seal the lid with glue. Glue pictures all around the container. Cover with clear contact paper. Cover the lid with textured contact paper.

Approach

Incorporation

Facilitation

Infants will learn that the slightest touch will send round cylinders rolling. Encourage the infants to pat, hit, and bang the container. If the infant is not yet mobile, then roll the container back and try to get a reciprocal game going.

For both the mobile and nonmobile infant, give simple descriptions of the pictures and relate what the baby sees to individual personal experiences: "Look at the baby playing in the water. Splash, splash." For the crawling infant, support a chase game with the container. Bring out the container when singing and use it as a drum. Banging the sides, top and bottom will produce different auditory results. The sounds produced from shaking will vary as well.

These early sensory experiences will assist infants in developing a keener ability to discriminate sounds.

Tin Can Stacking

Age
6–18 months

Curriculum Area
Motor

Curriculum Objectives
To improve eye-hand coordination; to explore spatial relations through motoric trial and error.

Anti-Bias Areas
Race, Ability, Age, Appearance

Anti-Bias Skill
To foster pride in personal accomplishments.

Materials
Three tin cans of varying sizes; skin-toned shelving paper; pictures of someone in a wheelchair, someone who is fat, a senior citizen involved in an activity; and cloth tape and contact paper.

Ensure that cans are safe by covering the edges with cloth tape. Place a different picture on each can and cover with clear contact paper.

Approach
Incorporation

Facilitation
Demonstrate putting a small can inside a big one or on top of another. Encourage the infants to imitate and discover size relations through their own experimentation. Comment on the pictures as they disappear or emerge from within the cans. Offer praise as infants attempt to nest or stack, and gently suggest correct choices if they seem to become frustrated.

Community Resource
Shelving paper is available in most department and hardware stores.

Bouncing Balloons

Age
8–18 months

Curriculum Area
Motor

Curriculum Objectives
To strengthen projectile management and movement; to increase targeting and goal–directed reaching of large muscles.

Anti-Bias Area
Race

Anti-Bias Skill
To expose infants to different skin tones.

Materials
Ten white balloons; nylon stockings of different shades; water, rice, popcorn kernels, and bells.

Partially blow up the balloons. Add small amounts of rice, water, popcorn kernels, or bells for sound variation. Encase each balloon in a nylon stocking to serve as a protective shell in case of balloon rupture.

Approach
Incorporation

Facilitation
Encourage the infants to practice a variety of motor skills by suspending, throwing, or bouncing the balloons. Reinforce all their movements in space by labeling their actions and emotional responses: "What a good kick/throw/catch. Listen, can you hear that sound? It sounds like a bell."

As the infants play with and visually inspect the balloons, point out the colors. "You are shaking the light brown balloon. Here's another brown balloon. Shake it. Does it sound the same?" The purpose behind the skin-toned nylons is to expose the children to different flesh colors in yet another way. The positive effect of such exposure is cumulative.

Diving Pool

Age
9–18 months

Curriculum Area
Motor

Curriculum Objectives
To increase large motor coordination and exploration of spatial relations; to enhance visual identification.

Anti-Bias Areas
Race, Gender, Culture

Anti-Bias Skills
To promote self-esteem and positive self-concept; to value uniqueness of one's own family and others' families.

Materials
Wading pool; pillows covered with culturally diverse patterns and fabrics; laminated photos of the children with their families; and masking tape.

Fill the pool with the pillows. Tape the photos all around the periphery of the pool.

Approaches
Modified Personalization and Incorporation

Facilitation
Mobile infants do not need much encouragement to climb into and out of enclosed spaces. For those just learning to coordinate going up or down stairs, the pool will provide the opportunity to practice hitching their legs and bottoms over an edge and turning their torsos in the appropriate direction. Use plenty of pillows to cushion clumsy landings or intentional falls. As the infants pull themselves out of the pool, focus their attention on the photo just in visual range. Get them to identify who is in the photo, either by pointing or naming their peer. Comment on what the child in the photo is doing and who the family members are. Ensure that each child eventually finds their own family photo.

Community Resources
Fabric stores and shops sell clothing and material from India, Southeast Asia, Eastern Europe, etc. An alternative which meets the criteria for differences in texture, but not cultural patterns, is the Giant Tactile Pillows (eight 9-inch washable pillows and their mini versions, available from Lakeshore/Wintergreen, #LC 1915).

Stickers on You and Me

Age

12–18 months

Curriculum Area

Motor

Curriculum Objectives

To strengthen targeting, and pincer grasp and release; to develop body awareness, and receptive and expressive language.

Anti-Bias Area

Gender

Anti-Bias Skills

To promote self-esteem and positive self-concept.

Materials

Variety of stickers, e.g., fruit, balloons, vehicles, etc.; mirror.

Approach

Modified Personalization

Facilitation

An infant's awareness of body parts gradually emerges through continuous caretaking routines, songs, and social games. Capitalize on children's growing ability to use pincer grasp skills and their love of pulling off and putting on things. Motivate the activity by focusing an infant's attention to a sticker you place on your nose. Say, "Look at the sticker on my nose. Can you put one on your nose?" Pat stickers on infants' hands, cheeks, toes, knees, tummies, etc.; allowing the infants to pull the stickers off and place them anywhere on their bodies or yours. Show your enjoyment of this game by laughing and labeling the body part that is sporting a sticker. Support all initiatives.

Direct the children's attention to the mirror, pointing out the reflection of the sticker on the named body part. Reinforce their observations of what they feel their bodies doing. Help make the connection between body parts and self-identity: "Who's that in the mirror with the sticker on his nose? It's Jamal."

Resources for Infants

The following books reflect diversity by depicting infants and families of different ethno-racial backgrounds participating in daily routines and building self-concept. A number of books are dual track and/or available in different languages (indicated by an asterisk). Other books depict infants involved in activities with grandparents and other older adults. A number have been cross-referenced with specific activities, both for infants and toddlers. The remaining selections can be read at any time to take advantage of a quiet, intimate moment with an infant.

Family Lullabies

Gilbert, Y. (1990). *Baby's book of lullabies and cradle songs.* New York: Dial Books.

Family Hide and Seek

Williams, V. B. (1990). *More, more, more said the baby.* New York: Greenwillow.

A Book of Me

Winter, S. (1994). *A baby just like me.** London: Mantra.
Hudson, C. W. (1992). *Goodnight baby.* New York: Scholastic.
Hudson, C. W. (1992). *Good morning baby.* New York: Scholastic.

Hand/Foot Water Play

Teague, K. (1990). *Arms and legs.** Toronto: Editions Renyi, Inc.

Mobile Mania

Teague, K. (1990). *Faces.** Toronto: Editions Renyi, Inc.

Family Puzzle

Bailey, D. (1994). *My mom and my dad.** Buffalo: Firefly Books.
Slier, D. (1991). *Me and my grandma.* New York: Checkerboard Press.
Slier, D. (1992). *Me and my grandpa.* New York: Checkerboard Press.

Diving Pool

Butterfield, M. (1995). *Baby faces.* Loughborough, England: Ladybird Books Ltd.
Ingle, A. (1992). *Rainbow babies.* New York: Random House.

Stickers on You and Me

Butterfield, M. (1995). *Baby words.* Loughborough, England: Ladybird Books Ltd.

Other Readings

Asch, F. (1985). *I can roar.* Toronto: Kids Can Press.
Asch, F. (1985). *I can blink.* Toronto: Kids Can Press.
Cooke, T. (1994). *So much.* London: Walker Books.
Dwight, L. (1992). *All my things.* New York: Checkerboard Press.
Dwight, L. (1992). *Babies all around.* New York: Checkerboard Press.
La hora de la comida. (1992). London: Dorling Kindersley Ltd.
Let's eat–Vamos a comer. (1992). New York: Simon and Schuster.
Oxenbury, H. (1987). *Clap hands, say goodnight, all fall down.* New York: Simon and Schuster.
Oxenbury, H. (1987). *Say goodnight.* London: Walker Books.
Oxenbury, H. (1987). *Tickle, tickle.* New York: Simon and Schuster.

Finger Plays, Action Rhymes, and Songs

Anti-Bias Goal

To build self-identity and sense of relationship to family

Age

Infant and Toddler

Songs, Rhymes, and Plays

The following have been adapted from originals in *This Little Puffin . . . Finger Plays and Nursery Games,* compiled by Elizabeth Matterson.

1. Here is the ______ short and stout.
Here is the ______ with children all about.
Here is the ______ tall you can see.
Here is the ______ with dolly on his/her knee.
This is the baby sure to grow.
And here is our family all in a row. (Page 14)

Fill in the blanks with appropriate family member's names while pointing to each finger in turn, starting with the thumb.

2. Two little eyes to look around.
Two little ears to hear each sound.
One little nose to smell what is sweet.
One little mouth that likes to eat. (Page 17)

3. Peek-a-boo, peek-a-boo
Who's that hiding there?
Peek-a-boo, peek-a-boo
______'s behind the chair. (Page 20)

4.

Roll, roll, roll, the baby	(baby on back, hold legs and
Roll, roll, roll, the baby	gently roll from side to side)
Pull, pull, clap, clap, clap	(hold baby's hands by the wrists stretch slowly to the side and clap hands together)
Roll, roll, roll, the baby	
Roll, roll, roll, the baby	(same action as first time)
Stretch, stretch, kick, kick, kick	(hold baby by ankles, stretch legs slowly to the side and clap feet together)

UNIT 3

Anti-Bias Activities for Toddlers

"Acceptance of a child does not happen automatically; it is a goal and not a given."

Rita Warren (1977)

Care and learning continue to occur simultaneously during the toddler years. Sensitive, ongoing observations provide caregivers with valuable information about a toddler's individual temperament, learning style, and preferences for relating to others. Quality development happens when:

- Adults recognize that toddlers are not "mini-preschoolers," but have distinct and unique physical, emotional, social, and intellectual needs.
- Adults understand that toddlers are driven by two opposing impulses; the need to feel safe, dependent, and protected often coincides with the need to feel carefree, unrestricted, and unencumbered in their exploration. When adults sensitively support these emotional needs toddlers learn to trust and feel secure in their world.
- Adults realize that toddlers' egocentrism drives events and actions to be interpreted only in terms of how it affects themselves.
- Adults enable toddlers to cope with painful separations as well as to establish new attachments.
- Adults provide a physical environment that allows toddlers to challenge their bodies safely and make decisions.
- Toys are plentiful so that sharing doesn't have to be an ongoing issue of conflict.
- Toddlers are allowed to practice self-help skills, even if it means they create messes in the process.
- Adults share toddlers' exuberance and enthusiasm while also understanding their mood swings.
- Adults provide an environment that is rich in sensory motor opportunities and adaptive to the toddlers' changing developmental skills.
- Toddlers are given opportunities to feel powerful and make things happen in their environment.
- Adults individualize routines and ensure that each toddler receives one-on-one nurturing several times a day.
- Adults spend the day encouraging, coaching, and responding to toddlers' varying abilities and competencies.
- Spontaneity and capitalizing on incidental learning experiences drive the interactions between toddlers and teachers.
- Parental knowledge and family involvement are highly prized in the child-care/education program.

Web for Toddlers Anti-Bias and Developmental Skills

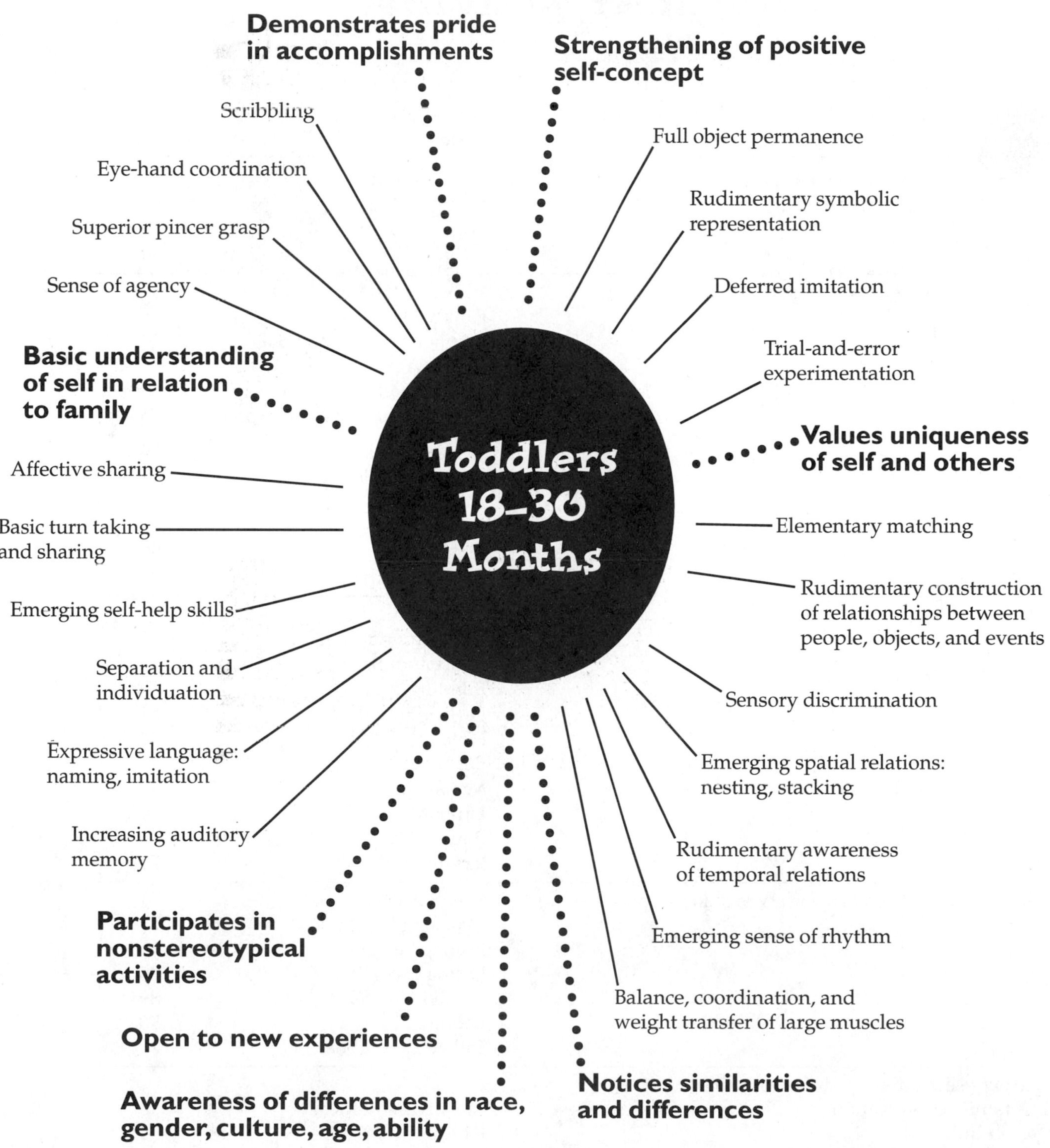

Summary of Anti-Bias Skills Toddler Activities

Anti-Bias Skills	Activity Title	Page Number
To promote a positive sense of self; to strengthen positive identity.	Bandage Time	56
	Handprinting	61
	Book of Routines	69
	Lacing Faces	86
To value uniqueness of self and others.	Hide and Find the Toddlers	57
	Family Place Mats	58
	Emotions Peek-a-boo Board	59
	Me Collage	60
	Book of Routines	69
	Opening and Closing Surprises	75
To strengthen basic understanding of self in relation to family.	Family Messages	54
	Are You My Mother?	55
	Family Place Mats	58
	Crying Babies	68
	Magnet Play	80
	Family Matchup	84
To expose toddlers to cultural differences in:	Ramp Fun	91
◎ textures and patterns;	Rock Around the Clock	61
	Bunches of Bags	67
	Building Spools	79
	Feeling Fingers	81
	Matching Fabrics	83
	Beanbag Toss	88
◎ rhythms and music;	Making Music	64
	Drum March	90
◎ smells and foods.	Bumpy Goop	65
	Jars and Lids	75
To expose toddlers to a variety of skin tones.	Silly Putty Silliness	64
	Matching Paint Chips	74
	Feeling Fingers	81
	Lacing Faces	86
	Stuffed Nylons	89
	Bandage Time	56
	Tall Body Felt Board	71
To expose toddlers to differences in:		
◎ family composition;	Ivory Snow® Smear	63
◎ ability;	Bathtime for Babies	54

Anti-Bias Skills	Activity Title	Page Number
	Ivory Snow® Smear	63
	Knobs in a Box	72
	Exploring Mobility Devices	87
◎ age;	The Obstacle Course	88
◎ appearance;	Mirror Reflections	67
◎ race and gender.	Bathtime for Babies	54
	Washing and Drying Clothes	60
	Tall Body Felt Board	71
	Laundry Scoops	76
	Building Spools	79
To build awareness of others' feelings.	Emotions Peek-a-boo Board	59
To encourage toddlers to try new experiences.	Vermicelli Play	63
	Bumpy Goop	65
	Noodles and Things	65
	Brown Dough Sticks	66
	Exploring Mobility Devices	87
To participate in nonstereotypic activities.	Bathtime for Babies	54
	Washing and Drying Clothes	60
	Bunches of Bags	67
To notice similarities and differences.	Buried Treasure	62
	Squishy Water Play	62
	Scrub Painting	66
	Mixed-up Suitcase	70
	Buttons and Beads	73
	Changeable Faces	77
	Gluing Faces	78
	Matching Fabrics	83
To promote positive association with the color brown.	Brown Dough Sticks	66
To increase a toddler's ability to interact with others who are differently abled.	Signing a Name	82
To build empathy.	Bandage Time	56
	Crying Babies	68
To support gender equity in play.	Baby Dressing	85
	House Cleaning	91

Bathtime for Babies

Age
18–30 months

Curriculum Area
Socio-emotional

Curriculum Objectives
To support a toddler's understanding of personal needs and the needs of others; to promote a sense of self.

Anti-Bias Areas
Gender, Race, Ability

Anti-Bias Skills
To participate in a nonstereotypic activity, and expose toddlers to differences in race, gender, and ability.

Materials
Multiracial dolls with a limb missing, a leg brace or glasses; wash basins; towels and face cloths from different cultures; variety of sponges (including sea sponges); large empty powder containers; and plastic training pants.

Approach
Incorporation

Facilitation
Capitalize on the toddler's passion for water play by providing the dolls, bathing props, and warm water. Encourage both the boys and girls to clean, shampoo, pat dry, powder, and nurture the dolls. Discuss any differences in racial appearance or ability that the children observe. Comment and reaffirm what they see in a natural and straightforward manner. State that all children, even those who might only have one leg or who wear glasses, enjoy having a bath and feeling the bubbly water.

Community Resource
Donation of leg brace or any other adaptive equipment.

Family Messages

Age
18–30 months

Curriculum Area
Socio-emotional

Curriculum Objectives
To work through issues of attachment and separation; to strengthen the child's sense of security.

Anti-Bias Areas
Family Composition, Gender

Anti-Bias Skill
To strengthen basic understanding of self in relation to family.

Materials
Paper, large crayons, envelopes, and stickers.

Approach
Incorporation

Facilitation
Suggest to the toddlers that their mothers/fathers/grandparents or other appropriate caregivers miss them a lot during the day and would love to receive a special message from them.

Put out the paper, stickers, and crayons and encourage them to scribble. As they are drawing, focus the conversation on the activities they have engaged in that day: water play, snack, outdoor play, puppets, etc. Give the children words for their emotions, using terms of endearment that are unique to each family. Write each child's name on their drawing; have the children stuff and decorate envelopes. Let the children carry the envelopes in a pocket or put the envelopes in a special place for safekeeping. Remind them at pickup time to give the special message to their caregivers.

Are You My Mother?

Age

18–30 months

Curriculum Area

Socio-emotional

Curriculum Objective

To work through attachment and separation issues.

Anti-Bias Area

Gender

Anti-Bias Skill

To strengthen basic understanding of self in relation to family.

Materials

Are You My Mother?, by P. D. Eastman; felt pieces of mother and baby animals; and felt figures of mothers and children in a variety of skin tones.

Approach

Incorporation

Facilitation

Read the picture book *Are You My Mother?* to the children. Use animated expressions and vary your vocal intonations and sounds. Involve the children by intermittently asking them if they think the pictured animal/object is the little bird's mother. When the bird and mother are reunited, talk about how sad or sometimes scary it feels when family members are separated and how happy and good it feels when they can be together.

Take out the felt pieces and see how the children match up mother and baby animals, as well as mother and child felt figures. Use the opportunity to label whatever felt pieces are manipulated and increase the toddlers' receptive and expressive abilities.

Bandage Time

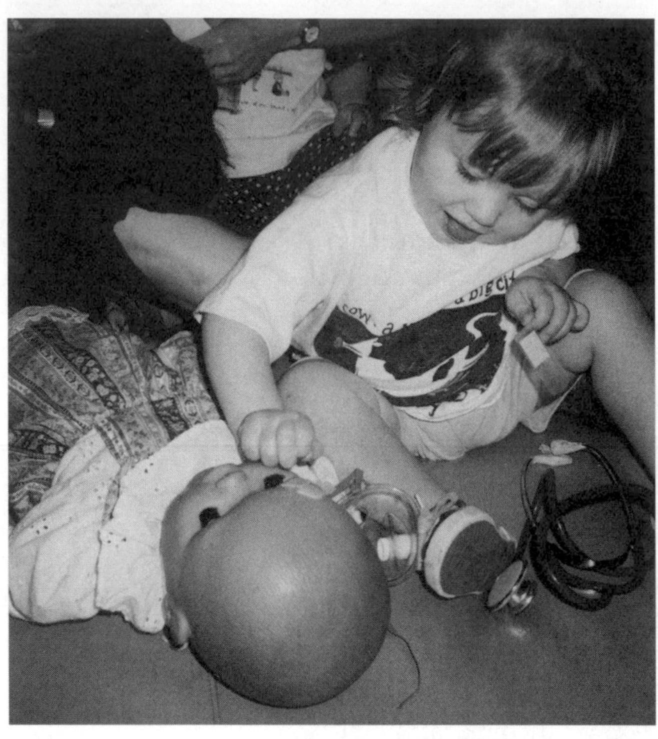

Nurturing dolls and building empathy.

Age

18–30 months

Curriculum Area

Socio-emotional

Curriculum Objectives

To strengthen self-identity; to build empathy.

Anti-Bias Areas

Race, Gender

Anti-Bias Skills

To promote positive sense of self; to strengthen positive identity; to build empathy.

Materials

Multiracial dolls; dolls with adaptive equipment: leg brace, glasses, hearing aid, etc.; and transparent bandages and rolled gauze.

Approach

Incorporation

Facilitation

Bring out the dolls and a basket full of bandages and gauze. Encourage both girls and boys to take care of the dolls that are "hurt." Assist the children as they manipulate the bandages. Support their actions by commenting on how they are making the dolls feel better, just like their families help them when they don't feel well. It is important to support the boys as they nurture side by side with the girls. Make casual reference to how you can see the skin color through the bandages.

Hide and Find the Toddlers

Age
18–30 months

Curriculum Area
Socio-emotional

Curriculum Objectives
To strengthen attachment relationships and work through any separation issues.

Anti-Bias Area
Race

Anti-Bias Skill
To value uniqueness of self and others.

Materials
Multiracial dolls

Approaches
Personalization and Incorporation

Facilitation
This enjoyable game can be played either on the playground or in the classroom.

Take one or two children by the hand and announce to another toddler that you are going to hide. Go to playground equipment, a tree, or another spot that partially obscures you and the other toddlers. Sing out: "Can you find us, Jacob? Where are Sean and Naomi?" When the toddler finds you, get the children to say "Boo" and you hug the "seeker." Continue playing as long as the children are enthusiastic. Have the children take turns seeking and hiding.

Play this game indoors by hiding dolls under chairs, under blankets, behind blocks, etc. Give toddlers verbal clues: "Where is the baby? Is he in the block corner?" Or offer physical assistance: "If we go this way will we find him? Do you think he is inside the box? Is he around the corner?"

Toddlers need to have control over disappearing and appearing people and objects as they work through attachment and separation issues common to this stage of development.

Family Place Mats

Age

18–30 months

Curriculum Area

Socio-emotional

Curriculum Objectives

To strengthen positive self-concept; to reinforce visual identification of family members and peers.

Anti-Bias Areas

Culture, Race

Anti-Bias Skills

To strengthen basic understanding of self in relation to family; to value uniqueness of self and others.

Materials

Photos of the toddlers with their families mounted on bristol board and covered with clear contact paper.

Approaches

Incorporation and Modified Personalization

Facilitation

Initially, bring out the place mats during a non-mealtime play situation. Spend time with each child visually examining the pictures and chatting about who is on the place mat and what they are doing. Taking time to talk about each child's family and pointing out family members of other toddlers helps each child feel valued and supports emotional attachments.

At mealtimes, randomly place the mats around the table and ask the toddlers to find their seats. Take the opportunity to encourage all expressive and receptive language skills that emerge: "Rebecca, can you find your place mat today? That's right, today you are sitting next to Monisha." Or, "Whose picture is on that place mat? Good for you. That is Matthew and his family. Can you find your picture?"

Create new place mats every six months to encourage ongoing discussions about family.

Emotions Peek-a-boo Board

Age
18–30 months

Curriculum Area
Socio-emotional

Curriculum Objectives
To identify simple emotions; to help toddlers learn to predict cause and effect.

Anti-Bias Areas
Race, Gender, Ability, Age, Culture

Helping toddlers to identify emotions.

Anti-Bias Skills
To build awareness of others' feelings; to value uniqueness of self and of others.

Materials
Large, clear photos of children with adults, representing a diversity of race, age, gender, ability. (The Moods and Emotions Poster Pack from Lakeshore/Wintergreen, LC 1184, has a selection of 20 good-sized photos.) Laminate or protect the photos with clear contact paper, and cover them with fabrics from different countries.

Approach
Incorporation

Facilitation
As the toddler lifts the cover, identify and describe simply how the child in the photo is feeling, linking it to a cause. Talk to the toddler about how different children feel during certain emotional situations. Assure toddlers that an adult will be there to support them whether they are happy, sad, or mad.

Follow up this simple activity with board books that give toddlers the opportunity to hear, see, and recognize a wide array of emotions. This will enable toddlers to understand and control their emotions.

Expansion
Read such board books as *Don't Say No,* by Anne Sibley O'Brien, as a follow-up discussion on toddler emotions.

Me Collage

Age
18–30 months

Curriculum Area
Socio-emotional

Curriculum Objective
To strengthen positive self-concept.

Anti-Bias Areas
Gender, Race

Anti-Bias Skill
To value uniqueness of self and others.

Materials
Mural paper; paints in various skin tones and primary colors; brushes; glue; and fabric and yarn.

Approaches
Incorporation and Personalization

Facilitation
Invite grandparents or other family members to participate in this creative experience. Trace and cut out the body shapes of the toddlers and family members. Provide small bowls of paint and/or glue pots with a wide assortment of materials that can be used by the toddlers to decorate their collages.

Support the children's creativity by labeling body parts and clothing, and describing the colors and textures of the materials chosen to decorate the body image.

Washing and Drying Clothes

Age
18–30 months

Curriculum Area
Sensory

Curriculum Objectives
To provide opportunities for sensory pleasure; to strengthen fine motor coordination.

Anti-Bias Area
Gender

Anti-Bias Skills
To participate in nonstereotypical activities; to expose toddlers to differences in race and gender.

Materials
Multiracial dolls; clothing; mild hypoallergenic dish detergent; clothesline and clothespins. (Large doll pins which slide easily on the line can be purchased from Lakeshore/Wintergreen, SC7-WD421.)

Approach
Incorporation

Facilitation
Capitalize on the toddler's eagerness to imitate chores they see family members doing, as well as their fondness for water play. Talk about why and when clothes need washing and what happens to clothes after they are wet. Support the toddlers' initiatives as they undress the dolls, and wash and hang up the clothing. Emphasize gender equity in this experience. Ask them how they think clothes are dried and then show them the equipment. Point out similarities and differences in the way families carry out this task.

Handprinting

Age
18–30 months

Curriculum Area
Sensory

Curriculum Objectives
To encourage visual and tactile exploration; cause and effect.

Anti-Bias Areas
Race, Gender

Anti-Bias Skills
To promote a positive sense of self; to strengthen positive identity.

Materials
Paper and paints in skin-toned colors.

Approach
Modified Personalization

Facilitation
Put out paper and place paints on a tray. Encourage the children to dip their palms flat into the paint and then onto the paper. Join in the toddlers' pleasure and surprise as their handprints appear. After the initial engrossment and sensory pleasure wanes, point out the fingers and count them with the toddlers. Emphasize how special handprints are because they are a part of each child.

If the children become involved in smearing paint on their hands and arms, allow them to explore not only the sensation but also the visual comparison they may be making about color. You can casually comment how one child's hands now look like another's.

Rock Around the Clock

Age
18–30 months

Curriculum Area
Sensory

Curriculum Objectives
To refine tactile discrimination; to encourage moving one's body in response to music

Anti-Bias Area
Culture

Anti-Bias Skill
To expose toddlers to cultural differences in textures and patterns.

Materials
Twelve pieces of material cut into large 12-inch squares; "rock-around-the-clock" song, and tape recorder.

Select a variety of textures (bamboo, quilt, velvet, corduroy, silk, cotton, batik, straw, burlap, etc.) with distinctive patterns. Tape these squares into the configuration of a clock.

Approach
Incorporation

Facilitation
Have the children remove their socks and shoes and invite them to dance barefoot on the different squares of material. Play the "rock-around-the-clock" song for rhythm and bounce. Encourage them to jump, twist, and dig their toes into the squares in order to explore the differences in texture. Comment on their movements as well as the sensations their feet are experiencing: "What terrific dancing, Amal. Does the burlap square tickle? Myra is jumping on the elephant from India. Go, Myra, go!"

Buried Treasure

Age
18–30 months

Curriculum Area
Sensory

Curriculum Objectives
To encourage visual and tactile exploration, sensory pleasure, and visual discrimination.

Anti-Bias Area
Culture

Anti-Bias Skill
To notice similarities and differences.

Materials
Sandtable/box and a variety of shells (clam, mussel, scallop, cones, etc.); spoons are optional.

Approach
Incorporation

Facilitation
Toddlers take great delight in pouring and digging through sand. Enhance their curiosity by hiding a number of different shells in the sand. Ask the children to find the surprise buried in the sand. Once they discover the shells, talk to them about color, shape, size, and the beach. Watch as they visually and tactilely compare the shells. Help them to understand that shells come in different shapes and sizes from all over the world. Supervise the toddlers with the very small shells.

Community Resources
It is best to have your own collection, however, if you are unable to visit the seashore then Constructive Playthings has a lovely assortment of shells (FEI-103).

Squishy Water Play

Age
18–30 months

Curriculum Area
Sensory

Curriculum Objectives
To encourage visual and tactile exploration; to understand cause and effect.

Anti-Bias Area
Culture

Anti-Bias Skill
To notice similarities and differences

Materials
Variety of sponges (sea, foam, loofah, scrubber, etc.); reusable cloth towels; and separate containers of water.

Approach
Incorporation

Facilitation
Set out containers half filled with water; place the sponges and other absorbing materials around the containers. Have the toddlers play with the water and experiment with the sponges. Model dunking a sponge and squeezing out the water. Encourage the children to dip the materials in the water and watch how the water runs out. Describe how the different textures feel and the amount of water that can be squeezed out. When water spills on the table, show the children how it can be mopped up by the sponges. Encourage them to imitate.

This activity provides another opportunity to investigate materials that have a similar function but are different in appearance and texture.

Ivory Snow® Smear

Age
18–30 months

Curriculum Area
Sensory

Curriculum Objectives
To encourage visual, tactile, and olfactory exploration; to stimulate sensory pleasure.

Anti-Bias Areas
Family Composition, Ability

Anti-Bias Skill
To expose toddlers to differences in family composition and ability.

Materials
½ cup warm water; 1 cup Ivory Snow® powder detergent; food coloring; mixing bowl; blender or hand mixer; and picture mats, covered with clear contact paper, that reflect the diversity in families (integrated, extended, same sex, etc.) and depict children who wear glasses, have a hearing aid, use a walker, etc.

Approach
Incorporation

Facilitation
Prepare the Ivory Snow® mixture with the toddlers so they can observe the process, perhaps turn the blender on and off, and listen to your commentary on what is happening in the bowl. Give each child a mat, then scoop out some mixture onto the mats. Encourage the children to freely explore the sensation of smearing the mixture on the mats. Support and extend their excitement as they make the pictures appear and disappear by describing their actions and what they see in the pictures. Keep all conversations casual: "Where's Miriam and her family? There they are. Can you cover her up again? Let's find Jyoti. See, she is wearing glasses just like me. Oh, where did she go?"

Vermicelli Play

Age
18–30 months

Curriculum Area
Sensory

Curriculum Objectives
To encourage visual and tactile exploration; to stimulate sensory pleasure.

Anti-Bias Area
Culture

Anti-Bias Skill
To encourage toddlers to try new experiences.

Materials
Hard, uncooked vermicelli dyed with two different food colorings and baked. Bins with pictures of other types of pasta.

Approach
Incorporation

Facilitation
This sensory experience provides a very different texture for the toddlers to explore. It may be a preferable alternative for those toddlers who have an aversion to wet, sticky substances. Allow maximum time for the toddlers to handle the vermicelli. Extend their physical manipulation with appropriate language: "You grabbed a big bunch of noodles. Listen to them scrunch. I like the way you are dropping the noodles slowly into the bin."

Compare the vermicelli with the pictures of different pasta on the bins. This is a first step to learning that different cultures have an assortment of grains.

Caution: This activity may violate policies on food usage. Use or discard according to your program's philosophy and policies.

Making Music

Age
18–30 months

Curriculum Area
Sensory

Curriculum Objectives
To enhance auditory and visual discrimination; to stimulate use of body movement in response to different rhythms.

Anti-Bias Area
Culture

Anti-Bias Skill
To expose toddlers to cultural differences in rhythms and music.

Materials
Maracas, castanets, tambourines, triangles, rain stick, rhythm sticks, etc.; tape recorder; and music from different countries. (Lakeshore/Wintergreen has an extensive selection of multicultural instruments and multiethnic music on cassette tapes.)

Approach
Incorporation

Facilitation
Invite the children to gather in a group and select a musical instrument to explore. Initially encourage them to listen to how each instrument sounds. Describe the type of sound each instrument produces, and label each child's actions. Put on a song tape and clap the rhythm for the group. Have the children play their instruments together in accompaniment to the different songs. Encourage any dance movements as the toddlers bang, shake, and hit their instruments.

Silly Putty Silliness

Age
18–30 months

Curriculum Area
Sensory

Curriculum Objectives
To encourage tactile and visual exploration; to stimulate sensory pleasure.

Anti-Bias Area
Race

Anti-Bias Skill
To expose toddlers to a variety of skin tones.

Materials
Recipe: 1 cup white nontoxic glue, 1 teaspoon people-colored tempera paint, 3 teaspoons Bacti-Stat® soap. Mix ingredients together to form a smooth, elastic consistency. Add more Bacti-Stat® if the mixture is too sticky, until smooth, rubber-like consistency is achieved.

Approach
Incorporation

Facilitation
The developmental benefit of any sensory activity is that toddlers can explore the medium in individual ways. This silly putty mixture provides toddlers with a wide range of small motor manipulation as they squeeze, poke holes, roll, twist, pull, and stretch the substance. The freedom to create, destroy, and re-create is left up to the toddler.

Once again, the use of different skin tones enhances the toddler's evolving ability to make visual discriminations in color shading. The likelihood of discomfort over racial differences becoming an issue later is considerably lessened with such repeated hands-on exposure to different flesh tones early in a child's socialization process.

Bumpy Goop

Age
18–30 months

Curriculum Area
Sensory

Curriculum Objectives
To enhance tactile, visual, and olfactory discrimination.

Anti-Bias Area
Culture

Anti-Bias Skill
To encourage toddlers to try new experiences.

Materials
Three bowls of differently colored goop, prepared by mixing equal parts cornstarch and water. Consistency will thicken when more cornstarch is added, or thin when more water is added. The mixture also will thicken if left to stand, and will dry completely if left out over a long period. Scent with almond extract, garlic, and cumin powders. Provide individual sheets of corrugated paper for toddlers to spread the goop on.

Approach
Incorporation

Facilitation
As the children explore the sticky consistency use opportunities to name the spices and label the smells, tastes, and colors. Talk about how some families use these spices in their cooking. Recall a lunch the toddlers shared in which any of these spices were included. Describe how it feels to spread the goop on the bumpy paper.

Expansion
Put out braille place mats which have pictures and braille for the children to explore.

Noodles and Things

Age
18–30 months

Curriculum Area
Sensory

Curriculum Objectives
To encourage visual and tactile exploration; to stimulate sensory pleasure.

Anti-Bias Area
Culture

Anti-Bias Skill
To encourage toddlers to try new experiences.

Materials
Two large basins of water, one filled with dry rice noodles, the other with softened rice noodles. Rice noodles come in a variety of widths. Scents and food coloring are optional.

Approach
Incorporation

Facilitation
As in every sensory experience for this age group, provide opportunities for lengthy exploration of the materials. Facilitate learning by providing commentary on the texture of the noodles (slippery, smooth, hard), the position of the noodles in the water (floating or on the bottom) and how the children use their hands to grasp, squeeze, pull, and release the noodles. Draw their attention to the differences between the soft and hard noodles as they move from one bin to another.

For older toddlers, scents and food coloring can be added to enrich both the sensory experience and language development.

Caution: The author is aware that the use of food in play is controversial. The inclusion of any such activity is discretionary and should be in line with your program's philosophy and policies.

Scrub Painting

Age
18–30 months

Curriculum Area
Sensory

Curriculum Objectives
To experiment with tools that are different in texture and size; to enhance tactile discrimination.

Anti-Bias Area
Race

Anti-Bias Skill
To notice similarities and differences.

Materials
Three small dish brushes with smooth mop-like bristles; three net scrubbies; three rough-surfaced dish sponges; construction paper in skin-toned colors; three different colors of paint, including brown; and tape.

Approach
Incorporation

Facilitation
Encourage toddlers to explore dipping, scrubbing, and painting with the variety of tools. Point out the different strokes and patterns that are made, as well as the different sounds that are produced. Make casual reference to skin color as they paint: "Nouran, look what's happening to your hands. The paint is making your hand darker. Look at Amy, her hand is purple."

Brown Dough Sticks

Age
18–30 months

Curriculum Area
Sensory

Curriculum Objectives
To encourage tactile and visual exploration; to enhance eye-hand coordination; to practice verbal negotiating skills.

Anti-Bias Area
Race

Anti-Bias Skills
To promote positive association with the color brown; to encourage toddlers to try new experiences

Materials
Flour, oil, salt, water; skin-toned paints; basin; and a large variety of sticks (popsicle, tongue depressors, stir sticks, straws, etc.).

Combine two parts flour, one part salt, one part water, and two tablespoons cooking oil. Add paints and mix well. Add flour if dough becomes sticky.

Approach
Incorporation

Facilitation
Invite children to a table and give substantial portions of playdough to each. Have the sticks sorted according to type in individual canisters. Be prepared as toddlers engage in hoarding behavior by supplying generous amounts of each type of stick. Encourage toddlers to poke and cut the dough; support their attempts at creating symbolic representations (birthday cake, porcupine, etc.). After the children have explored the dough, facilitate counting and sorting skills with the sticks. Describe the similarities and differences among the sticks.

Mirror Reflections

Age
18–24 months

Curriculum Area
Language

Curriculum Objectives
To receptively and expressively identify body parts; to promote recognition of self in relation to a mirror image.

Anti-Bias Area
Appearance

Anti-Bias Skill
To expose toddlers to differences in appearance.

Materials
Large pictures of people's faces and bodies taped to a mirror.

Approaches
Incorporation and Modified Personalization

Facilitation
Ask the toddlers to look at the pictures on the mirror. Have them point out body parts in the pictures. Ask them to show corresponding body parts either in their mirror image or on themselves. Observe if it is easier for them to relate to the mirror image or to their own body. Involve yourself in the game, asking them to identify your arm, nose, hair, knee, etc. Make sure the people in the pictures represent diversity in appearance: wearing glasses, skinny or large, white haired, differently abled, etc.

Bunches of Bags

Age
18–30 months

Curriculum Area
Language

Curriculum Objectives
To build a receptive and expressive vocabulary.

Anti-Bias Areas
Gender, Culture

Anti-Bias Skills
To participate in nonstereotypical activities; to expose toddlers to cultural differences in textures and patterns.

Materials
Collection of purses, money belts, shoulder bags, net bags, backpacks, etc., that reflects cultural variations in style and material.

Approach
Incorporation

Facilitation
Capitalize on the toddler's love of stuffing and toting carryalls with this collection of bags. Let the toddlers explore the interiors of the bags, as well as how to put them on. Encourage the children to select small objects to pack. Engage them in dramatic play as they stuff and carry, exercising their receptive and expressive language abilities. Talk about the size, color, and designs of the bags they are wearing. Add bags to the dramatic play center.

Community Resource
Continue to build on your collection of carryalls by seeking donations from different cultural groups in the community.

Crying Babies

Age

18–30 months

Curriculum Area

Language

Curriculum Objectives

To develop expressive labeling of baby's emotions, body parts, clothing, and accessories.

Anti-Bias Areas

Gender, Race

Anti-Bias Skills

To strengthen basic understanding of self in relation to family; to build empathy.

Materials

Several multiracial infant dolls; diapers and blankets; sleepers and bibs; toy bottles, pacifiers, and small hair brushes; doll-sized crib; a tape with sounds of infants crying; and a small tape recorder.

Approach

Incorporation

Facilitation

Hide the tape recorder in the crib and begin playing the tape of babies crying. Ask the children why they think the baby is crying? Do they think the baby is hungry? wet? tired? Does the baby need a hug and a kiss? Offer suggestions using available accessories, such as a diaper change, new sleeper, bottle, blanket wrap, and pacifier. Comment on the toddlers' actions, extend their language related to body parts or emotions. Give assistance to fine motor tasks. Talk about how well they are doing at being a big brother or sister. Play the tape from time to time to maintain role-playing atmosphere.

Book of Routines

Learning about objects and actions associated with routines.

Age
18–30 months

Curriculum Area
Language

Curriculum Objectives
To identify objects and actions associated with specific routines at home; to stimulate visual memory.

Anti-Bias Areas
Culture, Gender, Race

Anti-Bias Skills
To promote a positive sense of self; to value uniqueness of self and others.

Materials
"Routine Times" picture book cut up and bound with rings; box of common objects: toothbrush, hairbrush, comb, washcloth, bedtime book, pajamas, etc.

Approach
Incorporation

Facilitation
Show the homemade picture book to the toddlers and describe what is happening at each time of the day. Help the toddlers to become aware that everyone has routines they do in the morning and at night. Emphasize the commonalities and differences in approach. Bring out the box and let the toddlers identify the various objects. Ask them what they think people use the object for. Who helps them with this object? When do they use it, at night or in the morning? Keep the book out in the dramatic play center or available in the book area so that the children are free to examine it at their pleasure.

Community Resources
Routine Times is available in Canada from Sonsuh Educational Supplies, and in the United States from Trend Inc.

Mixed-up Suitcase

Age

24–30 months

Curriculum Area

Language

Curriculum Objectives

To practice sorting items according to function; to enhance expressive abilities.

Anti-Bias Areas

Culture, Ability

Anti-Bias Skill

To notice similarities and differences.

Materials

Suitcase; winter hat, baseball cap, scarf, sandal, sock, leg brace, slipper, pants, toy car, stuffed animal, block, book, eyeglasses, asthma mask, etc.

The clothing should be representative of different cultures.

Approach

Incorporation

Facilitation

Bring out the suitcase to a group of toddlers sitting on the floor. Tell them that you packed up things to *wear.* Ask them to please help find all the things to wear. Let each child pull out one item and ask each in turn, "What do you do with it?" If they label the object and point to a corresponding body part, then enhance the child's reply by confirming, "Yes, you do wear a shoe. You wear a shoe on your foot."

When a toy is pulled out and you help to clarify that you *play* with a toy, put the toy in a separate pile at a distance from the suitcase and say, "Let's put things to play in this pile." See what the children do with the other toys and equipment such as the glasses, leg brace, and asthma mask. Explain to the children that these objects are also worn and give them the reasons for wearing them. Leave the suitcase out and observe whether the children will engage in sorting objects spontaneously.

Tall Body Felt Board

Age

18–30 months

Curriculum Area

Cognitive

Curriculum Objectives

To increase body awareness; to practice visual discrimination and matching.

Anti-Bias Areas

Race, Gender

Anti-Bias Skill

To expose toddlers to differences in race and gender.

Materials

Large felt board body shape with cutout pieces of head, torso, arms, legs, hands, fingers, feet, toes in different skin tones; different textured hair pieces.

Approach

Incorporation

Facilitation

Bring out the body felt board with the body parts in a separate container. Allow the toddlers to engage in trial-and-error placement of the body parts. When they have made a successful match, comment and expand on their achievement: "Good for you. You put the legs and arm on. She only has one arm. Where do you think the hand/fingers go?" The activity should support the toddlers' enjoyment of putting things together and taking them apart. Comments or observations related to different colored body parts should be handled naturally without pressure to match colors (e.g., "You put on one brown leg and one white leg.").

Community Resources

Textured hair can be purchased in hobby or arts and crafts stores. Lakeshore/Wintergreen has Curly Doll Hair available in brown, black, copper, and blonde, SC7-TR125.

Knobs in a Box

Age

18–30 months

Curriculum Area

Cognitive

Curriculum Objectives

To improve visual discrimination for matching and sorting according to size; spatial relations; to improve fine motor manipulation.

Anti-Bias Area

Ability

Anti-Bias Skill

To expose toddlers to differences in ability.

Materials

Large box with lid that has five circular openings of different sizes cut out; plastic jars and containers to fit those holes; plastic knobs drilled and screwed into three of the lids; pictures of children with different abilities on the containers: in a wheelchair, with leg brace, glasses, etc.

Approach

Incorporation

Facilitation

Place this box on a table or the floor. Toddlers will pull out and insert the containers repeatedly to gain an understanding of how things of corresponding size fit together. The lids that have knobs on them are designed to assist those children with less developed muscle control and coordination, so toddlers of varying fine motor abilities can all enjoy this activity. As the children pull out each container, focus their attention on the pictures that reflect others of different abilities.

Getting competent with preliminary puzzles.

Buttons and Beads

Age
18–30 months

Curriculum Area
Cognitive

Curriculum Objectives
To strengthen visual discrimination and preliminary sorting skills.

Anti-Bias Area
Culture

Anti-Bias Skill
To notice similarities and differences.

Materials
Basket containing large buttons and beads from different countries; both beads and buttons need to have some similarities—number of holes, color, size, or shape.

Approach
Incorporation

Facilitation
Bring out the basket and shake it to attract the attention of the children. Let the toddlers use their own initiative to visually and physically explore the beads and buttons. For many, just the sight and sounds of these objects will be stimulating. Use teachable moments—when the children hold up two buttons that appear similar, point out in what ways the items are alike. Focus their attention to the many ways that two things can be similar—two big, two little, two red, two gold, two with one hole, two with a tube shape, etc. See if the children undertake any sorting by themselves.

Caution: This activity is for those toddlers who no longer put any small object in their mouths.

Matching Paint Chips

Exposure to similarities and differences in skin tones.

Age
18–30 months

Curriculum Area
Cognitive

Curriculum Objectives
To refine visual discrimination and preliminary matching skills.

Anti-Bias Area
Race

Anti-Bias Skill
To expose toddlers to similarities and differences in skin tones.

Materials
Ten to 20 large paint chips paired by color; the chips should all be the same size and reflect an appropriate range of skin tones.

Approach
Incorporation

Facilitation
Begin this game with only a few matched pairs of paint chips so as not to overwhelm the toddlers and to introduce them to the concept of matching. Spread out three paired cards that reflect distinctive color shades and observe what the toddlers do with them. Support any attempts to group, match the pairs, or even count. Once the toddlers seem to understand the concept, bring out more cards.

As in other activities, the underlying purpose is to begin the ongoing process of ensuring a comfort level with different skin tones. The toddlers may or may not observe similarities and differences to their own color. Seize any teachable moments that may arise if color comparisons are attempted.

Jars and Lids

Age
18–30 months

Curriculum Area
Cognitive

Curriculum Objectives
To encourage rudimentary construction of relationships between objects and elementary matching; to improve eye-hand coordination.

Anti-Bias Area
Culture

Anti-Bias Skill
To expose toddlers to cultural differences in smells and foods.

Materials
Six clear plastic jars of varying sizes with lids; and duplicate pictures of fruit.

Glue one of the pictures on the jar and the other inside the lid, e.g., pineapple, kiwi, apple, banana, lemon, mandarin

Approach
Incorporation

Facilitation
Set out the six jars and give the toddlers the opportunity to visually and physically examine them. Model how to twist the jar lid off and on. Allow time for trial-and-error experimentation as the toddlers try to discriminate the size of jar opening and seek out the appropriate lids. Focus the toddlers' attention on the fruit pictures and help them to find the matching lid. Support their efforts with praise and give them the names of the fruit as they search for the pair. This activity takes time to master, so make the jars available to the children for practice.

Opening and Closing Surprises

Age
18–30 months

Curriculum Area
Cognitive

Curriculum Objectives
To refine object permanence; to strengthen attachment relationships; to develop expressive language, specifically related to peers and teachers.

Anti-Bias Areas
Race, Gender

Anti-Bias Skill
To value the uniqueness of self and others.

Materials
Variety of wallets, boxes, and containers that have different ways of opening (snap, velcro, hinged lid, slide top, flap, etc.); and small laminated photos of the children and teachers in the group taped inside.

Approach
Modified Personalization

Facilitation
Bring out a basket full of these different wallets, small purses, and containers. Allow the children to explore them while asking them if something is inside. Once the photos have been discovered, encourage the toddlers to name who is in the photos. Discuss what the child is doing and lend verbal support to the friendships among the group members.

This activity capitalizes on a toddler's natural curiosity about what is inside an object, and challenges developing motor skills. The experience simultaneously supports emotional relationships and extends language opportunities.

Laundry Scoops

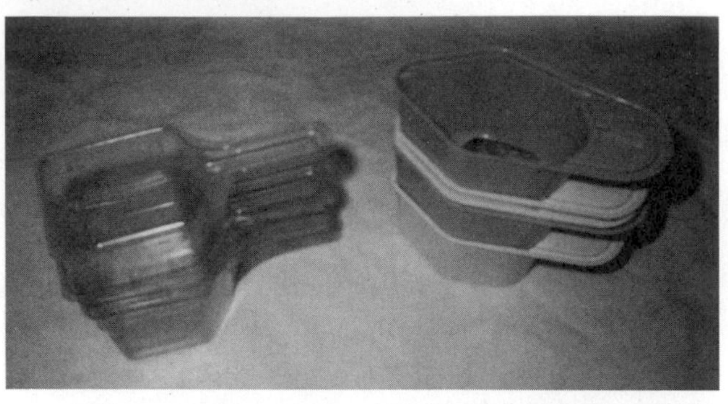

What fits? What matches? Figuring out relationships.

Age

18–30 months

Curriculum Area

Cognitive

Curriculum Objectives

To strengthen understanding of vertical spatial relations and preliminary matching skills.

Anti-Bias Areas

Race, Gender

Anti-Bias Skill

To expose toddlers to differences in race and gender.

Materials

Twenty laundry scoops (either green, white, or clear), found in most detergent boxes; pictures of multiracial babies and children that are taped either inside or on the side of the scoops.

Approach

Incorporation

Facilitation

As the toddlers explore the scoops by either nesting or stacking them, encourage the children to focus on the pictures. When they identify the pictures as "baby" or "boy," foster attempts to group or match: "You found another baby. Can you find more babies?"

Some toddlers will be engrossed solely in the physical manipulation of the scoops, while others will be attracted to the pictures. Support both approaches and extend wherever possible.

Changeable Faces

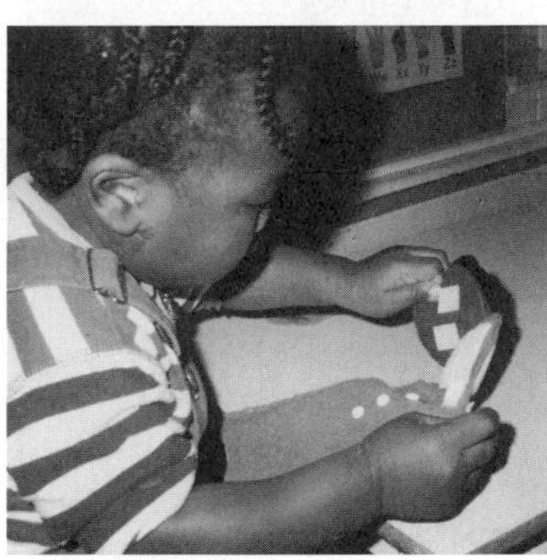

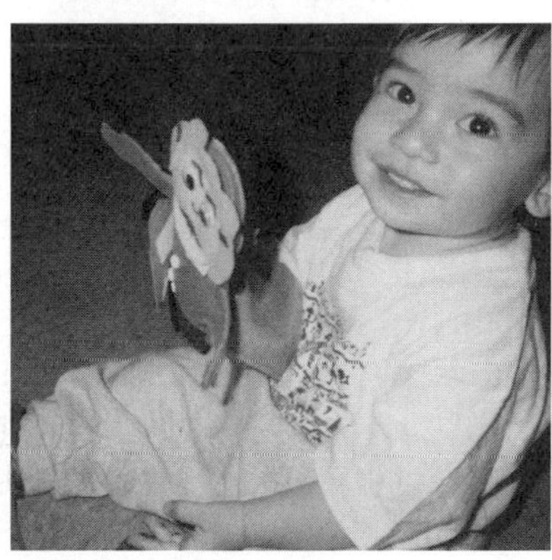

Noticing differences in faces.

Age

18–30 months

Curriculum Area

Cognitive

Curriculum Objectives

To strengthen body awareness and self-image through representational medium; to improve eye-hand coordination.

Anti-Bias Areas

Race, Gender

Anti-Bias Skill

To notice similarities and differences.

Materials

People-colored felt for faces; multicolored felt for clothes; felt for eyebrows, mouth, hair; and eyes, buttons, and velcro.

Create three pairs of double-sided puppets and six different faces, depicting different racial backgrounds and gender. Velcro should be sewn on the backs of the faces and front of the puppet heads.

Approach

Incorporation

Facilitation

Toddlers enjoy pulling things apart and putting them back together as they explore relationships between objects. Offer the double-sided puppets and demonstrate how the faces can be removed and replaced. Let the children experiment by visually inspecting the different faces and then selecting ones to put onto the puppet figures. Engage them in casual conversation by describing how the puppet looks (happy? sad? angry?); the color of skin and hair; what gender they consider it, etc.

Make the connection for them that all the puppets have faces, however, each face looks a bit different.

Community Resource

Constructive Playthings offers a flannel board set called "The Face" (GW-1) that provides a similar activity with 36 felt pieces in three skin tones, four hair colors, and three eye colors, along with self-teaching emotions picture cards.

Gluing Faces

Age

18–30 months

Curriculum Area

Cognitive

Curriculum Objectives

To strengthen self-image through representational pictures; to understand cause and effect; to improve fine motor coordination.

Anti-Bias Area

Race

Anti-Bias Skill

To notice similarities and differences.

Materials

Cut out a large assortment of face parts—eyes (with and without glasses) ears, noses, mouths (with and without teeth, braces, moustache/beard), eyebrows and hair that reflect diversity in shape, color, and size; people-colored paper cut in circles; glue and paddles.

Approach

Incorporation

Facilitation

Read *My Nose, My Toes,* which has large photographs of faces of young children, as an introduction to this activity.

Arrange the assortment of cutouts on small trays, grouped by face parts. As the toddlers select facial features, identify each one and help relate the representational part to their own faces. Direct the children to think about what's missing as the collage progresses, rather than telling them *where* to place the pieces.

For older toddlers point out differences in eye color, hair type, glasses, and skin color. The conversation should flow naturally from children's observations. Any negative comments made in relation to appearance should be clarified immediately.

Building Spools

Age
18–30 months

Curriculum Area
Cognitive

Curriculum Objectives
To explore vertical and horizontal spatial relations and cause and effect; to enhance visual discrimination and matching skills.

Anti-Bias Areas
Culture, Race

Anti-Bias Skills
To expose toddlers to cultural differences in textures and patterns, and race and gender.

Materials
A dozen plastic tool and dye spools covered with pictures of children and adults on each flat end, and wrapped with different fabric swatches from batik to woven cotton. Prepare six matched pairs.

Stacking and rolling means learning about spatial relations.

Approach
Incorporation

Facilitation
Toddlers can explore the spools in many ways; encourage rolling and watching the patterns change, or assist the children in cooperative stacking and building. Rows of matched spools can be created from finding the same picture at either end of the spool.

After the novelty wears off, remove fabric and pictures and place the spools in the water table for additional exploration.

Community Resources
Ask for donations of spools from local tool and dye manufacturers. Small cable spools might also be available from telephone repair companies.

Magnet Play

Age
18–30 months

Curriculum Area
Cognitive

Curriculum Objectives
To improve cause and effect and relational thinking; to improve eye-hand coordination.

Anti-Bias Areas
Race, Culture

Anti-Bias Skill
To strengthen basic understanding of self in relation to family.

Materials
Small photos of the children and family members; orange juice lids with magnetic strips glued to one side and photos to the other; and a metallic tray.

Approach
Modified Personalization

Facilitation
Assist the toddlers as they experiment with the scientific properties of magnets. They will pull off and drop the lids onto the tray repeatedly until the novelty wears off. Focus their attention on the pictures and describe who is doing what. Make up short scenarios about the children and their families as they play with the magnets. Point out, name, and describe family members of the other toddlers and what actions they are engaged in: "Who is this man with the beard? Yes, it's David's grandfather. He's lighting candles. David is celebrating Hanukkah. There's Madeleine. She is having a picnic with her family. I wonder what she is eating?"

Feeling Fingers

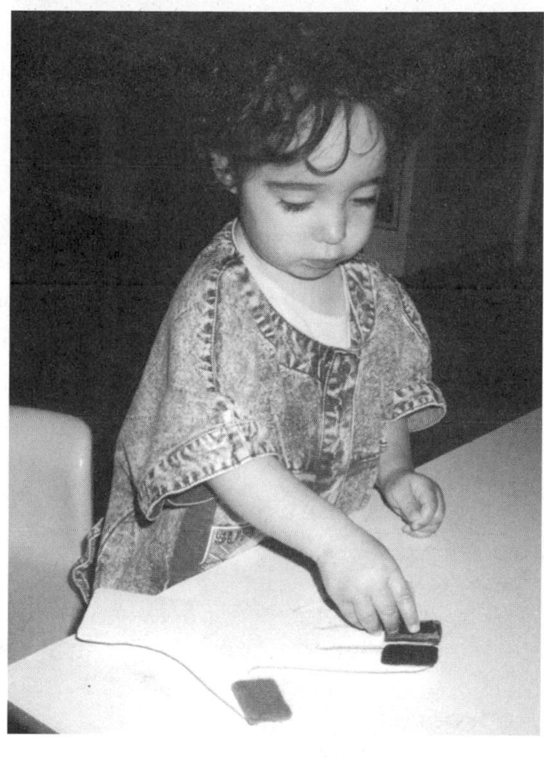

Age

18–30 months

Curriculum Area

Cognitive

Curriculum Objectives

To improve eye-hand coordination in targeting and using the pincer grasp; to understand cause and effect.

Anti-Bias Areas

Race, Culture, Ability

Anti-Bias Skills

To expose toddlers to a variety of skin tones; to expose toddlers to cultural differences in textures and patterns.

Materials

Bristol board cut into the shape of a hand with velcro tabs on the fingertips; and rectangular pieces of fabric, reflecting different cultural patterns and textures.

Cutout hands should be painted with a variety of skin tones, as well as differentiated by size and designed with and without a finger or thumb.

Approach

Incorporation

Facilitation

Toddlers enjoy practice at picking up small items. This activity combines this interest with the sensory pleasure of creating a sound.

Let the children explore the process of pulling off and sticking back on the different fabric pieces. Comment on the color, texture, and patterns of the material, as well as the fingers upon which they are placing the materials: "You stuck purple and black squares on the thumb." Compare their hand sizes with the bristol board cutouts and point out what finger may be missing. If the skin tone is similar, then casually comment on this aspect as well. Point out when the color of a hand is similar: "This hand looks like mine. Can you find one that looks like yours?"

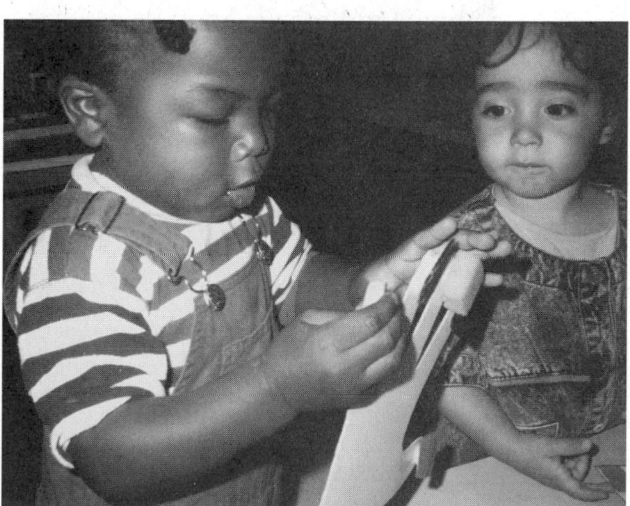

Exploring differences in skin tones and patterns.

This activity can be multisensory by adding scents to the materials.

Signing a Name

Age
18–30 months

Curriculum Area
Cognitive

Curriculum Objectives
To communicate an individual's name through signing initial letter; to improve visual discrimination and motor imitation.

Anti-Bias Area
Ability

Anti-Bias Skill
To increase a toddler's ability to interact with others who are differently abled.

Materials
Word Signs: A First Book of Sign Language; knowledge of hand sign for every child's name. (See Signed English Guide in appendix.)

Approach
Incorporation

Facilitation
Toddlers enjoy imitating hand gestures in action songs. For those who have been signing "Wheels on the Bus" and "Skinnymarink" gestures, this activity will be familiar.

Show toddlers the book *Word Signs* and demonstrate the hand gestures for the key words illustrated. Encourage all attempts at imitation. Go around the group and introduce the letter sign for your name and for each child's name by placing the hand sign visibly against your chest. Demonstrate the sign each time you call upon a child or use the child's name. Praise and encourage the toddlers' imitations.

If this signing activity occurs daily, over time toddlers will not only sign their own "letter" names, but also recognize and sign the letters of peer and staff names.

Matching Fabrics

Age
18–30 months

Curriculum Area
Cognitive

Curriculum Objectives
To refine visual discrimination, matching skills, and eye-hand and fine motor coordination.

Anti-Bias Area
Culture

Anti-Bias Skills
To expose toddlers to cultural differences in textures and patterns; to notice similarities and differences.

Materials
Four plastic tumblers; four different fabric patterns (e.g., material from Central America, Southeast Asia, Native America) glued around the cups; and 12 flat non-spring wooden clothespins that are covered with the corresponding fabrics. (Large flat clothespins are available from Lakeshore/Wintergreen, SC7-WD450. The 3¾-inch size has enough surface space upon which to glue the fabric.)

Approach
Incorporation

Facilitation
Spread out all the clothespins and cups on a table. Ask the toddlers if they know what the items are and what they can do with them. Demonstrate how the clothespin can fit on the cup, but allow them to follow their own initiative in exploring the materials. When matching occurs, reinforce how they found the clothespin that looks the same. Encourage matching and describe how the fabrics look the same or different in relation to design, pattern, and color. Choose patterns that are clearly distinctive and allow for expressive language practice. You can mention the fabric's country of origin: "This zigzag design is made by Native Americans. This silky fabric with birds on it is from Japan."

Community Resources
Fabrics may be found in dressmaker supply stores or stores specializing in Southeast Asian or Central American clothing.

Family Matchup

Age

20–30 months

Curriculum Area

Cognitive

Curriculum Objectives

To practice elementary matching; to encourage rudimentary construction of relationships between people.

Anti-Bias Areas

Race, Age, Family Composition

Anti-Bias Skill

To strengthen basic understanding of self in relation to family.

Materials

Family photos of children, mounted on bristol board, laminated and cut into matching sets with different configurations.

Approach

Incorporation

Facilitation

Initially place two sets of photo puzzles in front of the child. Support trial-and-error experimentation as the toddler tries to match the pair up either through the visual clues of the photo or the shapes of the puzzle pieces. Label and describe what the toddler is viewing and doing. Encourage the toddler to use expressive language skills while putting the puzzle pieces together: "Here's Lida. And you found Lida's 'baba.' Is it your birthday party? Lida is blowing out candles." Or "You found the piece that fits. Good matching."

As the children become more competent, add more sets to match.

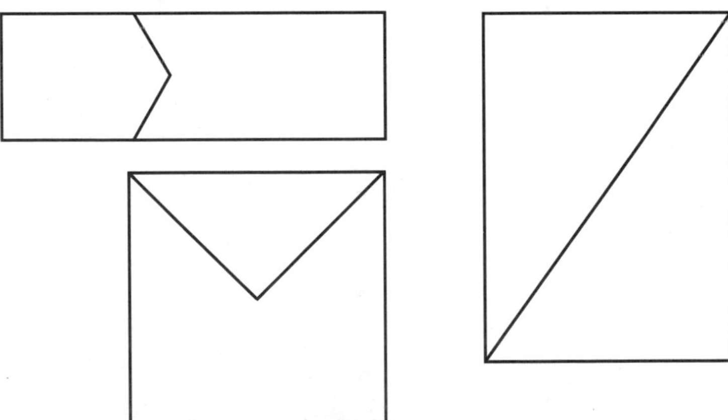

Observing how parts make up a whole.

Baby Dressing

Age

18–30 months

Curriculum Area

Fine Motor

Curriculum Objectives

To improve eye-hand coordination involving pincer manipulation, language related to emotional needs, and preliminary matching skills.

Anti-Bias Areas

Gender, Race

Anti-Bias Skill

To support gender equity in play.

Materials

Multiracial baby dolls of both genders; stretchy fabric hats; doll-sized terry cloth bibs, shaped in a square, triangle, and oval, with elastic necks to make dressing the dolls easier; matching appliqué shapes in red, yellow, and blue with velcro on the back; and a "snowsuit" bag with velcro fastener.

Approach

Incorporation

Facilitation

Baby doll play is extremely important to toddlers who need to exercise emerging autonomy and practice self-help skills.

Show the children the various dresswear for the naked dolls; encourage them to explore the materials and how they relate to the doll. Support all initiatives demonstrated—putting on hats and bibs, pulling on snowsuits and adjusting the velcro tabs, matching the appliqué shapes to the appropriately shaped bibs.

Talk about the need for wearing hats and snowsuits: "What does your baby need to wear when it's cold?" Discuss the different types of colored hats and snowsuits the toddlers have.

This activity allows toddlers to play at their own developmental level. It also reinforces the concept of gender equity around nurturing.

Lacing Faces

Age

24–30 months

Curriculum Area

Fine Motor

Curriculum Objectives

To improve eye-hand coordination for threading; sequencing of in and out

Anti-Bias Areas

Race, Gender

Anti-Bias Skills

To promote a positive sense of self; to expose toddlers to a variety of skin colors.

Materials

Tops from margarine or yogurt containers, with pictures of multiracial children's faces glued to outside. Cut out the eyes, nose, and mouth on each picture, creating four medium-sized holes. Prepare shoelaces with masking tape at one end and a large bead at the other which won't fit through the lid openings.

Approach

Incorporation

Facilitation

Show a small group of toddlers the faces on the lids, and help them to identify the facial features that are represented by the holes. These may look clearer on the inside of the lid where the holes are in a plain background. Give each child a lace and demonstrate how to bring it through one hole. The fine motor manipulation required to draw the shoelace through from the other side is complicated initially, so model and assist. Let the children explore threading the lace through any of the holes until they have gotten the hang of it. Focus their attention on the facial features emerging as lines appear between eyes, nose, and mouth on the lid.

Exploring Mobility Devices

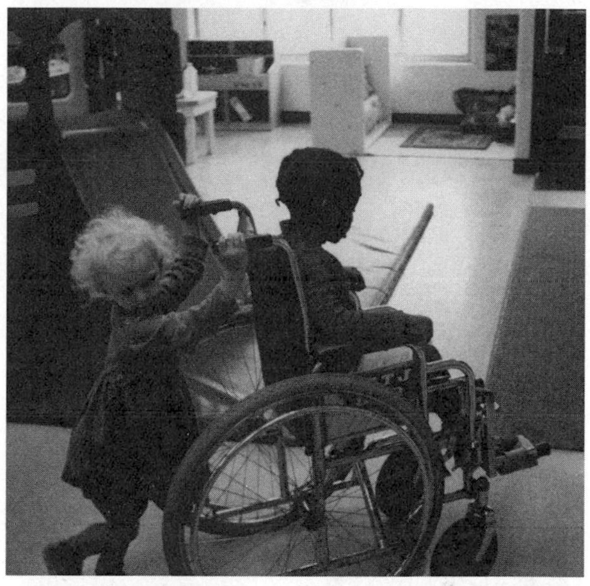

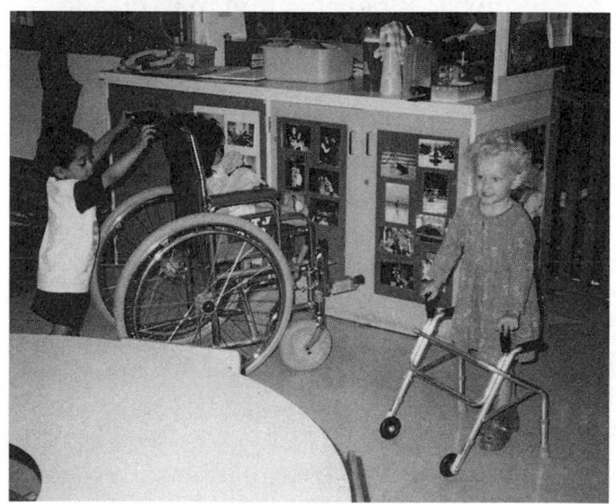

Learning to feel comfortable with those who are differently abled.

Age

18–30 months

Curriculum Area

Gross Motor

Curriculum Objective

To strengthen balance, coordination, and weight transfer of large muscles.

Anti-Bias Area

Ability

Anti-Bias Skills

To encourage toddlers to try new experiences; to expose toddlers to differences in ability; to increase a toddler's ability to interact with others who are differently abled.

Materials

Child-sized wheelchair, walker, small crutches, leg braces, and multiracial dolls.

Approach

Modified Personalization

Facilitation

Bring out a variety of mobility assistance equipment; support the toddlers as they explore the equipment by themselves or with the dolls. Sit in a wheelchair and have them push you and other toddlers around. The equipment will stimulate their curiosity and appeals to the toddler's urge to push wheeled things.

Comment casually on how some children/people need this equipment to help them walk. The novelty of the equipment will wear off with the frequency of toddler play. When they eventually see someone utilizing the equipment, the fear or discomfort that usually results from being confronted by the strange or the unknown will be considerably lessened. (Parents of toddlers who have experienced this activity said that their children, on different occasions, have approached people in wheelchairs, smiled, and wanted to help push them across the street.)

The Obstacle Course

Age
18–30 months

Curriculum Area
Gross Motor

Curriculum Objectives
To strengthen balance, coordination, and weight transfer of large muscles; to refine understanding of spatial relations.

Anti-Bias Area
Age

Anti-Bias Skill
To expose toddlers to differences in age.

Materials
Tunnel; low bench; vinyl mat; plastic recycling box; large cushion or beanbag.

Design large arrows and place them between pieces of equipment to create a path. Inside the arrows paste pictures of seniors, physically involved in a range of activities.

Approaches
Incorporation and Personalization

Facilitation
Design the obstacle course to maximize opportunities for jumping, crawling, stepping over, climbing, and balancing. Lead the toddlers through the course, commenting on their movements. Focus their attention on the arrows, not only as direction indicators but also as examples of older people being physically active. This kind of activity is equally effective indoors and outdoors as it provides the toddlers with different challenges on rugs or grass.

Inviting grandparents or other elder family members to participate in this active experience helps prevent common misconceptions about the abilities of older people from taking hold. Ageism is quite prevalent among children in the early primary years.

Beanbag Toss

Age
18–30 months

Curriculum Area
Gross Motor

Curriculum Objectives
To practice large muscle coordination and balance; to refine understanding of spatial relations; to enhance visual and olfactory discrimination

Anti-Bias Area
Culture

Anti-Bias Skill
To expose toddlers to cultural differences in patterns, textures, and smells.

Materials
Three baskets, each lined with different material; set of beanbags covered in cloth with distinctive patterns from different cultures.

Design the beanbags in different shapes and sizes. Enhance the bags with scents (vanilla, cinnamon, rose, etc.).

Approach
Incorporation

Facilitation
Set the three baskets on the floor at significant distances from each other. Offer the beanbags to the toddlers, encouraging them to shake, toss, and visually inspect them. Model walking over to the basket and tossing a bag in. Suggest that the toddlers dump out the basket and try throwing the bags in. Stand back and let them enjoy exploring the materials. Provide commentary on what they are doing and descriptions of the colors, shapes, and sizes of the beanbags. Ask the toddlers to smell a beanbag and label the scent for them.

Stuffed Nylons

Exploring differences in skin tones in another way.

Age

18–30 months

Curriculum Area

Gross Motor

Curriculum Objectives

To strengthen balance, coordination, and weight transfer of large muscles; to enhance projectile management and movement.

Anti-Bias Area

Race

Anti-Bias Skill

To expose toddlers to a variety of skin tones.

Materials

Ten pairs of nylons that reflect a range in skin color; newspapers.

Cut nylons, stuff with newspapers, and tie in order to make them easy to toss.

Approach

Incorporation

Facilitation

Bring out a bin of 20 stuffed nylon balls. Encourage the toddlers to practice a variety of motor skills by initiating rolling, tossing up in the air and catching, throwing gently, etc. Reinforce all large muscle activity and share in their enjoyment of this experience.

The toddlers may or may not notice the different shades in the nylons. As in all anti-bias experiences, the approach should be natural, never forced, and always responsive to the children's observations and questions. The purpose of the material is just to have children become familiar and feel comfortable with the range of skin color.

Drum March

Age

18–30 months

Curriculum Area

Gross Motor

Curriculum Objectives

To refine coordinated movements of arms; to stimulate use of body movement in response to different rhythms.

Anti-Bias Area

Culture

Anti-Bias Skill

To expose toddlers to cultural differences in rhythms and music.

Materials

Small- and medium-sized drums made from various lidded canisters (coffee, infant formula, etc.); contact paper with different patterns; wooden clothespins to use as drumsticks; and tapes of different drumming rhythms (African, South Pacific, Caribbean, Native American and Canadian, etc.).

A 5-inch rope can be attached to one side of the drum to act as a handle for carrying.

Approaches

Incorporation and Personalization: Invite a drummer/singer from a Native cultural center to demonstrate traditional drumming.

Facilitation

Gather children around and invite them to select a drum to play. Distribute the clothes pins and turn on the tape. Use their actions to describe the different sounds, pitches, and rhythms they are producing. Encourage the children to tap the drums in various positions—sitting, standing, and moving around the room.

Community Resources

Who is in your community who could bring in a display of different drums and demonstrate traditional drumming? Contact a Native American center or other ethnic community group in your area.

House Cleaning

Age
24–30 months

Curriculum Area
Gross Motor

Curriculum Objectives
To improve large muscle coordination and balance involved in carrying, stooping, scrubbing, and sweeping.

Anti-Bias Area
Gender

Anti-Bias Skill
To support gender equity in play.

Materials
Large rollers, paintbrushes; buckets; and brooms and dust pans.

Approach
Modified Personalization

Facilitation
Tell the toddlers that you really need their help to tidy up the inside and outside play spaces. Ensure that both girls and boys have the opportunity to experience sweeping and washing the surfaces. The washing task will probably be more appealing because it involves water. Let the children fill the buckets with water from a hose and direct them to fences and/or walls with large paint brushes and rollers. This activity allows the children to "mess" about with water under the guise of helping to clean. It is important to emphasize that both genders are equally competent to carry out the job, and to reinforce that their cooperative effort is important to the management of the play space.

Ramp Fun

Age
18–30 months

Curriculum Area
Gross Motor

Curriculum Objectives
To strengthen balance and coordination of large muscles; spatial relations.

Anti-Bias Area
Culture

Anti-Bias Skill
To expose toddlers to cultural differences.

Materials
Plastic toy vehicles; cardboard ramp covered with pictures of transportation vehicles from around the world: car, bicycle, plane, canoe, songthau (open air bus in Thailand), becak (pedal rickshaw), elephant, camel, wheelchair, etc. *National Geographic* is an excellent source for such pictures.

Approach
Incorporation

Facilitation
Move the ramp into an area with plenty of space for movement. Let the toddlers explore the ramp while you point out the vehicles. Bring out a bin with small, sturdy, wheeled toys and push a car down the ramp. Allow the children to experiment with the vehicles, and support their actions by describing what they are doing. You can refocus their attention on the pictures by saying, "Look, your car just passed the bus/canoe/camel, etc." Help them to make the connection between up and down as they push or pull the toys. String or yarn attached to the front of the toy helps toddlers pull the vehicles up the ramp.

Learning to take turns and share are additional developmental issues in this activity.

Resources for Toddlers

The following selection of board and soft books expand the toddler's world by focusing on relevant experiences and people in the child's world. The developmental needs of this age group—strengthening the sense of self, as well as relationships and social interactions with family members, and encouraging exploration of common objects and activities—are all represented using photographs and story lines that celebrate human diversity. Toddlers will gain exposure to differences in race, age, culture, gender, and ability as children and caregivers from a variety of backgrounds are depicted. This age group will particularly enjoy exploring the area of physical disabilities, with the introduction of such images as a mother in a wheelchair, Mother Goose rhymes in sign, and dual track books in braille. Books marked with an * are available in different languages.

Many activities are cross-referenced to specific books. Infant board books have also been included here for further literary support. The remaining books are for your reading pleasure with toddlers.

Bathtime for Babies

Playskool. (1994). *Bathtime.* Hasbro Canada.

Family Messages

Dijs, C. (1990). *Are you my mommy? A pop-up book.* New York: Simon and Schuster.
Nebratney, S. (1994). *Guess how much I love you.** London: Magi.
Cooke, T. (1994). *So much.* London: Walker Books.

Are You My Mother?

Eastman, P.D. (1960). *Are You My Mother?* New York: Beginner Books.

Bandage Time

Kissinger, K. (1994). *All the colors we are: The story of how we get our skin color.** St. Paul, MN: Redleaf Press.

Hide and Find the Toddlers

Asch, F. (1985). *I can roar; I can blink.* Toronto: Kids Can Press.

Family Place Mats

Ricklen, N. (1988). *Grandma and me; Grandpa and me; Daddy and me; Mommy and me;* New York: Simon and Schuster/Little Simon Super Chubby Board Books.
Reiser, L. (1993). *Margaret and Margarita.* New York: Greenwillow Books.
Greenfield, E. (1991). *Daddy and I.* New York: Black Butterfly Children's Books.
Ormerod, J. (1995). *Dad's back.* London: Walker Books.

Emotions Peek-a-boo Board

O'Brien, A.S. (1985). *Don't say no.* New York: Holt, Rinehart and Winston.
O'Brien, A.S. (1985). *I'm not tired.* New York: Holt, Rinehart and Winston.

Me Collage

Ricklen, N. (1990). *Baby's big and little.* New York: RGA Publishing Group.

Handprinting

Teague, K. (1990). *Arms and legs.** Toronto: Editions Renyi, Inc.

Brown Dough Sticks

Kissinger, K. (1994). *All the colors we are: The story of how we get our skin color.** St. Paul, MN: Redleaf Press.

Mirror Reflections

Groebel, R. (1995). *Two eyes, a nose, and a mouth.* New York: Scholastic Books.
Kreisler, K. and Rotner, S. (1994). *Faces.* New York: MacMillan Publishing.
Pinkney, A. and Pickney, B. (1997). *Pretty brown face.* San Diego: Harcourt, Brace and Co.
Tuxworth, N. (1996). *Funny faces—a very first picture book.* London: Anness Publishing.

Crying Babies

Henderson, K. (1988). *The baby's book of babies.* New York: Puffin Pied Piper.
Tuxworth, N. (1996). *Babies—a very first picture book.* London: Anness Publishing.

Book of Routines

Ormerod, J. (1995). *Reading; Sleeping.* London: Walker Books.
Playskool. (1994). *Mealtime.* Hasbro Canada.
Playskool. (1994). *Playtime.* Hasbro Canada.
Playskool. (1994). *Bedtime.* Hasbro, Canada.
Tuxworth, N. (1996). *Food—a very first picture book.* London: Anness Publishing.

Mixed-up Suitcase

Miller, M. (1991). *Whose Shoe?* New York: Greenwillow Books.
Playskool. (1994). *Playtime.* Hasbro Canada.

Matching Paint Chips

Kissinger, K. (1994). *All the colors we are: The story of how we get our skin color.* St. Paul, MN: Redleaf Press.

Jars and Lids

Tuxworth, N. (1996). *Food—a very first picture book.* London: Anness Publishing.

Laundry Scoops

Henderson, K. (1988). *The baby's book of babies.* New York: Puffin Pied Piper.
Dwight, L. (1992). *Babies all around.* New York: Checkerboard Press.

Changeable Faces

Kreisler, K. and Rotner, S. (1994). *Faces.* New York: MacMillan Publishing.
Tuxworth, N. (1996). *Funny faces—a very first picture book.* London: Anness Publishing.

Signing a Name

Slier, D. (1993). *Word signs—a first book of sign language.* New York: Checkboard Press.
Collins, H. S. (1994). *Mother goose in sign.* Eugene, OR: Garlic Press.

Family Matchup

Bailey, D. (1993). *Sisters.* Toronto: Annick Press.
Carter, A. R. (1997). *Big brother Dustin.* Mortin Grove, IL: Albert Whitman and Co.

Baby Dressing

Oxenbury, H. (1987). *Say goodnight; Clap hands, say goodnight, all fall down.* New York: Simon and Schuster.

Lacing Faces

Playskool. (1994). *My nose, my toes.* London: Reed Children's Books.
Groebel, R. (1995). *Two eyes, a nose, and a mouth.* New York: Scholastic Books.

Exploring Mobility Devices

Cowan-Fletcher, J. (1993). *Mama zooms.* New York: Scholastic Books.

Other Readings

Ehlert, L. (1992). *Moon rope.* San Diego: Harcourt, Brace and Jovanovich.
Greenfield, E. (1991). *My doll Keisha; I make music; Daddy and I; Big friend, little friend.* New York: BlackButterfly Children's Books.
Greenfield, E. (1997). *Kia Tanisha.* New York: HarperCollins.
Merriam, E. (1992). *Train leaves the station* (dual track). Boston: Bill Martin Books.

Finger Plays, Action Rhymes, and Songs

Anti-Bias Goal

To build self-identity and sense of relationship to family.

Age

Toddler

Songs, Rhymes, and Plays

1. With my broom I sweep, sweep, sweep,
   On my toes I creep, creep, creep,
   With my eyes I peep, peep, peep,
   On my bed I sleep, sleep, sleep. (Matterson, p. 33)

2. Lyn is very thin
   Pat is very fat
   Mort is very short
   Saul is very tall
   Kent is very bent
   Kate is very straight
   Isn't it fun to all be different? (Matterson, p. 167)

Anti-Bias Goal

To promote gender equity in actions.

3. Daddy's washing, daddy's washing
   Rub, rub, rub.
   Picked up _____'s little shirt,
   And threw it in the tub.
   Mommy's washing, mommy's washing,
   Scrub, scrub, scrub.
   Picked up _____'s little pants,
   And threw them in the tub.
   Brother's washing, brother's washing,
   Wring, wring, wring.
   Picked up _____'s little socks,
   And hung them on some string.
   We're all finished, we're all finished,
   Hip hip hooray.
   Now we'll have our clothes all clean,
   To wear for school today. (Matterson, p. 34)

Children can mime actions and fill in appropriate names. This version omits stereotyped gender roles and clothing.

4. The Grand Old Duke of York
   The Grand Old Duke of York
   He had 10,000 friends
   He marched them up to the top of the hill (marching steps)
   And he marched them down again.

When they were up they were up (marching standing)
And when they were down they were down (squatting)
And when they were only halfway up (standing)
They were neither up nor down. (squatting)

This rhyme is more inclusionary with substitution of "friends."

5. 5 Little Seashells (Use with *Buried Treasure* activity)

5 little seashells lying on the shore,
Swish went the waves and then there were four.

4 little seashells cozy as can be,
Swish went the waves and then there were three.

3 little seashells, all pearly and new,
Swish went the waves and then there were two.

2 little seashells sleeping in the sun,
Swish went the waves and then there was one.

1 little seashell left all alone,
Whispered "shhhhhh" as it took itself home.

From Leola Hayes, *A Fountain of Language Development for E.C.E. and the Special Child, Too.* New York.

UNIT 4

Anti-Bias Activities for Preschoolers and Kindergartners

"The teacher must become an active pluralist, who will imbue every aspect of the classroom with cultural and racial diversity. The classroom should become a microcosm of the pluralistic society the children do and will continue to live in. . . . The goal with preschoolers is not to teach history, but to inoculate them against racism."

Leilani Clark, Sheridan DeWolf, and Carl Clark (1992)

Key developmental requirements for this age fall into several categories.

Emergent Literacy

Children need to have many opportunities:

- to hear new and familiar stories;
- to hear stories that contain patterns, repetitions, and rhymes;
- to retell stories in various ways (felt board, dramatic play with props, puppet plays, etc.); and
- to practice visual and auditory discrimination.

Expressive Language

Children need to have:

- adults who listen respectfully, sustain conversations, answer questions, and support critical thinking;
- opportunities to practice visual and auditory memory by describing personal and group experiences;
- words to make their ideas take shape;
- opportunities to discuss problems and plan solutions; and
- encouragement to ask questions and make predictions, observations, and comparisons.

Socio-emotional Growth

Children need to have:

- opportunities to release tension, frustrations, and fears in socially acceptable ways;
- opportunities to make decisions and plan actions;
- environments that support cooperative projects, evolving pro-social skills, the belief that children can learn from one another, and self-discipline; and
- environments that promote independence in a variety of areas.

Knowledge, Skills, and Attitudes

Children should have:

- equitable opportunities for learning, regardless of gender, race, ability, or cultural background;
- exposure to both familiar and novel images, objects, events, people, and sensory experiences;
- opportunities to develop their own theoretical understanding of the physical (natural) and technological worlds;
- opportunities to discuss unfairness, stereotyping, similarities and differences in feelings, attitudes, and points of view;
- environments that provide resources for creative expression in a variety of art forms and media; and
- opportunities to play with ideas and environments that value divergent thinking, experimentation, and curiosity.

Mathematical Readiness

Children need to have:

- endlessly varied opportunities for exploring classification, seriation, matching, spatial relations, and problem solving;
- opportunities to create order, and perceive and create patterns;
- knowledge that ideas and experiences can be represented by sounds, shapes, print symbols, and numbers;
- rich exploration of math and other qualitative concepts such as shape, size, length, weight, volume, temperature, color, and texture;
- knowledge about numeracy; and
- a foundation for the higher level thinking skills of analysis, synthesis, and evaluation.

Web for Preschoolers and Kindergartners Anti-Bias and Developmental Skills

Summary of Anti-Bias Skills Preschool and Kindergarten Activities

Anti-Bias Skills	Activity Title	Page Number
To strengthen self-esteem and self-identity.	I Can Do Place Mat	109
	Mixed-up Creatures	110
	The Guessing Bag	126
	The Body Bingo Game	136
	Lacing Hands	172
To value uniqueness of self and others.	I Can Do Place Mat	109
	Mixed-up Creatures	110
	Emotion Books	111
	Shoe Sort Game	124
	The Guessing Bag	126
	Whose Voice Is That?	127
	Silhouette Guess	128
	People Puzzles	142
	Face-to-Face Puzzles	151
	Body Sounds	165
	Hair Beading	173
	Group Mural of Likes and Dislikes	182
	Sands of Many Colors	183
To value uniqueness of one's own family and others' families.	Ways of Carrying Babies	106
To strengthen basic understanding of self in relation to family.	Family Flannel Board	108
	The Family House	134
To expose children to cultural differences in:	Newspaper Collage	117
	Mystery Prop Game	123
	Memory Games	126
	Hats, Hats, Hats Lotto Game	138
	Seriated Surprise Boxes	146
	Holiday Dress	157
	Papier-mâché Creations	184
◎ textures and patterns;	Grain Play	116
	Pattern Match-up Board	145
	Fishing for Cultural Patterns	170
◎ rhythms and music;	Musical Scarves	175
	Painting to Music	181
◎ smells and foods.	Grain Play	116
	Grocery Matching	129
	Go Bake Card Game	135
	Bread Delivery	137

Anti-Bias Skills	**Activity Title**	**Page Number**
	Lots of Breads	155
	Tasting Milk	164
To foster familiarity with differences in:		
◎ skin color;	Ice Cube Melt	112
	Amazing Hair Dramatic Play	120
	The Body Bingo Game	136
	Friendship Dominoes	139
	Fun with Paint Chips	148
	Designer Shade	158
	More Fun with Paint Chips	160
	Spray Bottle Art	181
◎ ability;	Playdough in a Glove	113
	People Sponge Painting	114
	Memory Games	126
	The Body Bingo Game	136
	Worm Puzzle	171
	Barefoot Art	175
	Scooter Board Skills	178
	Cooperative Relay Game	179
	What's in a Name?	141
	Friendship Dominoes	139
◎ age.	The Body Bingo Game	136
To recognize and label similarities and differences.	People Sponge Painting	114
	Matching Feely Bag	127
	Silhouette Guess	128
	People Puzzles	142
	Who Is Underneath?	149
	Pasta Power	149
	Face-to-Face Puzzles	151
	Lots of Breads	155
	Classification Board Game	161
	Conservation Tasks Cards	162
	Don't Judge by Appearances	169
	Body Parts	169
To strengthen positive association with the color brown.	Brown Is Beautiful	115
	Matching Feely Bag	127
	It Looks Like Spilled Cocoa	144
To promote respect for human diversity in:	Stick Puppet Drama	118
	Language Cards	122
	Missing Parts	144
	Fun with Geometric Shapes	147
	Who Is Underneath?	149
	Diversity Puzzle	152
◎ culture;	Spice Match-up	153
	Word Picture Puzzles	154
	Musical Scarves	175
	Memory Games	126
◎ race;	The Friendship Square	107
	Counting Children	143

Anti-Bias Skills	Activity Title	Page Number
	Counting Board Game	156
	Changes in Appearance	167
	Lacing Hands	172
	Hair Beading	173
	Cheese Puzzle	174
	Friendship Dominoes	139
◎ gender;	The Friendship Square	107
	Counting Board Game	156
	What Belongs Together?	159
◎ ability;	Helping Hands for All	119
	People Sponge Painting	114
	The Body Bingo Game	136
	Books in Braille	121
	Letter Cards	128
	The Missing Pic Symbol	131
	What Does This Person Need?	132
	What's in a Name?	141
	What Belongs Together?	159
	Body Sounds	165
	Barefoot Art	175
	Outside Treasure Hunt	176
	Scooter Board Skills	178
	Ball Toss	180
	Designer Shade	158
◎ appearance;	The Friendship Square	107
	Puzzle by Number	163
	Shape Changes	166
	Changes in Appearance	167
	Amazing Hair Dramatic Play	120
◎ age.	What Belongs Together?	159
	Puzzle by Number	163
To increase ability to label feelings and emotions.	Emotion Books	111
To support emergent empathy.	What Can You Do to Help?	110
	Playdough in a Glove	113
	What If . . . ?	133
	Moving Through Space	177
	Scooter Board Skills	178
To encourage children to try new experiences.	Fun with Geometric Squares	147
	Spice Match-up	153
	Tasting Milk	164
	Barefoot Art	175
To encourage cooperation and teamwork.	Cooperative Relay Game	179
	Group Mural of Likes and Dislikes	182
To support and respect gender equity.	Unisex Dress-up for Dolls	105
	Sounds Are Us	130
	Job Cards	140
	Whose Job Is It Anyway?	150
	Dramatic Pulley Play	168

Anti-Bias Skills	Activity Title	Page Number
To support and respect racial equity.	Job Cards	140
	Whose Job Is It Anyway?	150
To support emergent ability to listen to another's point of view.	Let's Talk About . . .	118
To provide opportunities for children to interact with people who are differently abled.	What's in a Name?	141
	Worm Puzzle	171
	Helping Hands for All	119
	Books in Braille	121
	Letter Cards	128
	The Missing Pic Symbol	131
	What Does This Person Need?	132
	Moving Through Space	177
	Ball Toss	180
To challenge gender stereotyping.	Unisex Dress-up for Dolls	105
	Sounds Are Us	130
	What Belongs Together?	159
	Lacing Hands	172
	Hair Beading	173
To challenge age stereotyping.	Life Cycle in Sequence	125
	What Belongs Together?	159
To encourage children to act on behalf of others.	What Can You Do to Help?	110

Letter to Families of Preschool and Kindergarten Children

Dear Families,

We are currently working on helping our children become familiar and comfortable with the many different kinds of people that they are likely to encounter throughout their lives. We feel that learning to deal with human differences is an important aspect of their emotional development. Developing empathy and becoming sensitive to how others feel is essential for your child's ability to engage in positive interactions with children whose ethno-racial backgrounds, or religious orientations, or even physical abilities may be different.

In order to work toward this goal we will be inviting visitors throughout the year to spend time with our children and participate in many of our activities. Over the following two weeks we will be welcoming Les from the local Native Friendship Center, Suzanna and her seeing eye dog, Maurice from the Veteran's Organization, and Indra who is the chef at a local vegetarian restaurant. Since preschoolers are still at the stage where they learn best through concrete, hands-on experiences, we think that this personalized approach will enable the children to understand how people share similarities and differences in life's activities. We believe such continuous interactions will prevent children from forming stereotypical perceptions and hurtful behaviors toward others whom society has designated as different.

We wish to integrate visits from family and other community members into our program activities. Should you know of someone whose presence would enrich our children's understanding of differences, or if you or a family member wish to assist us with our efforts, please let us know! Your involvement and expertise are always encouraged and welcomed. We are looking forward to a cooperative effort that creates more accepting children in this world.

Sincerely,

Unisex Dress-up for Dolls

Age

3–5 years

Curriculum Areas

Socio-emotional; Perceptual Motor

Curriculum Objectives

To support the development of nurturance; to strengthen perceptual motor coordination.

Anti-Bias Area

Gender

Anti-Bias Skills

To respect gender equity; to challenge gender stereotyping.

Materials

Multiracial dolls of both genders; assortment of infant-sized clothing (sleepers, T-shirts, pants, overalls, sweaters, jackets, hats, etc.).

Approach

Incorporation

Facilitation

In this completely open-ended activity, children can select items of clothing to dress up their dolls. The teacher is there to assist in any difficulties with buttons, snaps, or zips. More importantly, the teacher should mediate any mistaken assumptions made by the children in relation to gender-specific colors or clothing: "only boys wear pants/overalls" or "only girls wear pink/purple T-shirts." Boys should be encouraged to participate in this activity side by side with the girls to dispel the notion that only females nurture children.

A good follow-up book to read to the children is *William's Doll,* by Charlotte Zolotow.

Community Resource

Donation of infant clothing.

Ways of Carrying Babies

Age
3–5 years

Curriculum Areas
Socio-emotional; Perceptual Motor

Curriculum Objectives
To become familiar with the variety of ways of carrying infants; to support the development of nurturance.

Anti-Bias Areas
Culture, Gender

Anti-Bias Skill
To value uniqueness of one's own family and others' families.

Materials
Snuggly; cloth wrap; cradle board; basket; car seat; stroller; Japanese square; and photos of mothers and children from all over the world.

Approach
Incorporation

Facilitation
Explore with the children how babies can be carried. Ask them to think about the many different ways they have seen babies transported. Show them photos and picture books that illustrate the variety of baby carriers used by families all over the world.

Hold up samples of a snuggly, a cradle board, and a cloth wrap. Explain their origins and have the children practice putting in dolls and wearing the carriers. Encourage both the boys and girls to explore the infant carriers and leave them out in the dramatic play area for further experimentation and role play.

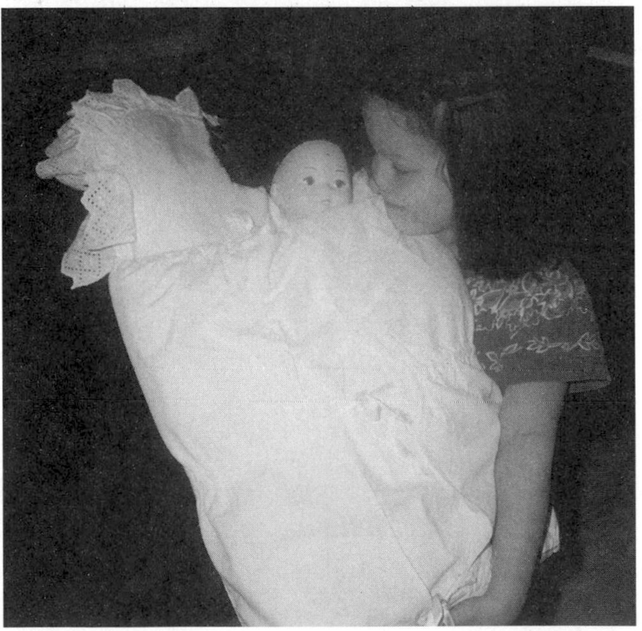

Discovering our nurturing selves.

Community Resources
Patterns for different baby carriers from community members; *Global Child: Multicultural Resources for Young Children*, by Maureen Cech, is a good reference for this activity.

The Friendship Square

Age

3–5 years

Curriculum Areas

Socio-emotional; Perceptual Motor

Curriculum Objective

To understand that friends come in all colors, shapes, and sizes.

Anti-Bias Areas

Race, Gender, Appearance

Anti-Bias Skill

To promote respect for human diversity in race, gender, and appearance.

Materials

Pictures of children and adults reflecting diversity in race and gender; wax paper squares; scissors; iron; hole puncher; and yarn.

Approach

Incorporation

Facilitation

This activity is a variation on waxed leaf hanging, a favorite autumnal creative art experience.

Invite the children to create a friendship square. Have children select two pictures each from a large collection of faces that reflect the diversity in racial backgrounds and gender. The older children can cut away any background to create a full frontal image; assist the younger ones in this task. Next, ask the children to place the pictures back-to-back so that the faces can be seen from *both* sides. Have the children place the pictures in between two pieces of wax paper and observe while a teacher/caregiver presses it with a warm iron. Punch a hole at the top and thread a piece of yarn through each square. Finally, get the children to tie their squares on a line low enough for all to see.

This activity allows teachers to get a sense of a child's comfort level with different genders and racial groups. If children clearly indicate they don't want a child of another gender or race in their square, then the challenge for the teacher is clear. It is important that the teacher take time to explore the child's feelings around such a comment and clarify individual perceptions before taking action.

After the squares are all hanging have the children talk about why they choose those children to put in the square. Reinforce how friends come in different colors, shapes, and sizes.

Community Resource

Crystal Designer Waxed Tissue is available from Lakeshore/Wintergreen, SC7-PE916, and comes in seven pastel colors on sheets sized 15″ × 20″.

Family Flannel Board

Age

3–5 years

Curriculum Area

Socio-emotional

Curriculum Objective

To become aware that families take different forms and have no set membership.

Anti-Bias Area

Family Composition

Anti-Bias Skill

To strengthen basic understanding of self in relation to family.

Materials

Flannel board and pieces representing a house, adults and children who are racially and gender mixed, dogs, and cats. The adult members can be the same shape, with children smaller, while the skin colors can be different. Make extra pieces from people-colored felt.

Approach

Incorporation

Facilitation

This activity introduces the concept that there is no one way to be a family. Invite the children to sit around the flannel board. Set up the task in the following way: "I'm filling up the house with the people who live here. Who should we put in the house?" Encourage the children to create a house membership from the available flannel pieces. Ensure they label each piece. This will give you the opportunity to evaluate the children's perception of what constitutes a family. Ask: "Is every house like this one? Who else can live in this house? Does everyone in the house have to be the same skin color? Have the same number of children?"

Teachers should be prepared to support those children who come from single, same-sex, or racially mixed homes if others in the group argue that those groupings don't constitute a "normal" family.

Community Resources

Commercially made family flannel board sets are available from Constructive Playthings and Kaplan.

I Can Do Place Mat

Age

3–5 years

Curriculum Area

Socio-emotional

Curriculum Objectives

To strengthen self-concept and self-esteem; to practice listening to others.

Anti-Bias Areas

Race, Culture, Gender, Ability

Anti-Bias Skills

To strengthen self-esteem; to value uniqueness of self and others.

Materials

Variety of child-focused magazines; scissors; crayons; glue; contact paper; and oaktag large enough for place mat shape.

Approach

Modified Personalization

Facilitation

Put out all the materials. Engage the children in a conversation that asks them to focus on things they enjoy doing, particularly the activities at which they feel they are good. Ask them to illustrate these activities by cutting out appropriate pictures, or drawing them. When the children have completed this experience, gather them in a circle so they can share their individual *I Can Do* place mats with the group.

This is a good opportunity to support those children with low self-esteem or any developmental weaknesses. Emphasize how any child can feel good about individual abilities and show a preference for certain activities. Point out to the group how unique they all are based on the place mats: some children are good at painting, others feel great riding trikes, while still others are terrific engineers in the sandbox, etc.

Place contact paper on the mats and use them for special snack occasions at least once a week. Get the children to distribute them as a reminder of their individuality.

What Can You Do to Help?

Age
4–5 years

Curriculum Areas
Socio-emotional; Language

Curriculum Objectives
To promote empathy and feelings for others; to encourage expressive language that facilitates problem solving.

Anti-Bias Areas
Class, Race, Culture, Ability

Anti-Bias Skills
To support emergent empathy; to encourage children to act on behalf of others.

Materials
Lazy Susan covered with four photos (one in each quadrant facing out) that depict children and/or adults in a variety of situations: pictures depicting people in physically demanding jobs; a blind person with a seeing eye dog or a white cane trying to get on public transportation; children playing games in run-down–looking neighborhoods; a person crying. Use masking tape to adhere pictures to the lazy Susan.

Approach
Incorporation

Facilitation
Give each child a turn to spin the lazy Susan. Have the children examine whichever photo faces them directly. Encourage the children to describe what they think is happening in the pictures, and ask what they could do for the people. Elicit divergent opinions and solutions. Replace the photos with four different ones after all perceptions and discussions have been exhausted.

Mixed-up Creatures

Age
4–6 years

Curriculum Areas
Socio-emotional; Creative Art

Curriculum Objective
To explore the imagination through the visual arts.

Anti-Bias Areas
Appearance, Ability, Race, Gender

Anti-Bias Skills
To strengthen self-esteem; to value uniqueness of self and others.

Materials
The Mixed-Up Chameleon, by Eric Carle; paper; and crayons.

Approach
Incorporation

Facilitation
Read the picture book *The Mixed-Up Chameleon.* Explore the feelings of wanting to look like someone else or the displeasure over one's own appearance. Help the children to appreciate their individuality and take pride in who they are.

To promote creative use of their imagination, ask them to invent a new animal. After they have drawn the picture, ask them to give it a special name and dictate a story about it to you. Write down their stories and display all the different animal pictures.

Emotion Books

Age

5–6 years

Curriculum Areas

Socio-emotional; Language

Curriculum Objectives

To recognize emotions and identify the sources for such feelings; to practice listening to others.

Anti-Bias Area

Culture

Anti-Bias Skills

To increase ability to label feelings and emotions; to value uniqueness of self and others.

Materials

Cardboard; paper; markers; scissors; and magazines.

Approach

Incorporation

Facilitation

It is important that young children be in a setting that values their unique personality. As part of understanding their identity—their strengths and weaknesses, or their preferences and dislikes—preschoolers need to understand what situations/behaviors make them respond in the emotional ways that they do.

This activity challenges the young child to think about the following topics:

- I laugh when . . .
- I get angry when . . .
- I cry when . . .
- I become afraid when . . .
- I don't like it when other people . . .
- I like to be first when . . .

Try one topic in a group discussion to get them sharing ideas, listening to, and learning about one another. Offer children the opportunity to make small booklets on any of the above topics. Let them choose to draw or cut out pictures from magazines, and dictate the end of the sentence for you to write on the page. Let the children share their books with one another by reading them aloud with your assistance.

Expansion

Share other books that deal with typical emotions of the preschool-kindergarten age group such as Joan Singleton Prestine's *Love Me Anyhow.*

Ice Cube Melt

Age

3–5 years

Curriculum Area

Sensory

Curriculum Objectives

To enhance understanding of causal relations; to provide opportunities for tactile and visual exploration; to stimulate sensory pleasure.

Anti-Bias Area

Race

Anti-Bias Skill

To foster familiarity with differences in skin colors.

Materials

Variety of ice cubes prepared with people-colored paints; white finger paint paper.

Approaches

Incorporation and Modified Personalization

Facilitation

Place ice cubes on a flat tray, after ensuring they are slightly thawed. This is an open-ended sensory activity in which the children can push the ice cubes around and watch as the colors emerge, run, and blend on the paper. Use any opportunity for incidental teaching about skin color through the children's own self-examination and comparisons. Have them compare ice cubes to their own skin and skin of others. Give them words for shades: lighter, darker, etc.

Playdough in a Glove

Age

3–5 years

Curriculum Area

Sensory

Curriculum Objectives

To enhance tactile discrimination and sensory pleasure; to stimulate curiosity; to practice fine motor coordination.

Anti-Bias Area

Ability

Anti-Bias Skills

To foster familiarity with differences in ability; to support emergent empathy.

Materials

Surgical gloves; playdough; and *Come Sit By Me,* by Margaret Merrifield.

Recipe for playdough: Combine 4 cups flour, 2 cups salt, 4 tablespoons cream of tartar, 4 cups water, and 2 tablespoons oil.

Approach

Incorporation

Facilitation

Read *Come Sit By Me* which explores the way a child with AIDS feels when exclusionary behavior is directed against him. Focus the follow-up discussion in a general manner on the endless medical treatments any child with a chronic illness must endure. Hold up a surgical glove, and ask if anyone knows what it is and what it is primarily used for. Explain the term "sterile" and the fact that children who spend a lot of time in the hospital often experience the touch of this glove.

Put out a number of surgical gloves that have playdough stuffed into the palm area. Tie up the open end, and give them to the children to explore. Encourage the children to try to squeeze the playdough into the fingers, and observe what strategies they use to accomplish this goal. Respect individual preferences—some children will derive enormous sensory pleasure from this activity, and others, who might have had intravenous experiences, may feel uncomfortable and refuse to play with it.

Expansion

Provide food coloring and eye droppers, and let the children add color to the playdough. After squeezing and manipulating the glove, they can observe what changes take place with the playdough mixture.

Community Resource

Bulk donation of gloves from a local pharmacy or pharmaceutical company.

People Sponge Painting

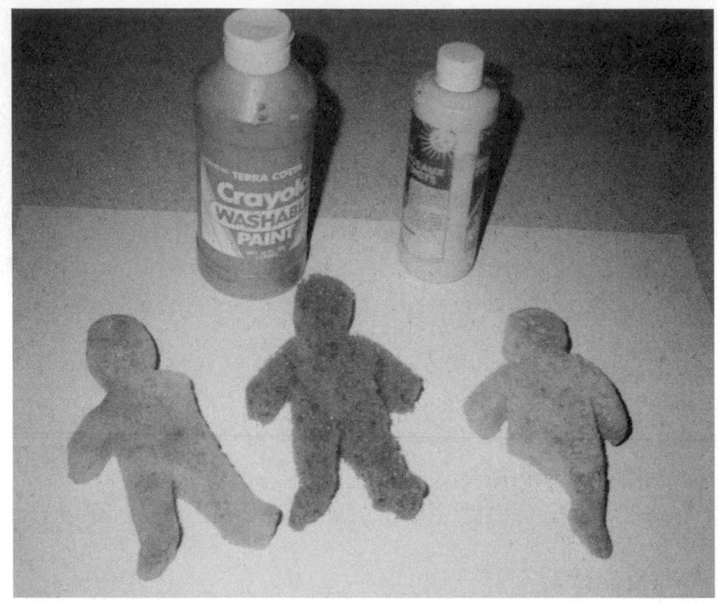

Noticing similarities and differences in people.

Age
3–5 years

Curriculum Area
Sensory

Curriculum Objectives
To strengthen perceptual motor coordination; to explore cause and effect.

Anti-Bias Areas
Ability, Appearance

Anti-Bias Skills
To recognize and label similarities and differences; to foster familiarity with differences in appearance and ability

Materials
People-shaped sponges with and without a leg and an arm; paint; paper; and clothespins. (Sponges available from Lakeshore/Wintergreen, SC7-DC71, are 6½ inches.)

Approach
Incorporation

Facilitation
Set out paint trays and a variety of sponges. Attach clothespins to the sponges. Guide the children to pick up and dip the sponges in the paint, then onto the paper. After the initial engrossment in the stamping process has subsided, ask the children how the sponge people look the same and different. Answer any questions or disquiet that may be triggered by the armless/legless figures.

Brown Is Beautiful

Age
3–6 years

Curriculum Area
Sensory

Curriculum Objectives
To enjoy the sensory exploration of baking materials; to practice measurement and observation.

Anti-Bias Area
Race

Anti-Bias Skill
To strengthen positive association with the color brown.

Materials
Black Is Brown Is Tan, by Arnold Adoff; baking utensils and ingredients; and picture cards depicting the baking sequence.

Approach
Incorporation

Facilitation
Read *Black Is Brown Is Tan.* Focus the follow-up discussion on favorite foods that are brown. Have the children offer examples of foods they like that are brown: hot chocolate, fudge brownies, peanut butter, most breakfast cereals, butterscotch or chocolate puddings, etc.

Select a food for a baking experience and proceed as usual with such an activity. Prepare picture cards that outline the ingredients needed in the recipe and the sequence involved. Highlight how the dry ingredients change in appearance during the mixing and baking process.

As in other activities, the more children develop positive associations with the color brown, the greater the likelihood that this attitude will be generalized to people.

Grain Play

Age
4–5 years

Curriculum Area
Sensory

Curriculum Objectives
To encourage visual and tactile exploration; to practice measuring and making comparisons.

Anti-Bias Area
Culture

Anti-Bias Skill
To expose children to cultural differences in textures and patterns, and in smells and foods.

Materials
Seven small basins filled with the following grains: rice, couscous, bulgur, oats, barley, rye, and buckwheat (kasha); variety of measuring spoons and cups; and sieves and funnels.

Approach
Incorporation

Facilitation
Invite children to explore the different grains in the sensory bins. Help them to describe the differences in size, color, weight, texture, and smell. As they scoop and pour the grains, have them count and compare the number of scoops required to fill a cup with oats as opposed to couscous. Have them examine the speed of flow through funnels and sieves, and compare the grains: large, small, flakey, hard, spherical, etc.

This activity is a follow-up to *Bread Delivery* and *Lots of Breads.*

Expansion
Bring out different crackers (rice, stonewheat, rye, etc.) for a snack or as a taste test.

Community Resource
Donations from bulk or health food stores.

Newspaper Collage

Age
3–5 years

Curriculum Area
Sensory

Curriculum Objectives
To enhance tactile and olfactory sensory pleasure; to practice perceptual motor coordination.

Anti-Bias Area
Culture

Anti-Bias Skill
To expose children to cultural differences.

Materials
Newspapers with different language scripts (Chinese, Russian, Persian, Hindi, Greek, etc.); flour and water paste sprinkled with powdered ginger; scissors; and paper.

Approach
Incorporation

Facilitation
This is an open-ended activity that gives children an opportunity to practice cutting and pasting with culturally diverse materials. Listen to observations and comments made by the children about either the paste's smell or the scripts. Label the scripts; ask if they know anyone who reads that language. Build on conversations that touch on the speaking and reading of different languages. Using these materials will enhance children's awareness that languages look different in print. For those who may be beginning to recognize print this can be a particularly stimulating activity.

Expansion
Introduce the book *Table, Chair, Bear,* by Jane Feder, which offers children a basic vocabulary of objects in thirteen different languages.

Stick Puppet Drama

Age
3–5 years

Curriculum Area
Language

Curriculum Objectives
To engage in imaginative dramatic play and the creation of story lines and stick puppets.

Anti-Bias Areas
Race, Gender, Appearance, Ability, Age

Anti-Bias Skill
To promote respect for human diversity.

Materials
Popsicle sticks; large circular pieces of paper; face photos of people who reflect the range of diversity; glue; and scissors.

Approach
Incorporation

Facilitation
Put out the creative materials and invite the children to design their own puppets. When they have completed this task, suggest that all the stick puppets introduce themselves; this will start the children thinking about the persona they are constructing and the direction their dramatic play may take. Let them play out roles and situations. Encourage the children to challenge stereotypical comments or situations that the puppets might make.

Puppets are a wonderful vehicle for exploring anti-bias issues. Create your own and join in the play to lend assistance in working through such issues.

Let's Talk About . . .

Age
3–5 years

Curriculum Area
Language

Curriculum Objectives
To improve expressive abilities; to recognize and talk about incongruencies.

Anti-Bias Areas
Gender, Race, Ability, Age

Anti-Bias Skill
To support emergent ability to listen to another's point of view.

Materials
Cardboard; glue; scissors; and a series of picture boards constructed from magazine pictures that reflect people/children of different backgrounds, ages, and abilities in an interesting setting. Find an object that is totally incongruous to the picture and paste it on. Examples include: an elderly couple walking on a beach and a picture of a bed glued in the water; a woman rock climbing and a picture of an iron on the cliff; or a toddler in the bath and a picture of a crutch in the tub. Use mail order catalogs for the unusual objects.

Approach
Incorporation

Facilitation
The use of humor and incongruity is a tried-and-true method of getting children involved and thinking. The depth of your discussion will depend on the nature of your pictures and the objects that you choose. The range of human diversity can be subtle as in the elderly couple enjoying a walk on the beach, or it can be pointed as in the case of the female rock climber. Pretend there is nothing wrong with the picture, and then laugh along with the children once they have expressed the reason behind the incongruency. Seize any opportunities to discuss discriminatory or stereotypical comments that may emerge.

Helping Hands for All

Age
3–5 years

Curriculum Area
Language

Curriculum Objectives
To recognize that a picture represents an action; to strengthen visual memory; to take collective responsibility for the classroom's management.

Anti-Bias Area
Ability

Anti-Bias Skills
To provide opportunities to interact with people who are differently abled; to promote respect for human diversity.

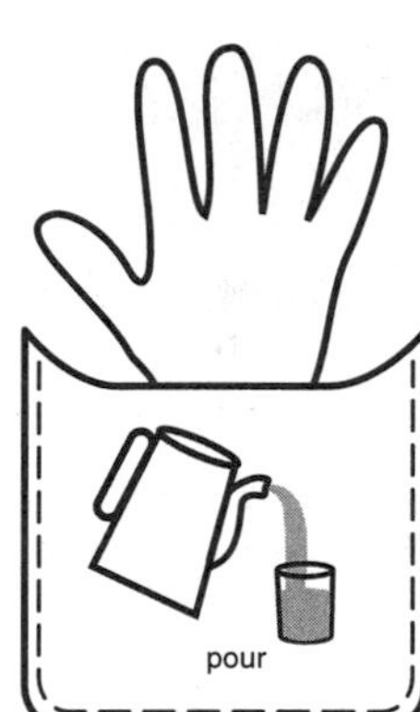

Making classroom management an inclusive experience.

Materials
Photos of each child with velcro on back; five large hands cut from bristol board with velcro tabs glued to each in order to attach children's photos. Pocket stapled to bulletin board. On each pocket place a "pic" symbol illustrating a routine in the classroom (see Appendix 10 and Mayer-Johnson's *Picture Communication Symbols* books).

Approach
Modified Personalization

Facilitation
This activity is a modified duties/chores wheel that includes all the children in the classroom. The tasks illustrated—sweeping, watering the plants, wiping up the table after snack, pouring juice/water, putting away the blocks—remain constant, while the children's photos on the hands are changed every 2–3 days. The pic symbols selected are usually used with children with nonverbal abilities. The use of these symbols here is to design a more inclusive classroom and to familiarize children with alternative methods of communication.

Community Resources
Invite an augmentative communication specialist to introduce the staff to the Mayer-Johnson's resource, *Picture Communication Symbols.* Contact early intervention services in your community for suggestions on how to reach speech therapists.

Amazing Hair Dramatic Play

Age

3–5 years

Curriculum Area

Language

Curriculum Objectives

To engage in symbolic play; to label and explore different hair types and how they relate to people.

Anti-Bias Areas

Race, Gender

Anti-Bias Skill

To foster familiarity with differences in skin color.

Materials

Amanda's Perfect Hair, by Linda Milstein and Susan Meddaugh; wigs of different colors and textures; curlers, combs, and brushes from different cultures; ribbons, elastics, barrettes/clips, hairnets, etc.; and multiracial dolls that have different textured hair.

Approaches

Incorporation and Extension: Introduce children to the concept that some children and people have lost their hair because of illness. Should they be treated differently? Why or why not?

Facilitation

Read *Amanda's Perfect Hair* which uses humor and exaggeration to probe the dilemma of a young girl whose long, thick, and curly hair is the only focus of everyone's attention. Explore the variety of hair types across the races, and discuss the children's perceptions about who has what color, texture, and length of hair. Let the children feel each other's hair and clarify any misconceptions.

Ask if they believe all women have long hair and all men have short hair? Can either gender have different lengths of hair? Why or why not? Ensure they deal with the fact that hair length is not associated with gender identity.

Extend the exploration of these ideas in the dramatic play center.

Community Resources

Multiracial dolls with different hair textures are available in the United States from Lakeshore Company, and in Canada from Snailbrush and Wintergreen, among other sources.

Books in Braille

Age

3–5 years

Curriculum Area

Language

Curriculum Objectives

To increase vocabulary; to improve expressive abilities; to introduce a familiar story in a different language.

Anti-Bias Area

Ability

Anti-Bias Skills

To promote respect for human diversity in ability; to provide opportunities to interact with people who are differently abled.

Materials

The Very Hungry Caterpillar, in braille; and cards with each child's name written in braille (see Appendix for Braille Alphabet Guide).

Approaches

Incorporation, Personalization, and Extension.

Facilitation

Discuss with the children the fact that a book can be written in two languages. Let them explore the raised braille patterns, and then identify the configurations of their individual name cards. Talk about how people who are visually impaired use their fingers to read. Invite a visitor from the community to demonstrate how braille is read.

Ask the children to think about all the things we need to read in our daily lives, about what people who are blind need to use to help them everyday, to get to school, go grocery shopping, cook, talk on the phone, etc.

Ask them who can be blind (other children? grandparents? others?).

Expansion

Make braille cards for important features/structures in the room: water/sand table, bookshelf, toilet, sink, signs for the allowed number of children per activity area, etc.

Community Resource

The Children's Braille Book Club, National Braille Press, has dual track books. For a catalog, write to: National Braille Press; 88 St. Stephen Street, Boston, MA 02115; (617) 266-6160.

Language Cards

Familiarizing children with the differences among people.

Age

3–5 years

Curriculum Area

Language

Curriculum Objective

To increase the expression of imaginative creative thinking.

Anti-Bias Areas

Age, Race, Culture, Gender, Appearance, Ability, Class, Family Composition, Belief

Anti-Bias Skill

To promote respect for human diversity.

Materials

Cut out pictures from *National Geographic* that illustrate interesting events or relationships between people that preschoolers can relate to. Mount them either individually or in a series on cardboard and cover with clear contact paper for durability.

Approach

Incorporation

Facilitation

Hold up each card and give the children time to describe who and what they see. Assist with vocabulary they may not have. Ask open-ended questions about what might be happening and what the person(s) may be feeling and why. Encourage as much divergency in their thinking as possible.

Community Resources

Take community walks and snap photos of objects, events, and people that would be an interesting source for discussion (billboards, construction sites, window displays, houses and shops, people and their pets, or different modes of transportation, etc.).

Mystery Prop Game

Promoting relational thinking.

Age

3–5 years

Curriculum Area

Language

Curriculum Objective

To promote the expression of relational thinking.

Anti-Bias Area

Culture

Anti-Bias Skill

To expose children to cultural differences.

Materials

Wooden honey dipper; goose-feathered basting brush; bamboo painting brushes (Chinese brushes come in a set that are attached so the width can be changed); and pastry brush

Approaches

Incorporation, Personalization, Extension

Facilitation

Present a selection of utensils from different cultures to the children in a mystery container. Have the children guess the functions of the utensils, and explain their hypotheses. Supply the correct labels for these objects in the necessary languages. Encourage children to see how objects that share similar characteristics can be used for different functions.

Invite people from your community to demonstrate how these utensils are used in their culture. Assess gender bias by asking children if they think men/boys could use these items and for what purposes?

Expansion

Provide an opportunity to use these items creatively with paint and have children assess the differences that result from the various materials.

Community Resources

Hardware or specialty cooking stores.

Shoe Sort Game

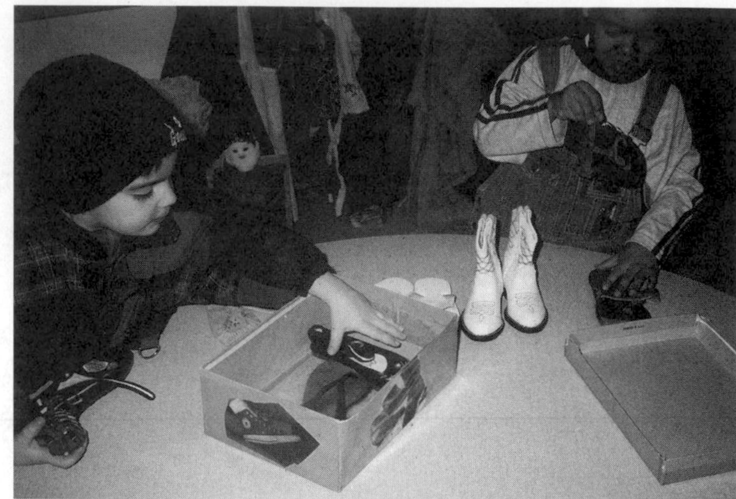

Broadening thinking and challenging stereotypes.

Age
3–5 years

Curriculum Area
Language

Curriculum Objectives
To strengthen expressive abilities in reasoning and challenging stereotypes; to broaden vocabulary.

Anti-Bias Areas
Gender, Culture, Age, Ability

Anti-Bias Skill
To value uniqueness of self and others.

Materials
A collection of shoes that reflects a wide variety of footwear (adult sandals, child-sized running shoes, thongs, Chinese slippers, cowboy boots, moccasins, clogs, snowshoes, ballet shoes, etc.).

Approaches
Incorporation and Extension

Facilitation
Bring out the shoes and use one of your favorite types of shoes to begin a discussion on footwear. Ask the children to describe, label, and discuss who, when, and where the shoes would be worn. Listen to their assumptions, perhaps even stereotypes, about gender, age, and ability in footwear.

Challenge such statements as "Old people only wear slippers" with "Why do you think that?" Help them to understand misperceptions: "Do you think only girls can wear ballet shoes? Can girls wear cowboy boots?"

Expansion
Put the shoe collection out in the dramatic play center for exploration.

Read the book *Two Pairs of Shoes,* by Esther Sanderson, which tells the story of a young girl who receives a pair of dress shoes that she has longed for and a pair of beaded moccasins from her blind grandmother. The story explores how the girl must learn when and how to wear each pair of shoes.

Community Resources
Bata Shoe Museum in Toronto, 327 Bloor St. West; local museum collections; dollar stores; and garage sales.

Life Cycle in Sequence

Sequencing from the very youngest to the oldest.

Age

3–5 years

Curriculum Area

Language

Curriculum Objectives

To practice sequencing; to develop relational thinking.

Anti-Bias Areas

Age, Gender, Ability, Belief

Anti-Bias Skill

To challenge age stereotyping.

Materials

Laminated picture cards that depict the cycle of aging from pregnancy through childhood and adolescence to adulthood (young, middle, and old). The people on the cards should reflect diversity in race, culture, gender, ability, and belief. The pictures should portray people engaged in activities and experiences that are both nonstereotypical and stereotypical in order to promote discussion.

Approach

Incorporation

Facilitation

The focus of this activity is to help children understand the physical changes that happen to people over time and the process of growing and aging. As the children look at and arrange the cards, engage them in discussions that may reveal misconceived notions about how abilities relate to age. Explain how *ageism* (actions that discriminate against the young or the old) happens; clarify that just because people are older, or have wrinkles, does not mean they cannot do active things (ski, bike, hike, etc.).

Expansion

Read the story *How Does It Feel To Be Old?*, by Norma Faber. Have a follow-up discussion about the advantages and disadvantages of being old. Continue to encourage empathy and discourage stereotypical ideas.

The Guessing Bag

Age
3–5 years

Curriculum Area
Language

Curriculum Objectives
To improve listening skills and expressive problem solving.

Anti-Bias Area
Culture

Anti-Bias Skills
To strengthen self-esteem; to value uniqueness of self and others.

Materials
Flannel draw bag; children's special items from home or school.

Approach
Modified Personalization

Facilitation
Invite two to three children to bring in a favorite item from home and hide it in the flannel draw bag. The task for these children is to give clues about the object instead of just describing it. The other children are actively involved by using this information to guess what the items are. Emphasize the uniqueness of each child's special item. Repeat this activity once a week so every child has an opportunity to feel special.

If children are unable to share a special object from home due to economic conditions, then suggest they may present something from the classroom or the school (library, etc.). No child should ever feel disadvantaged.

Memory Games

Age
3–5 years

Curriculum Area
Language

Curriculum Objective
To improve visual memory.

Anti-Bias Area
Culture

Anti-Bias Skill
To expose children to cultural differences.

Materials
South American worry dolls; Matroshka dolls; variety of items such as dishes, utensils, toys that reflect cultural diversity (bamboo steamer, wooden carved plate, etc.); and a large cloth.

Approach
Incorporation

Facilitation
In a small group of five to six children put out three or four items and determine if they know the correct label for each object. Give them the proper name and a brief description of its function for each item. Cover the objects with a cloth and while they close their eyes, remove an object. Have them guess which item was taken away. Depending on the ages and abilities of your group, increase the game's level of complexity by adding more items and rearranging the order of the objects remaining.

Expansion
Repeat the same activity but refocus the anti-bias area to reflect ability. Substitute miniature figures in leg braces, crutches, miniature wheelchair, hearing aid, glasses, asthma mask, etc., for the cultural items. This game can be made more difficult by combining objects from the two areas once the children are familiar with all the items.

Whose Voice Is That?

Age
3–5 years

Curriculum Area
Language

Curriculum Objective
To improve auditory discrimination and memory.

Anti-Bias Areas
Gender, Culture

Anti-Bias Skill
To value uniqueness of self and others.

Materials
Tape recorder and tape.

Approach
Modified Personalization

Facilitation
Circulate around the class as the children play, and tape the conversations taking place. If necessary, create situations to engage children in a dialogue in order to capture every child's voice on tape. During snack or large group time play the tape back and encourage the children to identify themselves and their peers by the voices heard. Emphasize how each child's voice is special and unique.

Matching Feely Bag

Age
3–6 years

Curriculum Area
Language

Curriculum Objectives
To improve tactile discrimination and memory; to extend expressive vocabulary.

Anti-Bias Area
Race

Anti-Bias Skills
To strengthen a positive association with the color brown; to recognize and label similarities and differences.

Materials
Flannel bag and two each of the following brown objects: chestnuts, emery boards, kiwi fruit, wooden blocks, pompoms, pieces of hard clay, and swatches of corduroy/velvet or burlap on cardboard.

Approach
Incorporation

Facilitation
Place one set of objects in the flannel bag and set out the others on a tray. Each child should select one object from the tray, feel it, and describe its texture, shape, and color, before reaching into the bag and attempting to find its match. As the child is rummaging through the bag, repeat the object's description and encourage the child to look at the object in hand. Increase the number of objects according to the children's abilities. After the game is over, discuss how all the objects are similar and different.

As with other activities, continuous, hands-on exploration of brown objects will instill children with a positive attitude toward this color and reduce the discomfort that may arise later in life.

Silhouette Guess

Age
4–5 years

Curriculum Area
Language

Curriculum Objectives
To practice part-whole relational thinking; to promote expressive, descriptive language.

Anti-Bias Area
Gender

Anti-Bias Skills
To value the uniqueness of self and others; to recognize and label similarities and differences

Materials
People-colored paper; markers; and overhead projector.

Approach
Modified Personalization

Facilitation
Use this traditional activity of tracing a child's profile and hair to work on perceptions linked to gender. After all the silhouettes are completed, hold up each paper and ask the children to describe what they see in terms of hair length and style, and any other facial features. Seize the opportunity to clarify any stereotypical perceptions about gender identity and assumed hair length or style: "That's not Gareth. It has long hair so it must be Alicia." If any children laugh about someone's features, emphasize how the parts of our face/head are what makes each one of us special.

Read *Somos un arco Iris: We Are a Rainbow,* by Nancy Maria Grande Tabor, to round out this experience.

Letter Cards

Age
4–6 years

Curriculum Area
Language

Curriculum Objective
To support emergent understanding of sound-symbol relationship.

Anti-Bias Area
Ability

Anti-Bias Skills
To promote respect for human diversity in ability; to provide opportunities to interact with people who are differently abled.

Materials
Set of letter cards with appropriate pictures that illustrate the initial phonetic sound. On the other side is the same letter with both the braille and sign equivalents (see appendix for braille and Signed English guides).

Approach
Incorporation

Facilitation
These cards should be a staple item among your reading readiness materials, so the children can explore them on an individual basis, one-on-one with the teacher, or in pairs.

For older children who have mastered letter recognition, encourage them to practice identifying the braille configuration by covering the letter or signing the letter by looking at the picture.

Grocery Matching

Age

4–6 years

Curriculum Area

Language

Curriculum Objectives

To develop auditory discrimination of initial sounds; to support emergent understanding of sound-symbol relationship.

Anti-Bias Area

Culture

Anti-Bias Skill

To expose children to cultural differences in smells and foods.

Materials

Large paper bags; cards with initial consonants; containers; boxes; foods representing selected consonant sounds; and proper storage for perishable fruits and vegetables which will be out for a limited time.

Approach

Incorporation

Facilitation

Decide which consonant or vowel sounds you would like the children to explore and learn. Provide enough materials so they can sort them according to the letter symbols attached to the paper bags. Encourage them first to look at the letter and make the correct phonic sound. Help them by holding up one object and asking what they think it is. Once they have labeled the item, help them to focus on the beginning sound of the word and look for the appropriate bag that matches the sound. For those who are more print aware, point out the word on the package to build word recognition.

Follow up this activity with a discussion about what foods they would eat for breakfast, dinner, or dessert. What could they drink? What could they eat raw and what has to be cooked?

M
mango
maple syrup
melon
milk (soy, coconut as well)
mint
mandarin

P
pita bread
pineapple
pear
peanut butter
papaya
pancake batter
parsley
potatoes

C
coconut
carrot
cabbage
corn
Cheerios
cauliflower
coriander
cream cheese
cucumber

B
broccoli
beet
banana
breadstick
bagel
bread
bean sprouts
bulgur

L
lime
lemon
lemongrass
lasagna noodles

A
avocado
apple
alfalfa sprouts
apricot

(continued)

Expansion

Select from the variety of fruits and vegetables and let the children prepare a fruit salad or vegetable snack. Illustrate a simple recipe that encourages children to read symbols and follow directions. Example: pita bread with cream cheese, cucumber, and alfalfa sprouts.

Read the story *The Food We Eat*, by Bobbie Kalman and Susan Hughes.

Sounds Are Us

Age

4–6 years

Curriculum Area

Language

Curriculum Objectives

To develop auditory identification, discrimination, memory, and auditory association skills.

Anti-Bias Areas

Gender, Age, Ability

Anti-Bias Skills

To support and respect gender equity; to challenge gender stereotyping.

Materials

Tape recorder and recording of domestic sounds and outside sounds. (A commercial tape, *Around the World Sound Tracks*, is available from Kaplan.)

Approach

Incorporation

Facilitation

Have the children listen to the taped sounds which should not be presented in any grouped order. Ask the children to identify each sound. Follow this with a discussion about where they might hear the sounds, and what or who might be producing these sounds.

Encourage the children to challenge preconceived assumptions about sex roles, and help them to understand that one's gender, age, or ability doesn't necessarily limit one's capacity to do things.

Domestic		Outside	
vacuum cleaner	washing machine	lawn mower	car engine starting
blender	alarm clock ringing	fire truck siren	leaves being raked
toilet flushing	dishes/cutlery	steam shovel digging	snow shoveling
musical instrument		train/airplane	

Expansion

Read *The Work People Do*, by Betsy Imershein.

Community Resource

Check the library for sound track tapes.

The Missing Pic Symbol

Exposure to augmentative communication.

Age
4–6 years

Curriculum Area
Language

Curriculum Objectives
To improve visual memory and closure; to learn about the association between a picture and its printed equivalent.

Anti-Bias Area
Ability

Anti-Bias Skills
To promote respect for human diversity in ability; to provide opportunities to interact with people who are differently abled.

Materials
Assortment of pic symbols from Mayer-Johnson's *Picture Communication Symbols,* photocopied and cut out. Create situations for which the symbols are logical solutions.

Approach
Incorporation

Facilitation
Tell the children they are going to create simple stories using picture symbols. Do one with a small group as a demonstration: "Today we went to the zoo/farm and we saw . . ." Put out the pic symbols for "everybody looking" and an assortment of animals. Or try: "We took a bus to the store to buy . . ." Provide correct pic symbols that can be arranged by the children. Let them explore the symbols and play with the sequences to create a story line.

After interest in the activity has waned, discuss with the group that many children aren't able to speak and their hands don't do what their brains tell them. The only way for them to communicate with others is by pointing to the pictures.

Expansion
Cut out more pictures, such as emotions, to increase the children's storymaking opportunities.

What Does This Person Need?

Age

4–6 years

Curriculum Area

Language

Curriculum Objectives

To introduce a new language and improve expressive abilities.

Anti-Bias Area

Ability

need
Move right N downward one time

want
Five shape both hands, palms up, fingers slightly curved. Draw back to body.

Trying to communicate using a different system.

Anti-Bias Skills

To promote respect for human diversity in ability; to provide opportunities to interact with people who are differently abled.

Materials

Signed English book *The Things I Like to Do*; five to ten pictures of objects in *The Comprehensive Signed English Dictionary*; and signs for "I want" and "I need."

Approach

Modified Personalization

Facilitation

Read the Signed English book *The Things I Like to Do*, accompanied with signing. Teach the children the signs for "I want" or "I need." Put out the 10 pictures giving directions for signing objects and let the children select what sentence they would like to sign. Help them practice their individual sentences. Gather all the children back together and let the children take turns signing their sentences. It is important for children to learn that many people communicate using this system.

Expansion

Take a song such as "Sunshine on My Shoulders" and teach the children how to sign it. Sing and sign the song during music time to keep the experience alive.

Community Resources

Invite an augmentative communication specialist to teach the staff key signs and review the resource, *The Comprehensive Signed English Dictionary*. Check with organizations that provide early intervention services for suitable personnel.

What If . . . ?

Age

4–6 years

Curriculum Area

Language

Curriculum Objectives

To engage in problem solving and divergent thinking using expressive language; to be able to think about how someone else may be feeling.

Anti-Bias Area

Class

Anti-Bias Skill

To support emergent empathy.

Approach

Incorporation

Facilitation

Gather the children in a circle and tell them you have a new thinking game. Begin by saying that you have some problems and could really use their help to solve them. Have some "what if" situations prepared. Examples: What if someone didn't have a bed, where would he sleep?; what if someone didn't have a car, how would she get to work?; what if someone didn't have winter boots, how could he walk around in the wet weather?; what if someone was all dressed up and a car on the street drove through a puddle and splashed her new coat?; what if a mother gave her child 25 cents to buy juice in school and by the time the child got to school he realized he had lost it?

Encourage the children to brainstorm as many different solutions as possible. Ask them how they think that person might feel. This exercise represents a beginning in sensitizing young children to the economic discrepancies that exist among families and communities and building empathic feelings.

The Family House

Age

4–6 years

Curriculum Area

Language

Curriculum Objectives

To improve matching a picture with its word symbol; to support emergent recognition of word patterns; to develop finger dexterity.

Anti-Bias Area

Family Composition

Anti-Bias Skill

To strengthen basic understanding of self in relation to family.

Materials

Several blank houses cut from bristol board; photos of children's family members; and matching word cards labeling family members (mum, daddy, or child's special name for a person). Affix velcro to the houses, photos, and word cards so they can be attached.

Approach

Modified Personalization

Facilitation

Have the children create visual representations of their families by attaching photos of family members to the houses. For those who show reading readiness, set out word cards that they can match with the appropriate photo. Teachers need to remind children that families come in different sizes and with different memberships in case any child's family house is made fun of.

Expansion

Do this same activity but have the children wear gloves as they try to place the cards and photos on the family house. The difficulty the children will encounter is akin to the poor motor planning and dexterity that children with physical limitations, such as cerebral palsy, experience. This expanded activity will sensitize children to those who are differently abled.

Read the book *All Kinds of Families*, by Norma Simon.

Go Bake Card Game

Age

4–6 years

Curriculum Area

Language

Curriculum Objectives

To strengthen expressive abilities; to practice labeling in different languages.

Anti-Bias Area

Culture

Anti-Bias Skill

To expose children to cultural differences in smells and foods.

Materials

Enlarge previously made bread cards by adding another matched set (see *Lots of Breads,* p. 155).

Approach

Incorporation

Facilitation

Introduce the game Go Bake; explain that the goal is to acquire as many matched pairs of cards as possible. Review the names of the different kinds of breads the children explored previously (bao, bagel, scone, matzo, naan, baguette, pita, chapati, tortilla, challah, breadstick, toast, etc.). Keep the instructions simple. Each child gets five cards and each child, in turn, asks, "Do you have a ___?" If the other child is holding such a bread card she hands it over. If the child doesn't have what is asked for she says, "Go bake." This prompts the asking child to take a card from the pile. The same process is repeated by the next child. Once a matched pair is found, the two cards are put together off to one side. At the end of the game the children list the different kinds of bread they "baked" successfully.

Expansion

Read the book *The Bagels Are Coming,* by Arlene Kingston.

The Body Bingo Game

Age
3–5 years

Curriculum Area
Reading Readiness

Curriculum Objectives
To improve visual discrimination, auditory memory, and matching skills.

Anti-Bias Areas
Race, Ability, Age

Anti-Bias Skills
To strengthen self-esteem and self-identity; to foster familiarity with differences in skin color, ability, and age.

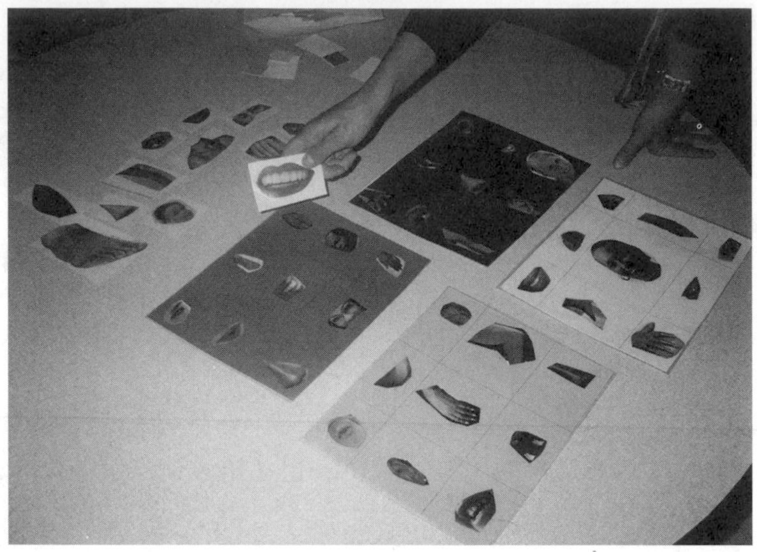

Improving visual discrimination and learning about racial differences.

Materials
Homemade game boards with nine squares each containing cutout magazine pictures of facial features and body parts. Include pictures of eyes with glasses, ears with a hearing aid, and other body parts that reflect diversity in race, age, and ability; provide a set of similar pictures to use as markers. Cover with clear contact paper.

Approaches
Incorporation and Extension: call out body parts in French, Spanish, or any other different language represented by children and staff.

Facilitation
Show the book *Two Eyes, a Nose and a Mouth,* by Roberta Groebel. Introduce the concept of this game that requires the children to cover a square of the body part that is called out. They must find the same type of card and place it in the appropriate position on the board. If children have queries about the pictures, respond with accurate information about racial differences. Let children look at each other and compare the differences in their physical appearances. Reinforce that each child is unique and special.

Bread Delivery

Age
4–5 years

Curriculum Area
Reading Readiness

Curriculum Objectives
To improve visual discrimination and matching skills.

Anti-Bias Area
Culture

Anti-Bias Skill
To expose children to cultural differences in smells and foods.

Materials
Bread baskets with color-coded paper; bread cards color coded to match baskets; map of countries where breads are found, with corresponding color codes; pictures of people eating or making the bread, placed inside the baskets; and the names of the countries printed on the baskets in the same colors.

Approach
Incorporation

Facilitation
Show the children a modified map of the world and point out the countries where the breads they have been learning about are usually baked. Tell them that they need to deliver bread to empty baskets hidden all over the room. Ask the children individually to select a bread card, identify it if possible, look at the map, and identify its color. Read the name of the country for the child, if necessary, and reiterate that the basket for "pita," as an example, will be marked by a yellow sticker, just like the round sticker on the card. When the children find the proper basket, they should bring it back with the card, show the photo inside, and describe to the others what's happening in the picture.

Leave the baskets and bread cards out for children to play with. Encourage matching and any attempts at reading bread and country labels. This is a follow-up activity to *Lots of Breads.*

Hats, Hats, Hats Lotto Game

Learning about different types of headwear.

Age

4–5 years

Curriculum Area

Reading Readiness

Curriculum Objectives

To increase visual discrimination, and visual and auditory memory.

Anti-Bias Areas

Culture, Gender, Belief

Anti-Bias Skill

To expose children to cultural differences.

Materials

Hats, Hats, Hats, by Ann Morris; photocopies of select headwear, mounted and laminated on boards (seven per board); and buttons as markers.

Approach

Incorporation

Facilitation

Read the book *Hats, Hats, Hats.* Give the children the correct names for each type of hat. Discuss on whom and where such hats are found, as well as what the person does. Follow up this experience with homemade lotto game boards. Call out the hat, using the correct name, and have the children cover up the appropriate pictures in response. Address any misconceptions about gender stereotyping in relation to headwear. Some common stereotypical statements children make are: "She can't be a fireman because girls never wear helmets. Only boys wear cowboy hats and baseball caps. He can't be an Indian. Where are his feathers?"

Expansion

Begin a collection of hats donated from families as well as from community resources to enrich the dramatic play area. Always disinfect headwear on a regular basis.

Names of Headwear

Straw hat; chef hat; baseball cap; sun hat; hood; chullo; firefighter hat; cowboy hat; ten-gallon hat (adult male in distinction to child's); kaffiyeh; kerchief; chicken feather ceremonial hat; helmet; basket hat; head scarf (for Indian women in contrast to the kaffiyeh for men), etc.

Friendship Dominoes

Understanding that friends come with different abilities and different skin colors.

Age
4–5 years

Curriculum Area
Reading Readiness

Curriculum Objectives
To improve visual discrimination and matching skills.

Anti-Bias Areas
Gender, Race

Anti-Bias Skill
To foster familiarity with differences in skin color.

Materials
Domino cards that have children of different races and gender in red, blue, yellow, or green pants, dresses, or shoes. Cards can be made from the All Kinds of Kids trimmer, TS Denison 2368-2, which depicts children from different racial backgrounds and with different physical abilities wearing just such clothing and shoes.

Approach
Incorporation

Facilitation
Encourage those playing with the cards to match the children by color of clothing or shoes so that children of different races, gender, and ability will be friends.

Job Cards

Age

4–6 years

Curriculum Area

Reading Readiness

Curriculum Objectives

To improve memory and visual discrimination.

Anti-Bias Areas

Gender, Race

Anti-Bias Skill

To support and respect gender and racial equity.

Materials

Prepare a set of twenty cards depicting 10 occupations that are bias free in terms of gender and race, or genders in nontraditional roles—male and female doctors, electricians, firefighters, mail carriers, construction workers, plumbers, orchestra conductors, carpenters, computer programmers, and police officers.

Approach

Incorporation

Facilitation

Let the children explore the cards initially to familiarize themselves with the occupations and personnel. Take the opportunity to challenge any stereotypical perceptions the children may have about who can do a job, by helping them to understand that everyone who aspires and studies can perform that job.

Put the cards face down in 4 rows of 5, or 5 rows of 4, or 2 rows of 10. Have the children take turns selecting two cards, turning them face up, and remembering their position on the table. The task is to match up all 10 pairs. As the cards are turned over, encourage the children to verbalize the name of each profession to strengthen their vocabulary at the same time.

Expansion

Keep career puzzle sets that are free of racial and gender stereotyping out in the play area for reinforcement.

Community Resource

Cards can be made by cutting, mounting, and laminating borders showing occupations represented by nonsexist, multiracial depictions of people. (The closest approximation to such a border is the Children International Series: At Work, available from Lakeshore/Wintergreen, The Children's Factory catalog, CF221-526.)

What's in a Name?

Age

5–6 years

Curriculum Area

Reading Readiness

Curriculum Objectives

To strengthen letter recognition, matching skills, and visual discrimination.

Anti-Bias Area

Ability

Anti-Bias Skill

To foster familiarity with differences in ability.

Materials

Grid boards for each child with the name spelled vertically and the corresponding letters in different spatial arrangements in horizontal rows; matching letter cards with raised braille dots under the letter.

Approach

Incorporation

Facilitation

Invite children to solve a name puzzle. Elicit identification of the individual letters, and encourage them to find and point out the same symbol in each row. Let them find a matching letter card from the tray and place it in the correct position. Ensure they feel the corresponding braille arrangement of dots that are under each letter. For those children who have been practicing identification of braille letters, make matching letter cards with only the raised dots.

Remind children that many people read books and elevator floor numbers by touching the raised dots.

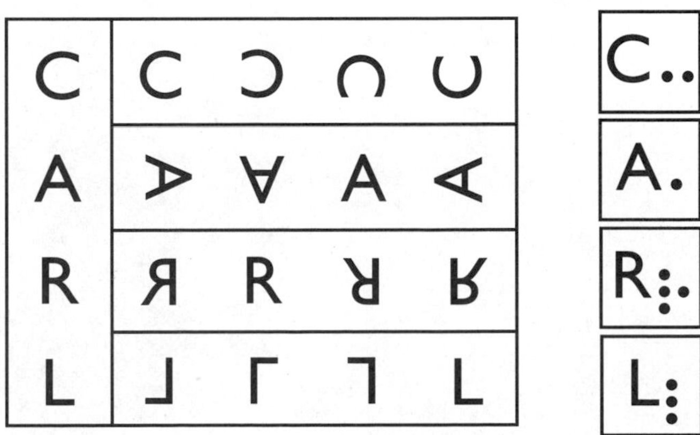

Becoming aware that some people read using their fingers instead of their eyes.

People Puzzles

Age

3–4 years

Curriculum Area

Mathematics

Curriculum Objectives

To improve visual discrimination; to practice figure-ground matching.

Anti-Bias Areas

Appearance, Ability

Anti-Bias Skills

To recognize and label similarities and differences; to value uniqueness of self and others.

Materials

Assortment of people cookie cutters in different sizes and shapes traced onto bristol board. Block off an arm or a leg on two of the traced figures; cutouts for matching. Create four different boards.

Approach

Incorporation

Facilitation

Put out the assortment of people-shaped cutouts with the puzzle boards. Encourage the children to find the cutout shape that matches or looks just the same as the one on the board. For the three-year-olds ensure that both the traced outlines and the cutouts share matching colors for added visual clues. The four-year-olds should not have to rely on color clues, but should try and focus on the shape for more refined visual discrimination practice.

Ask the children to tell you how they know that these people match. If they cannot, then describe the matchups by size, shape of head, body, two-legged or one-armed, etc.

This is a natural way to expose children to the fact that some people have different physical shapes and abilities.

Counting Children

Improving one-to-one correspondence and counting skills.

Age
3–5 years

Curriculum Area
Mathematics

Curriculum Objectives
To improve one-to-one correspondence and counting; to match pictures with the appropriate number symbol.

Anti-Bias Area
Race

Anti-Bias Skill
To promote respect for human diversity in race.

Materials
Math cards created with thick cardboard, minimally 6 inches square, numbered 1–5. Cut up the border Kids Are Great, T-8513 by Trend Enterprises, in which photos of children of different racial backgrounds are represented. Create a matching set of 15 face cards, 2 inches square in size, to be used as counters.

Glue 1, 2, 3, etc. pictures of children at the head of the board. Draw a thick line across the top under the pictures to delineate space.

Approach
Incorporation

Facilitation
These hands-on math boards will give children the opportunity to work through the numerical concepts of 1–5. Offer cards for children to place underneath the line. Help them to count and see how they are to match the *number* of children, not the faces. In this way, race does not become a factor and children of different races are naturally integrated into a counting game. Depending on the children's developmental abilities, offer the number cards to see if they can place the correct symbol on the math board after counting the children's faces.

Expansion
Peg-It Number Board (Kaplan) is another variation using the manual hand alphabet to indicate the corresponding number.

Community Resource
Kids Are Great border can be ordered from the Lakeshore/Wintergreen Elementary Teacher Catalog, *Your Classroom.*

Missing Parts

Age
3–5 years

Curriculum Area
Mathematics

Curriculum Objectives
To practice part-whole relational thinking, making hypotheses, and drawing conclusions.

Anti-Bias Areas
Race, Gender, Age

Anti-Bias Skill
To promote respect for human diversity.

Materials
Magazine pictures mounted on cardboard. The pictures can depict adults/children of different ethno-racial backgrounds, as well as age and gender, involved in activities. Select a significant feature or element either in the person, or the object, and cut it away: child in a wheelchair without a wheel; toddler holding a hand, but the adult's face is missing, etc.

Approach
Incorporation

Facilitation
Bring out the cards and invite the children to join you in a guessing game. Tell them that in each picture something is missing and they need to identify the thing that has disappeared. Their perceptions may or may not yield interesting opportunities for an anti-bias discussion. As an example, the picture of the toddler holding someone's hand may evolve into a conversation of who else besides mommy can take care of a baby?

This activity gives the preschool child an opportunity to practice visual closure and association using anti-bias materials.

It Looks Like Spilled Cocoa

Age
3–5 years

Curriculum Area
Mathematics

Curriculum Objectives
To practice part-whole relational thinking, and making hypotheses.

Anti-Bias Area
Race

Anti-Bias Skill
To strengthen a positive association with the color brown.

Materials
Felt board; pieces of brown felt cut into the shape of a bear, tree trunk, crayon, bird, raisins, chocolate ice cream cone, horse, etc.; and cover paper with different shaped openings.

Approach
Incorporation

Facilitation
This guessing game is a twist on the original spilled milk concept. The objects are partially revealed and the teacher can give verbal rhyming clues to assist the children's thinking:

- You might see it at a zoo or fair, it is a big, brown (*bear*).
- It gallops, it trots, it canters of course, that's because it is a graceful (*horse*).

All the hidden items are brown to reinforce a positive association with things that are brown.

Pattern Match-up Board

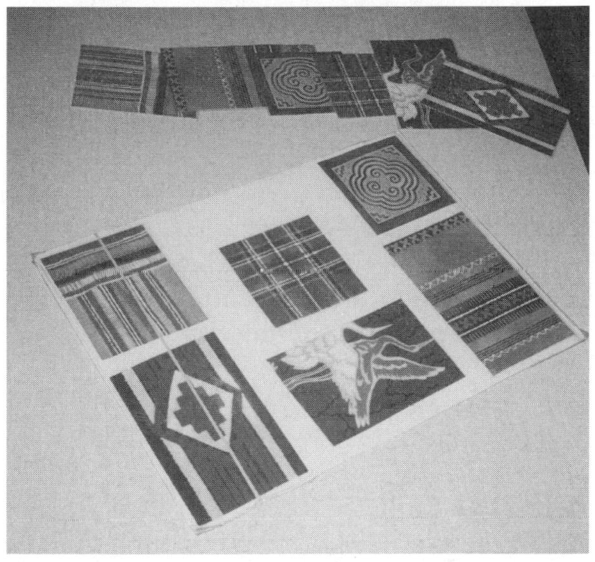
Fostering familiarity with different cultural patterns.

Age

3–5 years

Curriculum Area

Mathematics

Curriculum Objectives

To refine visual discrimination and matching skills.

Anti-Bias Area

Culture

Anti-Bias Skill

To expose children to cultural differences in textures and patterns.

Materials

Cut display borders (Cultural Trimmers, Trend Inc.) that reflect Indian, Hmong, Guatemalan, African, Navajo, and Japanese traditional patterns into 3-inch squares. Cover cardboards with at least four to six different squares. Finish with contact paper for durability. Make three or four different boards. Make a duplicate set of cards to match each game board and a master set for the caller.

Approach

Incorporation

Facilitation

Set out the boards and invite the children over to play a form of bingo. Hold up a card and encourage the children to find its match. When they have decided on a match, they cover up the square with the corresponding card. Once the children are familiar with the game, begin to call out the ethnic group whose pattern is represented on each square. Ensure that each child takes a turn being the caller.

Bring out an atlas and show the children where the people who designed these patterns live in the world.

Seriated Surprise Boxes

Age

3–5 years

Curriculum Area

Mathematics

Curriculum Objectives

To strengthen visual discrimination for seriation, and perceptual motor coordination for problem solving.

Anti-Bias Area

Culture

Anti-Bias Skill

To expose children to cultural differences.

Materials

Four boxes with lids that fit one into another; pictures that depict people in activities from different cultural backgrounds pasted in the bottom of each box.

Approach

Incorporation

Facilitation

By the time children have reached this age, they have experimented endlessly with objects of different sizes. This activity creates an additional challenge to understanding size gradation with the inclusion of box lids. As the children pull off the lids, the pictures present yet another focus for them.

Strengthening problem-solving skills.

Present all four lidded boxes side by side. Let the children explore the boxes and engage them in simple discussions about the pictures. Ask them to think about how all the boxes could fit together. Support all their trial-and-error problem solving.

Community Resources

Most dollar stores or stationery stores carry these kinds of boxes.

Fun with Geometric Shapes

Age
3–5 years

Curriculum Area
Mathematics

Curriculum Objectives
To experiment with and problem solve spatial arrangements using geometric shapes.

Anti-Bias Areas
Gender, Age, Ability

Anti-Bias Skills
To encourage children to try new experiences; to promote respect for human diversity.

Materials
Twenty-four homemade geometric shapes (six circles, three large, three small; six squares, three large, three small; six rectangles, three large, three small; six triangles, three large, three small), each one covered with individual pictures of people representing different ages, races, gender, and ability, mounted on cardboard and laminated. Outlines of different objects (boat, house, airplane, animal shapes, etc.) on white cardboard.

Approach
Incorporation

Facilitation
Let the children first explore the geometric puzzle pieces for shape and size patterning. Put out puzzle boards which range in complexity from simple (six-piece outline) to the more difficult (all 24 pieces). Each puzzle board has a shape outline that requires filling in, like a tangram or parquetry. Indicate on the back of the board the number and kind of shapes required to complete the puzzle. This guide also functions as a self-correcting tool.

Community Resources
A variety of commercial pattern blocks task cards are available for use as outlines or puzzle boards.

Fun with Paint Chips

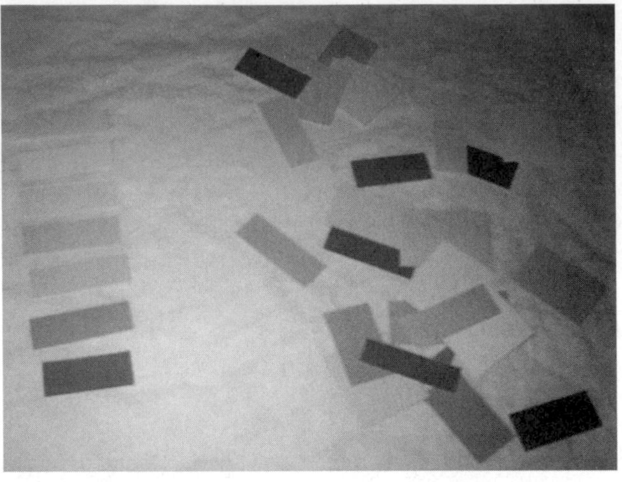
Labeling similarities and differences in skin tones.

Age
3–5 years

Curriculum Area
Mathematics

Curriculum Objective
To refine visual discrimination for matching and seriation.

Anti-Bias Area
Race

Anti-Bias Skill
To foster familiarity with differences in skin color.

Materials
Collect a double set of paint chips in various flesh tones from pale beige to dark brown. Cut the cards into small strips of colors. Alternatively, leave one card with the five tones intact and cut the duplicate into matching strips.

Approaches
Incorporation, Personalization, and Extension: If we close our eyes, can we match the colors? (Ability)

Facilitation
Let the children explore the materials, supporting their attempts to sort, match, and seriate the hues from dark to light or light to dark. The conversation related to each child's and teacher's skin color should be casual, pointing out how very different everyone's skin color truly is. Both staff and children can be involved by finding a paint chip to match their own skin color.

Questions that indicate confusion between social color—being White or Black—and general color, should be answered simply. Help children to understand that the term *Black* is used to identify the group of people to which a family feels they belong. Black people can have different shades of brown skin, as do White people: "Yes Natasha, you are correct. This is brown. Some people call themselves Black even though their skin comes in many shades of brown." Reinforce that we all get our skin color from our families.

Teachers need to be aware that cognitive limitations of this age group result in the inability to understand multiclass inclusion—racial identity and cultural affiliation.

Expansion
Read the book *All the Colors We Are: The Story of How We Get Our Skin Color,* by Katie Kissinger, to reinforce the concept.

Community Resources
Paint chips are available from hardware or paint stores.

Who Is Underneath?

Age
3–5 years

Curriculum Area
Mathematics

Curriculum Objectives
To practice part-whole relational thinking, making hypotheses, and drawing conclusions.

Anti-Bias Areas
Race, Gender, Age

Anti-Bias Skills
To recognize and label similarities and differences; to promote respect for human diversity.

Materials
Pictures of adults reflecting diversity in age, race, and gender. Cover each picture with paper and leave a square window revealing only a part of the picture underneath.

Approach
Incorporation

Facilitation
Present this activity as a guessing game to the children. Place the opening in a different position on each picture, so the children will have to predict who is hidden underneath based on such key, partially visible features as hair, eyes, nose, or mouth.

As the children work their way through the pictures you can help them to draw the conclusion that everyone, regardless of race, gender, or age, has the same facial features. Everyone needs hair, eyes to see, a nose to smell, ears to hear, and a mouth with which to eat and speak. These features may be of a different shape, color, size, or even have coverings such as a moustache or glasses, but we all have them.

Pasta Power

Age
3–6 years

Curriculum Area
Mathematics

Curriculum Objectives
To improve visual discrimination and grouping skills.

Anti-Bias Area
Culture

Anti-Bias Skill
To recognize and label similarities and differences.

Materials
Collection of different shaped pasta (penne, rotini, rigatoni, shells, fettuccine, lasagna, rice vermicelli, Chinese egg noodles, etc.); baskets; and paper and crayons.

Approach
Incorporation

Facilitation
Provide a bin full of assorted pasta and ask the children to find the ones that look the same. As they group the pasta, have them identify the critical characteristic. For example, if they place all the "long" pasta in one basket, then have them design a card that reflects this grouping and place it in front of the container. Encourage them to continue in this way until all the pasta has been sorted into the baskets.

Afterwards talk about the fact that although all the noodles look different, they still have things in common—the cooking process, nutritional value, they all belong to the grain family. Help them to see the parallel to themselves—children can look different but still have many things in common with one another.

Whose Job Is It Anyway?

Selecting the right person for the job.

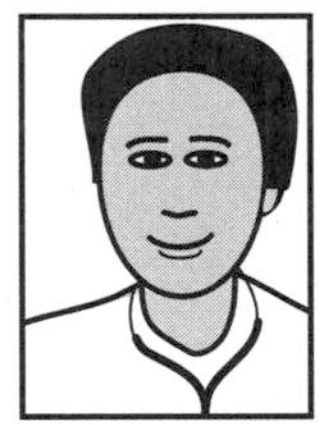   

Age

3–6 years

Curriculum Area

Mathematics

Curriculum Objectives

To practice visual association, one-to-one correspondence, and counting.

Anti-Bias Areas

Race, Gender

Anti-Bias Skill

To support and respect gender and racial equity.

Materials

Design a board game in an *S* shape. Make squares; on every fourth square paste a picture of an object that requires a match from a particular occupation: a burning building, musical instruments, spaceship, leaky tap and wrench, telephone pole and truck, stethoscope, etc. Create a set of cards depicting corresponding occupations: a firefighter, drummer, astronaut, plumber, electrician, doctor. To ensure gender and racial equity, make both male and female figures to represent each occupation. Make a homemade dice with only four numbers and bingo chips as counters.

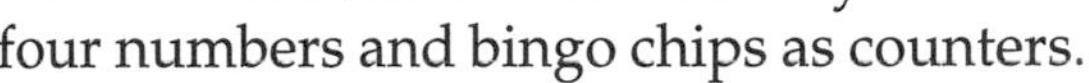

Approach

Incorporation

Facilitation

This game is multipurpose. On the simplest level it evaluates the child's ability to make associations between job-related objects or situations and the people who carry out those occupations. As the children are selecting the appropriate person, the teacher also has the opportunity to assess the children's perceptions about who can do the job. The mathematical level involves counting the number of dots and moving the corresponding squares to the next pictorial situation.

Challenge any stereotypical assumptions the children may show by helping them to understand that anyone who works hard and has a desire can perform that occupation.

Face-to-Face Puzzles

Age
4–5 years

Curriculum Area
Mathematics

Curriculum Objectives
To improve matching skills, visual closure, and problem solving.

Anti-Bias Areas
Race, Gender

Anti-Bias Skills
To recognize and label similarities and differences; to value uniqueness of self and others.

Materials
Close-up photos of the children's faces, cut into three strips: mouth, nose, and eyes and hair.

Approach
Modified Personalization

Facilitation
For preschoolers, scramble up the face photos of only four or five children at a time; for older children add more photos to increase complexity. Encourage the children to work in pairs so they can engage in discussions of comparison and problem solving. Help them to see the uniqueness of each child as they piece the faces of their peers together, while emphasizing the commonalities of everyone.

Diversity Puzzle

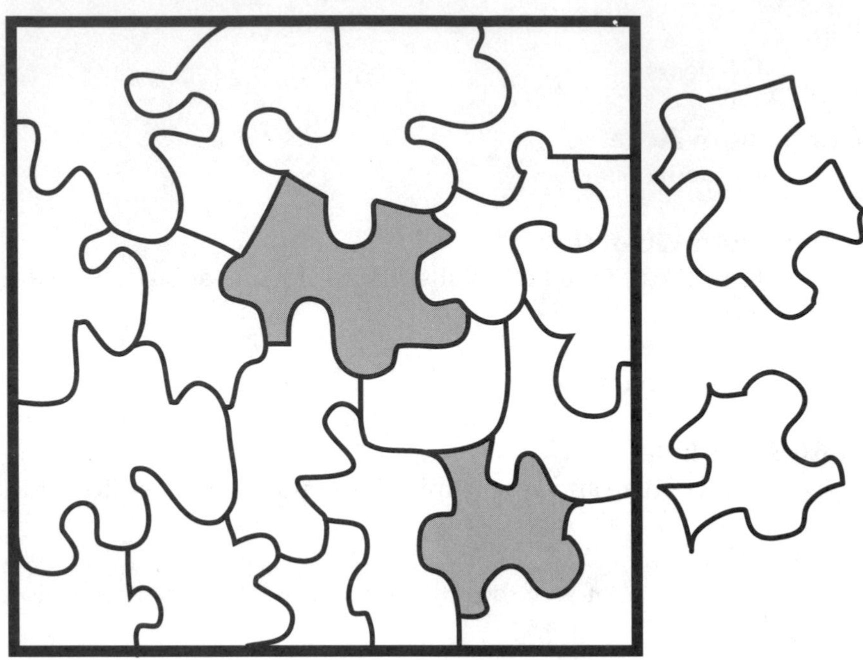

Age

4–5 years

Curriculum Area

Mathematics

Curriculum Objectives

To improve visual discrimination and figure-ground matching skills; to encourage expressing opinions.

Anti-Bias Areas

All areas

Anti-Bias Skill

To promote respect for human diversity.

Materials

An assortment of pictures depicting children and adults working, playing, or interacting, reflecting the various areas of diversity. Cut the pictures into interesting shapes, mount them on stiff cardboard, and laminate. The pictures should join as one huge jigsaw puzzle. Create a puzzle board with lines that outline the various shapes of the picture pieces.

Approach

Incorporation

Facilitation

Put out the pictures and puzzle board, and let the children explore how the pictures fit together or into the appropriately lined contours. Take the opportunity to engage the children in brief descriptions of what they see. Ask them if they would like to play with this person or child? Why or why not? Listen to any pre-prejudicial comments that might emerge in relation to race, appearance, gender, etc. Take the time to correct any misconceptions or assumptions with factual information.

For maximum conversation select out-of-the-ordinary people in different settings and situations.

Spice Match-up

Experimenting with part-whole relations.

Age
4–5 years

Curriculum Area
Mathematics

Curriculum Objectives
To practice visual and olfactory discrimination; to make comparisons; to improve understanding of part-whole relations.

Anti-Bias Area
Culture

Anti-Bias Skills
To promote respect for human diversity in culture; to encourage children to try new experiences.

Materials
Small jars with perforated lids or spice jars with clear lids; and an assortment of spices in their whole and powdered forms (cinnamon, nutmeg, garlic, coffee, chili, cloves, ginger, etc.).

Approaches
Incorporation and Personalization

Facilitation
Have the children explore the smelly jars and try to match up the spices. Encourage them to provide descriptions and reasons for the pairing. Engage the children in a discussion about how families use different ingredients in their cooking. Ask children to indicate which smells they like and dislike. If children comment that a smell is "yucky," help them to understand that different people like different spices. Tell them it is okay to dislike a particular smell, but it is not okay to label something as "yucky," because that hurts the feelings of people who do like it.

Have a family member assist in a cooking activity using particular spices. If the visitor is male and of a different racial background, then you have added two other areas of bias (gender and race).

Community Resource
Go to a bulk food store to buy spices for a cooking activity.

Word Picture Puzzles

Age

4–5 years

Curriculum Area

Mathematics

Curriculum Objectives

To improve visual discrimination and matching skills (representational image to corresponding word).

Anti-Bias Area

Culture

Anti-Bias Skill

To promote respect for human diversity in culture.

Materials

Oaktag rectangles cut into two pieces in a variety of puzzle shapes. Glue either photocopied photos or hand-drawn illustrations on one side and the printed word on the other. Vary the complexity of the puzzle contours.

Approach

Incorporation

Facilitation

This activity can be introduced after the *Hats, Hats, Hats Lotto Game* activity. Make the cards available and let the children explore finding the matching half to the puzzle card. Have them verbally identify the type of hat and who wears it for what situation. Increase the children's knowledge of headwear by adding other types of hats to the list created from *Hats, Hats, Hats* by Ann Morris.

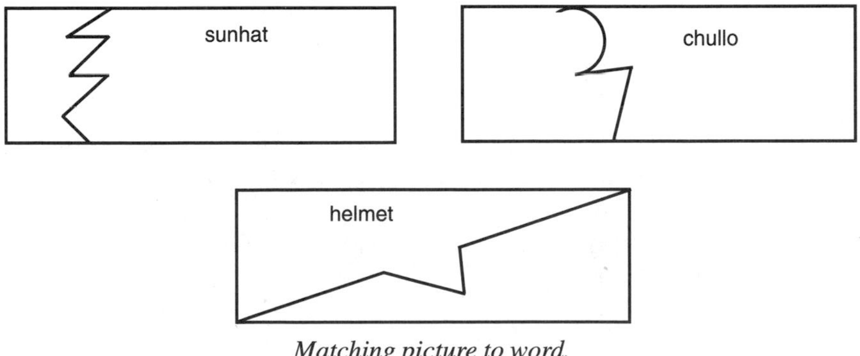

Matching picture to word.

Lots of Breads

Age

4–5 years

Curriculum Area

Mathematics

Curriculum Objectives

To practice grouping; to improve visual discrimination

Anti-Bias Area

Culture

Anti-Bias Skills

To recognize and label similarities and differences; to expose children to cultural differences in smells and foods.

Materials

Bread, Bread, Bread, by Ann Morris; representative sample of breads; illustrated cards of breads; pockets designated by shape on bristol board; and basket of plastic breads from around the world.

Approach

Incorporation

Facilitation

Read *Bread, Bread, Bread.* Ask the children to name some of their favorite breads and describe what they look like: round with a hole, or thin and flat, or long like a sausage, etc. Bring out the bread collection in several baskets and encourage the children to identify the shape of each. Give them the geometric form along with the proper name of the bread. Cut the breads into small pieces so each child can try two or three very different tasting breads, for example, chapati, bagel, and bao. Show the illustrated card and encourage the children to sort them according to the shapes identified:

- circular—bagel, bao, scone
- rectangular—matzo, white, and pumpernickel
- oval—naan, challah
- triangular—pizza slice
- long—baguette, breadstick
- flat—pita, chapati, tortilla

Leave the game out so the children can practice visual discrimination skills. Place the basket of plastic multicultural breads in the dramatic play center for further exploration and learning.

Counting Board Game

Age

4–6 years

Curriculum Area

Mathematics

Curriculum Objectives

To improve visual discrimination, and matching and counting skills.

Anti-Bias Areas

Race, Gender, Ability

Anti-Bias Skill

To promote respect for human diversity in race and gender.

Materials

Large bristol board designed with a curved path or squares drawn in connecting horizontal or vertical columns. Pictures of children from different racial backgrounds, cut from borders, serve as matching playing cards and board markers. Glue a variety of children's pictures two to four squares apart on the board. Provide counters.

Approach

Incorporation

Facilitation

Bring out the board and explain to the children how pieces can be moved from one end of the path to the other. Pieces are moved forward by picking a card from the pile and moving the counter to the matching face on the board. The card is then returned to the bottom of the pile to keep the supply of faces full. There are no winners or losers and the game can continue for as long as the children show interest.

The children depicted on the TS Denison trimmer will challenge the preschool-kindergarten group to observe carefully when attempting to match cards to boards. Many of the figures are wearing similar colored clothing and have similar hair coloring, but differ in gender and skin color. Children in wheelchairs are also prominent.

Community Resources

TS Denison #2368-2 (All Kinds of Kids) Trimmers That Teach; an alternative border is Children at Play from the International Children Border Series available from Lakeshore/Wintergreen, CF 221-524.

Holiday Dress

Age
4–6 years

Curriculum Area
Mathematics

Curriculum Objective
To improve visual discrimination for one-to-one correspondence.

Anti-Bias Area
Culture

Anti-Bias Skill
To expose children to cultural differences.

Improving visual discrimination for one-to-one correspondence.

Materials
Cutout dolls wearing holiday clothing. Paper doll models with 18 outfits are designed and ready for mounting on cardboard in Maureen Cech's *Globalchild: Multicultural Resources for Young Children;* or cut up the Children in Traditional Costume border from the International Children Border Series, Lakeshore/Wintergreen, CF 221-522. Provide clothespins (large spring-type pins are available in hardware stores or from educational supply catalogs), short clotheslines, and baskets.

Approach
Incorporation

Facilitation
String two clotheslines, one under the other, and provide one basket for clothespins and another basket for the cutouts dressed in holiday outfits. Before you bring out the materials, introduce the concept that on holidays people usually dress differently. Ask the children what kind of clothing their families wear on such occasions. Show the children photos of people in different countries, including North America, celebrating their traditional holidays. Pull out the cutouts and identify what country the figures are from, as well as essential background information such as names and uses of the outfits. Encourage the children to describe the clothing, footwear, and head gear. Emphasize that people all around the world have fancy dress clothes and everyday clothes.

To carry out the activity the children must select a cutout, peg it on the line, and find the matching outfit to hang underneath it. This activity can be made more complicated by cutting the outfits in half and having the children find the matching halves.

Community Resources
Community members who have examples of holiday clothes that they are willing to show and share with the class.

Designer Shade

Age
4–6 years

Curriculum Area
Mathematics

Curriculum Objectives
To experiment with creating and changing colors and shades; to improve visual discrimination and seriation.

Anti-Bias Area
Race

Anti-Bias Skill
To foster familiarity with differences in skin color.

Materials
Six-hole muffin tins (enough for a small group); white and brown paint in small paper cups; ⅛ teaspoon measuring spoons for each muffin tin; popsicle sticks; cotton buds; and white paper.

Approach
Incorporation

Facilitation
Set out the art materials and encourage the children to place different amounts of white and brown paints in each muffin hole. Stir with the popsicle stick. Observe how the children experiment with creating darker or lighter shades of brown.

After the children have created six different paint shades, have them dip a cotton bud into the paint samples and dab them onto a piece of paper. As the six paint shades are lined up see if the children can point out which is the lightest and darkest shade of brown they have made. Encourage the children to sequence the colors from dark to light or vice versa, using the cotton buds as paintbrushes.

Talk with the children about how they designed these different shades. Guide them in their observations to make the connections that adding white lightens a color while adding more of a color darkens the shade.

Expansion
Let the children discover the fun of making symmetrical designs by dabbing all six colors on half of a folded piece of paper. Refold and press the two halves together. Open and see what colors and designs have now been created. Children can do this as often as they like and the shades will continue to change.

Read the book *You Be Me, I'll Be You,* by P. Mandelbaum, which explores feelings about skin color within an interracial family.

What Belongs Together?

Age

4–6 years

Curriculum Area

Mathematics

Curriculum Objectives

To increase logical thinking by creating matched sets, and drawing relationships between objects.

Anti-Bias Areas

Ability, Gender, Age

Anti-Bias Skills

To promote respect for human diversity in ability, gender, and age; to challenge gender stereotyping.

Materials

Collection of 10 objects (miniature toy props available from catalog companies); 15 pictures (inventory below) mounted on bristol board and laminated.

Approach

Incorporation

Facilitation

Set objects out and let the children visually and physically inspect them. Provide a box of picture cards for the children to look through and ask them to decide which picture belongs with which object. As they place the card in front of the object, ask the children to explain the reason why the object and picture go together. Probe matchups that reflect assumptions about age, ability, and gender: a wheelchair and picture of a senior citizen, an earring and picture of a female, etc.

Ask the children to consider who else can use a wheelchair? Why and why not? Can men wear earrings? Why or why not?

Objects		Pictures	
hearing aid	bracelet	ear	young boy
glasses	wheelchair	eyes	young girl
diaper pin	white cane	baby	male senior citizen
Q-tip	crutch/walker	hands	female senior citizen
eye patch	toothbrush	teeth	nose
ring	hair comb	hair	

Because there is no one-to-one correspondence between pictures and objects, they can be arranged differently each time.

Community Resource

The following adaptive equipment for dolls is available from Lakeshore/Wintergreen:

Wheelchair	LC 1143	Leg braces and forearm crutches	LC 1145
Hearing aid and glasses	LC 1147	Protective helmet	LA 1201
Walker	LC 1151	Guide dog, harness, and cane	LC 1149

More Fun with Paint Chips

Age
4–6 years

Curriculum Area
Mathematics

Curriculum Objectives
To improve counting, one-to-one correspondence, grouping, and seriation.

Anti-Bias Area
Race

Anti-Bias Skill
To foster familiarity with differences in skin color.

Materials
Twenty-five popsicle sticks; sets of paint chips in various skin tones, from pale beige to dark brown, cut and pasted onto the sticks; five containers each marked with a number from 1–5, as well as an equivalent number of dots, and shaded from light to dark.

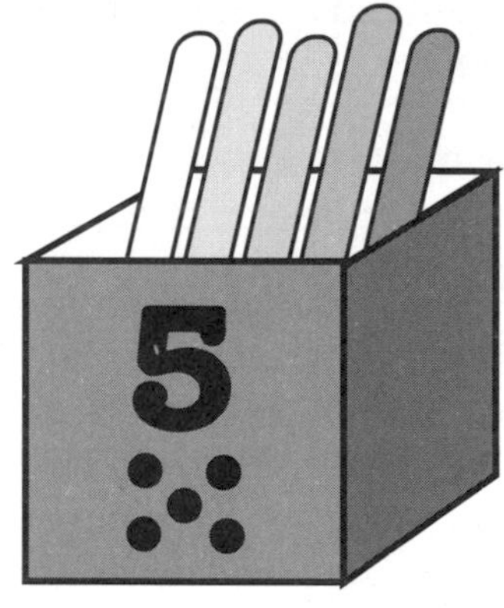

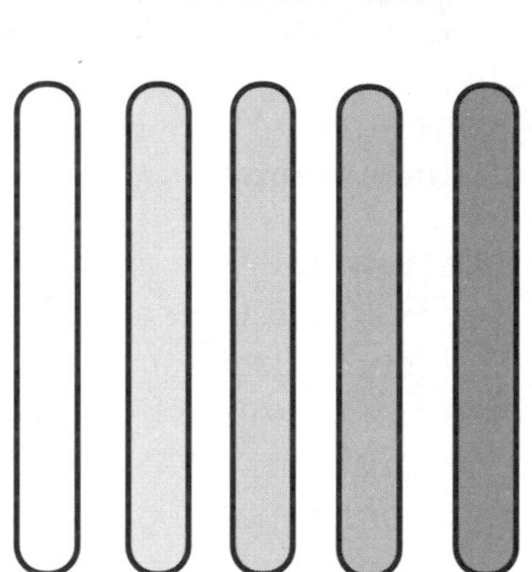

Counting, grouping, and sequencing skills—all in one activity.

Approach
Incorporation

Facilitation

This activity is a follow-up to the previous paint chip experience. The focus in this activity is counting, grouping, and seriating. The children will attempt to master the concept of quantification by counting the dots and placing the equivalent number of sticks as required by the container. Initially they may focus only on the counting and the one-to-one correspondence. Older children should be encouraged to group sticks by color and then find the necessary number required. The final task would be to seriate the sticks from light to dark and place them in the appropriate containers.

For primary level children this game can be extended into simple addition and subtraction. Throw in a die and ask children how to combine sticks in order to produce the number. See if they can combine multiple groupings to produce the number 5 or 6.

Classification Board Game

Age
4–6 years

Curriculum Area
Mathematics

Curriculum Objectives
To improve classification and grouping skills.

Anti-Bias Areas
Ability, Race, Culture, Gender

Anti-Bias Skill
To recognize and label similarities and differences.

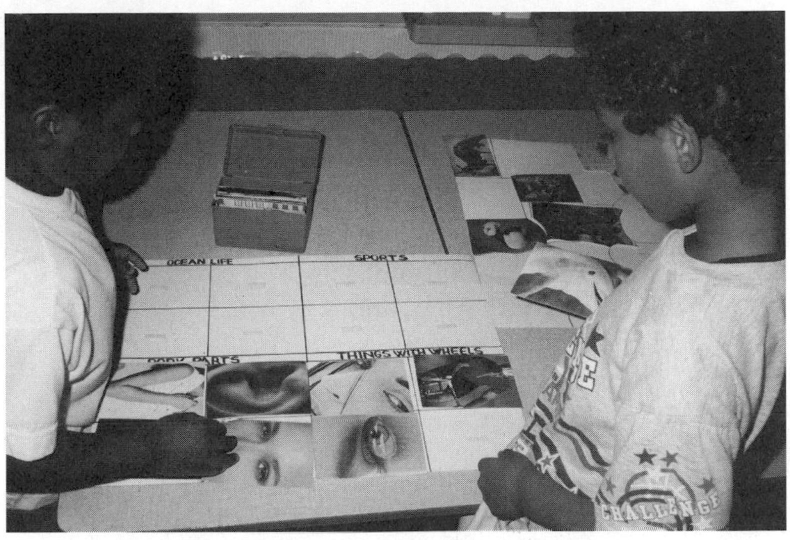

Practicing classification skills.

Materials
Large bristol board. Divide the board into four major sections and label: Body Parts, Things with Wheels, Ocean Life, and Sports. Subdivide each section into four squares. Cut out and mount on index cards pictures of people, animals, and objects that reflect the classification criteria and simultaneously meet the requirements for diversity in the areas of race, culture, ability, and gender. Glue velcro strips to both the cards and the board spaces.

Approach
Incorporation

Facilitation
Bring out the board and the box containing all the picture cards. Explain the game and facilitate a few card placements by asking the children (1) what does this picture show, and (2) where do they think this card should go? Let the children explore the pictures. Stand back and observe their classification skills. Discussions about how people/objects/animals are similar and different can happen over the shelf life of the game. Reinforce children's spontaneous observations of similarities and differences.

Conservation Task Cards

Labeling similarities and differences using several attributes.

Age

4–6 years

Curriculum Area

Mathematics

Curriculum Objectives

To improve formation of sets, counting, comparing, and developing conservation.

Anti-Bias Areas

Gender, Race

Anti-Bias Skill

To recognize and label similarities and differences.

Materials

Bristol board or oaktag cards, cut into 4-inch squares; stickers or border pictures of children of different races and gender; and clear contact paper.

Each set of cards has the identical number of stickers but placed in a different configuration on the card. Design the cards to challenge conservation skills in logical progression, for example, a matched pair that only reflects one attribute such as gender to the more complex pair that shows gender and race.

Approach

Incorporation

Facilitation

Put out the matched set of cards depicting only one attribute. Mix them up and have the children find the matching pair. Encourage the children to count, identify the children on the cards by gender or race, and discuss the comparisons. Move the children who are developmentally competent to the more complex cards.

Puzzle By Number

Age

5–6 years

Curriculum Area

Mathematics

Curriculum Objectives

To improve counting, one-to-one correspondence, figure-ground matching, and part-whole thinking.

Anti-Bias Areas

Appearance, Age

Anti-Bias Skills

To promote respect for human diversity in appearance and age.

Model figure. *Corresponding pieces by numerical dots.*

Materials

Large magazine photos of people representing the diversity of appearance and age, mounted on bristol board and laminated. Pictures should reflect images of people actively involved in sports, leisure activities, or work. Create a duplicate outline of the picture and then cut the photos into six pieces. On the back of each puzzle piece place round ¼-inch stickers in the configuration of dice. The same number of dots should be placed in the space of the outline where the puzzle pieces should be matched. Provide a die.

Approach

Incorporation

Facilitation

This puzzle game encourages children to manipulate math concepts on a more complex level. Place the puzzle outline in front of a child and explain that the pieces need to be filled in one by one by throwing the dice. After each throw the child needs to count the number of dots, find the corresponding piece with the equivalent number of dots, and then find the appropriate space on the outline board. This can be done either by figure-ground matching or by matching the dots once again. Once the puzzle is completed ask the child to look at the person and discuss what is happening in the picture.

Place pieces on blank model form to complete the puzzle.

Clarify any mistaken assumptions made about a person's age or appearance with respect to ability to perform actions.

Tasting Milk

Age

3–5 years

Curriculum Area

Science

Curriculum Objectives

To practice taste discrimination, and making comparisons and predictions.

Anti-Bias Area

Culture

Anti-Bias Skills

To expose children to cultural differences in smells and foods; to encourage children to try new experiences.

Materials

Variety of milk: cow, goat, soy (and soybean), buttermilk, coconut (if possible bring in a whole coconut as well), powdered baby formula, lactose-free milk; and plastic cups.

Approach

Incorporation

Facilitation

Engage the children in a general discussion about milk: Where does it come from? How many different kinds do they know? Dispel their assumptions that milk comes only from cows by showing the coconut and the soybean.

Ask them to predict whether all the milk will taste the same, and if not, how might they taste different? Pour samples into small cups and get the children to describe the taste and texture. Survey the group to find out who drinks different types of milk. If children turn up their noses or make disparaging remarks, remind them that everyone has different taste preferences and needs. For example, many children are allergic to cow's milk and get very sick unless they drink goat or soy milk. Make it clear that it is not acceptable to make fun of foods that others may like.

Community Resource

Health food stores.

Body Sounds

Age

4–5 years

Curriculum Area

Science

Curriculum Objectives

To increase body awareness and verbal skills.

Anti-Bias Areas

Gender, Ability

Anti-Bias Skills

To value uniqueness of self and others; to promote respect for human diversity in ability.

Approach

Modified Personalization

Facilitation

Start the activity by whistling. Encourage the children to think divergently about all the different kinds of sounds people can make using their bodies. Get them to demonstrate their ideas and have everyone imitate. The possibilities include: snapping fingers, stamping feet, clicking tongues, singing, head tapping, cheek slapping, tongue rattling against upper teeth, blowing, hissing, gasping, teeth chattering, etc.

Expansion

Ask the children to consider what gestures or body language they could use to communicate if they couldn't speak.

Shape Changes

Age
4–6 years

Curriculum Area
Science

Curriculum Objectives
To refine visual discrimination; to make observations and draw conclusions; to explore scientific concept of change.

Anti-Bias Area
Appearance

Anti-Bias Skill
To promote respect for human diversity in appearance.

Materials
Convex, concave, regular, and magnifying mirrors, all available from Lakeshore/Wintergreen, CF 332-340, The Children's Factory; magnifying mirror

Approach
Modified Personalization

Facilitation
Invite the children to explore the mirrors. Tell them to look at themselves in the regular mirror first. Then have them move over to the concave mirror. Ask them if they think their appearance or how they look has changed. If so, could they describe in what way? Help them with vocabulary. Repeat the procedure with the convex and magnifying mirrors. If children laugh at others or comment on how fat and funny they look, remind them it is wrong to make fun of and judge people based on appearance. Children need to be aware that even when they look different in the mirrors, they are still the same person.

Expansion
The concept of change needs to have a lot of hands-on exploration. This activity should be extended as a science experiment by encouraging the children to collect objects from the classroom and view them in front of the different mirrors. Help them to articulate the changes in shape that they observe.

Read *The Biggest Nose*, by Kathy Caple.

Community Resource
An alternative to using large standing mirrors is the Flexible Wall Mirror that flexes and twists and constantly changes the face it reflects. It comes in a handheld version (12″ × 18″, CF 332-155) or a slightly bigger size (24" × 16", CF 332-156) both from Lakeshore/Wintergreen.

Changes in Appearance

Age
4–6 years

Curriculum Area
Science

Curriculum Objectives
To refine visual discrimination; to make observations and draw conclusions; to explore scientific concept of magnification.

Anti-Bias Areas
Race, Appearance

Anti-Bias Skill
To promote respect for human diversity in appearance and race.

Materials
Magnifying sheets; cellophane sheets in different colors; and people pictures.

Approach
Incorporation

Facilitation
This is a follow-up activity to the *Shape Changes* activity, and maintains the same focus of change in people's appearance. Select a range of large photos of people and ask the children to place the magnifying sheet over each photo. Engage them in a discussion of how the facial features or body parts look. If children reply that bigger is scarier, help them to work out their discomfort with size. Try a similar task with the different colored cellophane sheets. Watch for judgmental statements made on the basis of color.

It is important for children to work through the notion that people come in all shapes, colors, and sizes. They need to hear that judgments or feelings of preference or exclusion cannot be based on how a person looks.

Expansion
Read the book *Being Big*, by Sharen Liddell, to illustrate the feelings of pain and confusion a child experiences because of her size.

Dramatic Pulley Play

Age
4–6 years

Curriculum Area
Science

Curriculum Objectives
To explore causal relations and the scientific concept of energy; to engage in cooperative and creative problem solving.

Anti-Bias Areas
Gender, Culture

Anti-Bias Skill
To support and respect gender equity.

Materials
Big bucket; rope; and pulley set up in a corner where dramatic play occurs. Dramatic play center can be a grocery store with empty food containers/boxes representing food items from different cultures, or a home center with cookware, utensils, foods, etc., also from different cultures.

Approach
Incorporation

Facilitation
Introducing a pulley to the dramatic play center can add an entirely new dimension to how children act out roles, socialize, and problem solve. The pulley will stimulate curiosity, observation, testing, and discovery of the causal relation of pulling and lifting. Depending on the size of the room, the pulley system can be a simple load and lift or it can transport items horizontally across a small space. If the center is a store then you can stimulate the play by bringing out a large bin of food packages that have just been "delivered." The children can "stock" the shelves by unloading the bins of supplies using the pulley.

The point of this experience is to get both girls and boys involved in (1) exploring machinery and constructing knowledge about how technology works, and (2) engaging in cooperative dramatic play where roles can be rotated.

Don't Judge by Appearances

Age
4–6 years

Curriculum Area
Science

Curriculum Objectives
To practice sensory discrimination, observations, making comparisons, and drawing conclusions.

Anti-Bias Area
Race

Anti-Bias Skill
To recognize and label similarities and differences.

Materials
Clear jars individually filled with coarse salt, baking powder, bleached flour, sugar, and cornstarch.

Approach
Incorporation

Facilitation
Put out the jars and have the children explore the white substances, using each sense in turn: sight, touch, hearing, taste, and smell. After each round of sensory exploration, ask the children to describe how the white powders seem different and the same. Assist them by providing taste, texture, and olfactory words. When the children attempt to label the substances, ask them why they believe it is salt or sugar, etc.

At the end of the activity provide the correct names for the substances. Discuss the notion that even though things may look the same, they can taste, smell, and feel different. Make the connection to people. We can't judge people by appearances only, but need to get to know them better by playing, working, sharing meals, etc., together.

Body Parts

Age
4–6 years

Curriculum Area
Science

Curriculum Objective
To understand that the human body is held together by the skeletal system.

Anti-Bias Areas
Appearance, Gender

Anti-Bias Skill
To recognize and label similarities and differences.

Materials
X-rays of bones; large picture of human skeleton; and *People*, by Peter Spier.

Approach
Incorporation

Facilitation
Ask the children to feel their own wrist, ankle, jaw bones, ribs, and spine. Hold up an X ray of a spine or rib cage to help the children visualize what their bones look like. Point out the major bones on the skeleton picture and discuss how our bodies are held together. Hold up other X rays and have the children guess what bones they are looking at. Ask them to hypothesize whether the X ray belongs to a girl or boy and why they think so?

This activity will help children understand that despite how differently we may look on the outside, we all have the same skeletal, muscular, and circulatory system. Read Peter Spier's book *People* for additional exploration of similarities and differences among people.

Community Resource
X-ray diagnostic clinics willing to donate old X rays.

Fishing for Cultural Patterns

Using eye-hand coordination to find matching cultural patterns.

Age

3–5 years

Curriculum Area

Perceptual Motor

Curriculum Objectives

To refine eye-hand coordination; to improve understanding of spatial relations; to practice visual discrimination and matching skills.

Anti-Bias Area

Culture

Anti-Bias Skill

To expose children to cultural differences in textures and patterns.

Materials

Cut display borders that reflect the distinctive patterns of India, Japan, Hmong, Navajo, Guatemala, etc., into 2-inch squares. Cover with clear contact paper, place a large paper clip on each, and create a set of matching cards. Make fishing rods from small dowels and magnets attached to string.

Approaches

Incorporation and Extension: Ask children how they could fish if they had no arms (Ability).

Facilitation

Encourage the children to explore the cause-and-effect process involved with magnets. As each square is lifted, comment on the images, designs, and colors particular to that culture.

Expansion

After the fishing game is completed, encourage the children to find the pairs of cultural patterns or make a board game for matching.

Community Resources

Cultural Trimmers are available from SONSUH Educational Supplies in Toronto, Canada, and Trend Enterprises in the United States.

Worm Puzzle

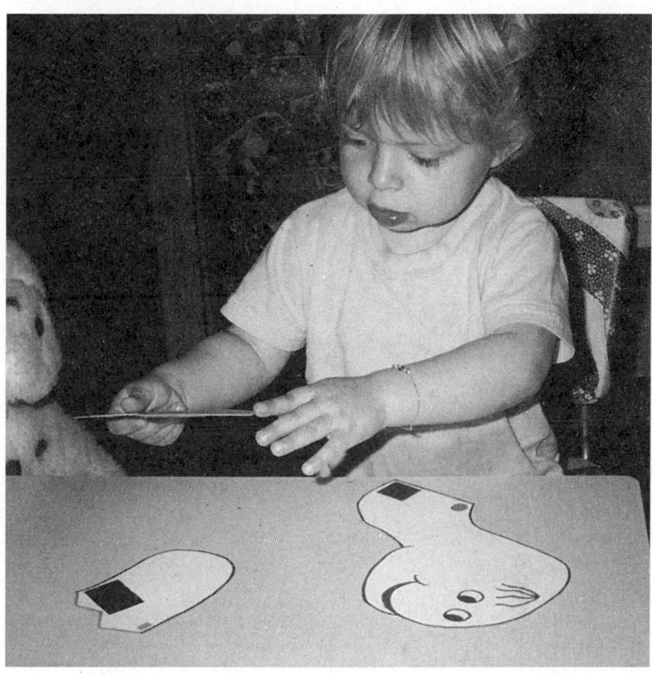

Becoming familiar with those who are differently abled.

Age

3–5 years

Curriculum Area

Perceptual Motor

Curriculum Objectives

To refine visual and tactile discrimination; to practice matching skills.

Anti-Bias Area

Ability

Anti-Bias Skill

To foster familiarity with differences in ability.

Materials

Draw a large wiggly worm on large bristol board, and cut into segments. At the end of one segment and beginning of next one place a matching color dot and underneath it a matching braille configuration. The raised dots can be made either by gluing lentils in place, covered with clear contact paper for further security, or by pounding a flat nail into the back of the board in order to create a bump on the other side. Place self-correcting symbols on the back of each piece.

Approach

Incorporation

Facilitation

This puzzle can range from simple to complex based on the number of pieces created. Depending on the children's perceptual motor skills the puzzle can be approached three ways. For the younger child the pieces can be matched by shape—the contours and curves. Children who can visually discriminate colors can use the color dot as another clue in the matching process. For children who need a further challenge, encourage them to match the pieces by feeling the raised dots. All the children can use the self-correcting symbols on the back to gauge their success.

This activity contains elements that assist a child with visual impairment. As children work through the puzzle, discuss with them how children with such physical challenges use different strategies to solve puzzles. Such experiences will sensitize children to those who are differently abled.

Expansion

For more competent children, blindfold and encourage them to assemble the puzzle solely by using the braille.

Lacing Hands

Age
3–5 years

Curriculum Area
Perceptual Motor

Curriculum Objectives
To improve eye-hand coordination and sequencing.

Anti-Bias Area
Race

Anti-Bias Skills
To promote respect for human diversity in race; to strengthen self-esteem and self-identity.

Materials
People-colored paper cut in the shape of different-sized hands and feet; contact paper; yarn or shoelaces; and hole puncher.

Approach
Incorporation

Facilitation
Have children select the shape they would like to lace. Assist younger children in the sequence required for manipulating the yarn through the holes. Ask the children to look at each other's lacing cards and describe how they are alike and how they are different.

After the cards are laced they can be sequenced according to size and skin color, or grouped into hand and foot piles.

Expansion
This same activity can be done by mounting pictures of adults and children reflecting diversity in age, race, culture, gender, appearance, and ability on hand/foot shapes.

Community Resource
Hand shapes in 10 people-colored shades can be purchased from Lakeshore/Wintergreen, SC7-PE742.

Hair Beading

Valuing individual creativity.

Age

3–5 years

Curriculum Area

Perceptual Motor

Curriculum Objectives

To improve eye-hand coordination and sequencing skills.

Anti-Bias Areas

Race, Gender

Anti-Bias Skills

To promote respect for human diversity in race; to challenge gender stereotyping; to value uniqueness of self and others.

Materials

Cut out large pictures of males and females from different racial backgrounds. Glue them onto bristol board and laminate. Punch out four holes around the head area and thread shoelaces through the holes. Knot the laces in the back and let them dangle like hair strands in the front. Provide assorted beads in small individual trays.

Approach

Incorporation

Facilitation

Have both girls and boys bead the laces in any fashion. Encourage older preschoolers to create patterns and ask them to identify the color sequence they are following.

Discuss differences in hairstyles, color, and racial backgrounds, and assess the children's perceptions about who wears what hairstyle. Help children to challenge the stereotype that only girls play at hairdressing or make jewelry.

Expansion

Read the book *Hats Off to Hair,* by Virginia Kroll, for a more in-depth exploration of hairstyles.

Community Resources

The best place to buy beads and leather laces in bulk is at a specialty beading shop. If this doesn't exist in your community, then hobby or arts and crafts stores usually have packages of plastic beads. (Lakeshore/Wintergreen offers S & S Guildcraft Lacing in black, brown, and yellow, SC7-LA255; faceted beads in an assortment of sizes from 6–10mm, SC7-BE838; or Plastic Goldilock Tri-Beads that come in solid or transparent jeweled colors in 11mm sizes, SC7-BE9071.)

Cheese Puzzle

Working with mathematical concepts.

Age

3–5 years

Curriculum Area

Perceptual Motor

Curriculum Objectives

To improve visual closure, part-whole thinking, and counting skills; to recognize and match number symbols to pictorial representation.

Anti-Bias Area

Race

Anti-Bias Skill

To promote respect for human diversity in race.

Materials

Five round cheese boxes that can be stacked, covered with pictures of children of different races. On each level place a portion of one picture, the requisite number of dots for each level (one on the bottom, two on the next level, etc.), and the matching number symbol. The pictures, dots, and numbers should be aligned one under the other so that five distinct columns will appear when the boxes are correctly stacked.

Approach

Incorporation

Facilitation

Place the five cheese containers side by side and invite the children to assemble the puzzle. Constructing a puzzle vertically will be a novel experience and a difficult concept to grasp. Let the children experiment by stacking and twisting the boxes randomly until, with some guided facilitation, they start to use the pictures as visual cues. Help them see the columns that are emerging. After the picture is completed, focus the children's attention on the dots for an opportunity to practice counting. Similarly, point out the equivalent number symbols and review the correspondence between the abstract and pictorial representations. Have this activity available for many opportunities to practice and master.

Barefoot Art

Age
4–6 years

Curriculum Area
Perceptual Motor

Curriculum Objective
To explore creative materials using body parts other than hands.

Anti-Bias Area
Ability

Anti-Bias Skills
To encourage children to try new experiences; to promote respect for human diversity in ability.

Materials
Large mural paper; tempera paints; brushes; markers; feathers; and sand.

Approach
Modified Personalization

Facilitation
Ask the children to think about how people without the use of their hands would paint a picture. Encourage them to try out their ideas with the materials provided. This experience is best done in small groups for maximum exploration. During the process ask the children what they find difficult about making their pictures: Is it easier to paint with the brush or the feather? Why? Is it easier to paint standing up or sitting down?

As a conclusion, the children should put their footprint somewhere on the paper. This reinforces the concept that everyone is unique and has a footprint that is different and special.

Musical Scarves

Age
3–5 years

Curriculum Area
Creative Movement

Curriculum Objectives
To improve body expressiveness and movement.

Anti-Bias Area
Culture

Anti-Bias Skill
To strengthen awareness and respect for different cultures.

Materials
Woven ribbons/belts; scarves from different countries; batik sarongs; and musical tapes representing different cultures.

Approach
Incorporation

Facilitation
Children love to twirl ribbons and scarves while moving their bodies. This becomes a multicultural experience when they use scarves, sarongs, and ribbons from many different countries, while moving creatively to melodies and rhythms from different cultures. Vary the beats and melodies. Provide strong rhythms such as Native American chanting and drumming. Contrast with predictable and repetitive songs such as "Macarena."

Outside Treasure Hunt

Age
3–5 years

Curriculum Area
Gross Motor

Curriculum Objectives
To improve understanding of spatial relations; to practice locomotion and large muscle coordination.

Anti-Bias Area
Ability

Anti-Bias Skill
To promote respect for human diversity in ability.

Materials
Each child gets three cards depicting one letter of the alphabet in three different alphabets: the capital letter, the braille equivalent with the represented letter underneath, and a picture of the letter in sign. A matched set is hidden all around the playground. (See appendix for the braille and Signed English alphabets.)

Approaches
Incorporation and Personalization: Invite a visitor from the community to tell a familiar story in sign language. The children can learn to retell it with simple but accurate gestures.

Facilitation
This game is a follow-up to the *Books in Braille* activity, which exposed the children to the concept of braille. Here the children use their matching skills in a more physically active way as they stretch, bend, reach, and move through space and around objects in order to find the set of cards. Encourage children to assist one another in the visual recognition of letters.

Moving Through Space

Age
4–6 years

Curriculum Area
Gross Motor

Curriculum Objectives
To improve balance, coordination, and body and spatial awareness.

Anti-Bias Area
Ability

Anti-Bias Skills
To provide opportunities to interact with people who are differently abled; to support emergent empathy.

Materials
Crutches; snowshoes; can stilts; wheelchair; flippers; walking cane; and blindfold.

Approach
Modified Personalization

Facilitation
Set up an obstacle course that requires children to climb over a barrier, go up and down a slope, maneuver around corners, and go under a barrier. Have five children at a time explore the course, each using a different walking device. Focus their attention on how it feels. Ask them to describe what they find easy or difficult and why? Ask them to consider under what circumstances would each device be used? Have them discuss anyone they know who uses these devices.

Expansion
Conduct a Simon Says game where children are asked to imitate jumping on two feet, spinning around, skipping or hopping on one foot. Try with the devices and discuss the results.

Community Resource
Crutches, wheelchairs, and canes can be rented from home health care stores; sporting goods stores might be willing to loan the snowshoes and flippers if you present a good case and promise free advertising in the future.

Scooter Board Skills

Age
4–6 years

Curriculum Area
Gross Motor

Curriculum Objectives
To improve visual-motor coordination, understanding of spatial relations, and general body awareness.

Anti-Bias Area
Ability

Anti-Bias Skills
To support emergent empathy; to promote respect for human diversity in ability.

Materials
Scooter boards; pylons; masking tape; balls; and hoops.

Approach
Incorporation

Facilitation
Design varied tasks that challenge the children's visual motor coordination as well as judgment of spatial relations.

1. Set up pylons in clusters and with distances in between.
2. Tape a line along one pathway with a hoop propped up/suspended at the end.

Children will explore the first obstacle course by lying on their stomachs and only pushing with their arms. They can go full circle around the pylons, and go in and around the remaining ones; this same course can be tried with the hands on the scooter while using only the legs for power and the body for steering. The alternate course is to push a ball along the taped line and to get it through the hoop at the end.

Ask the children to think about how it felt maneuvering themselves using only the upper or lower half of their bodies. If they enjoyed themselves, ask them to consider how they would feel if they always only had the use of one part of their body for all the other activities they enjoy. Do they think they could manage with the same enjoyment? Discuss children who are wheelchair bound, and help them to listen to the opinions, emotions, and ideas expressed by the group.

Cooperative Relay Game

Age
4–6 years

Curriculum Area
Gross Motor

Curriculum Objectives
To improve large motor coordination; to promote cooperative efforts.

Anti-Bias Area
Ability

Anti-Bias Skills
To foster familiarity with differences in ability; to encourage cooperation and teamwork.

Materials
Trike, scooter, wagon, wheelchair, and stroller; and twenty-five 4–10-piece puzzles at five different "problem-solving" stations.

Approach
Modified Personalization

Facilitation
Explain to the children that this relay game emphasizes taking turns and working together with wheeled toys and puzzles. Set up five stations in different areas of the outdoor play space, each with five wooden puzzles. Tell the children they have to use a different wheeled vehicle to visit each station. Once they get there they have to solve a puzzle together. They can take turns pushing one another in the wheelchair and stroller, pulling one another in the wagon, and using the trike and scooter. No more than 10 children should participate at one time in order to support the cooperation needed between pairs. Have the five puzzles disassembled at each station. This will eliminate the need to return to each station as soon as the next pair arrives to assemble a puzzle. Reinforce all teamwork and problem-solving strategies with praise.

This activity is intended to sensitize children to those who are physically challenged but who can still be productive and helpful team players.

Ball Toss

Age
4–6 years

Curriculum Area
Gross Motor

Curriculum Objectives
To strengthen large muscle coordination and balance; to refine understanding of size and spatial relations.

Anti-Bias Area
Ability

Anti-Bias Skills
To provide opportunities to interact with people who are differently abled; to promote respect for human diversity in ability.

Materials
Three different-sized balls (tennis, volley, and beach); small, medium, and large containers to hold the balls; and sunglasses smeared with petroleum jelly.

Approach
Modified Personalization

Facilitation
Children will have the opportunity to practice ball throwing with limited physical and visual abilities. Set up the containers at a close distance and explain to the children that they can only throw the balls in four ways:

1. one-handed with one arm behind the back from a sitting or standing position;
2. with their feet while sitting;
3. with both hands from a sitting or standing position; and
4. with the blurry sunglasses on.

As the children play, talk to them about the difficulties they may experience. After the game is concluded, ask the children to consider how others who need wheelchairs, who only have the use of their feet (no hands), or who can only see things blurry, manage the same ball-throwing skills. Support any comments that express empathy. Reassure the children that throwing a small ball into a small container is hard for everyone, and that's why everyone needs the opportunity to practice until they feel successful.

Spray Bottle Art

Age
3–5 years

Curriculum Area
Creative Art

Curriculum Objectives
To experiment with water and paint.

Anti-Bias Area
Race

Anti-Bias Skill
To foster familiarity with differences in skin color.

Materials
Clear plastic spray bottles with nozzles and trigger handles; mural paper taped to the wall or outside fence; and various shades of skin-toned water in jugs.

Approach
Incorporation

Facilitation
In this activity children explore the medium of watercolor. Young children will enjoy observing and influencing the process of colors merging and trickling down the paper, and generally changing and creating new colors and patterns. The added bonus is screwing and unscrewing the bottles, filling them with colored water of their choice, and squeezing the nozzle lever. Comment on how the colors become darker and lighter.

Painting to Music

Age
3–6 years

Curriculum Area
Creative Art

Curriculum Objectives
To stimulate creative expression; to explore the paint medium creatively.

Anti-Bias Area
Culture

Anti-Bias Skill
To expose children to cultural differences in rhythms and music.

Materials
Paper; easels or outside fence; paintbrushes; paints; tape recorder; and tapes reflecting distinctive musical styles from around the world.

Approach
Incorporation

Facilitation
Children enjoy the process of painting at any time. Enhance their sensory integration by having them listen to music and think about how it makes them feel. Select music with distinctive styles, such as the tango, yodeling, steel drumming, or polka, that will stimulate different approaches to brush strokes or color use. Keep selections short to accommodate various attention spans. Give the children feedback to keep them focused: "I like those zigzags or dots. It looks like you hear something loud/sharp/strong in the music."

Group Mural of Likes and Dislikes

Age

3–5 years

Curriculum Area

Creative Art

Curriculum Objectives

To participate in a cooperative and collective creative experience; listening to others; perceptual motor skills.

Anti-Bias Areas

Race, Culture, Gender

Anti-Bias Skill

To value uniqueness of self and others.

Materials

Magazines; scissors; glue; mural paper; and crayons.

Approaches

Modified Personalization and Incorporation

Facilitation

A mural project requires a preliminary discussion with the children to help them focus on the topic. Introduce the subject of individual preferences and dislikes. Talk about how we all have different feelings about foods, animals, stories, play activities, etc. Get them to talk about what things they really like to do, eat, see, etc., and what things they really don't like. Show the large mural paper taped to the floor. On the left side is a happy face and on the right side is a sad face. Working in small groups, have the children look through magazines; when they find pictures of things they like and don't like, they cut them out and paste them in the appropriate spaces on the paper. Encourage those who are able to write their names under or next to the picture; help the younger children write their names.

Review the mural with the entire group before hanging it up. Children can identify their pictures and speak about what their likes and dislikes are. Have the children listen to one another and hear how they may or may not share preferences or dislikes.

It is important for children to understand that everyone has the right to be respected, even if one doesn't share the same feelings.

Sands of Many Colors

Age
4–6 years

Curriculum Area
Creative Art

Curriculum Objectives
To improve problem solving and eye-hand coordination; to promote creative expression.

Anti-Bias Area
Culture

Anti-Bias Skill
To value uniqueness of self and others.

Materials
Clear bags filled with sand of different textures; food coloring or tempera paints; baby food jars with lids; plastic containers or cups; scoops; forks, butter knives; pencils; and books on different beaches and sands.

Approach
Incorporation

Facilitation
Introduce the fact that sands come in many different colors. Show them pictures of the red sand found in Prince Edward Island or Australia, and the black sand found on some Hawaiian beaches. Discuss some of the reasons for this: clay and mineral deposits and lava flows, etc.

Put out the bags of sand and plastic containers. Have the children place the sand into the plastic cups and add a few drops of food coloring (or paint) at a time. Stir with a fork until the desired color appears. Children will take turns creating a different cup of colored sand. Pour the sand out on a newspaper to dry briefly and then return it back into the cups. Ask the children to scoop small amounts of sand into the baby food jars to make layers. Have them use a pencil or butter knife to create dips, rises, or zigzag patterns, adding layers of sand until the jar is full.

Expansion
This activity can be extended into another visual art experience by having children create pictures with sand and glue.

Community Resource
Bright Fine Sand comes in neon-colored hues if you wish to skip the coloring step; it is available from Lakeshore/Wintergreen, SC7-SP3938.

Papier-mâché Creations

Age

4–6 years

Curriculum Area

Creative Art

Curriculum Objective

To use imagination and creativity in designing a three-dimensional structure.

Anti-Bias Area

Culture

Anti-Bias Skill

To expose children to cultural differences.

Materials

Newspapers with different language scripts (Chinese, Russian, Persian, Greek, Hindi, Spanish, etc.); flour and water paste; cardboard; scissors; pencils; and tape.

Approach

Incorporation

Facilitation

In this activity, the children are free to design any creature, person, or object of their choice. Provide cardboard upon which to sketch out an image and assist them to cut out the shape. They can crumble and tape the newspaper to add dimension to the shape. Tear newspapers into strips and demonstrate how to dip the strips into the paste mixture, then wrap the strips around the newspapered form. The children can add as many layers as they wish. To add finer details, such as facial features, or accentuate certain dimensions of their animal/object, show the children how they can mold the desired shape by wetting the newspapers in the paste, sticking it onto the correct spot, and covering it with more paper strips. Once the creature is dry they can finish it by painting or decorating with yarns and fabric scraps.

As the children are involved in this process, watch and see if any observations or comments are made about the language scripts. You can casually point out who reads these newspapers and ask if they know anyone who speaks this language.

Community Resources

Different cultural presses in the community.

Resources for Preschoolers and Kindergartners

This is by no means an exhaustive list; it is intended to suggest supplementary books and provide bibliographic information for the activities provided in this chapter. Refer to the resource section in the appendix, which contains over 100 annotated titles, for additional support materials for the preschool-kindergarten age group.

Family Flannel Board

Bonnici, P. (1985). *Amber's other grandparents.* London: The Bodley Head.

Emberley, R. (1990). *My house, mi casa: A book in two languages.* New York: Little, Brown and Co.

I Can Do Place Mat

Cheltenham Elementary School Kindergartners. (1991). *We are all alike . . . We are all different.* New York: Scholastic, Inc.

Mixed-up Creatures

Carle, E. (1984). *The mixed-up chameleon.* New York: Harper and Row.

Emotion Books

Prestine, J. (1987). *Love me anyway; Sometimes I'm afraid; Me first.* Los Angeles: Price/Stern/Sloan Publishers.

Ice Cube Melt

Kissinger, K. (1994). *All the colors we are: The story of how we get our skin color* (bilingual). St. Paul, MN: Redleaf Press.

Playdough in a Glove

Merrifield, M. (1990). *Come sit by me.* Toronto: Women's Press.

Brown Is Beautiful

Adoff, A. (1973). *Black is brown is tan.* New York: Harper and Row.

Newspaper Collage

Feder, J. (1995). *Table, chair, bear: A book in many languages.* Boston: Houghton Mifflin Co.

Helping Hands For All

Bednarczyk, A., and Weinstock, J. (1997). *Happy birthday* (sign book). New York: Star Bright Books.

Bednarczyk, A., and Weinstock, J. (1997). *Opposites* (sign book). New York: Star Bright Books.

Amazing Hair Dramatic Play

Milstein, L., and Meddaugh, S. (1993). *Amanda's perfect hair.* New York: Tambourine Books.

Books in Braille

Carle, E. (1987). *The very hungry caterpillar* (braille). New York: Philomel Books.

Shoe Sort Game

Sanderson, E. (1990). *Two pairs of shoes.* Winnipeg: Pemmican Publishers.

Badt, K. L. (1994). *On your feet.* Chicago: Children's Press.

Roy, R. (1992). *Whose shoes are these?* Boston: Houghton Mifflin Co.

Life Cycle in Sequence

Farber, N. (1979). *How does it feel to be old?* New York: Puffin Unicorn.

Silhouette Guess

Tabor, N. M. G. (1995). *Somos un arco iris: We are a rainbow.* Watertown, MA: Charlesbridge Publishing.

Letter Cards

Baker, P. (1986). *My first book of sign.* Washington, DC: Gallaudet University Press.

Grocery Matching

Kalman, B., and Hughes, S. (1986). *The food we eat.* New York: Crabtree Publishing Co.

What Does This Person Need?

The things I like to do. Signed English. (1974). Washington, DC: Gallaudet College Press.

Bornstein, H., Saulnier, K., and Hamilton, L. (1983). *The comprehensive signed English dictionary.* Washington, DC: Gallaudet University Press.

The Family House

Dorros, A. (1992). *This is my house.* New York: Scholastic Books.

Simon, N. (1976). *All kinds of families.* Chicago: Albert Whitman.

Go Bake Card Game

Kingston, A. (1988). *The bagels are coming.* West Bloomfield, MI: Child Time Publishers.

Body Bingo Game

Groebel, R. (1995). *Two eyes, a nose, and a mouth.* New York: Scholastic Books.

Hats, Hats, Hats Lotto Game

Morris, A. (1989). *Hats, hats, hats.* New York: Lothrop, Lee and Shepard Books.

Roy, R. (1987). *Whose hat is that?* Boston: Houghton Mifflin Co.

Friendship Dominoes

Cheltenham Elementary School Kindergartners. (1991). *We are all alike . . . We are all different.* New York: Scholastic, Inc.

Job Cards

Grossman, P. (1991). *The night ones.* San Diego: Harcourt Brace Jovanovich.

Fun with Paint Chips

Kissinger, K. (1994). *All the colors we are: The story of how we get our skin color* (bilingual) St. Paul, MN: Redleaf Press.

Whose Job Is It Anyway?

Imershein, B. (1990). *The work people do.* New York: Simon and Schuster Trade.

Ziefert, H. (1992). *Where's mommy's truck?* New York: HarperCollins.

Lots of Bread

Morris, A. (1989). *Bread, bread, bread.* New York: Mulberry Paperback Book.

Holiday Dress

Cech, M. (1990). *Globalchild: Multicultural resources for young children.* Ottawa, Canada: Health and Welfare Canada.

Designer Shade

Mandelbaum, P. (1990). *You be me, I'll be you.* Brooklyn, NY: Kane/Miller.

Shape Changes

Caple, K. (1985). *The biggest nose.* Boston: Houghton Mifflin.

Changes in Appearance

Liddell, S. (1994). *Being big.* Toronto, Canada: Second Story Press.

Body Parts

Spier, P. (1980). *People.* New York: Doubleday.

Hair Beading

Kroll, V. (1995). *Hats off to hair.* Watertown, MA: Charlesbridge Publishing.

Other Readings

Jukes, L. (1995). *I'm a girl.* Boca Raton, FL: Cool Kids Press.

Kuklin, S. (1992). *How my family lives in America.* New York: Bradbury Press.

Finger Plays, Action Rhymes, and Songs

Anti-Bias Goal

To build self-identity.

Age

Preschool

1. Lyn is very thin
   Pat is very fat
   Mort is very short
   Saul is very tall
   Kent is very bent
   Kate is very straight
   Isn't it fun to all be different? (Matterson, p. 167)

Anti-Bias Goal

To promote gender equity in actions.

2. Daddy's washing, daddy's washing,
   Rub, rub, rub,
   Picked up ____'s little shirt,
   And threw it in the tub.

   Mommy's washing, mommy's washing,
   Scrub, scrub, scrub,
   Picked up ____'s little pants,
   And threw them in the tub.

   Brother's washing, brother's washing,
   Wring, wring, wring,
   Picked up ____'s little socks,
   And hung them on some string.

   We're all finished, we're all finished,
   Hip hip hooray,
   Now we'll have our clothes all clean,
   To wear for school today. (Matterson, p. 34)

Children can mime actions and fill in appropriate names. This version omits stereotyped gender roles and clothing.

3. This is the way we play with our friends,
      play with our friends,
      play with our friends,
   This is the way we play with our friends,
      in our fun-filled classroom.

   Some like to paint and some like to climb,
      paint and climb,
      paint and climb,
   Some like to paint and some like to climb,
      in our fun-filled classroom.

Others play in water and sand,
water and sand,
water and sand,
Others play in water and sand,
in our fun-filled classroom.

Who has the puzzles, who has the blocks,
puzzles and blocks,
puzzles and blocks,
Who has the puzzles, who has the blocks,
in our fun-filled classroom.

I like to run and you like to jump,
run and jump,
run and jump,
I like to run and you like to jump,
in our fun-filled classroom (Original by Nadia Saderman Hall).

Sing to the tune of "Here We Go Round the Mulberry Bush."

4. The Grocer

1 grocer worked hard weighing rice.
2 grocers worked hard packing spice.
3 grocers worked hard sorting teas.
4 grocers worked hard wrapping cheese.
5 grocers worked hard stacking jam.
6 grocers worked hard slicing ham.
7 grocers worked hard cutting meats.
8 grocers worked hard opening sweets.
9 grocers worked hard selling bread.
10 grocers tired out went home to bed.

The grocers can be any gender, from any ethno-racial background, with diverse abilities. (From *Bright Ideas: Teacher Handbooks, Language Resources.*)

5. Manuel Road (Jamaican folk song done with bean bags)

Go down Manuel road, girl and boy	
We go break rock stone	
Break them 1 × 1 girl and boy	(every child passes a bean bag to the person sitting to their right)
Break them 1 × 1	(repeated until one bag is dropped; child sits outside of circle and continues to clap the rhythm)
Break them 2 × 2	(two bags are passed until they are dropped and so on)

(*Bright Ideas,* 132)

6. Johnny's Hammer (Alternate boy's and girl's name to achieve equity)

Johnny works with one hammer one hammer, one hammer Johnny works with one hammer Then he works with two	(one fist on right or left knee)

Ayesha works with two hammers two hammers, two hammers Ayesha works with two hammers Then she works with three	(add both fists on right and left knees)
Jamal works with three hammers	(add tapping right foot with fists)
Maria works with four hammers	(add tapping both feet with fists)
Boris works with five hammers	(move head left and right to other actions)

The children are so tired
so tired, so tired,
They are all so tired this fine day.

(From Hayes, *A Fountain of Language Development for E.C.E. and the Special Child, Too*).

7. The More We Get Together (Sung to the tune of "Have You Ever Seen a Lassie?")

The more we get together, together, together,
The more we get together the happier we'll be.
Because your friends are my friends and
My friends are your friends,
The more we get together the happier we'll be.

The more we play together, together, together,
The more we play together the happier we'll be.
There's ____ and ____ and ____ and ____.
There's ____ and ____ and____ and ____.
The more we play together the happier we'll be.

Insert the names of children in your group.

Anti-Bias Goal

To promote respect for ability.

Age

Preschool–Kindergarten

8. Do you plant your cabbages/taro/zucchini (any other food can be substituted for cultural diversity)
In this way, in this way?
Do you plant your cabbages
In this way if you please?

You can plant them with your hand
With your hand, with your hand,
You can plant them with your hand
In this way if you please. (Matterson, p. 85)

Refrain: You can plant them with your foot, elbow, head, wheelchair, leg brace, etc.

9. My Wellington boots go squish, squish, squish to splash in
My wooden clogs go clack, clack, clack to walk in
My running shoes go squeak, squeak, squeak to run in

My sandals go click, click, click in the warm weather
My slippers go swish, swish, swish, to keep my feet warm
My wheelchair goes whirr, whirr, whirr, to get me someplace quickly

(Adapted from Matterson, p. 140)

Invent other verses using different noun, sound, and functional relationship patterns.

10. Can you walk on two legs, two legs, two legs,
Can you walk on two legs,
Round and round and round.

I can walk on two legs, two legs, two legs,
Yes I can walk on two legs,
Round and round and round. (Matterson, p. 143).

Can you hop on one leg?
Can you speak with two hands?
Can you read with one hand?
Can you paint with one foot?

Invent other verses that explore different abilities.

11. I can tie my shoelace.
I can brush my hair.
I can wash my hands and face,
And dry myself with care.
I can clean my teeth too,
And fasten up my frocks.
I can say 'How do you do'
And pull up both my socks.

(*Round and Round the Garden* by Sarah Williams.)

12. The Anti-Bias Song

Sticks and stones may break my bones
But name-calling certainly hurts me
Teasing is wrong
Insulting is worse
But caring for others makes us strong (Original by Nadia Saderman Hall)

For multicultural folk rhymes, finger plays, and rhyming verses consult *Folk Rhymes from Around the World,* edited by Evelyn Neaman, and *Sleep Rhymes Around the World,* edited by Jane Yolen.

UNIT 5

Anti-Bias Activities for Elementary School Children

"Not everything that is faced can be changed, but nothing can be changed until it is faced."

James Baldwin

"I do not want my house to be walled in on all sides and my windows to be stuffed. I want the cultures of all the lands to be blown about my house as freely as possible. But I refuse to be blown off my feet by any of them."

Mahatma Gandhi

Key developmental requirements for elementary school children can be grouped under the broad categories of Knowledge, Skills, and Attitudes. This wide range, 6–11 years, should be viewed as a continuum.

Beginning of logical thought.	Ability to conserve area, mass, and volume, and classify ideas into logical systems.
Recognizes numeral and letter symbols.	Understands mathematical notations and develops accuracy in calculation.
Decodes and derives meaning from print.	Uses reading experiences for gaining information, problem solving, recreation, and personal growth.
Uses physical manipulation to figure out how things work and generalizes about cause-and-effect relationships.	Thinks abstractly about casual relationships.
Limited understanding of time.	Beginning to understand historical time.
Moral reasoning based on the rightness or wrongness of an action and its conformity to established rules.	Making moral judgments based on logical reasoning and taking into account others' perspectives.
Dependent upon adult approval and praise for self-esteem.	Enhancement of self-esteem derived by working in own areas of competency.
Exploring geometrical relations of two- and three-dimensional structures.	Makes use of geometrical properties and symmetries in solving practical problems.
Explores and makes discoveries using creative media.	Purposeful usage of varied techniques in the creative arts.
Gaining coordination and learning to move in a variety of physical activities.	Demonstrates control and accuracy in physical activity, with and without use of equipment.
Beginning awareness of self.	Identification of personal strengths, capabilities, and interests.
Awareness of cultural diversity.	Appreciation and empathy for cultural diversity.
Beginning use of language for gaining information, listening, and analyzing.	Comprehension and expressive language skills of interpreting, analyzing, synthesizing, and evaluating.

Web for Elementary School Children Anti-Bias and Developmental Skills

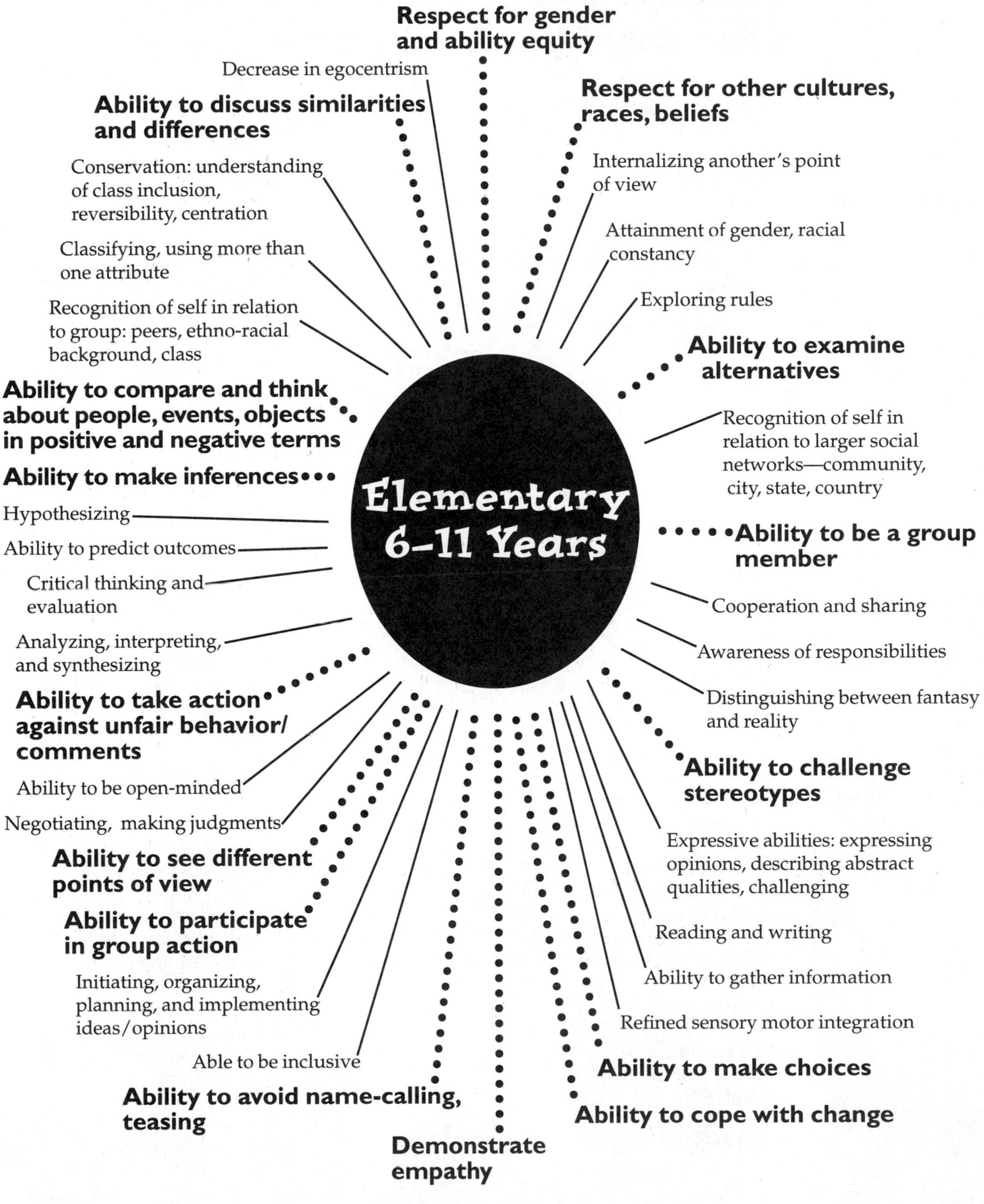

Elementary 6–11 Years

Respect for gender and ability equity

Decrease in egocentrism

Respect for other cultures, races, beliefs

Internalizing another's point of view

Attainment of gender, racial constancy

Exploring rules

Ability to examine alternatives

Recognition of self in relation to larger social networks—community, city, state, country

Ability to be a group member

Cooperation and sharing

Awareness of responsibilities

Distinguishing between fantasy and reality

Ability to challenge stereotypes

Expressive abilities: expressing opinions, describing abstract qualities, challenging

Reading and writing

Ability to gather information

Refined sensory motor integration

Ability to make choices

Ability to cope with change

Demonstrate empathy

Ability to avoid name-calling, teasing

Able to be inclusive

Initiating, organizing, planning, and implementing ideas/opinions

Ability to participate in group action

Ability to see different points of view

Negotiating, making judgments

Ability to be open-minded

Ability to take action against unfair behavior/comments

Analyzing, interpreting, and synthesizing

Critical thinking and evaluation

Ability to predict outcomes

Hypothesizing

Ability to make inferences

Ability to compare and think about people, events, objects in positive and negative terms

Recognition of self in relation to group: peers, ethno-racial background, class

Classifying, using more than one attribute

Conservation: understanding of class inclusion, reversibility, centration

Ability to discuss similarities and differences

Summary of Anti-Bias Skills Elementary School Activities

Anti-Bias Skills	Activity Title	Page No.
To strengthen self-identity and increase self-esteem.	The Story of a Name	260
	Why Am I So Different?	284
	A Gift for You	287
	Name Anagrams	295
To value uniqueness of self, others, and families.	Dinosaur Acrostics	201
	Name Play	208
	Who's in My Family	213
	Dictionary of Family Names	216
	The Importance of a Name	221
	Getting to Know One Another	254
	Who Goes? Who Stays?	257
	Oral Histories	258
	Poster Ads	268
	Commemorative Stamps	269
	Puppet Dreaming	275
	Special Gifts	276
	Similes About Myself	284
	Individual Coat of Arms	294
	Creative Holidays	256
To recognize, label, and discuss similarities and differences.	*Bruno Brontosaurus*	198
	Dinosaur Sort	199
	Dinosaur Eggs	203
	Stellaluna	204
	Cultural Celebrations I	217
	Rock Garden	219
	Multiple Meanings	232
	The Inuit and Ecology	233
	Spirits of the North	235
	Arctic Nutrition	236
	Contributions Made by Immigrants	241
	Work and Leisure	259
	Picture Story Writing	283
	People Sort	306
	People Living in My Home	307
	Trees Are Like Us	311
	You've Come a Long Way	312
	Food Stories Created by Sound	314
To appreciate how people use objects differently.	Rock Garden	219
	Homes and Houses	262
	Tool Sort	304
To promote awareness of and respect for diversity in:		
◎ culture (art forms, homes, food, language, etc.)	Lifestyle Differences	200
	Can We Be the Same and Different?	205
	Star-Moon	207
	Mrs. Katz and Tush	215
	Who's in My Family	213
	Dancing Time	216
	Cultural Celebrations II	218
	Geography Web	218
	Mayan Math	228
	Tiktala	229
	Building a Dome	230
	Constructing an Igluvigak	231
	Multiple Meanings	232
	Carving Experience	234
	I Can't Understand You	240
	Getting to Know One Another	254
	Houses Around the World	263
	Houses on the Move	264
	Mapping a Neighborhood	266
	M is for Mum	274
	Mama Will You Love Me?	281
	Musical Find-a-Chair	282
	Why Am I So Different?	284

Anti-Bias Skills	Activity Title	Page No.
	Storytelling with Objects	287
	Creating Legends	301
	Comic Strip Authors	303
	A Tangram Tale	308
	Food Pyramid	310
	Somewhere in Africa	315
	Making an American Quilt	316
	Art Forms of Aboriginal Peoples	317
	Who Belongs Here? II	245
◎ race	*Mrs. Katz and Tush*	215
	Picture Card Scramble	278
	No One Loved Horace	281
	Comic Strip Authors	303
	Bandage Science	312
◎ gender	Comic Strip Authors	303
◎ age	*Mrs. Katz and Tush*	215
◎ appearance	Dinosaur Acrostics	201
	Bones and Bodies	202
	Flying Animal Match Game	209
	Abuela's Weave	220
	Swimmy Felt Board Story	272
	No One Loved Horace	281
	An Aesop Fable	298
◎ ability	Experiences in Vision	206
	Flying Animal Match Game	209
	Flight Patterns	210
	In Other Words	249
	No One Loved Horace	281
	Helpful Communication	300
	Hardware Handiness	305
◎ family composition	Who's in My Family	213
	People Living in My Home	307
◎ belief	Lifestyle Differences	200
	Creative Holidays	256
	Who's in My Family	213
	Omens and Signs	222
◎ class	Money Jars	247
To promote respect for gender and racial equity.	What Do Moms Do?	246
	Houses of the Future	265
	What's Happening in This Picture?	273
To encourage openness to new experiences.	Cultural Celebrations I	217
	Cultural Celebrations II	218
	Rock Garden	219
	Weaver's Booth Game	226

Anti-Bias Skills	Activity Title	Page No.
	Contributions Made by Immigrants	241
	Augmentative Communication Experience	250
	Mechanical Busy Board	250
	Riding in Someone Else's Wheelchair	251
	Signing In	280
	Art Forms of Aboriginal Peoples	317
To interact comfortably with cultural diversity.	Weaver's Booth Game	226
	Who Goes? Who Stays?	257
To interact comfortably with people who are differently abled.	Experiences in Vision	206
	The Bat Sensory Cave	208
	Oral Motor Practice	279
	Modem Pal	288
	Who Goes? Who Stays?	257
To listen to and value other points of view.	Living out of a Bag	212
	Patterns All Around	223
	Yarn Pictures	224
	Community Project	247
	In Other Words	249
	Caption It	255
	Dreams for a Better Future	303
	Food—Past and Present	313
To encourage cooperative group efforts.	Cultural Celebrations II	218
	Rock Garden	219
	Yarn Pictures	224
	The Sharing Quilt	225
	Ecology Debate	237
	Construction Time	248
	Famous Homes	265
	Community Calendar	268
To challenge stereotypes.	What Do Moms Do?	246
	What's Happening in This Picture?	273
	Nursery Rhymes Biases	289
	Witches Get Bad Press	291
	An Aesop Fable	298
	Television Advertising	299
	Drama Improvisation	302
To examine alternatives.	Writing without Hands	252
	Sports Logos	285
	Dreams for a Better Future	303
	Tool Sort	304

Anti-Bias Skills	Activity Title	Page No.
To gather information and draw conclusions based on facts.	Mistaken Perceptions	292
	Bandage Science	312
To make inferences.	Caption It	255
	Television Advertising	299
To effectively cope with change.	Coping with Change	309
To describe fair and unfair behavior, and recognize prejudice.	Story Scramble	271
	Picture Card Scramble	278
	Big Is Beautiful	270
To think critically about people and events.	Interviewing for Information	239
	Recipes for Peace	243
	The Gossip Sheet	267
	Sports Logos	285
To avoid name-calling.	I Can't Understand You	240
To demonstrate empathy.	*Fly Away Home*	211
	The Value of Money	212
	Poverty and Families	214
	Abuela's Weave	220
	The Sharing Quilt	225
	Who Belongs Here?	238
	Who Belongs Here? II	245
	Chair for My Mother	246
	Augmentative Communication Experience	250
	Mechanical Busy Board	250
	Riding in Someone Else's Wheelchair	251
	Writing without Hands	252
	Communication Machine	253
	Big Is Beautiful	270
	Story Scramble	271
	Puppet Dreaming	275
	Pass the Beanbag, Please	277
	Signing In	280
	Being Differently Abled	296
	Following Instructions	297
	Dogs Who Work	298
To participate in group action on behalf of others.	Nutrition is . . .	213
	Poverty and Families	214
	The Many Forms of Proactivism	244
	Community Project	247
	Writing without Hands	252
	Swimmy Felt Board Story	272
To be proactive in helping others.	The Sharing Quilt	225
	Political Activists	242
	Community Project	247
	Access for Everyone?	267
	Ma Liang and the Magic Brush	319
To be proactive against discriminatory behaviors.	Recipes for Peace	243
	Fact Sheet on Discrimination	286
	Witches Get Bad Press	291
	Killer Statements and Gestures	293
	Drama Improvisation	302

Letter to Families of Elementary School Children

Dear Families,

Over the next few weeks the children will be exploring the concepts of poverty and homelessness. As part of this experience we will examine the children's perceptions of homelessness and any judgments related to their beliefs. As they explore personal values related to home and security, I will try to promote empathy and a sensitivity for those who live differently. An important part of this process is to help children think about what they could do to make situations better for those whose lives may not include the basic necessities.

At this point I do not know what suggestions the children may come up with, however, I certainly intend to support their ideas. I am anticipating that a clothing, toy, or food drive may be among their suggested actions. I am asking your assistance in discussing this topic at home and reinforcing the concept that helping others means sharing and giving of yourself or something that you have. Ask your child what he or she could contribute for the benefit of some other child or family. If they say they have no money to buy anything, reinforce that volunteering time and effort is another way to take action. In this way we can work together to enable the children to think critically about fair and unfair situations in life and what actions could make a situation better.

I shall be sending a permission form home soon indicating the time and date for a trip either to a food bank or a shelter. If you are able to accompany us and lend a helping hand, your presence will be much appreciated. Your involvement in this proactive event will model strongly what it means to act on behalf of others.
As always, I thank you for any support that you may be able to offer. I am looking forward to our working partnership throughout this venture.

Sincerely,

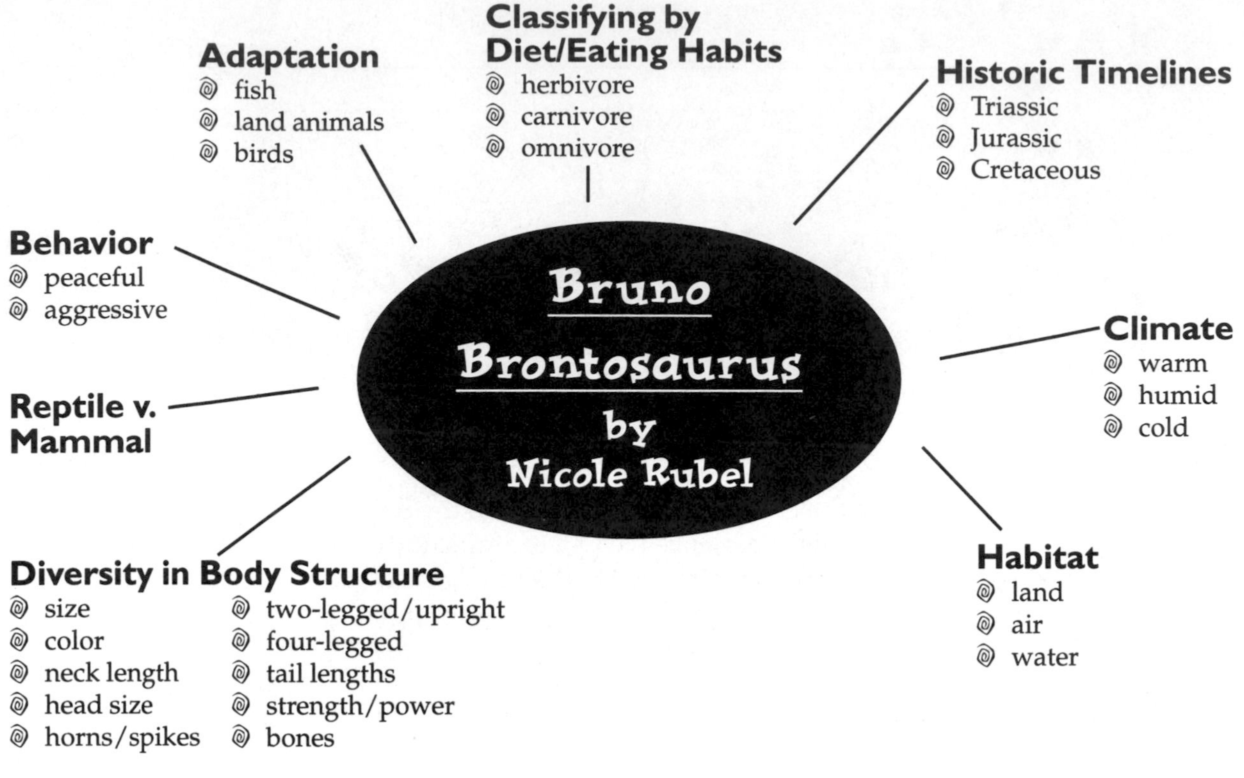

Bruno Brontosaurus

Age
6–8 years

Curriculum Area
Language Arts

Curriculum Objectives
To develop critical thinking through expressive language, and listening comprehension.

Anti-Bias Area
Appearance

Anti-Bias Skill
To recognize, label, and discuss similarities and differences.

Materials
Bruno Brontosaurus, by Nicole Rubel; chart paper; and marker.

Approach
Incorporation

Facilitation
Read *Bruno Brontosaurus* to the class. In the follow-up discussion get the children to generate a list of differences, both physical and behavioral, for both the Tyrannosaurus rex and the Brontosaurus. Record their answers in chart form so they will have these characteristics to refer back to for future activities. Assist the children to infer how diversity in body structure helped these dinosaurs survive.

Ask questions related to discrimination:

- What behaviors, either actions or words, do the other dinosaurs make toward Bruno?
- How do you think it makes Bruno feel?
- How does Bruno solve his problem?

Define the term "discrimination" for the children. Ask them to think about a time when someone said or did something negative because of the way a child looked (appearance) or performed (ability)? Do they hear teasing or name-calling of others in class or on the playground because of physical appearance? Have them brainstorm possible strategies to deal with such behaviors.

Dinosaur Sort

Age

6–8 years

Curriculum Area

Mathematics

Curriculum Objectives

To group by specific attributes; to create sets; to match pictures/word cards to physical attributes.

Anti-Bias Area

Appearance

Anti-Bias Skill

To recognize, label, and discuss similarities and differences.

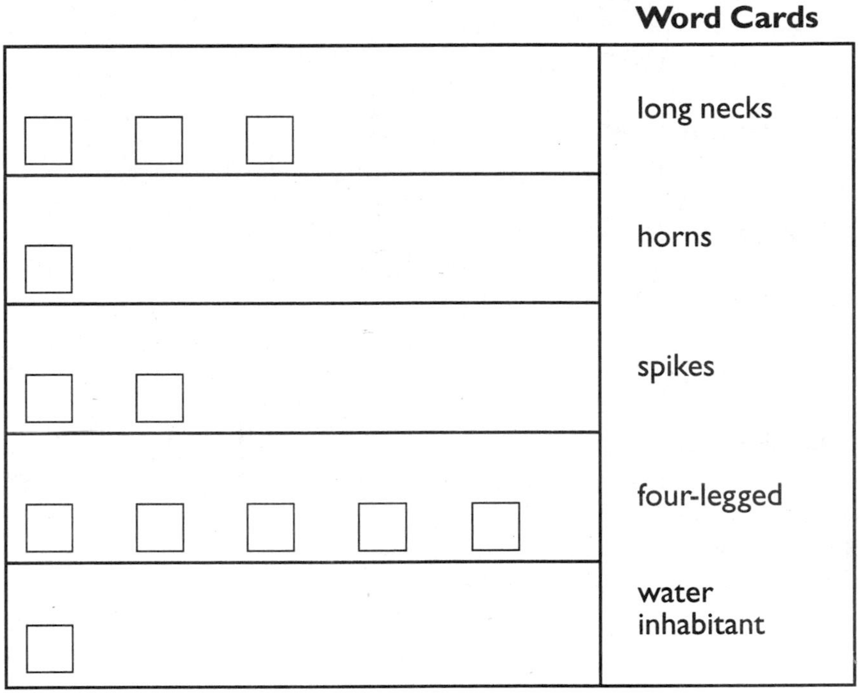

	Word Cards
☐ ☐ ☐	long necks
☐	horns
☐ ☐	spikes
☐ ☐ ☐ ☐ ☐	four-legged
☐	water inhabitant

Grouping dinosaurs by specific attributes.

Materials

Plastic models or pictures of dinosaurs mounted on laminated cards (stegosaurus, diplodocus, brontosaurus, pteradactyl, triceratops, velociraptor, brachiosaurus, dimetrodon, tyrannosaurus, compsognathus, etc.; consult *100 Dinosaurs from A to Z,* by Ron Wilson); grid on poster boards; and word cards of physical characteristics with illustrations.

Approach

Incorporation

Facilitation

Allow the children to explore the pictures/models and devise their own groupings. Help them to focus on the many different characteristics by reviewing the chart that was created by the class in the *Bruno Brontosaurus* activity. Keep the chart posted nearby for quick referencing.

Give older children the grid boards and word cards for additional classification and reading practice.

Physical Characteristics

long tails	short tails	four-legged	round claws
horns	wings	sharp claws	dull teeth
spikes	bony shield	sharp teeth	water inhabitant
long necks	short necks	land inhabitant	
big heads	small heads	two-legged	

Lifestyle Differences

Age
6–8 years

Curriculum Area
Mathematics

Curriculum Objectives
To categorize and classify differences in eating, diet, and habitat.

Anti-Bias Areas
Culture, Belief

Anti-Bias Skill
To promote awareness of and respect for differences in culture and belief.

Materials
Plastic models or pictures of dinosaurs on small laminated cards; and two bristol boards, one divided into three columns labeled *Land, Air, Water,* and the other divided into three columns labeled *Herbivore, Carnivore, Omnivore* (you can use picture or word titles).

Approach
Incorporation and Modified Personalization

Facilitation
Begin this activity with a general discussion of how people differ in eating preferences and how they prepare their foods. Ask the children if they know friends or family members who are vegetarians? Or those with dietary restrictions? Give children examples of what a vegetarian diet might include. Discuss the terms *kosher* and *halal* for those practicing the Jewish and Muslim faiths, and the restrictions on eating pork, shellfish, etc.

Introduce the bristol boards with the dinosaur cards. Have children review the different food diets and habitats of the dinosaurs studied. Leave the materials out in the cognitive area for children to explore. The cards can be self-correcting by placing the initial consonants of the columns on the reverse side for verification.

Dinosaur Acrostics

Age
6–8 years

Curriculum Area
Language Arts

Curriculum Objectives
To develop vocabulary; to practice problem solving, counting, and one-to-one correspondence.

Anti-Bias Area
Appearance

Anti-Bias Skills
To promote awareness of and respect for diversity in appearance; to value uniqueness of self, others, and families.

Materials
Laminated dinosaur crossword puzzles and water soluble markers. Create the puzzles by listing words on the silhouette form of the dinosaur with the requisite number of squares in the acrostic formation provided.

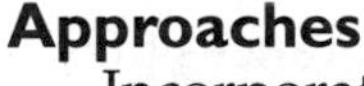

Approaches
Incorporation and Modified Personalization

Facilitation
Devise an assortment of dinosaur puzzles so children can practice them repeatedly. Give children tips on counting the letters and finding the appropriate number of matching squares.

Have the children design their own individual word puzzles by creating a list of words to describe themselves and then the appropriate square formation.

Example: For younger children have the word squares unconnected.

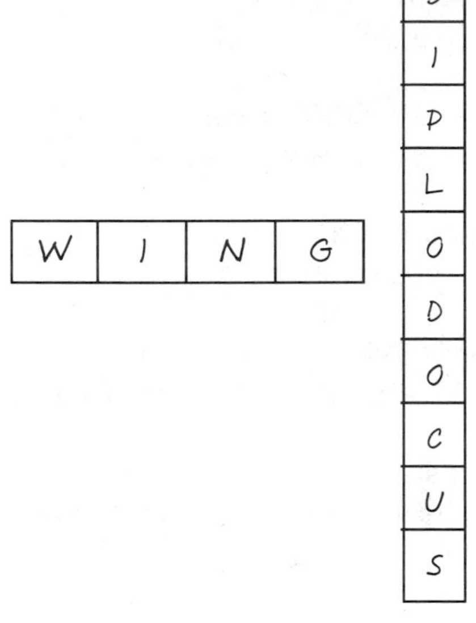

For older children it might look like this:

spiny
plates
plant eater
small teeth
stegosaurus

Dinosaur Acrostics.

Bones and Bodies

Age

6–8 years

Curriculum Area

Science

Curriculum Objectives

To make comparisons, analyze, categorize, hypothesize, and synthesize information.

Anti-Bias Area

Appearance

Anti-Bias Skill

To promote awareness of and respect for diversity in appearance.

Materials

One fish unfilleted; chicken or turkey skeleton and bones, boiled clean; and large picture of human skeleton.

Approach

Incorporation

Facilitation

Show a picture of the human skeleton and discuss how bones hold our bodies together. Point out key bones and identify them for the children if they are unable to name them. Compare the differences in sizes of ribs, legs, toes, arms, and wrists.

Have the children feel their own bodies to discover where and how small or large the following bones are: skull, jaw, ankle, spine, ribs, hip, wrist. Discuss the differences they discover in shape, length, and thickness.

Bring out the fish. Have the children predict what the skeleton will look like. Fillet it in front of the children and see if their hypotheses were correct. Let them analyze the bone structure. Finally bring out the boiled chicken bones and see if they can put the skeleton together.

This activity should be preceded or followed by a trip to a museum to explore dinosaur skeletal exhibitions.

Expansion

Fossil making is a fun extension to this activity. Have the children make imprints of the different bones or set them into clay and bake.

Dinosaur Eggs

Age

6–8 years

Curriculum Area

Science

Curriculum Objectives

To practice hypothesizing, observing, comparing, and drawing conclusions.

Anti-Bias Area

Race

Anti-Bias Skill

To recognize, label, and discuss similarities and differences.

Materials

Half dozen each brown and white eggs, small and large sizes; bowls; saucepan and heat source; and scales.

Approach

Incorporation

Facilitation

Bring out the eggs and ask the children to pretend that the brown eggs belonged to the Tyrannosaurus rex family and the white eggs belonged to the brontosaurus family. Ask them if they think the eggs are the same. Have them hypothesize what the differences between the two might be.

Solicit ways that they could use to test their hypotheses. Be prepared to crack the eggs open to examine the color of the shell inside, the color of the yolk and the albumen. Boil two eggs for the same amount of time, and have the children peel the hard-boiled eggs to compare results. Provide a scale for weighing.

During this activity help the children to identify similarities and differences, and assist them to make the connections with human beings. Ask them to think about assumptions and judgments that people make on the basis of one's skin color. Get the children to enumerate ways we could get to know people before leaping to a conclusion based on appearance.

Expansion

Boil up remaining eggs and have the children peel them. Offer some children the opportunity to make egg salad for snack and the others can crush the shells to either compost or use in a creative activity.

Another activity could focus in on size comparisons. Obtain pictures to show the difference in shape and size of an emu or ostrich egg compared to the egg of a duck, goose, seagull, etc.

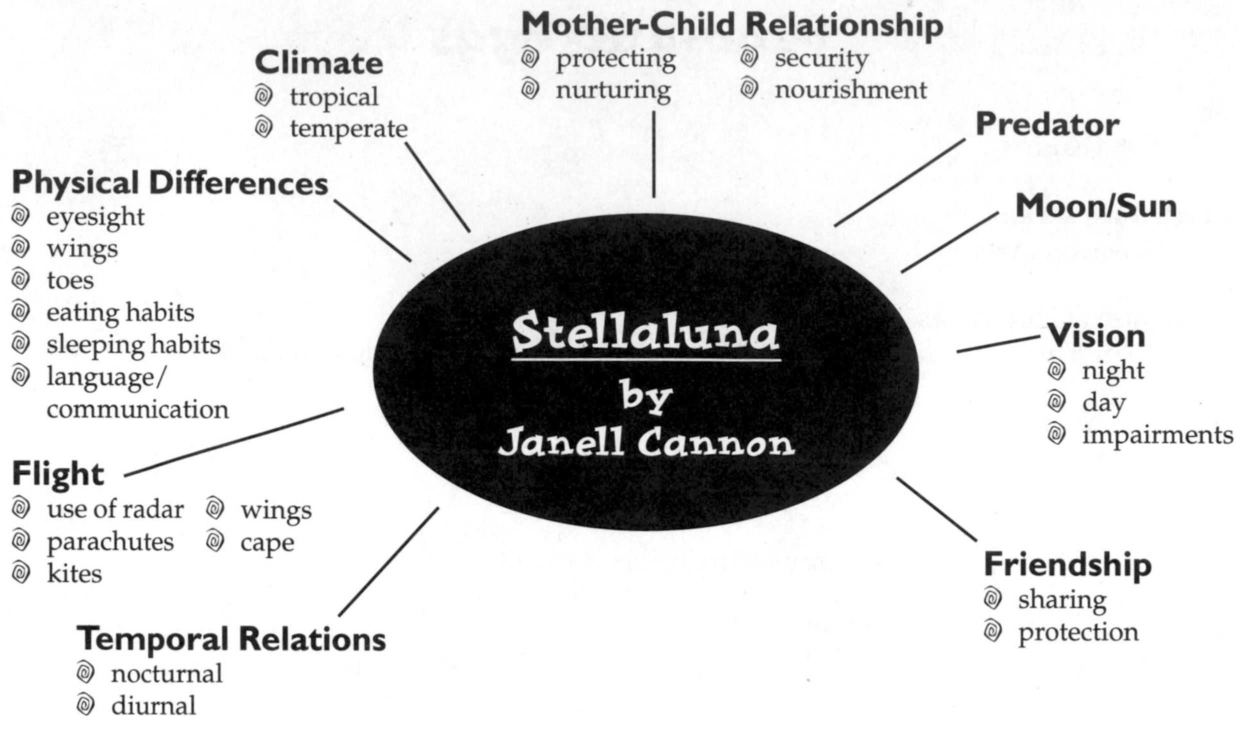

Stellaluna

Age

7–8 years

Curriculum Area

Language Arts

Curriculum Objectives

To increase comprehension and critical thinking skills.

Anti-Bias Area

Appearance

Anti-Bias Skill

To recognize, label, and discuss similarities and differences.

Materials

Stellaluna, by Janell Cannon; flip chart paper; and pen.

Approach

Incorporation

Facilitation

Read *Stellaluna* to the children. Focus the discussion on interpreting the question, "How can we be so different and feel so much alike?" Elicit the underlying message that friendship means sharing with and protecting one another despite any physical differences.

Generate a list of differences they discover between the two flying animals:

- eyesight
- wings/flying structure
- toes
- eating habits
- sleeping habits
- language/communication

Expansion

Begin a unit on birds. Let the children research books and make their own *Facts on Birds* book that includes the great diversity in the shapes and functions of bills, wings and feet; flying versus non-flying birds; and characteristics that exempt them from the mammal class.

Can We Be the Same and Different?

Age

7–8 years

Curriculum Area

Language Arts

Curriculum Objectives

To strengthen listening skills and learn how to organize information into a set framework.

Anti-Bias Areas

Race, Culture, Appearance

Anti-Bias Skill

To promote awareness of and respect for diversity in culture.

Materials

Paper and pencils.

Approach

Personalization

Facilitation

Prepare a model interview sheet that is divided into large columns titled *Things We Like* and *Things We Don't Like.* Down the left-hand side list four categories such as *Food, Sports, Books, and Music,* and encourage children to add other areas important to them. Within each column create two subheadings, ME and MY FRIEND. Have children work in pairs, interviewing one another and filling out individual forms. At the end, the children will have a visual chart of how you can like a friend and share similarities and differences.

For those who are more competent in writing, ask them to write a short paragraph describing how they can be so different yet feel so much alike.

Things We Like		**Things We Don't Like**	
Me	**My Friend**	**Me**	**My Friend**
Food			
Sports			
Books			
Music			

Experiences in Vision

Age
7–8 years

Curriculum Area
Science

Curriculum Objective
To learn about the function of vision in living organisms.

Anti-Bias Areas
Ability, Appearance

Anti-Bias Skills
To interact comfortably with people who are differently abled; to promote awareness of and respect for diversity in ability.

Materials
Sunglasses; petroleum jelly; waxed paper; scissors; toilet paper rolls; longer tubes such as paper towel or wrapping paper rolls; variety of differently colored cellophane pieces; glue; tape; and child-sized binoculars and telescope available in science stores or educational supply catalogs.

Amazing Bats, by Greenaway and Young, is a good additional resource.

Approaches
Incorporation and Modified Personalization

Facilitation
Introduce the words *nocturnal* and *predator.* Ask the group if they have ever seen animals' eyes shining at night and if they know why this happens.

Explain the term *nocturnal,* or night active, in relation to Stellaluna and other animals such as deer, porcupine, opossum, owls, raccoons, bats, mice, and skunks who are able to hunt at night because they have special night vision.

Ask if anyone has ever camped out at night; have those children describe the visual experiences they had. What could(n't) they see—trees, flowers, parts of a car, fences, etc. Darken the room or lead the group into a room that is very dark. Ask them to comment on what objects they can see better than others? What senses are they using to help out? How long does it take their eyes to adjust? What can they see now that they couldn't see a short while before? (This experiment can be repeated by the children at home. As they get ready for bed and turn off the lights, ask them to remember the things in the room they couldn't see at first; then, after a few minutes, what things could they recognize?)

Return to the original question about nocturnal animals and explain how these animals have a shiny layer on the back inner surface of their eyes. This surface helps to reflect light back to enable the animal to see better in the dark. In the human eye we have two structures called rods and cones. The cones help us to see color while the rods are useful in night lighting. Ask the class to hypothesize what a person without cones in the eyes could see.

Bring out the assortment of sunglasses/regular glasses that have one lens smeared with petroleum jelly or covered with waxed paper; binoculars, telescope, paper tube rolls, and cellophane paper. While some children construct their own colored glasses, binoculars, and telescopes with the cellophane paper and tubes, others will experiment with the materials simulating visual impairments or producing effects of size magnification or diminution.

Ensure the children use all the materials so you can have a summary discussion about how things can look differently depending on how your eyes work. Get the children to reflect on how they felt looking at things that were colored differently, blurred, or smaller or larger than usual.

Expansion

Generate a list of nocturnal occupations/jobs that people hold and discuss the advantages and disadvantages of working at night. Read *The Night Ones,* by Patricia Grossman.

Community Resource

Request a visit from a representative of the local Institute for the Blind in Canada.

Star-Moon

Age

7–8 years

Curriculum Area

Language Arts

Curriculum Objectives

To recognize key vocabulary in English and other languages; to recognize visual and aural patterns among languages.

Anti-Bias Area

Culture

Anti-Bias Skill

To promote awareness of and respect for diversity in culture.

Materials

Pictures of space objects; color-coded cards for different languages; and a variety of English-other language dictionaries.

Approach

Incorporation

Facilitation

Bring out large pictures of space-related objects such as a star, the moon, the sun, the earth, and other planets. Show the cards in Italian—*stella* for star and *luna* for moon with the appropriate pictures. Ensure the class makes the connection that the title of the book are words in a different language.

Prepare color-coded cards for languages represented in the class and for others not spoken. Hold up pictures and fill the cards out with the children who know the corresponding words. Have the children look in the dictionaries for the words that are not readily recalled. Let the children match the words cards to the pictures and say the words out loud. Post the pictures with the language cards underneath. Ask the children to analyze the words for similar patterns in sound and letters: the initial *s* sound, and in some languages the *sol* sound pattern.

Example:

SUN—	sol	Spanish
	sole	Italian
	soleil	French
	sonne	German
	sol'ntse	Russian
	shams	Arabic
	o-hi-sama	Japanese

The Bat Sensory Cave

Age
7–8 years

Curriculum Area
Science

Curriculum Objective
To improve discrimination of texture, shape, and size.

Anti-Bias Area
Ability

Anti-Bias Skill
To interact comfortably with people who are differently abled.

Materials
Large appliance cardboard box; textured scraps in different shapes and sizes, such as burlap, fake fur, bamboo, corduroy, gauze, silk, sandpaper, sticky contact paper, and bubble wrap; and a blindfold.

Approaches
Incorporation and Modified Personalization

Facilitation
Remind the children how a bat uses different senses to navigate and find food. Invite them to explore the bat sensory cave using their sense of touch rather than sight. After the children have investigated the interior have them draw up a list of textures they felt, describing their sizes and shapes.

Name Play

Age
7–8 years

Curriculum Area
Mathematics

Curriculum Objectives
To collect information and construct appropriate bar graphs.

Anti-Bias Areas
Culture, Gender

Anti-Bias Skill
To value uniqueness of self, others, and families.

Materials
Paper; pen; and name dictionary (optional).

Approach
Incorporation

Facilitation
Write the name *STELLA* on the board and give the class the following task. In pairs, generate a list of as many names as possible that begin with the letter *S*. Next to each name identify the number of letters, syllables, and whether the name can be used by a boy or a girl or both: Shawn or Sean, etc. They can consult books if they need help.

Afterwards have the class create a bar graph representing *S* names with three, four, five, etc. letters; bar graphs illustrating the number of syllables; bar graphs depicting names according to gender or gender-neutral names.

	# Letters	# Syllables	Gender
Shawn	5	1	Girl
Sean	4	1	Boy
Sergiou	7	3	Boy

Flying Animal Match Game

Age

7–8 years

Curriculum Area

Language Arts

Curriculum Objectives

To improve visual discrimination, identification, and matching; to strengthen cooperation and pro-social skills.

Anti-Bias Areas

Ability, Appearance

Anti-Bias Skill

To promote awareness of and respect for diversity in appearance and ability.

Materials

Forty-eight picture cards comprised of four sets of 12 pictures of different flying animals; three different kinds of bats, five different kinds of birds (ostrich, owl, condor, starling, parrot, etc.), and four other flying animals (flying squirrel, sailfish, porpoise, frog, etc.); and four different bingo boards each with nine pictures showing 9 of the 12 different animals.

Approach

Incorporation

Facilitation

The game should be entirely facilitated by the children. Up to five children can play at one time (four have boards and one calls out the name of the animal on the card). As the animal is called out, those who can place the corresponding card on the board should name one fact that they have learned about the animal—nocturnal, flightless, predator, its habitat, etc. Eliminate competition by having the children place cards on one another's boards to complete the entire series rather than promote individual winners.

Flight Patterns

Age
7–8 years

Curriculum Area
Science

Curriculum Objectives
To discover how energy can be utilized by differing forms of technology; to stimulate curiosity, prediction, and problem solving.

Anti-Bias Area
Ability

Anti-Bias Skill
To promote awareness of and respect for diversity in ability.

Materials
Picture books on different types of flying crafts: helicopter, hot air balloons, rockets, gliders, etc.; construction and heavy-weight paper; light-weight nylon material; ruler; and scissors.

Approach
Incorporation

Facilitation
Ask the children to describe the differences in the way birds and bats fly. Encourage them to guess what man-made aircraft corresponds to the different wing structures found in these two animals.

Bring out the nylon material and have two children, taking two ends each, toss it over their heads. As the material catches air, have the class describe what type of flying craft would use this principle. In contrast, have one child rest the end of a piece of paper (2 in. × 8 in.) on her chin and blow. The harder she blows, the higher the paper will fly. Explain the basic principle of aerodynamics—air needs to move over and under wings to help the aircraft gain height. The more pressure beneath the wing in contrast to weaker pressure on top, the higher the craft will fly. Move outdoors to facilitate the remainder of the activity.

Encourage the children to make different airplanes, modifying the shape (angled, curved, or straight) and length of the wings. Get them to predict what will happen with the change of shape. Focus their efforts on problem solving the design in order to meet their predicted outcome. Back inside, have them write brief descriptions of their flying models and the flight consequences.

Help them to make the connection that any changes or alterations to a physical structure will have corresponding effects on performance. They can see this in the different ways animals fly and people walk.

Community Resource
Commercial kites and gliders are available from educational supply companies for a more involved exploration of aerodynamics.

Fly Away Home

Age
6–10 years

Curriculum Area
Language Arts

Curriculum Objectives
To improve listening comprehension and expressive ability to describe abstract ideas.

Anti-Bias Areas
Class, Family Composition

Anti-Bias Skill
To demonstrate empathy.

Materials
Fly Away Home, by Eve Bunting.

Approaches
Incorporation and Personalization: Invite a community member who lives in a shelter to speak with the class. Get the children to generate ideas for activities they can organize to lend assistance.

Facilitation
Follow up the reading with a discussion that probes children's perceptions of homelessness; deal with any judgmentalness. As the children explore personal values related to home and security, point out alternative perspectives in order to foster empathy for those who live differently. Some questions to pose include:

- What makes a place a home?
- If you didn't have a place to call home where would you live? Why?
- When someone mentions the word *bums* or *bag ladies* what image comes into your head? (clothing, appearance, smells)
- Do all homeless people look alike? If so, how?
- How do you think they feel?
- What do you do when you see a person sleeping on a park bench? on a doorstep?
- Why do you think people are afraid of the homeless?
- What are some ways in which we could help the homeless?

Expansion
Support the proactive initiatives that emerge from the children's brainstorming. Lend guidance and assistance around resources and organizations.

Living out of a Bag

Age
6–10 years

Curriculum Area
Language Arts

Curriculum Objectives
To identify and examine the meaning of security and family belonging; to respect others' values.

Anti-Bias Areas
Class, Family Composition

Anti-Bias Skill
To listen to and value other points of view.

Materials
Paper and pen.

Approaches
Modified Personalization and Incorporation

Facilitation
Ask the children to think about the following scenario:

> Your father lost his job a month ago. Your mother has gone away to live with her parents who are very ill and need her help. You have been evicted from your apartment. For the time being, you and your dad will be living in the bus terminal. Your dad told you that you can only take one small bag with your belongings. What would you choose to pack?

Get the class to make a list of the items they would take.

Ask the children to pack such a bag at home and bring it to school the next day. Everyone will share what they chose to take and why.

Expansion
Look through Bernard Wolf's *Homeless,* a photo essay on homeless people and living in poverty, for additional discussions.

The Value of Money

Age
8–10 years

Curriculum Area
Mathematics

Curriculum Objectives
To practice calculations; to increase critical thinking.

Anti-Bias Area
Class

Anti-Bias Skill
To demonstrate empathy.

Materials
Classified ads; food store flyers; and paper and pen.

Approach
Incorporation

Facilitation
Have the children recall what Andrew and his father, in the book *Fly Away Home,* were saving their money for. Divide the children in small groups of three. Give each group a paycheck with differing amounts of money. Distribute classified ads for rental properties and flyers from different grocery stores to each group. Remind the children what public transportation costs are in the city. Draw a chart on the board with four columns labeled *Shelter, Food, Transportation, Other Costs.* Have the children look for a rental property and create a week's shopping list, then place costs under the appropriate column.

While doing numerical calculations of addition, subtraction, and division, assist them to see how critical it is to try and make money stretch to accommodate basic human needs.

Who's in My Family

Age
6–10 years

Curriculum Area
Social Studies

Curriculum Objectives
To fill out a family tree graph; to develop recognition of self in relation to family and larger social networks.

Anti-Bias Areas
Culture, Family Composition, Class, Belief

Anti-Bias Skills
To promote awareness of and respect for diversity in culture and family composition; to value uniqueness of self, others, and families.

Materials
Family tree graph; and pencils.

Approach
Incorporation

Facilitation
In *Fly Away Home*, Andrew and his father reflected one kind of family composition. They also experienced the support and sharing of other community members who acted like family. Discuss this concept of what makes a family with the children before distributing a family tree graph for each child in the class. The focus of this graph is only on family members, their occupations, and where they live(d). Let the children add boxes to the basic graph as they deem necessary. Allow the children to take the family tree home and finish working it through with their families. When the children are ready to present their trees, encourage the inclusion of photos.

During the class discussion it is important to remind all the children that each family is unique and special, and that there is no one way to be a family.

Nutrition Is . . .

Age
6–10 years

Curriculum Area
Science (Health Education)

Curriculum Objectives
To increase empathy and work cooperatively toward a common goal.

Anti-Bias Areas
Culture, Family Composition, Class

Anti-Bias Skill
To participate in group action on behalf of others.

Materials
Paper and pens; plastic bags; and donated food.

Approach
Personalization

Facilitation
Based on the book, *Fly Away Home*, have the children recall the kind of food that Andrew and his dad ate in the airport cafeteria. Ask them to compare the breakfast and dinner food items with those that the children usually have. In the comparison process, highlight how everyone's family prepares the basic food groups in distinctive ways. Devise a list of foods that Andrew and Dad should have for their breakfast and dinner.

Invite a staff member from the local food bank to come and discuss its function. Assist the children to solicit donations (school newsletter, community flyer, etc.) and arrange for a morning of volunteer help at a local food bank.

Community Resource
Local food bank.

Poverty and Families

Age

6–10 years

Curriculum Area

Social Studies

Curriculum Objectives

To encourage awareness of what poverty means to a family; to understand the effects of poverty on families.

Anti-Bias Areas

Family Composition, Class

Anti-Bias Skills

To demonstrate empathy; to participate in group action on behalf of others.

Materials

Chart paper; and markers. Refer to *Fly Away Home*, by Eve Bunting.

Approach

Incorporation

Facilitation

As a follow-up discussion to *Fly Away Home* have the children think about the nature of poverty and its developmental implications by asking these questions:

- What kinds of things do families buy for their children and themselves? (List responses: food, clothing, toys, books, etc.)
- What do you ask your family to buy for you?
- If your family didn't have enough money to buy things that you really wanted and needed, how do you think it would make you feel? How do you think you might behave?
- If your family didn't have enough money to feed you breakfast and you had to come to school hungry, do you think you would be able to do your math or reading? Why/why not?
- If you came to school worried about not having warm clothing or enough food, do you think you would be able to study well?
- What else could be hard for children who live in poor families?
- What could we do to help these families?

Expansion

Invite staff from a local shelter to come in and discuss the needs of the families in residence. Encourage the children to sponsor a drive for used clothing, toys, and books. Let the children drop off the collected items as a class.

(Adapted from "Tell Me About Your Family," Canada Committee for the International Year of the Family 1994, Ottawa.)

Community Resource

Local hostel or shelter for families.

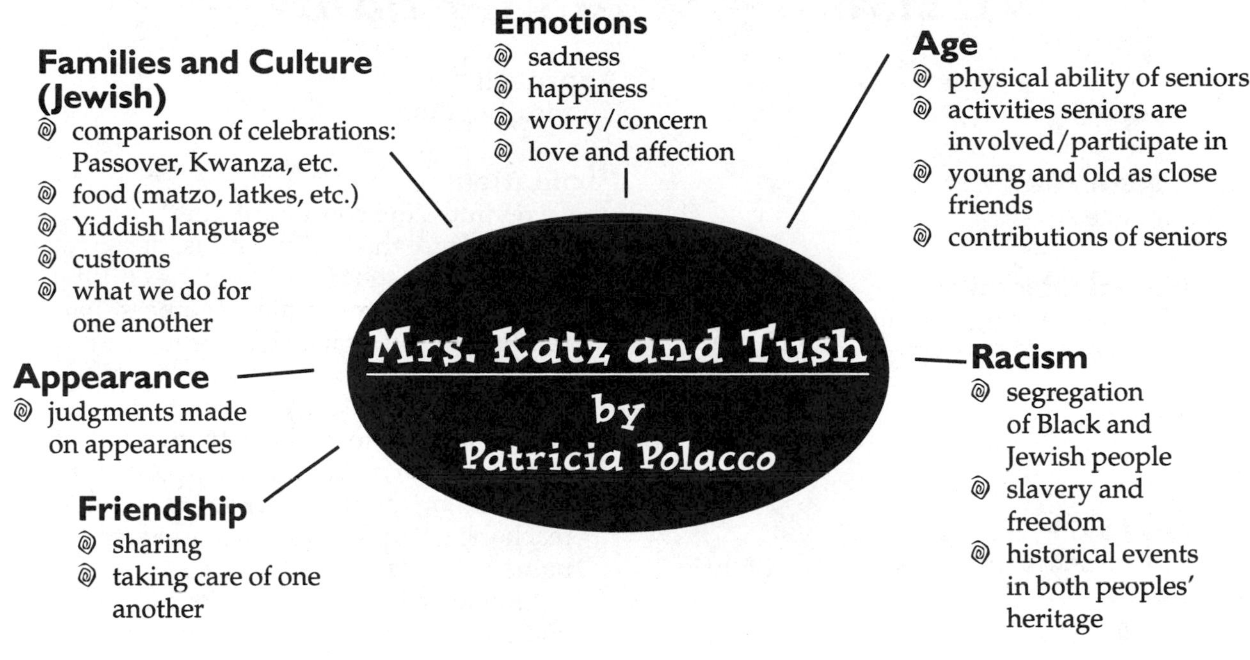

Mrs. Katz and Tush

Age
7–9 years

Curriculum Area
Language Arts

Curriculum Objectives
To increase comprehension skills; to strengthen interpretive ability.

Anti-Bias Areas
Age, Race, Culture

Anti-Bias Skill
To promote awareness of and respect for diversity in age, race, and culture.

Materials
Mrs. Katz and Tush, by Patricia Polacco.

Approaches
Incorporation and Personalization: Senior citizens on an ongoing basis

Facilitation
Read *Mrs. Katz and Tush.* Focus the discussion on two major points:

1. How taking care of one another, sharing and building a friendship can transcend the barriers of age, race, and culture. Ask the children to think about all the things that we do for a good friend or family member.
2. How both Larnel's and Mrs. Katz's ancestors were slaves; despite the past, both Black and Jewish people still struggle against prejudice in the present.

Begin a seniors outreach component in your program. Invite a senior as a helper and guest speaker to follow up the story. Involve the children in generating a list of tasks that the seniors could lend a hand with on an ongoing basis. Ensure that the tasks are active and not passive in nature. Intergenerational integration will prevent children from stereotyping people based on age and will help them challenge negative assumptions or perceptions made by others.

Community Resource
To involve senior citizens on an ongoing basis, contact community agencies involved in supporting senior citizens or a senior citizen center in your community.

Dictionary of Family Names

Age
7–9 years

Curriculum Area
Language Arts

Curriculum Objectives
To practice printing or cursive writing; to recognize words in different languages.

Anti-Bias Area
Culture

Anti-Bias Skill
To value uniqueness of self, others, and families.

Materials
Colored paper and fine-point markers.

Approach
Incorporation

Facilitation
To reinforce the concept of how fundamental the family unit is, design a name tree for the class. Have the children bring in names for family members that reflect the ethno-racial background of each child—*bubee* is grandmother in Yiddish, *baba* in Russian, etc. Depending on developmental level, have them print or use cursive to produce family name cards to mount on the tree. Each child should teach the group how to pronounce the name(s) they contribute.

Review all the different languages used and see if the children find similarities in initial consonants or phonic patterns among these different terms.

Dancing Time

Age
7–9 years

Curriculum Area
Music and Movement

Curriculum Objectives
To increase ability to perform movement patterns and coordination required for skipping and turning; to enhance rhythmic and counting ability.

Anti-Bias Area
Culture

Anti-Bias Skill
To promote awareness of and respect for diversity in culture.

Materials
Polka music; rhythm and blues music; tambourines.

Approach
Incorporation

Facilitation
Play a sample of polka music and encourage the children to clap out the rhythm with the strong and weak beats. Teach the group the basic skipping pattern and have them dance to the music in pairs. Have some children provide accompaniment by hitting out the proper rhythm on the tambourines.

For a change of rhythm and style, play a selection of rhythm and blues music with harmonica, guitar, and bass instrumentation. Observe the changes in movement in response. Ask the children to reflect upon the different moods created by the different types of music.

Cultural Celebrations I: A Two-part Experience

Age
7–9 years

Curriculum Area
Social Studies

Curriculum Objectives
To learn the historical and cultural significance behind the celebrations of Passover and Kwanza; to develop vocabulary.

Anti-Bias Area
Culture

Anti-Bias Skills
To recognize, label, and discuss similarities and differences; to encourage openness to new experiences

Materials
Stories about Passover and Kwanza; candlestick holder and candles; music; and clothing. Refer to *Mrs. Katz and Tush,* by Patricia Polacco.

Approach
Personalization

Facilitation
Remind the children that Mrs. Katz was Jewish and Larnel an African American. In each respective culture there are celebrations that have an important historical significance, in particular, those that mark a struggle toward freedom.

Invite either children's family members or members from the community to relate the stories behind Passover and Kwanza. Explain the word *symbol.* Illustrate the symbolic significance of the food for Passover and the lighting of the seven candles for Kwanza.

Prepare word cards that reflect key vocabulary for each celebration including:

seder (feast)	karamu (feast)
matzo (food)	ribunzi (food)
ten plagues (punishment)	zawadi (gifts)
haroset (food)	kinara (candleholder)
pharaoh (enslaver)	umoja (kinship/unity)
bitter herbs (food)	ujamaa (cooperation)

Have the children compare these celebrations and others they may know, such as the lighting of eight candles during Hanukkah or the communal feasting during Diwali.

Community Resource
Families who are willing to visit and relate both historical and personal stories about these holidays.

Cultural Celebrations II

Age
7–9 years

Curriculum Area
Social Studies

Curriculum Objective
To work cooperatively in preparing cultural feasts.

Anti-Bias Area
Culture

Anti-Bias Skills
To promote awareness and respect for diversity in culture; to encourage cooperative group efforts.

Materials
Food ingredients: matzo, parsley, salt water, hard-boiled egg, apple, nuts, honey, collard greens, black-eyed peas, cornbread, rice pudding, and ears of corn.

Approaches
Incorporation and Personalization

Facilitation
Decide ahead of time with community members which dishes can be made with relative ease in the classroom and which items require advanced preparation at home. Ask parents to contribute to the feast. Volunteers will be needed to work with the children in small groups to prepare a number of different dishes.

Enjoy the communal feast together and remind the children of the symbolism of the celebration: many people sacrificed their lives in the fight to be free; and sharing the first fruits of harvests and resources with family is a tribute to the human spirit and ancestors of the past.

Geography Web

Age
7–9 years

Curriculum Area
Mathematics

Curriculum Objectives
To introduce map-reading skills; to calculate distances using map scales.

Anti-Bias Area
Culture

Anti-Bias Skill
To promote awareness of and respect for diversity in culture.

Materials
Large wall map; rulers; string; pencils; paper; pins with flags attached; and reference books on flags. Refer to *Mrs. Katz and Tush,* by Patricia Polacco.

Approach
Incorporation

Facilitation
Show a small flag of Poland and ask the class if they remember where Mrs. Katz was born. Bring out a large map and show the seven continents of the world. Find Europe and place a pin on Warsaw for Mrs. Katz. Based on previously assigned homework, have the children locate where their ancestors are from. Let them construct flag designs and attach the pins to the map.

Construct a map scale using string and a ruler. Have the children calculate the distances traveled by their ancestors from the point of origin to their final destination. For further practice, ask each child to calculate the difference in miles traveled by Mrs. Katz and their family members.

Graph the various distances within the class and visually compare shortest and longest journeys.

Rock Garden

Age
7–9 years

Curriculum Area
Visual Arts

Curriculum Objectives
To create expression and imagination in design; to explore the aesthetics of an artistic medium.

Anti-Bias Area
Culture

Anti-Bias Skill
To encourage openness to new experiences; to appreciate how people use objects differently.

Materials
Rocks; variety of brushes; paints; pictures of inukshuks, pyramids, Stonehenge, and Easter Island. Refer to *Mrs. Katz and Tush,* by Patricia Polacco.

Approach
Incorporation

Facilitation
Ask the children if they remember what Mrs. Katz, and later Larnel, brought to the cemetery? Explain the custom of leaving a rock in memory of someone you loved. Have the children decorate a rock to commemorate someone.

Bring out pictures of rock sculptures such as those on Easter Island or Stonehenge or the pyramids. Explore with the class how rocks have been used to express emotions; as a tribute to honor someone; or as help as in the case of inukshuks in the far North.

Ask the children to design a rock garden in a cordoned-off area in the playground. Have them write about its significance and post the story by the garden for the other children in the school to experience.

Expansion
Trip to a cemetery to explore different headstones.

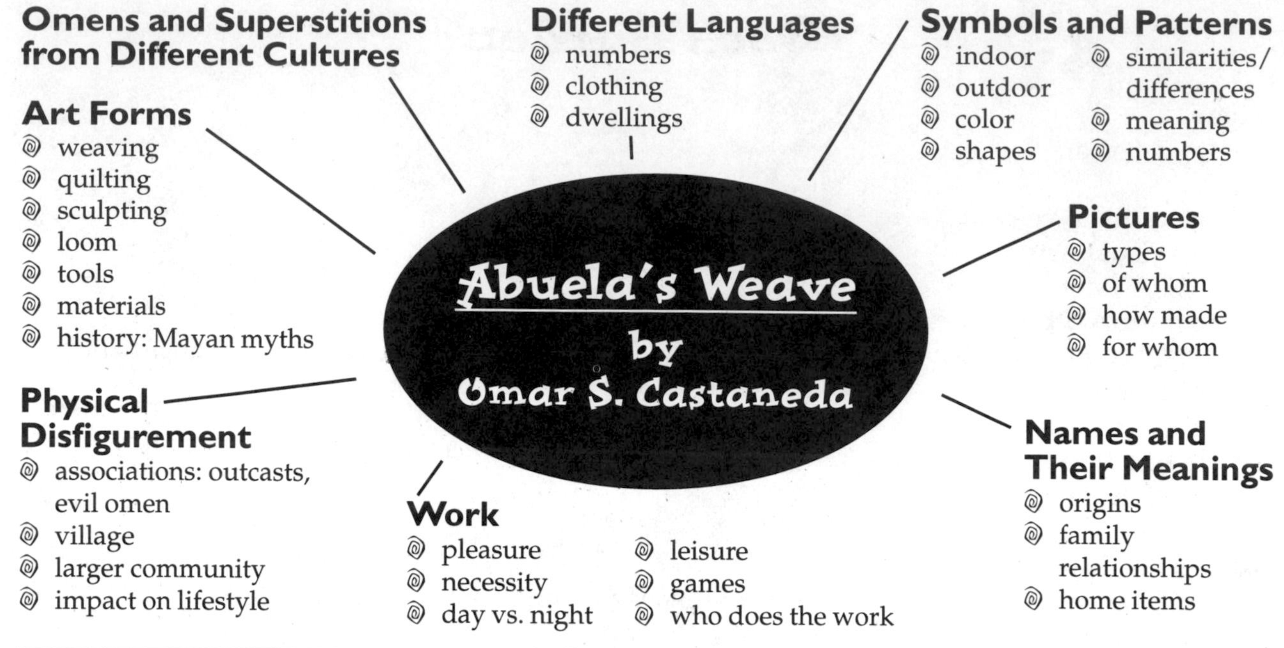

Abuela's Weave

Age
8–10 years

Curriculum Area
Language Arts

Curriculum Objective
To understand the cause and effect relationship of remarks and actions.

Anti-Bias Area
Appearance

Anti-Bias Skills
To demonstrate empathy; to promote awareness of and respect for diversity in appearance.

Materials
Abuela's Weave, by Omar S. Castaneda; and pictures depicting culturally diverse people with various facial incongruities: birthmarks, freckles, large noses, crooked noses, droopy eyelids, blackened or decayed teeth, etc.

Approach
Incorporation

Facilitation
As a follow-up discussion to *Abuela's Weave,* help the children focus on the issue of physical appearance and the emotions it can evoke both internally and externally. Show the pictures to the children and ask the following questions:

- Who might this person be (mother, brother, grandparent) in a family?
- If your mother, brother, grandfather, etc., looked like this, would you sit beside them on the bus? Why? Why not?
- Would you invite them to play with you and your friends? Why? Why not?
- Which one of these people would you *not* want to sit close to on a park bench? Why?

Discuss how Esperanza felt about her grandmother. Explore the reasons why the grandmother absented herself when Esperanza set up the stall in the marketplace. Have the children hypothesize how Abuela felt riding by herself on the bus, and how Esperanza felt. Use the questions and pictures as context for this discussion. Encourage the class to compare their thoughts about the book and photos with how they would feel if someone refused to sit beside one of their family members.

Conclude by eliciting from the group actions or statements that one could use to make people feel all right about how they look.

The Importance of a Name

Age

8–10 years

Curriculum Area

Language Arts

Curriculum Objectives

To encourage awareness of the meanings associated with names; to understand the effects of a name change on one's self-esteem.

Anti-Bias Area

Culture

Anti-Bias Skill

To value uniqueness of self, others, and families.

Materials

Abuela's Weave, by Omar S. Castaneda; names other than the children's own on self-sticking name tags; dictionary of names.

Approaches

Incorporation and Personalization: Invite a community member or family member, whose ethnic background is different from the majority of the children in the group, to share the experience of having undergone a name change.

Facilitation

As a follow-up discussion to the book, have the children identify the name of the granddaughter in the story. Ask the class to guess the meaning of Esperanza (Hope). Discuss with them whether it is an appropriate name for this character. Why do they think so?

Have them share the name that their families gave them at birth, and the name they are being called now. What meaning do they associate with their name? As they explore this, point out to each child where their name originated and what it means: Valerie means being valued and is from the Latin *valere,* etc. If there are any children who are called by a different name than the one originally given them, ask how they feel about it: Michael for Miguel, etc.

Before the visitor's arrival, explain to the group that each child will receive a tag with a new name. The visitor will call them by that name. After the visitor's story ask the following questions:

- How did they feel when the visitor called them by the new name?
- How did the visitor feel when his name had been changed?
- Did the children feel the same way? Why?

Talk about any discomfort that results by being issued a new identity through a new name. Discuss what action they might take in the future if someone tries to change their name, or if they are in a situation where it is being done to another child, for example, changing a name to make pronunciation easier, such as Rena for Inthiranee.

Community Resource

Immigration resettlement program in Canada.

Omens and Signs

Age
8–10 years

Curriculum Area
Language Arts

Curriculum Objectives
To strengthen critical thinking and evaluation skills.

Anti-Bias Areas
Belief, Culture

Anti-Bias Skill
To promote awareness of and respect for diversity in belief.

Materials
Pictures of sun, moon, eclipse, erupting volcano, raven, black cat, bat, long black robe, person with large scar on face; chart paper; and markers. Refer to *Abuela's Weave,* by Omar S. Castaneda.

Approaches
Incorporation and Extension: Discuss symbols associated with holidays celebrated by the children's families.

Facilitation
Show pictures of the sun, moon, lunar or solar eclipse, erupting volcano, raven, black cat, long black robe, bat, dark windswept countryside, person with a facial or hand scar. Ask the children to identify which picture reflects *good* and *bad* ideas. List them on a chart under the appropriate columns. Elicit other items that have a positive or negative association. Encourage the children to give reasons for their responses: black cat = bad luck or older woman with a scar on her face is a witch = evil; sun is equated with gold = good fortune, etc. Answers will depend on children's own experiences and backgrounds.

Discuss feelings associated with each of their answers. Possible answers could be fear, hatred, disgust, acceptance, or happiness. Refer to *Abuela's Weave* and ask what associations people made about Esperanza's grandmother. What was the reason (birthmark), and what was the result of this type of thinking? Ensure that the children connect how people are treated in response to negative/positive omens and signs.

Expansion
Read *The Winter Solstice,* by Ellen Jackson, and expand on symbols and omens associated with seasonal celebrations.

Patterns All Around

Age
8–10 years

Curriculum Area
Mathematics

Curriculum Objectives
To analyze, duplicate, and describe patterns.

Anti-Bias Areas
Culture, Age

Anti-Bias Skill
To listen to and value other points of view.

Materials
Abuela's Weave, by Omar S. Castaneda; pattern blocks and geometric tiles; paper; and pastels.

Approach
Incorporation

Facilitation
To introduce the topic of patterns have the children look at key pages in *Abuela's Weave* that depict symbols on the tapestry, a tree, and on several rocks. Have the children convey what those symbols mean to them. Point out to the group how some children may have identified the same images but arrived at very different conclusions as to what they represented: *eyes* versus *balls* or *ears* versus *beak.* It is important that they begin to value individual perspectives and understand that there is more than one way to view the same thing.

Direct their attention to the bottom of each page on which there is an illustration of material that has a distinctive pattern. Encourage them to describe the pattern verbally—what shapes and colors were used in what sequence. Set out pattern blocks and geometric tiles and ask the students to create their own special patterns. Ensure they understand the concept of pattern making. When they have completed their design they can re-create the pattern in pastels. Mount and hang each pattern so the children can observe how individual each design is.

For older children, provide tessellation tiles and ask them to create number patterns that increase and decrease.

Yarn Pictures

Age
8–10 years

Curriculum Area
Visual Arts

Curriculum Objectives
To strengthen problem-solving and design skills; to promote creative aesthetics.

Anti-Bias Areas
Culture, Ability

Anti-Bias Skills
To listen to and value other points of view; to encourage cooperative efforts.

Materials
Glue; assortment of yarns, wools, and thin strips of material of various colors, thickness, length, and texture; and construction paper in assorted shapes, sizes, and colors. Refer to *Abuela's Weave,* by Omar S. Castaneda.

Approaches
Incorporation and Extension: During the activity ask open-ended questions specific to how the children are using their eyes and hands. Ask whether they believe everyone can use their eyes or hands in the same way as they can. How might someone be able to hold or see the yarn if they were missing a thumb or blind?

Facilitation
Ask the children if they remember any of the patterns and hidden pictures in the tapestry that Abuela and Esperanza had woven. Discuss what shapes and patterns might be important to them. Encourage them to arrange the yarns, wools, and cloth pieces in order to create pictures or designs that might be meaningful to themselves or their families. When all the pictures are completed, have the children try to find the hidden pictures in each other's work. The artists need to share the significance of these pictures within the pictures.

Explore with the group how someone who is differently abled might create similar pictures.

Community Resource
A variety of weaving looms are available depending on program goals and curriculum considerations. Lakeshore/Wintergreen has three distinct styles in stock:

1. Prenotched Chipboard loom in three sizes (SC7-LM136, 6½″ × 13″; SC7-LM137, 9¾″ × 13″; and SC7-LM138, 13″ × 13″).
2. Friendly loom allows up to four children to weave simultaneously. The height adjustment allows for children to stand, sit, or kneel (SC7-LM131, 30″ × 36″).
3. Lilette Loom is a hardwood loom, suitable for weaving place mats, chair pads, bags (SC7-LM35, 15″ × 20″).

The Sharing Quilt

Age
8–10 years

Curriculum Area
Visual Arts

Curriculum Objectives
To compose a narrative using an art form; to explore the historical significance of quilts.

Anti-Bias Areas
Culture, Age, Gender

Anti-Bias Skills
To demonstrate empathy; to encourage cooperative group efforts; to be proactive in helping others.

Materials
Selina and the Bear Paw Quilt, by Barbara Smucker; pieces of material from special items belonging to the children, both at home and at school; thread; easy-to-thread sewing needles; large piece of material for liner.

Approaches
Incorporation and Modified Personalization

Facilitation
This is a long-term project. Begin a discussion about other types of textured art forms besides the tapestry weaving found in *Abuela's Weave:* rugs, silk prints, tie-dyed dresses, moccasin beading, batiking, quilts, etc. Read *Selina and the Bear Paw Quilt* and review the main points of the story:

- that every piece and pattern in the quilts that Selina's grandmother, aunts, and other family members used had a history and memories attached to them; and
- that the quilt is like a bond that keeps the family, even though miles apart, together in spirit.

Discuss the use of quilts in their homes and where the quilts came from. If no one has a quilt, then discuss generally what they think is the purpose of a quilt—warmth, comfort, sense of belonging, etc.

Have the class consider what pieces of clothing or other textured items are meaningful to them. Ask the children to contribute pieces so the class can create one large sharing quilt that would eventually be shared with someone who really needs warmth and comfort. Get the class to problem solve who that might be: a homeless person, someone living in a hostel or shelter, etc.

Once the children have brought in the material pieces for the quilt, explain how various patterns can be arranged and sewn (refer to the back cover of the book for instructions). Let the class decide on a sharing pattern. Provide daily opportunities for the completion of this group project.

Assist them as they work through an action plan for the quilt's donation or loan. Follow up on their decision and facilitate the exchange of their effort to an agency or individual.

Expansion
Visit a textile museum or exhibit. Arrange for a quiltmaker to demonstrate and share skills.

Community Resources
Craft and hobby organizations.

Weaver's Booth Game

Age
8–10 years

Curriculum Area
Mathematics

Curriculum Objectives
To develop accuracy in math calculations.

Anti-Bias Areas
Culture, Ability

Anti-Bias Skills
To encourage openness to new experiences; to interact comfortably with cultural diversity.

Materials
Variety of trims or borders with different cultural designs or patterns; bristol board; clear contact paper; cardboard "people" shapes; small square box; marker; and paper.

Approach
Incorporation

Facilitation
To make the game, cut the bristol board so that six strips of borders can be arranged vertically across its width. Length is optional as long as the borders are all equal. Glue the borders. With the marker, divide the board into 2-inch squares and laminate. To make the dice, cover a portion of each of the six sides of the square box with one of the cultural trims that was used on the board, so there is a different one on each side. For each side of the dice, write the numbers from 1 to 6 from a choice of six different languages in words. Numbers in braille and/or Signed English can be used as additional languages. Laminate the entire dice. Cover each of the six cardboard people shapes with "clothes"—one from each of the cultural patterns. Each person shape should have a pattern that coincides with a pattern on the dice and on the game board.

The purpose of the game is to get the "weavers" from their homes (at the bottom of the board) to their market booths (at the top of the board). Each weaver's home and booth has the same pattern as the weaver. A maximum of six players can play at one time.

Each child chooses a weaver; the pattern on the weaver's clothes becomes the child's pattern. Weavers are lined up at their homes and the children take turns rolling the dice. The dice will always land with a cultural pattern and a word-number facing upward. After each roll, the child must identify the number word and the pattern on the dice. The child can now move the weaver toward the booth in the quickest way possible. Movement can be forward, sideways, or backwards, according to the number indicated, however, the weaver may only land on a square that matches the pattern on the dice. So for example, if the dice face shows *drei, chi, trois, dree,* or *shalosh* and a hand with thumb, index, and middle fingers up, then that weaver can move three squares provided it can land on the pattern indicated by the dice. If this is not possible, the player loses a turn. The game is completed either when all the weavers have reached their respective booths, or with the arrival of the first weaver at the booth. The children can decide which rule to play by before beginning the game.

For older children, numbers from 6 to 10 can be substituted and the operations of subtraction, multiplication, or division can be used to challenge math skills. For example with each roll the number showing must be multiplied by 3, or 5, or 7, etc.

Numbers in Languages

Russian: odin, dva, tri, chteri, pyat, shest'

German: eins, zwei, drei, vier, fünf, sechs

French: un, deux, trois, quatre, cinq, six

Africaans: ien, twee, dree, feer, vyf, ses

Hebrew: achat, shteye-eem, shalosh, arba, chamesh, sheysh

The Weaver's Booth game.

Mayan Math

Age
8–10 years

Curriculum Area
Mathematics

Curriculum Objectives
To decode another numerical system; to understand the relationship between two symbols.

Anti-Bias Area
Culture

Anti-Bias Skill
To promote awareness of and respect for diversity in culture.

Materials
Secret code sheet with Mayan number symbols; a secret message. Refer to *Abuela's Weave,* by Omar S. Castaneda.

Approach
Modified Personalization

Facilitation
Ask the class if they can remember what country Abuela and Esperanza lived in. Ask them to locate Guatemala on the map. Give some historical background on Abuela's ancestors. The Mayans had a very rich civilization. They had an advanced understanding of math and astronomy. It was the Mayans who were the first to develop the concept of zero.

Introduce the class to the numerical system designed by the Mayan people thousands of years ago. Let the class look over the symbols and see whether they can identify the pattern used in the math symbols. Distribute the code sheet with the secret message on the bottom. Have the children decode this message.

Expansion
Have the students write secret messages to one another using this system.

Introduce Roman numerals as another numerical system to practice basic number operations.

Secret Code of the Mayan Indians

A B C D E F G H I J
1 2 3 4 5 6 7 8 9 10

K L M N O P Q R S T
11 12 13 14 15 16 17 18 19 20

U V W X Y Z
21 22 23 24 25 26 40 60 80

Secret Message

Decoding a secret message.

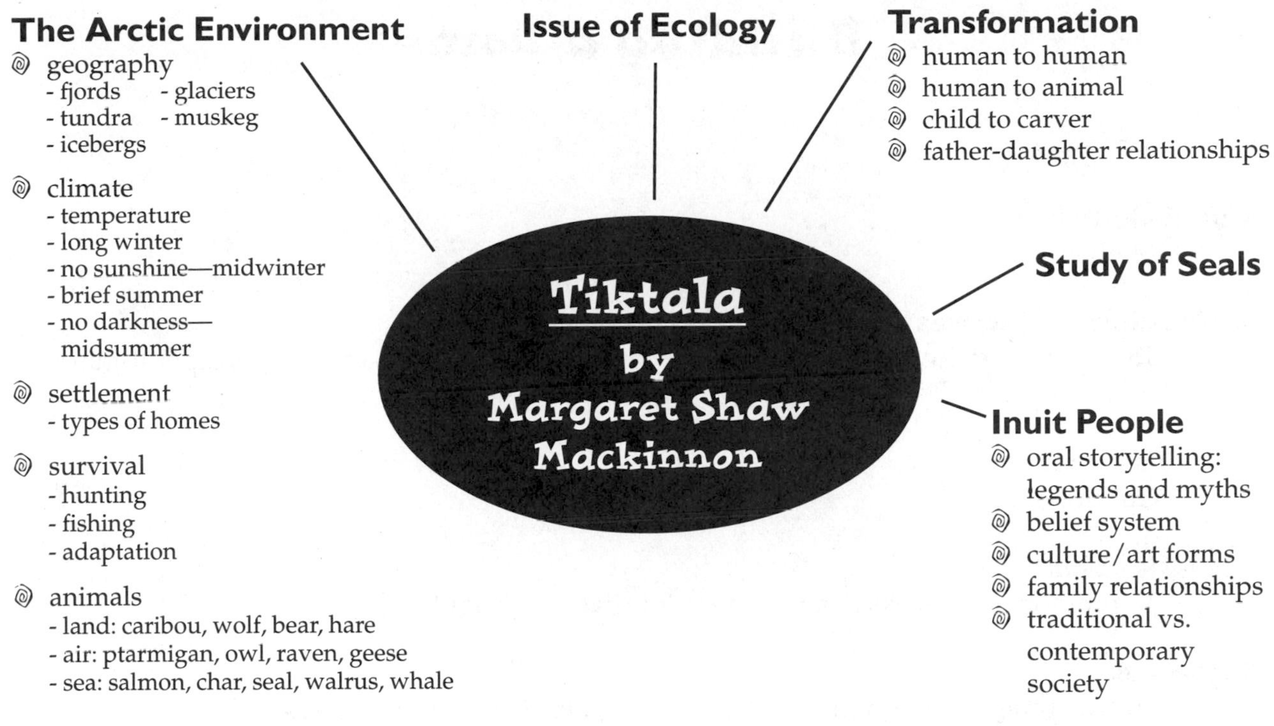

Tiktala

Age
9–11 years

Curriculum Area
Language Arts

Curriculum Objectives
To improve listening comprehension and expressive writing skills.

Anti-Bias Area
Culture

Anti-Bias Skill
To promote awareness of and respect for diversity in culture.

Materials
Tiktala, by Margaret Shaw Mackinnon; paper and pencils; resources on animals.

Approach
Incorporation

Facilitation
Read *Tiktala.* Focus the discussion on the act of transformation and see if the children can identify how it happens on at least three levels in the text: human to animal; child to carver; change in her father.

Use questions to elicit the children's understanding of some of the underlying issues of this book:

1. loss of traditional ways and beliefs due to White European influences;
2. Inuit belief in spirits that guide and teach;
3. meaning behind Inuit carvings;
4. reason behind the seal's fear and hatred of humans;
5. Arctic environment—habitat for humans, animals and fish; and
6. life in the far North—traditional versus contemporary.

As a follow-up activity ask the children to select an animal and write a short story about their own transformation from human to animal. Refer them to the appropriate resources so they can blend factual information with their imagination.

Building a Dome

Age
9–12 years

Curriculum Area
Mathematics

Curriculum Objectives
To understand the properties of solids; to improve measurement and perceptual-motor coordination skills.

Anti-Bias Area
Culture

Anti-Bias Skill
To promote awareness of and respect for diversity in culture.

Materials
Straws; pipe cleaners; felt material; scissors; pencils; glue; and rulers.

Approach
Incorporation

Facilitation
Prior to this activity, the students need to be familiar with geometric solids as part of the math curriculum (two surfaces, flat and curved, half-circle shape). It is important for the class to learn that the dome shape of the Inuit's traditional snow home is critical to its success in the harsh northern environment. The secret is based on the lack of a roof or any other framework requiring beam supports. In this way the strong Arctic winds sweep over and down around the snow structure not against. It is precisely the wind pressure over the curved shape that makes the building stronger.

Set out the materials and present the task for pairs or individual students. Have a solid dome as a model. The students will need to experiment with the pipe cleaners and straws as they create the dome frame and then use the felt material as the covering.

Remind the students that the word *igloo* means a house of any kind. Igloos were primarily constructed as temporary shelters by hunters during their winter outings.

Constructing an Igluvigak

Age
9–11 years

Curriculum Area
Mathematics

Curriculum Objectives
To recognize gradation as one of the properties of domeness; to improve perceptual-motor coordination and measurement skills.

Anti-Bias Area
Culture

Anti-Bias Skill
To promote awareness of and respect for diversity in culture.

Materials
Styrofoam trays; large chunks of insulating materials; glue; cardboard base; rulers; scissors; and *Frozen Land. Vanishing Culture,* by Jan Reynolds.

Approach
Incorporation

Facilitation
This activity is intended as a follow-up to *Building a Dome.* Inform the students that the snow homes were primarily used as temporary shelters during hunting trips; traditional homes were built partially underground using rocks and mounds of earth. Remind students that today the Inuit live in prefab wooden houses.

Students should be familiar with the steps involved in the actual construction of the Inuit's snow home before starting this task. A good resource to share initially with the students is *Houses of Snow, Skin, and Bones,* by Bonnie Shemie. Step-by-step directions include:

1. Mark a circle in the snow, measuring 1 yard long, 2 feet wide, and ½ foot thick.
2. Cut first blocks of snow out from the center.
3. Lay these blocks on edge, not flat, along the contours of the circle.
4. Shave off the tops at an angle, sloping upward and slanting inward.
5. Lay the next row on top with each block tilting inward to close the circle. Each successive row continues to spiral up towards the top of the dome.
6. A low entrance tunnel is cut near the bottom, and is always lower than the inside living space.

This activity can be done individually or in small groups. Have the children create single homes or family homes that are connected by passages.

Expansion
Have the students do additional reading on the historical use of igloos, as well, to learn more about the living space and the scientific principles involved in warming the interior.

Students can also do a comparative study of the different housing constructed by the Alaskan Eskimos.

Multiple Meanings

Age
9–11 years

Curriculum Area
Language Arts

Curriculum Objectives
To learn about prefixes; to develop encoding skills; to increase vocabulary.

Anti-Bias Area
Culture

Anti-Bias Skills
To promote awareness of and respect for diversity in culture; to recognize, label, and discuss similarities and differences.

Materials
List of root words on chart paper; dictionaries; paper and pens.

Approach
Incorporation

Facilitation
As part of the exploration of Inuit culture, the children can explore Inuktitut, which has no relation to any other spoken languages. Inuktitut is complicated because one word may have many meanings. In the Inuktitut language, the words and word roots are used to form complete thoughts or sentences. Remind children that as toddlers, they too used one word to mean a whole idea—more = I want more milk to drink).

As an example: *Igdlo,* meaning house, can be changed to mean big house by adding the suffix *-rssuag;* a person who builds a big house is called *igdlorssualiopoq.* So prefixes and suffixes are an integral part of the Inuktitut language.

The English language also makes use of prefixes and suffixes. This activity focuses on adding the prefix *dis* to a selection of root words. The students have to choose 8–10 root words, add the prefix, and check the meaning of the newly formed word in the dictionary if they are unsure. They need to create sentences that show the meaning of the new word. Elicit from the group that adding the prefix *dis* changes the meaning of a word to something negative.

Root Words

allow	behave	guise	miss
appear	card	illusion	arm
agree	claim	locate	advantage
appoint	close	like	credit
approve	count	own	please

The Inuit and Ecology

Age
9–11 years

Curriculum Area
Science

Curriculum Objectives
To learn about ecology; to create a tree diagram.

Anti-Bias Area
Culture

Anti-Bias Skill
To recognize, label, and discuss similarities and differences.

Materials
Experience chart paper; colored markers; resource books on Arctic peoples.

Approach
Incorporation

Facilitation

Begin a discussion with the entire class about the Inuit's belief that harmonious interaction with the environment is necessary for their survival. Describe the harsh climate and environment of a land that is a polar desert for nine months of the year. Ask the students to list the daily challenges to survival faced by the Inuit. A partial list would include: food, clothing, shelter, tools, weapons, heat, and light.

With the Inuit value of "everything is scarce and nothing is to be wasted" guiding daily existence, ask the class to brainstorm all the possible uses of the caribou. A tree diagram should emerge from this activity:

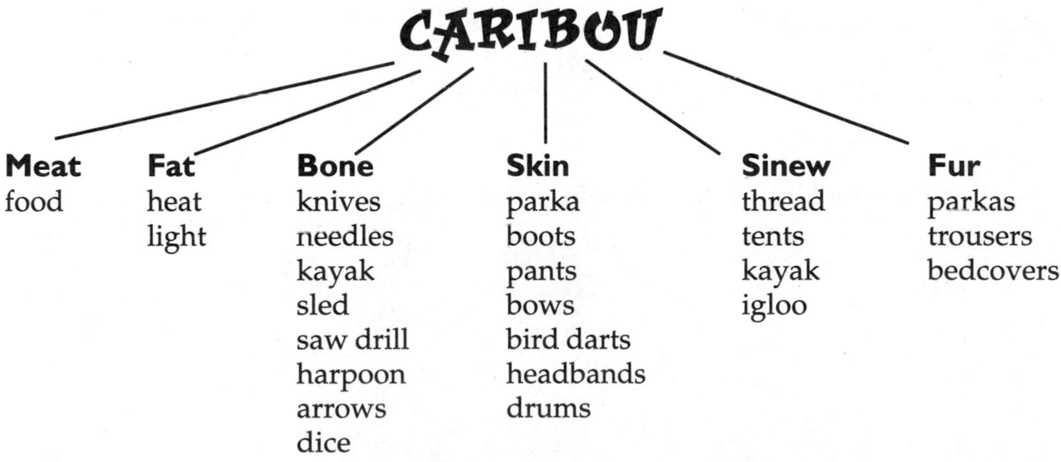

For another opportunity to practice organizing information, have the students individually create their own tree diagram for the other important Arctic animals, such as the seal, whale, and polar bear.

Carving Experience

Age

9–11 years

Curriculum Area

Visual Arts

Curriculum Objectives

To learn sculpting techniques; to experiment with three-dimensional art materials.

Anti-Bias Area

Culture

Anti-Bias Skill

To promote awareness of and respect for diversity in cultures.

Materials

Photos of Inuit soapstone/whalebone/ivory carvings, masks, and stone-cut prints; clay; soap; and sculpting utensils. Refer to *Tiktala,* by Margaret Shaw Mackinnon.

Approach

Incorporation

Facilitation

The focus of Tiktala was her desire to become a great carver. Supply the students with background information about this Inuit art form. Discuss the belief by Inuit carvers that the shape of the animal/person already exists in the stone, ivory, or whalebone, so they must talk to it, hold it, feel it, even sing to it, before they can release the hidden shape. The carvers always finish the carving process on the same day. The finishing process includes smoothing the carving with another stone; soaking it in seal oil for a few days; and hand-rubbing it to make it shine.

Make available the sculpting materials of clay and/or soap. The latter is a more difficult medium and the children's abilities and perceptual motor coordination need to be taken into consideration. Encourage them to really think about the animal's shape and characteristics before attempting to carve it.

Expansion

Stencil cutouts and ink art form; sewing fabric with bone needles and thick thread.

Spirits of the North

Age

9–11 years

Curriculum Area

Language Arts

Curriculum Objectives

To increase ability to compare and think critically.

Anti-Bias Area

Belief

Anti-Bias Skill

To recognize, label, and discuss similarities and differences.

Materials

List of spirits that affect daily life; chart paper; and markers. *Goddesses, Heroes and Shamans: A Young People's Guide to World Mythology* is a useful resource. Refer to *Tiktala,* by Margaret Shaw Mackinnon.

Approaches

Incorporation and Modified Personalization

Facilitation

Remind the class that Tiktala's journey of discovery was assisted by a spirit who transformed her body. Lead the class in a discussion of the Inuit belief system. Encourage the children to compare Inuit ideas with those that might be similar to their own family's beliefs or practices, or those of friends. Here are the most fundamental principles to discuss:

1. The supernatural is a normal part of everyday life. Get them to define *supernatural.*
   - The world of nature is controlled by spirits who can help people or play tricks on them: Sedna is the sea spirit who lives at the bottom of the sea and is responsible for seals, fish, and whales; Sila is the air spirit and watches over birds; Tarqeq is the moon spirit who lives in the sky and watches over humans.
   - It is important to keep these spirits happy otherwise they will drive away the animals, causing poor hunting and fishing.
   - Good spirits live in the upper worlds; bad spirits, in the lower worlds.
2. Inuit believe everything has a soul and when someone or something dies, the spirit can enter another living creature and be reborn. When a person dies, part of the soul is reborn in a new baby. When an animal dies, part of the soul is reborn and they become another hunted animal. (Similar to the concept of reincarnation in Buddhism.)
3. No one supreme god exists (like gods and goddesses in Hinduism).
4. The shaman is the only person with power to contact the spirits directly. He can get answers to important questions and problems (role of priests).
5. Inuit have many taboos (discuss the meaning). For example, they are not allowed to handle land and sea animals together. That means the caribou and seal can not be eaten on the same day (like the dietary habits of both Jews and Muslims).

(*continued*)

6. Inuits wear amulets (religious charms) to protect against evil spirits: owl claws mean strong hands; caribou ears mean good hearing (role of the cross, worry dolls, and other items in various religions).

Develop a comparative chart with the students. Ask them to research these belief concepts at home or in their community. Return to this topic in a week's time to fill in the chart and make comparisons. Remember to include the children whose families may be atheists.

Arctic Nutrition

Age

9–11 years

Curriculum Area

Science

Curriculum Objectives

To learn about the role of vitamins/minerals in nutrition; to develop a positive attitude toward healthy eating habits.

Anti-Bias Area

Culture

Anti-Bias Skill

To recognize, label, and discuss similarities and differences.

Materials

Comparison chart; markers; and food guide illustrating vitamins derived from key foods.

Approach

Incorporation

Facilitation

Gather the class around the comparison chart drawn on the board. Across the top of the chart list the basic foods of the Inuit. Underneath fill in the spaces with the appropriate vitamins and minerals derived from these foods. In another colored marker, write in foods the children eat that have the same nutritional value.

Discuss how the human body needs certain vitamins and minerals in order to grow and keep healthy, however, the sources of these vitamins can be very different depending on what is available in one's environment.

Inuit	seal	vetch roots	blubber	wild berries	fish	whale skin	bird eggs
	Vitamin A Vitamin D	fiber	essential fatty acids	Vitamin C	calcium	Vitamin C	iron
North American					milk		liver

Comparing how dietary needs are met in different cultures.

Ecology Debate

Age
9–11 years

Curriculum Area
Language Arts

Curriculum Objectives
To strengthen critical thinking skills and seeing two points of view; to express opinions and thoughts on challenging issues and concepts.

Anti-Bias Area
Culture

Anti-Bias Skill
To encourage cooperative group efforts.

Materials
Chart paper and markers.

Approach
Incorporation

Facilitation
Explain to the class the basic framework and principles of a debate. Draw a chart with *Pro* and *Con* columns, and title the topic "The Slaughter of Seals Is Necessary." Get the class to brainstorm and discuss the issues relevant to killing seals by the Inuit versus the people from south of the Arctic. Help them to see the ecological concerns (held not only by the Inuit but also by many in North America) and values attributed to both cultures.

Divide a group of six children into a panel with three for and three against massive seal killings. Have them prepare short arguments based on the information derived from the large group discussion. Try another topic, such as "Industrial Pollutants Cause the Decay of the Inuit Way of Life," on another day to sustain practice in this skill area.

Who Belongs Here?

Age
9–11 years

Curriculum Area
Social Studies

Curriculum Objectives
To explore the reasons for immigration; to introduce the term *refugee.*

Anti-Bias Areas
Race, Culture

Anti-Bias Skill
To demonstrate empathy.

Materials
Who Belongs Here? An American Story, by Margy Burns-Knight.

Approaches
Incorporation and Personalization

Facilitation
Read *Who Belongs Here?* Engage the class in a discussion about the reasons why people need to leave their countries and emigrate to another. List factors such as famine, civil war, unemployment, social change resulting in exclusionary government policies, etc. Define the terms *immigrant* and *refugee.* Invite visitors from the community to speak to the class about their experiences and feelings related to the immigration process. Ensure that the children understand their fears and anxieties about coming to a strange land. Ask the children to write letters thanking the guests for sharing their time and information.

Community Resources
Centers for new immigrants; English as Second Language training centers.

Interviewing for Information

Age
9–11 years

Curriculum Area
Language Arts

Curriculum Objectives
To organize, plan, and implement an interview; to practice writing, organizing, and presenting information.

Anti-Bias Areas
Race, Culture

Anti-Bias Skill
To think critically about people and events.

Materials
Paper and pen.

Approach
Personalization

Facilitation
As a follow-up to the *Who Belongs Here?* activity, have the students work in small groups of four to devise a list of questions that they would like to ask of someone who has immigrated to this country. In preparation, review the kinds of information they learned from the previous day's visitor. Facilitate this task by brainstorming a number of questions as a large group. Emphasize more open-ended questions that begin with words such as how, why, who, what, where, and when.

Students can either interview families within the school or larger community. The teacher will need to research and seek assistance from community agencies that support newcomers in order to make the necessary arrangements for the students.

The second part of this activity focuses on organizing and presenting the information they obtain. Students have a choice to:

- write a story;
- design a newsletter; or
- provide a dramatic re-creation of the event.

Expansion
Each group can do further research on the country of origin for the family involved. Booklets containing information on geography, climate, currency, agricultural/industrial products, population, language(s) spoken, and religion(s) practiced can be compiled and shared.

Additional Resources
Lerner Publications has produced an excellent series about families who were driven from their own countries, and the struggles and adjustments they had to make resettling in the United States as immigrants.

I Can't Understand You

Age
9–11 years

Curriculum Area
Language Arts

Curriculum Objectives
To explore the rules of expressive language; to increase auditory discrimination and recognition skills.

Anti-Bias Area
Culture

Anti-Bias Skills
To promote awareness of and respect for diversity in culture; to avoid name-calling.

Materials
Paper and pen; drum; blindfolds (optional).

Approach
Incorporation

Facilitation
Divide the class into groups of four and ask them to develop a language that will be unique to their group. After each group is finished, mix the students up by having them walk around to a drum beat. Next, ask them to close their eyes and from where they are standing, begin talking in their "language." Still blindfolded or with eyes closed, students should try to locate other members of their group by listening for familiar vocalizations.

Debrief after the activity concludes with a discussion on how they felt when they:

- couldn't understand what anyone was saying?
- suddenly heard a familiar word?
- found someone who understood them?

Help students connect how immigrants must feel in a new country, and what gives them feelings of comfort and security. Ask the students to stop and consider what they felt before about children who always spoke a different language with one another. Did they ever hear name-calling and teasing directed against these children? Let them discuss their feelings on this topic. Encourage feelings of empathy and tolerance.

Contributions Made by Immigrants

Age

9–11 years

Curriculum Area

Social Studies

Curriculum Objectives

To recognize similarities across groups and differences within groups; to see oneself as a member of a larger group.

Anti-Bias Areas

Culture, Race

Anti-Bias Skills

To recognize, label, and discuss similarities and differences; to encourage openness to new experiences.

Materials

Word cards: kindergarten, poltergeist, weiner, hamburger (German); bungalow, bandanna, jungle, loot (Hindi); tea, mandarin (Chinese); tycoon (Chinese-Japanese); judo (Japanese); tattoo (Tahitian); pictures of jeans, rice, tortillas, etc. Refer to *Who Belongs Here?* by Margy Burns-Knight.

Approaches

Incorporation and Modified Personalization

Facilitation

Have a discussion about the many facets of daily life that reflect cultural traditions: clothing, food recipes, music, stories, games, dances, hobbies, dishes/utensils, and language. As the class shares similarities and differences within these areas, point out how much of what we experience has been because of what immigrants from all over the world have contributed.

Present word cards to demonstrate how many English words are foreign in derivation. Ask students to think about games, common foods, and forms of entertainment they enjoy that have their origins in other countries.

Return to the original question posed in the book—What if everyone who lives in the United States now, but whose ancestors came from another country, was forced to return to their homelands? Who would be left? Who belongs here?

Expansion

Have the children research games, songs, or stores traditional to their families. Over the course of a week ask each child to share and/or teach something to the whole group.

Political Activists

Age

9–11 years

Curriculum Area

Social Studies

Curriculum Objectives

To use written texts as sources of information; to increase knowledge about historical figures who were political activists.

Anti-Bias Areas

Race, Culture

Anti-Bias Skill

To be proactive in helping others.

Materials

History texts; paper and pen. Refer to *Who Belongs Here?* by Margy Burns-Knight.

Approach

Incorporation

Facilitation

Begin this activity with the question: What does *freedom* mean to you? Ask the class for their responses to some political situations fairly common around the world. How do you think you would feel if:

- it were unsafe to walk outside?
- you were not allowed to go to school?
- your parents were arrested?
- you were denied entrance to a sporting club?
- you were not permitted to socialize with certain groups of people?
- you and your siblings were sent away to live with distant relatives for safety?

Use the information about Dith Pran from *Who Belongs Here?* as an example of a political activist who fought to bring about changes and peace in Cambodia.

Distribute texts or simple narratives on the lives of other significant political activists: Nelson Mandela, Dolores Huerta, Dr. Martin Luther King, Jr., Mahatma Gandhi, Aung San Suu Kyi, etc. Have the class read the texts for information. Group the students by political figure and have each group present key facts about the cause and what the activist did (is doing) to bring the struggle to the attention of the rest of the world.

Expansion

Read *Fighters, Refugees, and Immigrants. A Story of the Hmong,* by Mace Goldfarb.

Recipes for Peace

Age
9–11 years

Curriculum Area
Language Arts

Curriculum Objectives
To increase vocabulary related to prejudice and intolerance; to promote dictionary and thesaurus skills.

Anti-Bias Areas
All Areas

Anti-Bias Skills
To think critically about people and events; to be proactive against discriminatory behaviors.

Materials
Dictionaries; thesauruses; paper and pen; recipe cards; and a box. Refer to *Who Belongs Here?* by Margy Burns-Knight.

Approach
Incorporation

Facilitation
Discuss the children's understanding of the words *prejudice* and *discrimination.* Refer back to the incidents/situations depicted in *Who Belongs Here?* as illustrations of these terms. Bring out a list of words that are critical to the students' understanding of bias:

- intolerance
- hate mongering
- verbal and physical harassment
- advocacy
- equity
- negotiation
- peace
- caring
- respect

Divide the class into small groups and distribute dictionaries, thesauruses, and cards. The task for each group is to:

1. come up with a definition for each term;
2. decide what ingredients are usually needed for it to happen; and
3. decide what procedures need to be followed for the terms denoting positive actions and what things need to change for the terms associated with negative actions.

Review the cards as a class and make necessary revisions. This enables the entire group to learn about the barriers and solutions to living respectfully in a diverse society.

Each group will design its own recipe card and a box will be presented as a gift to the school.

Expansion
Read *The Bracelet,* by Yoshiko Uchida and Joanna Yardley, which depicts the internment of Japanese Americans during World War II.

The Many Forms of Proactivism

Age

9–11 years

Curriculum Area

Language Arts

Curriculum Objectives

To develop expressive writing skills; to develop a spirit of proactivism.

Anti-Bias Areas

All Areas

Anti-Bias Skill

To participate in group action on behalf of others.

Materials

Word cards; paper and pen.

Approach

Incorporation

Facilitation

Prepare cards with the following words: boycott, march, starvation strike, jail, writing letters, circulating petitions, demonstrations. Introduce the topic with a brief overview of how people, in the past and present, have used a variety of methods to fight against discrimination and inequality, or be proactive. Have the class try to predict what is involved for each form. Ask the students to think about the following questions:

- On what issue would you take a stand?
- What form would your proactivism take?
- What changes would you like to make?
- What do you think might happen to you in response to your proactivism?

After a class brainstorming of issues that are either school-, community-, or city-related, have the students design individual written answers. Bring the class together to review and discuss the proactive suggestions. Ask the class to prioritize the issues, and facilitate the implementation of the suggested strategies.

Who Belongs Here? II

Age

8–10 years

Curriculum Area

Social Studies

Curriculum Objectives

To learn about the first peoples of America and reflect on mistreatment of Native Americans.

Anti-Bias Area

Culture

Anti-Bias Skills

To promote awareness of and respect for diversity in culture; to demonstrate empathy.

Approach

Incorporation

Facilitation

Introduce this topic with the following story.

> Once upon a time a new leader traveled from a faraway country to take over the ruling of this land. In his speech to the natives of this land, who were terrified of losing their traditional way of life, he told them not to be alarmed or worried as nothing would change. He said:
>
> "You will be able to keep your homes, however, all the homes will be moved to a place called a reservation (reserves in Canada). This will be the only land available for you to live on, but it is yours. You will not be allowed to rent or lease land anywhere else. This will give more space to my people who are coming to this land.
>
> "You will be able to continue educating your children, but they will attend special schools where they will be taught our language, our religion, and our philosophy of life. They will be just like our children who are coming from my country. The children will be great friends.
>
> "You will be able to eat your usual foods, but your fishing and hunting privileges will be restricted to make food available for my people who will be arriving shortly.
>
> "So as you can see, nothing has changed and you can live exactly the same as before. We will all share this land and live cooperatively together on it."

Ask the class to evaluate what they just heard, hypothesize what life would be like, and draw conclusions about the fate of the people in this story. Explain that the people in this story were Native Americans and that historically they were the first inhabitants of North America. Take the opportunity to introduce the different nations of Native Americans as a new unit of study.

Chair for My Mother

Age
7–8 years

Curriculum Area
Language Arts

Curriculum Objectives
To improve listening comprehension and expressive writing skills.

Anti-Bias Areas
Family Composition, Class

Anti-Bias Skill
To demonstrate empathy.

Materials
Chair for My Mother, by Vera B. Williams.

Approach
Incorporation

Facilitation
Read *Chair for My Mother* and ask the children to imagine that their friend's or neighbor's home has burned down. Ask them what they would personally be willing to give up in order to make it better for their friend/neighbor?

Emphasize that support for people can come from three sources:

1. family;
2. friends; and/or
3. community.

Ask them to think about an experience they or their family had, where a family member, friend, or community member helped them out. Have the class write a short paragraph describing what happened, who helped, and what kind of assistance they received.

What Do Moms Do?

Age
7–8 years

Curriculum Area
Language Arts

Curriculum Objectives
To discuss the issue of job equity; to classify people using two or more abstract attributes.

Anti-Bias Area
Gender

Anti-Bias Skills
To promote respect for gender and racial equity; to challenge stereotypes.

Materials
Mommies at Work, by Eve Merriam.

Approach
Incorporation

Facilitation
As a follow-up to the *Chair for My Mother* activity, read Eve Merriam's book *Mommies at Work.* Engage the children in a discussion about all the possible employment opportunities available to women. Have them comment on the job options presented in the book and support any challenges made by the children to stereotypical thinking.

Ask the children to consider how many roles mothers generally have? Point out that most have a nurturing role and a professional role. Get the children to write a short paragraph on the variety of tasks their primary caregiver does for the family. Read *Daddies at Work* by the same author to present a full perspective.

Money Jars

Age
7–8 years

Curriculum Area
Mathematics

Curriculum Objectives
To practice computation problems; to practice place value with money.

Anti-Bias Area
Class

Anti-Bias Skill
To promote awareness of and respect for diversity in class.

Materials
Jars with nickels, dimes, quarters; grocery store flyers; pencils; and paper.

Approach
Incorporation

Facilitation
Fill up the jars with nickels, dimes, and quarters. Have some groups work at this task in rotation to ensure everyone has the opportunity to manipulate the required materials. Distribute the food flyers and ask the children to make a list of all the foods they could buy using different combinations of money. Another task would be to calculate the total amount of money in the jar and detail what food purchases they could make to within the final nickel.

Ask what food items they would have liked to purchase but couldn't afford. Review the food purchases and discuss which items are nutritious and necessary for good health. If they didn't include dairy, grains, or fruits/vegetables, ask them to justify their selections.

Have them think about the connection between eating healthy foods (growing strong) and the ability to pay.

Community Project

Age
7–8 years

Curriculum Area
Social Studies

Curriculum Objectives
To enhance community awareness and civic responsibility.

Anti-Bias Areas
Class, Culture, Race

Anti-Bias Skills
To participate in group action on behalf of others; to be proactive in helping others.

Materials
Paper and pencils.

Approaches
Incorporation and Personalization

Facilitation
Invite a worker from a community agency that works with families in need. Have them describe what life is like for these families and what they need to make their lives better. Let the class discuss the variety of projects they could undertake and then decide as a group which one they would like to try: winter clothing drive, toy collection, bake sale with proceeds to an agency, etc.

Have the students plan and organize the project, and deliver the proceeds. Facilitate and expedite where necessary, but it is important that the children take the responsibility from beginning to end in order to derive personal satisfaction from their achievement.

Community Resources
Consult with community agencies that support families in need, local shelters, and social workers.

Construction Time

Age
7–8 years

Curriculum Area
Visual Arts

Curriculum Objectives
To apply measurement, problem-solving, and design skills in combination with refined eye-hand coordination; to promote creative expression.

Anti-Bias Areas
Gender, Class

Anti-Bias Skills
To listen to and value other points of view; to encourage cooperative group efforts.

Materials
Variety of construction materials: boxes, containers, tubes, wood in varying sizes, etc.; nails; hammer; safety goggles; stuffing; fabric samples; needles and thread; rulers; pencil; bristol board; markers; string; scissors; glue; and tape.

Approach
Incorporation

Facilitation
Present the task of furnishing a home. Discuss the available materials and have the class generate a list of the furniture they would like to make. Facilitate division of groups according to the categories of furniture to be created. Encourage divergent approaches to design and production. Remind the class that not all families have the same kind or quantity of furniture because of their economic status. Lend assistance where necessary.

Community Resource
Donations of building materials.

In Other Words

Age

8–10 years

Curriculum Area

Language Arts

Curriculum Objectives

To increase comprehension and critical thinking skills; to increase ability to describe personal feelings and make personal decisions.

Anti-Bias Area

Ability

Anti-Bias Skills

To listen to and value other points of view; to promote awareness of and respect for diversity in ability.

Materials

In Other Words, by John C. Walker.

Approach

Incorporation

Facilitation

Preface the reading by brainstorming about communication methods other than talking or writing. Read the book and focus the discussion on the following questions:

- How would you let people know what you are feeling and thinking about if you couldn't talk?
- What do you think other children might feel about you if they asked you a question and you didn't answer them? How do you think it might feel if people didn't understand you?
- How do you think it might feel to be left out of activities with other children? What do you think children's feelings about your wheelchair might be?
- Who do you think arrived on the spaceship?
- Which decision would you make if you were in the character's position? Would you go or stay? Why?

This text gives children the opportunity to explore their feelings about others who are unable to communicate verbally. If children exhibit fears or make pre-prejudicial comments, help them to recognize the source of their discomfort.

Ensure the class understands that despite the characters' lack of mobility, comprehensible speech, and coordination, they were able to sustain a relationship of deep friendship and understanding.

Augmentative Communication Experience

Age
8–10 years

Curriculum Area
Language Arts

Curriculum Objectives
To learn how to communicate in a different language; to strengthen visual memory.

Anti-Bias Area
Ability

Anti-Bias Skills
To encourage openness to new experiences; to demonstrate empathy.

Materials
Sufficient copies of Mayer-Johnson's *Picture Communication Symbols.*

Approaches
Modified Personalization and Personalization

Facilitation
Introduce the pic symbols as the system that children and adults with nonverbal abilities use to communicate. Invite a communication facilitator from the community who can explain and teach this augmentative communication system to the class. Have the children work in groups of four to arrange the symbols in response to one another's communication efforts. For example:

- I bought a pair of shoes and they are too big.
- I need money for a snack.
- I don't know how to get to the museum.

Afterwards, discuss with the class what they needed to learn, what they found difficult, and what they found enjoyable.

Community Resource
Communication facilitator from local agency working with autistic children.

Mechanical Busy Board

Age
8–10 years

Curriculum Area
Social Studies (Values and Attitudes)

Curriculum Objectives
To strengthen eye-hand coordination; to use problem-solving strategies.

Anti-Bias Area
Ability

Anti-Bias Skill
To encourage openness to new experiences; to demonstrate empathy.

Materials
Mechanical board with switches that need to be flipped and pulled; bolt; chain lock; and knob to open door.

Approach
Modified Personalization

Facilitation
Instruct the children to operate the variety of mechanical hardware (1) without the use of their fingers and (2) with the use of one hand only.

Afterwards have the children discuss the emotions they experienced and the strategies they used to cope with the challenges.

Riding in Someone Else's Wheelchair

Age

8–10 years

Curriculum Area

Social Studies (Values and Attitudes)

Curriculum Objectives

To discover motor coordination and spatial relations required for nonambulatory people; to evaluate obstacles and generate solutions.

Anti-Bias Area

Ability

Anti-Bias Skills

To encourage openness to new experiences; to demonstrate empathy.

Materials

Wheelchair.

Approach

Modified Personalization

Facilitation

Rent a wheelchair for a day. Have the children take turns running errands to the office or participating in normal daily routines: moving around the classroom for supplies, getting a drink from the water fountain, getting jackets from corridor hooks, enjoying recess activities, going to the bathroom, etc., all in the wheelchair. Have the children work in pairs so they can make a list of difficulties and obstacles they encounter during their turns. At the end of the day, have the children read their lists and compare issues. Ask them to generate short- and long-term solutions to the problems they identified.

Write the word *handicap* on the board and ask them to think about its meaning. Have them discuss the issue of whether an individual is handicapped or if the physical environment is handicapping.

Writing without Hands

Age

8–10 years

Curriculum Area

Language Arts

Curriculum Objective

To demonstrate ability to write letters for different purposes.

Anti-Bias Area

Ability

Anti-Bias Skills

To demonstrate empathy; to participate in group action on behalf of others.

Materials

Computer or typewriter(s); and headpointers for writing.

Approach

Modified Personalization

Facilitation

Give the class the task of writing a short letter using the headpointer on the keyboard of the computer or the typewriter. The children can work in pairs to facilitate the process. They can select a topic for a letter from the following options:

- a thank-you note to the visitor from the local community agency;
- a note to parents describing what they have learned about nonverbal communication;
- a note to the principal describing the challenges/barriers of being a wheelchair-bound student in the school; or
- a note to the principal discussing short- and long-term solutions for those who come to school in wheelchairs.

Explain the function of the headpointer for children and adults who have poor motor coordination, which in addition to the above, can be used to operate any adapted-touch device such as remote control for television, lights, etc.

Community Resource

Headpointer may be borrowed from community agencies devoted to working with people who have physical challenges and communication disorders.

Communication Machine

Age
8–10 years

Curriculum Area
Science

Curriculum Objective
To design new technology to assist people who are nonverbal.

Anti-Bias Area
Ability

Anti-Bias Skills
To demonstrate empathy; to examine alternatives.

Materials
Paper; colored pencils; and markers.

Approach
Incorporation

Facilitation
The task for the class is to invent a machine that will transmit feelings. Have the children draw a diagram to show how it will work, and write a brief description of how to operate it.

Expansion
Read *Silent Lotus,* by Jeanne Lee, to create an uplifting mood about children who are unable to communicate verbally.

Getting to Know One Another

Age
7–11 years

Curriculum Area
Social Studies

Curriculum Objective
To appreciate diversity among classmates.

Anti-Bias Areas
Gender, Race, Culture, Ability, Family Composition, Belief

Anti-Bias Skills
To value uniqueness of self, others, and families; to promote awareness of and respect for diversity in culture.

Materials
An introduction sheet with a list of 20 questions for each child in the class.

Approach
Modified Personalization

Facilitation
Distribute the introduction sheet to each student. Instruct them to ask each other any of the questions but that they can only use a classmate's name *once.* After the sheets are filled in, have the groups review the little-known, special facts about one another.

This exercise is a good way to introduce the class to the anti-bias approach, because it demonstrates concretely how the different areas of bias are integrated some way into everyone. It also helps to move the scope of understanding beyond the classroom.

Getting to Know One Another

1. ______________ has eaten calamari.
2. ______________ knows someone who uses a hearing aid.
3. ______________ has traveled to Europe/Asia/South America.
4. ______________ speaks another language.
5. ______________ has relatives in Central America.
6. ______________ has a grandparent who lives with them.
7. ______________ has a parent born outside the United States.
8. ______________ has eaten dim sum.
9. ______________ knows where Tagalog is spoken.
10. ______________ has been to 10 or more states.
11. ______________ knows someone who can prepare sushi.
12. ______________ can read and write Spanish/Hebrew/Vietnamese.
13. ______________ can perform folk dances from other countries.
14. ______________ has been to a Passover seder.
15. ______________ likes roti and curry.
16. ______________ has friends from other cultures/religions.
17. ______________ listens to steel band music.
18. ______________ has a friend in a wheelchair.
19. ______________ has a friend who wears a hijab.
20. ______________ knows a family whose parents have an interracial marriage.

Caption It

Age
7–11 years

Curriculum Area
Social Studies

Curriculum Objective
To interpret reality through creative expression.

Anti-Bias Areas
All Areas

Anti-Bias Skills
To make inferences; to listen to and value other points of view.

Materials
Newspaper and magazine photos in a clear file; paper and pen.

Approach
Incorporation

Facilitation
Start a collection of magazine and newspaper photos that depict people of different backgrounds, belief systems, abilities, and ages involved with others or in a specific situation. The photos should allow for divergent interpretations. For this activity divide the children into small groups and distribute a number of photos. Challenge them to create their own captions. Ask the children to read the captions and justify the decisions behind their thinking.

Expansion
Cut out articles related to issues of bias and snip off the headline. Paste the headlines and stories on separate cards and place in separate containers. Have the children select an article, read it, and find the correct matching headline.

Creative Holidays

Age

8–11 years

Curriculum Area

Social Studies

Curriculum Objective

To discover commonalities and differences in traditions and elements central to festive celebrations around the world.

Anti-Bias Area

Culture, Belief

Anti-Bias Skill

To promote awareness of and respect for diversity in class.

Materials

Flip chart paper and marker.

Approach

Incorporation

Facilitation

Tell the class that an alien from outer space is planning on visiting them tomorrow, and it wants to obtain information about the kinds of holidays that earthlings celebrate. Get the children to brainstorm answers to these questions:

- What kinds of events are causes for celebrations?
- What is the meaning of these occasions?
- Who celebrates them?
- Do people prepare special foods or do they fast?
- Do people celebrate publicly or privately at home?
- Do people get dressed up or put on special clothes?
- Are there people who do not celebrate any holidays?

From this discussion the class should get a sense of the great variety of approaches that exist to holiday celebrations, and that each family has its own way of acknowledging special events that need to be valued.

Expansion

As a follow-up activity have the children, in small groups, invent a new holiday. Each holiday should have a name, a purpose, a list of participants, and a description of how it will be celebrated.

Who Goes? Who Stays?

Age
9–11 years

Curriculum Area
Social Studies

Curriculum Objective
To discover how discrimination becomes institutionalized in society.

Anti-Bias Areas
All Areas

Anti-Bias Skill
To value uniqueness of self, others, and families.

Materials
List of candidate names and their backgrounds, enough for six groups; pens.

Approach
Modified Personalization

Facilitation
Describe the following scenario to the class.

> It is the year 2010 and a new planet, Orpheo, has been discovered. Your parents have been charged with the responsibility of colonizing this planet with scientists, engineers, and a medical team from around the world. You have been delegated the task of selecting the first group of students to study there. Over 100 eager youth applied for this mission, and the list has been cut down to 10. Unfortunately, there is only space for five on the shuttle. You need to make the final decision of who goes and who stays. You will be required to state your reasons.

Distribute the candidate list to each group. Tell them to circle the numbers of the successful candidates. Circulate around the groups to facilitate and to observe the students' comments. Bring the class together and record their decisions on a chart. Have the class analyze the basis for their decisions; if they had difficulty, explain why. For those with overt prejudicial opinions, help them to see how discrimination happens in society and who really holds the power. Allow the children to express their discomforts, and over the year, help them work through these issues of ignorance and fear.

Candidates

1. Fatuma—female, from Somalia, who excels in physics and chemistry. She wears a traditional hijab and needs to be veiled in the presence of men. Age 16.
2. Gregory—male, of African-American descent, is an air force cadet who graduated in the top 10 of his class. Age 17.
3. Natalie—female, of Ukrainian descent, received top marks in national math competitions. She is deaf and has some visual impairment. Age 16.
4. Permida—female, from China, speaks six languages fluently. Age 17.
5. Joy—female, a Sioux Indian, has expertise in botany and traditional healing. Age 16.
6. Jorge—male, born in Mexico, is an expert in agriculture and horticulture. Age 17.
7. Nancy—female, of Italian descent, won awards all through high school for her leadership abilities. Age 17.
8. Nguyen—male, born in Vietnam, won a scholarship to Harvard University to pursue studies in geology. Age 17.
9. Devon—male, of Jamaican descent, is an accomplished musician. Age 16.
10. David—male, Jewish, was the national champion in survival skills before an accident left him paralyzed in a wheelchair. Age 16.

Oral Histories

Age

9–11 years

Curriculum Area

Social Studies

Curriculum Objective

To discover factors that influenced lifestyles of preceding generations.

Anti-Bias Areas

Culture, Class

Anti-Bias Skill

To value uniqueness of self, others, and families.

Materials

Family questionnaire.

Approach

Modified Personalization

Facilitation

This activity continues the search into individual family identity by exploring the histories of grandparents, aunts/uncles, etc. Have the class generate a list of questions that will be compiled into a questionnaire for each child to take home and complete. Ask them to think about what aspects of daily living would they like to learn about from that generation, especially things that are important to them. For example:

- When and where were you born?
- Where did you go to school?
- How did you get to school?
- How many students were in the classroom?
- What subjects did you study?
- How did the teachers keep order?
- What games did you play at recess? after school?
- What books did you enjoy reading?
- How were children punished?
- What did you bring for lunch?
- What responsibilities did you have at home?
- What did you do for entertainment at night?
- What were your favorite activities on weekends?
- Did you get an allowance? How much per week?

The children can decide which family member to ask depending on availability. If family members are not available, then surrogate family members/friends are equally suitable. Once all the questionnaires are completed, have the class compare their answers.

Ensure children understand that each family's history is special and differences stem from a variety of factors: economic, cultural values, environmental, etc.

Expansion

If possible, children can record these interviews. An added bonus would be to hear family members relating these events in their own dialects.

Work and Leisure

Age

9–11 years

Curriculum Area

Social Studies

Curriculum Objective

To explore the economic and social organization of society.

Anti-Bias Areas

Culture, Gender, Age, Ability, Race, Class

Anti-Bias Skill

To recognize, label, and discuss similarities and differences.

Materials

Flip chart paper and markers.

Approach

Incorporation

Facilitation

Put up the words *work* and *leisure* as two separate headings and have the class brainstorm their meanings. Focus the discussion on the universal necessity of work to ensure the basics of life as well as the universal necessity for leisure time. What people do as "work" and "leisure" is influenced by their cultural background, age, where they live, and perhaps physical health. Have the group consider:

- what jobs/chores they do as part of the family;
- the concept of paid work versus volunteering;
- the number of hours people work; and
- what jobs need specialized training.

Under the leisure column get them to list the popular hobbies and sports in which they are involved.

For future discussion during the week, ask the children to interview two people:

1. Their parents or another adult to find out what jobs they have had. Which did they enjoy the most? If they could do anything, what would they choose? Why?
2. A retired adult/relative or friend to find out what do they do now that they have stopped working. Would they prefer to be working? Why or why not?

Have each student report back to the class, then compare and contrast the answers they obtained.

The Story of a Name

Age

10–11 years

Curriculum Area

Social Studies

Curriculum Objective

To learn about the origins of family names.

Anti-Bias Area

Culture

Anti-Bias Skills

To strengthen self-identity and increase self-esteem.

Materials

List of names and corresponding definitions.

Approach

Incorporation

Facilitation

Ask the class to hypothesize what they think the meaning of their family name might be. Explain that our ancestors had names that described:

1. their trade or profession;
2. their physical appearance;
3. their place of origin (usually referring to nature);
4. their moral character;
5. their nationality; or
6. their relationship to another person (Richardson, son of Richard, etc.).

Divide the class into five small groups and hand out lists of names that correspond to the first five major categories outlined above. Let the groups guess the meanings. Provide answer sheets afterwards. Have the children analyze the origin of their surnames.

Group 1 Trade/Profession

Archer __________
Century __________
Fowler __________
Sawyer __________
Skinner __________
Levine __________
Tyler __________
Fischer __________
Trotter __________
Wagner __________

Group 2 Physical Appearance

Black __________
Quartermain __________
Klein __________
Swift __________
Blundell __________
Gross __________
Read __________
Schwartz __________
Weiss __________
Cruikshank __________

Group 3 Place of Origin

Rivera ____________
Banks ____________
Stein ____________
Berg ____________
Torres ____________
Sutherland ____________
Rosenberg ____________
Goldstein ____________
Craig ____________

Group 4 Moral Character

Noble ____________
Hardy ____________
Hartman ____________
Fox ____________
Giddy ____________
Darwin ____________
Curtis ____________
Friedman ____________

Group 5 Nationality

Norman ____________
Frances ____________
Germain ____________
Scott ____________
Brett ____________
Cornell ____________
Dennis ____________
Roman ____________
Wallace ____________

Answer Sheet, *The Story of a Name*

Group 1: Trade/Profession (only the least obvious are provided)

Century—belt maker
Fowler—wild bird hunter
Sawyer—sawer of wood
Levine—wine dealer
Tyler—tile maker
Trotter—messenger
Wagner—wagon driver

Group 2: Physical Appearance (descendants of . . .)

Quartermain—man with four hands; mail gloves
Klein—small man
Blundell—blonde man
Gross—fat or large man
Read—red hair
Schwartz—darkish or swarthy
Weiss—white-haired/skin
Cruikshank—crooked legs

Group 3: Place of Origin

Rivera—near a brook or river
Stein—significant stone or rock
Berg—mountain
Rosenberg—rose mountain
Goldstein—goldsmith

Group 4: Moral Character

Darwin—dear friend
Curtis—educated and courteous
Friedman—peaceful man

Group 5: Nationality

Norman—France
Germain—Germany
Brett—Brittony
Dennis—Denmark
Wallace—Wales
Cornell—Cornwall

Homes and Houses

Age

8–11 years

Curriculum Area

Social Studies

Curriculum Objectives

To survey homes and discover differences in style within communities; to collect data, analyze information, and present results in graph form.

Anti-Bias Areas

Culture, Class

Anti-Bias Skill

To appreciate how people use objects differently.

Materials

Paper and pencils.

Approach

Incorporation

Facilitation

Types of housing, depending on if you live in a rural or urban setting, can either be distinctive among different parts of a city or homogenous in style. Have the students conduct a survey in their own neighborhoods, or take a small field trip to other communities in the city for a more thorough survey of housing styles. Create a checklist with the group beforehand to facilitate data collection and analysis. The checklist can include: types of building materials (wood, brick, stucco, or concrete); number of stories (bungalow, two-story, apartment building); architectural style (Victorian, Tudor, ranch, Georgian, villa); colors; those with driveways; etc.

After the group completes the survey, get them to organize the data and create bar graphs to represent visually the kind of housing that is in the area. Ask the students to think about the historic reasons for the diversity (or homogeneity), and how different cultural backgrounds influenced the way homes were designed.

Note: *Homes and Houses* and the next four activities can be treated as a single topic of study and are paginated sequentially even though the curriculum areas are mixed.

Houses around the World

Age
8–11 years

Curriculum Area
Social Studies

Curriculum Objective
To understand how geographic factors and social structure influence the construction of homes.

Anti-Bias Area
Culture

Anti-Bias Skill
To promote awareness of and respect for diversity in culture.

Materials
Come Over to My House, by Theo Le Sieg; *The Mud Family,* by Betsy James; flip chart paper and markers; reference books such as *Welcome Home,* by Sylvia White, or *A Children's Book on Houses and Homes,* by Carol Bowyer; and *National Geographic* magazines.

Approach
Incorporation

Facilitation
Read *Come Over to My House* or *Houses and Homes* as an introduction to the great diversity of homes that exist all over the world. Ask the class to generate a list of the different types of homes, and try to identify what climatic conditions would typically influence the design of such homes. Create columns on the flip chart that include hot/dry, jungle/rain forest, high mountainous, icy cold, and temperate. See if they can remember how to classify the houses under the appropriate headings.

Create another list that focuses on commonly used building materials: stone, brick, mud, wood, bamboo/grasses/canes, and wools/skins. Have the children try to match appropriate building materials with climatic groupings. Help them to connect that people all over the world build shelters, and that their design is dictated by the weather, available building materials, and social structure of the society.

Put out selected *National Geographic* magazines and reference books on houses around the world. Ask the children to select one area to conduct a more in-depth examination of people's homes; for example:

- Nabdam in Northern Ghana or Masakin in Sudan
- Yanomano Indians of Brazil
- Anatolian farms of Turkey
- Huichols of Western Mexico
- Traditional homes in Japan
- Dayaks in Borneo
- Tunnel homes in Coober Pedy, Australia

Have the children compare what they learned about these dwellings with what they know about North American homes. What do they think are the major differences and the reasons for them?

Expansion
For three-dimensional creative construction, introduce the resource *Pyramids to Pueblos. 15 Pop-up Models for Students to Make.*

Community Resources
Posters and photographs of houses from around the world. Collect brochures from travel agencies.

Houses on the Move

Age

8–11 years

Curriculum Area

Social Studies

Curriculum Objectives

To continue learning about the influences of geography and social structure on the construction of homes.

Anti-Bias Area

Culture

Anti-Bias Skill

To promote respect for diversity in culture.

Materials

Same as the *Houses around the World* activity; *Who Am I?* cards based on descriptions of house design and location.

Approach

Incorporation

Facilitation

This activity continues to explore the diversity in dwellings. The focus here is on homes that are either temporary or movable. Ask the children to think about why some people don't live in one place permanently, and what kinds of homes would be examples of such a wandering lifestyle.

Create two columns on flip chart paper labeled *Land* and *Water.* Fill in the columns with such responses as tents (Bedouin), caravans (Gypsies), Yurts (nomadic families in Mongolia, Iran), mobile homes, houseboats, lipas, sampans, tree houses, etc. Again, the discussion should emphasize that other people are just as comfortable in their homes as we are in our homes. The differences in design are what makes us all special.

To review the facts presented over the week, play a guessing game. With younger children, the teacher can create the riddle cards, while older children can design their own riddle cards to present to the class. For example:

1. My house is located in the marshlands of the Tigris river. It is built of giant reeds that are bent into a semicircular framework. The walls and roof are made of mats that I helped to weave from reeds. (marsh Arab from Southern Iraq)
2. My home is in a hot place where we don't have many trees. It is a very unusual type of home since I live inside cone-shaped volcanic rocks and have to climb a ladder to get into a window. (Anatolian cave dweller in Turkey)
3. My home is made of wood and is insulated with fiberglass because it gets quite cold in the winter. The roof is made of shingles and is gently sloped so that the snow will stay on for added warmth. (Northern United States and Canada)

Expansion

Let the children experiment with the construction of small-scale dwellings using a variety of materials: popsicle sticks, clay, and cane for weaving; mud bricks hardened outside by the sun and grasses for thatching; wood and tongue depressors, etc.

Famous Homes

Age
8–11 years

Curriculum Area
Language Arts

Curriculum Objectives
To practice reading and reporting skills.

Anti-Bias Area
Culture

Anti-Bias Skill
To encourage cooperative group efforts.

Materials
National Geographic magazines; pictures of famous homes; and reference books.

Approach
Incorporation

Facilitation
This activity focuses on famous houses and asks the children to read reference books to obtain specific information on these structures. Get the group to brainstorm the topic of famous homes and to guess who lives (or lived) in them.

Break the class into small groups and have each group investigate such places as the White House, Buckingham Palace, the Taj Mahal, the pyramids, etc. Each group should report back to the whole group on what they found out about:

- who designed it;
- in what year;
- any special features;
- materials used to construct it; and
- who are the residents.

Houses of the Future

Age
8–11 years

Curriculum Area
Science

Curriculum Objective
To appreciate how technology can be affected by environmental and social factors.

Anti-Bias Areas
Gender, Culture

Anti-Bias Skill
To promote respect for gender and racial equity.

Materials
Paper and pencils; markers and colored pencils; and rulers.

Approach
Incorporation

Facilitation
To complete this cycle of activities exploring homes, have the students, either in pairs or individually, take the opportunity to design futuristic homes. These houses can be constructed in a variety of environments: outer space, deep sea, underground, or on land. Encourage the students to apply the ideas they learned about communal living, choice of building material, and the physical environment to their designs.

This activity should also highlight that both girls and boys have the aptitude to become architects and engineers.

Mapping a Neighborhood

Age

10–11 years

Curriculum Area

Social Studies

Curriculum Objective

To become aware of the physical and social environments that comprise a community.

Anti-Bias Areas

Age, Belief, Gender, Ability

Anti-Bias Skill

To promote awareness of and respect for diversity in culture.

Materials

Sketch pads; pencils, colored pencils, and markers.

Approach

Incorporation

Facilitation

Have the class discuss the ways in which people depend on one another as a way to define the term *community.* Assign each student to draw streets within a certain grid area of the immediate neighborhood. As a group the class can devise a legend to identify key physical and social structures in the community: schools, parks, places of worship, senior citizen homes, fire and police stations, movie theater, library, recreational centers, hospital, transportation services, etc. Stores should be clearly identified to distinguish variety: hardware, butcher, bakery, shoes, grocery, etc.

Compile the separate maps into a single unit and have the class make a summary of services available in the community. Ensure that the students include observations on the wheelchair accessibility of all physical structures and streets that are on the map.

Note: *Mapping a Neighborhood* and the following five activities can be treated as a single unit of study and are paginated sequentially even though the curriculum areas are different.

Access for Everyone?

Age
10–11 years

Curriculum Area
Mathematics

Curriculum Objective
To collect, organize, display, and interpret data about one's community.

Anti-Bias Areas
Age, Culture, Gender, Class

Anti-Bias Skill
To be proactive in helping others.

Materials
Chart paper; markers and crayons

Approach
Incorporation

Facilitation
This analysis of data is a follow-up activity to the mapping experience. The focus here is twofold: (1) graphing and (2) evaluation of who has and who does not have access to services.

Ask the students to classify the types of services available in the community, and construct bar graphs to display that information. Get the class to ascertain the number of services that are and are not wheelchair accessible; services for a particular gender; and the number of free services.

Have the class make comparisons and draw conclusions. This exercise should activate students' concern and sense of social responsibility for others.

Expansion
Encourage student initiatives in writing letters to appropriate government offices to protest obvious instances of discrimination.

The Gossip Sheet

Age
10–11 years

Curriculum Area
Social Studies

Curriculum Objective
To collect, organize, and think critically about information related to the local community.

Anti-Bias Areas
All Areas

Anti-Bias Skill
To think critically about people and events.

Materials
Construction paper; plain paper; and markers.

Approach
Incorporation

Facilitation
Have students interview people and scan local advertisements, flyers in shop windows, billboards, and community newspapers to find out about positive events or situations involving people in the community, as well as actions/situations undertaken by people that warrant a complaint. Students need to take particular interest in developments that are either beneficial to community members or disadvantageous to others. Instances of unfairness or inequity should be discussed and follow-up action should be taken.

Community Calendar

Age
10–11 years

Curriculum Area
Social Studies

Curriculum Objectives
To identify key physical and social environments of a local community; to strengthen understanding of the relation of self to larger social networks.

Anti-Bias Areas
Ability, Age

Anti-Bias Skill
To encourage cooperative group efforts.

Materials
Photographs; sketches; bristol board; and markers.

Approach
Incorporation

Facilitation
Assign students the task of either taking photographs or drawing sketches of significant physical structures and social occasions in their community. Have them compile, organize, and create a calendar for the next year that celebrates these important aspects of their community. Get students to write captions or descriptions under the photos/illustrations.

Poster Ads

Age
10–11 years

Curriculum Area
Visual Arts

Curriculum Objective
To synthesize collected information in a creative form.

Anti-Bias Areas
Culture, Age, Gender

Anti-Bias Skill
To value uniqueness of self, others, and families.

Materials
Bristol board; material scraps; glue; scissors; construction paper; colored pencils; and markers.

Approach
Incorporation

Facilitation
Have students discuss what their community means to them. Have them identify the various areas of diversity: how the members of different ethnic backgrounds are represented; how seniors are supported; how people with different abilities are recognized; etc.

Assign the task of creating a poster advertising their community. The poster should entice people to visit and reflect community pride.

Expansion
Invite a photographer from a local community newspaper to take photos of the posters for publication.

Commemorative Stamps

Age
10–11 years

Curriculum Area
Social Studies

Curriculum Objective
To discover historical facts related to people and/or events in the community.

Anti-Bias Areas
Gender, Culture, Race, Ability

Anti-Bias Skill
To value uniqueness of self, others, and families.

Materials
Construction paper; markers; scissors; glue; photocopies of old newspaper clippings; brochures; and historical photos.

Approach
Incorporation

Facilitation
Distribute the historical memorabilia to small groups for reading and research purposes. As you circulate, facilitate the students' understanding of key historical facts and dates, such as founding members, first school opening, who settled where originally, and other significant events and personalities.

Assign the class the task of designing a stamp that commemorates individuals, events, and/or animals significant to the community.

Big Is Beautiful

Age
6–7 years

Curriculum Area
Language Arts

Curriculum Objectives
To improve listening comprehension, critical thinking, and expressing opinions.

Anti-Bias Area
Appearance

Anti-Bias Skills
To describe fair and unfair behavior, and recognize prejudice; to demonstrate empathy.

Materials
Big Al, by Andrew Clements; and pictures of underwater sea creatures.

Approach
Incorporation

Facilitation
Read *Big Al.* Have the children describe Al's physical characteristics and ask them to think about:

- Why were the smaller fish so afraid of Al?
- Why is being big so scary?
- What positive qualities did Big Al possess?
- Did he have any negative qualities?
- How does it feel to be left out of a group?
- Can people have big eyes/big teeth and still be kind and generous?
- What are some ways the children use to achieve a sense of belonging?

Show pictures of underwater sea creatures to stimulate further thinking about these ideas.

The focus of this discussion should be two-pronged:

1. how people usually make judgments about others based on appearance; and
2. how people then act upon those judgments with discriminatory behaviors.

It is important that the children begin thinking critically about what qualities in people can be considered positive or negative, and to begin recognizing unfair behavior in response to how people look.

Expansion
Read *David's Father,* by Robert Munsch, as an example of judging people by their appearance.

Story Scramble

Age

6–7 years

Curriculum Area

Language Arts

Curriculum Objectives

To improve visual memory and identification; to practice sequencing and expressive language.

Anti-Bias Area

Appearance

Anti-Bias Skills

To describe fair and unfair behavior, and recognize prejudice; to demonstrate empathy.

Materials

Pictures of key episodes from *Big Al,* by Andrew Clements, mounted on cards.

Approach

Incorporation

Facilitation

Represent the following scenes from the picture book on cards:

1. Big Al crying at the bottom of the ocean.
2. Big Al camouflaged in shells and seaweed with no fish around.
3. Big Al buried in the sandy bottom with a few fish hovering above.
4. Big Al watching as small fish are scooped up into a net.
5. Big Al chewing through the net.
6. Big Al being dragged away up into a boat with fish looking on.
7. Big Al swimming happily with all the other fish.

Scramble the cards and ask the children to describe what is happening in each picture. Ask them to think about the order of events: which action happened first, next, and so on until the conclusion.

Leave the cards out and encourage the children to use them to retell the story to one another.

Swimmy Felt Board Story

Age

6–7 years

Curriculum Area

Language Arts

Curriculum Objectives

To develop critical thinking about someone who is different; to practice making predictions and divergent problem solving.

Anti-Bias Area

Appearance

Anti-Bias Skills

To participate in group action on behalf of others; to promote awareness of and respect for diversity in appearance.

Materials

Felt board pieces of characters and ocean plant life based on *Swimmy,* by Leo Lionni.

Approach

Incorporation

Facilitation

This activity is a natural follow-up to *Big Al* because the focus of this fish story is how group action can solve the problem of survival. Assist the children to understand that although the leader is different in appearance, it is he who is able to conceive of a plan and marshall the others into action.

The text is beautifully simple to use in conjunction with the felt pieces. Get the children involved by asking questions in key narrative spots:

- What was Swimmy's favorite activity? Why was that a problem for the little fish?
- How was Swimmy different from the red fish in appearance and behavior?
- Was Swimmy afraid of the big fish? How do you know?
- What do you think Swimmy and the red fish should do?
- Why was Swimmy such a hero?

Expansion

Have the children identify a classroom or school issue that is important enough to take group action to resolve. Get them to generate a list of possible actions to take. Help them to follow through on the solution of choice.

What's Happening in This Picture?

Age

6–8 years

Curriculum Area

Language Arts

Curriculum Objectives

To improve visual discrimination; to express reasons for visual association.

Anti-Bias Areas

Gender, Age, Ability, Race

Anti-Bias Skills

To promote respect for gender and racial equity; to challenge stereotypes.

Materials

Cut out and mount magazine photos of people doing various activities on card-sized paper. Paste heads that reflect diversity in gender, age, race, and ability on top of the bodies.

Approach

Incorporation

Facilitation

Put out the pictures and encourage the children to describe what they see happening in them. Wait and see if they can make correct visual discriminations. If they notice the incongruity and then make stereotypical statements related to gender or age or ability, you can ask them to explain why they believe this is so. Provide the opportunity for children to listen to one another, and support challenges to stereotypical assumptions.

Help children to understand that one's age, gender, race, or ability should never be a reason to limit someone's participation in an activity, and that denying a person a chance to engage in an activity is called discrimination.

M Is for Mum

Age
6–8 years

Curriculum Area
Language Arts

Curriculum Objectives
To improve auditory discrimination of initial sound; to recognize a consonant sound as the same in other languages.

Anti-Bias Area
Culture

Anti-Bias Skill
To promote awareness of and respect for diversity in culture.

Materials
Cards with the word *mother* printed in 12 languages.

Approach
Incorporation

Facilitation
Take this opportunity to reinforce the different languages spoken in your group, teaching staff, and community. Ask the children to share the word they use when calling their mother. As the English range of mum, mommy, ma, etc., is produced, have the children listen to the beginning sound of each word. Once they have identified the *m* sound, try to elicit the terms for mother in other languages. To offset the absence of other cultural groups bring out the cards and share the names used in other countries. Get the children to repeat the new words and learn which language is being used. Introduce the idea that because the *m* sound is used almost globally for mother, children have this word in common with others all around the world.

French: Mère
Greek: Meetera
Hebrew: Imma
Russian: Mat'
Portugese: Mãe
Tamil: Amma

Hindi: Mata ji
Chinese: Má mā; múgin
German: Mutter
Vietnamese: Me
Norwegian: Mor
Persian: Mādar

Puppet Dreaming

Age
6–8 years

Curriculum Area
Language Arts

Curriculum Objectives
To promote critical and empathetic thinking about those who are differently abled; to strengthen expressive abilities.

Anti-Bias Area
Ability

Anti-Bias Skills
To demonstrate empathy; to value uniqueness of self, others, and families.

Materials
Puppets with added props: glasses, wheelchair, leg braces, asthma mask, etc.

Approach
Incorporation

Facilitation
Set up a puppet show with these differently abled puppets. Begin the show by having two puppets talk to one another about their dreams. One puppet may wish for a friend. She can explain that sitting in a wheelchair scares away most of the children and she would like very much to have a buddy to play ball with. The other puppet agrees and tells about his dream. Rotate the puppets among the children and let each child speak about a dream on behalf of the puppet. Have the children interact by providing solutions so these dreams might come true.

Young children will probably focus on common wishes such as toys, places to go with family, etc. In this way, children will hear that everyone has the same kinds of wishes and dreams, even if physically they are different.

Special Gifts

Age
6–8 years

Curriculum Area
Language Arts

Curriculum Objective
To improve comprehension and ability to discuss the main idea of a story.

Anti-Bias Areas
Age, Culture

Anti-Bias Skill
To value uniqueness of self, others, and families.

Materials
Gifts, by Jo Ellen Bogart and Barbara Reid.

Approaches
Incorporation and Extension: Have a discussion on age and ability. Do they believe grandparents can undertake such active and exciting trips or is their perception that elderly people need wheelchairs? Why or why not?

Facilitation
Read *Gifts* and discuss the nature of the special relationship that existed between the grandmother and her granddaughter. Focus on several points:

1. Explore how family members can still love one another and have a strong relationship even when separated or living apart. This may be true for many children in the group. Discuss their feelings.
2. The special gifts that the grandmother sent were not monetary, nor even always materialistic. It is important to emphasize that sharing experiences becomes a valuable memory for families and should be cherished.
3. Explore the countries that grandmother visited by letting the children see where she traveled on a picture map. Provide picture books on people who live in these countries, such as the *Children of the World* series.

The children can create individual boxes of special memories with family members, pets, friends, and events. Let each child share and discuss their special memories.

Pass the Beanbag, Please

Age

6–8 years

Curriculum Area

Language Arts

Curriculum Objective

To help children express how they feel.

Anti-Bias Areas

Ability, Class, Culture

Anti-Bias Skill

To demonstrate empathy.

Materials

Beanbags; safety pins; collection of pictures from *National Geographic* that depicts children in daily life situations around the world; cassettes and tape recorder.

Approach

Incorporation

Facilitation

Gather the children in a circle and introduce this variation on the Pass the Parcel game. Ahead of time, prepare at least 10 beanbags with pictures pinned on them. As the music plays pass at least three bags around from child to child. When the music stops the children holding the bags will look at the picture and describe what they see to the others. Ask the children and the group how the pictures make them feel and why. For example, a child may laugh at a naked toddler in a jungle clearing. Talk about how babies love to be free without clothes, especially when it is hot. Get them to think about how they like to dress in the middle of summer. The success of this activity depends on the selection of the pictures. If they are relevant to the children's range of experiences, then personal connections can be made. Keep the pace lively and all children involved to sustain interest.

Picture Card Scramble

Age

6–8 years

Curriculum Area

Language Arts

Curriculum Objectives

To practice sequencing; to develop descriptive writing skills.

Anti-Bias Area

Race

Anti-Bias Skills

To describe fair and unfair behavior, and recognize prejudice; to promote awareness of and respect for diversity in race.

Materials

Laminated picture cards based on *The Swimming Hole,* by Jerold Beim; paper and pencils.

Approach

Incorporation

Facilitation

Illustrate *The Swimming Hole* on picture cards.

> One hot and sunny day a group of three children, Tom, Jake, and Harry, went swimming in a nearby river. While they were playing, another boy came along wanting to enjoy the cool waters. The boys looked at the other child and shouted that he couldn't swim in the river because he was Black and had dirty skin. The boy turned away sadly and walked off. Tom and Jake swam for a bit longer, but Harry stayed all day. When Harry returned home he was all sunburned.
>
> The next day, Harry went to the river again to join his friends. His two buddies didn't recognize him because he was bright red, instead of his usual color. Tom and Jake shouted that he wasn't allowed to swim in the river because he had ugly red skin. Harry felt very hurt and sad. He walked away leaving his friends frolicking in the cool waters.

Ask the children to arrange the pictures in the correct order, and write simple sentences and dialogue to place beneath the appropriate picture card. At the end of the picture story, ask the children to answer these questions:

- What lesson do you think Harry learned?
- What do you think he might do the next time another child of a different race wants to swim in the river?
- What do people call the behaviors demonstrated by the children toward the Black child?

Oral Motor Practice

Age

6–8 years

Curriculum Area

Language Arts

Curriculum Objectives

To learn about the importance of the tongue in oral communication; to develop language-learning awareness.

Anti-Bias Areas

Ability, Culture

Anti-Bias Skill

To interact comfortably with people who are differently abled.

Materials

Honey, hummus, soy sauce, ketchup; popsicle sticks.

Caution: watch for any allergies.

Approach

Modified Personalization

Facilitation

Gather the children in a large group and ask them if they ever thought about how they could speak without the use of their tongue. As an example, ask them to vocalize "la, la, la" and describe what the tongue is doing. Now repeat, "la, la, la" without letting the tongue go up and rest against the front teeth or roof. What sound did they produce? Could they actually distinguish the *l* sound?

The activity will focus the children's awareness of how the tongue has to work and where it has to be positioned to make critical sounds in English. Dab a small amount of each substance at the far corners of the mouth (near the cheek), over the top lip, and under the bottom lip near the chin. Have the children stretch their tongues to try to reach the four different tastes. Discuss what feels difficult and make the connection to the way the tongue has to work in different languages: guttural or clicking sounds, glottal stops, etc.

If you have children whose first language is not English, have them speak a sentence in their native tongue and focus on the sounds that would be difficult for a nonnative to produce. Extend this discussion to children who have poor muscle control, such as those with cerebral palsy or Down's syndrome. Ask the children to try forming words with the tongue not going where it is supposed to because of weakness.

This activity will help children build empathy by experiencing the frustration and embarrassment of those children learning English as a second language and those with oral motor problems.

Signing In

Age
6–8 years

Curriculum Area
Language Arts

Curriculum Objectives
To learn to interpret body language and communicate in a different language; to refine visual memory.

Anti-Bias Area
Ability

Anti-Bias Skills
To encourage openness to new experiences; to demonstrate empathy.

Materials
My Sister's Silent World, by Catherine Arthur, or *Words in Our Hands* by Ada Litchfield; *Mother Goose in Sign,* by Harold S. Collins; and signing alphabet chart.

Approach
Personalization

Facilitation
Invite a community member to participate in the usual reading time. Ask the visitor to sign a familiar and simple story, such as "Goldilocks and the Three Bears" or "Little Red Riding Hood," while you read it aloud. Have the visitor teach the children key words or phrases in sign language.

Bring out *Mother Goose in Sign* and ask for five volunteers. During the day assist the children to learn the signs for the short rhymes. Before the end of the day regroup the children and ask them to watch and guess what rhymes their peers are signing.

Ask them to consider what it would be like if they couldn't hear someone speaking to them, and if they didn't have the words to express themselves. How would they make themselves understood?

Extend the activity over a week to give each child the opportunity to learn and demonstrate signing a story or rhyme to the group. Sustain signing as another form of communication in your class during routines and transitions. As children become more competent in signing, they will begin to feel more comfortable interacting with people who are differently abled.

No One Loved Horace

Age
6–9 years

Curriculum Area
Language Arts

Curriculum Objectives
To discuss the concept of discrimination and to problem solve solutions.

Anti-Bias Areas
Appearance, Gender, Ability, Race

Anti-Bias Skill
To promote awareness of and respect for diversity in race, ability, and appearance.

Materials
No One Loved Horace, by Lynn Green.

Approach
Incorporation

Facilitation
Read *No One Loved Horace.* Engage the children in a discussion about the reasons why the other animals ostracized Horace. Ask them how they would feel if they were Horace. Explore the children's feelings about differences in others: those who are born in other countries and speak English with an accent; those who have different physical abilities; or those who look different, etc. Discuss ways that we can help one another accept and value differences in others.

Mama Will You Love Me?

Age
6–10 years

Curriculum Area
Language Arts

Curriculum Objective
To appreciate aspects of daily life in other cultures.

Anti-Bias Area
Culture

Anti-Bias Skill
To promote awareness of and respect for diversity in culture.

Materials
Mama Will You Love Me?, by Barbara Jaosse.

Approach
Incorporation

Facilitation
Read *Mama Will You Love Me?* Ask the children to describe the ways in which the little girl is the same and different from them. Help them to understand that unconditional love between child and parent is universal, and so is misbehavior! Explore the daily aspects of life for the Inuit people and identify objects/animals/events that are significant to this culture. Ask the children to think about how these aspects of life compare to their own.

Older children can write versions of *Mama/Papa Will You Love Me?* that are rooted in their own family's culture.

Expansion
Extended study of the Inuit culture for grades 4–6; see the following activities presented earlier: *Tiktala, Building a Dome, Constructing an Igluvigak, Multiple Meanings, The Inuit and Ecology, Carving Experience, Spirits of the North, Arctic Nutrition,* and *Ecology Debate.*

Musical Find-a-Chair

Age

6–10 years

Curriculum Area

Language Arts

Curriculum Objective

To refine visual and auditory discrimination skills.

Anti-Bias Areas

Culture, Belief

Anti-Bias Skill

To promote awareness of and respect for diversity in culture.

Materials

Enough chairs for each child; tapes of songs from different cultures; tape recorders; and matching pictures of buildings with distinctive architectural features. These can include both religious structures (temples, mosques, synagogues, and cathedrals) and nonreligious buildings such as the Taj Mahal, Buckingham Palace, skyscrapers, the White House, etc.

Approach

Incorporation

Facilitation

Set up chairs in the same style as for Musical Chairs. Hand out the picture cards to the children and tell them they will need to find the same building on a card that is stuck on a chair. To make the game more manageable, play it with no more than 10 children at a time. Review the instructions of walking around the chairs while the music is playing and stopping in front of a chair when the music stops. If the picture on the chair matches the one the child is holding, then the child sits down. The game continues until everyone finds a chair. Take time to talk about the buildings: function, shape, colors, and location.

Picture Story Writing

Age

7–9 years

Curriculum Area

Language Arts

Curriculum Objective

To practice composition and presentation skills.

Anti-Bias Areas

All Areas

Anti-Bias Skill

To recognize, label, and discuss similarities and differences.

Materials

Pictures of children from different countries depicting the primary emotions of joy, sadness, fear, and anger; paper and pens.

Approach

Incorporation

Facilitation

Explain to the children that they will write simple stories based on pictures they select. Each child will pick three photos and do a *P.B.E.* In the *P(hysical)* column, they should list all the physical details or characteristics: hair, eye and skin color, height, clothing, etc. In the *B(ehavioral)* column, they should list actions and objects in or with which the pictured child is engaged. In the *E(motions)* column, they should identify the emotion the child is feeling and what they believe is the cause. After they complete their P.B.E., the children should use the lists to generate paragraph stories.

The children can work on writing over an extended period of time. Once completed the children should choose one story to read to the class. In the course of discussion, have the children think critically about the relationship between experiencing emotions and one's skin color, physical ability, age, class, etc. The goal is for them to be able to express that no matter where one lives, what kind of clothing one wears, or how one looks, children feel the same emotions.

Community Resource

Lakeshore/Wintergreen offers a selection of photo cards that would be suitable for this activity: Let's Talk About Feelings Photo Cards (LT 866) or Children of the World Poster Pack (LC 936). The latter includes facts and key questions that allow for a further expansion of this activity.

Similes About Myself

Age
7–9 years

Curriculum Area
Language Arts

Curriculum Objective
To learn how to use similes in describing physical and emotional characteristics.

Anti-Bias Areas
Appearance, Gender, Race, Ability

Anti-Bias Skill
To value uniqueness of self, others, and families.

Materials
Quick as a Cricket, by Audrey Woods.

Approach
Modified Personalization

Facilitation
Read *Quick as a Cricket* and explain the use of simile as a method of literary comparison. Ask the children to draw up a list of their physical and emotional characteristics, and then to create similes about themselves. Afterwards, read the similes to the class, and have the children guess which similes refer to which classmates. Support everyone's individuality and strengths.

Why Am I So Different?

Age
7–9 years

Curriculum Area
Language Arts

Curriculum Objective
To refine critical and divergent thinking skills.

Anti-Bias Areas
All Areas

Anti-Bias Skills
To promote awareness of and respect for diversity in culture; to strengthen self-identity and increase self-esteem.

Materials
Why Am I So Different?, by Norma Simon; flip chart paper; and marker.

Approaches
Incorporation and Modified Personalization

Facilitation
Ask the children what would happen if everyone in the world was alike/the same. Have them think what the effects of this statement would be for them. Ask the children to consider the various ways in which people can be different.

Read *Why Am I So Different?*, and ask them to recall the differences specified in the story: physical traits, allergies, family composition, class, cultural and religious values, etc. List these on chart paper for additional reading practice and recognition of areas of diversity.

Have the children write a list of things they believe are different about themselves and of which they are proud. Get them to share their opinions with the rest of the class.

Sports Logos

Age

7–10 years

Curriculum Area

Language Arts

Curriculum Objective

To refine critical thinking skills.

Anti-Bias Areas

Race, Culture

Anti-Bias Skills

To think critically about people and events; to examine alternatives.

Materials

Banners, hats, and jerseys from baseball, hockey, football and basketball teams; flip chart paper; and markers.

Approach

Incorporation

Facilitation

Divide the class into four groups; have each group generate a list of names belonging to the major sports teams in hockey, baseball, football, and basketball. Let each group present its list and describe what the logo for each team looks like. Ask the children to analyze the origin of these names. What seem to be the predominant categories or sources for team names (animals, people, alliterative names, colors, etc.)? Ask them to evaluate if the images associated with these names are positive or negative.

Encourage the children to examine the hats or banners from the Cleveland Indians, Edmonton Eskimos, Atlanta Braves, Washington Redskins, Kansas City Chiefs, Chicago Blackhawks, Montreal Canadiens, etc., and ask them to consider what is different about these team names. The discussion that follows should sensitize the children to how images of people, Native Americans in particular, have been used. Ask them how they might feel about a new team named the Jersey Jews, or the New York Negroes, or the Indiana Irish?

Assist the children to understand how easy it is to devalue people who are not of the predominant culture. Brainstorm alternative names for the teams which do devalue people.

Fact Sheet on Discrimination

Age
7–10 years

Curriculum Area
Language Arts

Curriculum Objectives
To practice problem solving, identification, and written language skills.

Anti-Bias Area
Dependent upon discriminatory behaviors.

Anti-Bias Skill
To be proactive against discriminatory behaviors.

Materials
Black Like Kyra. White Like Me, by Judith Vigna; and fact sheet.

Approach
Incorporation

Facilitation
Read *Black Like Kyra. White Like Me,* by Judith Vigna, to create the context for the following activity. Either use the events depicted in the book or use an incident that occurred during which a child was teased, called names, unfairly treated, or discriminated against due to appearance, ability, gender, racial or cultural background. Distribute the fact sheets to the class to fill out. Ask the children to place themselves in the victim's shoes.

Facts on Discrimination

1. List five or more words (adjectives) that describe how you are feeling.
   1.
   2.
   3.
   4.
   5.
2. List three or more actions to solve the problem.
   1.
   2.
   3.
3. Write a sentence to tell the person who has treated you unfairly how you feel.

4. Write a sentence to tell that person what should be done to solve the problem.

Expansion
Read *Let's Talk About Racism,* by Angela Grunsell, for further exploration of this topic.

A Gift for You

Age
7–11 years

Curriculum Area
Language Arts

Curriculum Objective
To express positive attitudes in writing.

Anti-Bias Areas
All Areas

Anti-Bias Skills
To strengthen self-identity and increase self-esteem.

Materials
Photo or drawing of each child; 3 × 5-inch index cards cut in half, enough for each child to write something for each member of the group; and tape.

Approach
Modified Personalization

Facilitation
This activity can extend over a week as the children think about specific, positive comments they will make about one another. They can attach their positive assessments about ability, characteristic behavior, or personality traits to cards taped below photos of their peers. The teacher should participate as well.

When everyone has completed the task, each child will be able to take home an inventory of personal strengths. Ask the class how it feels to give and receive positive feedback.

Storytelling with Objects

Age
7–11 years

Curriculum Area
Language Arts

Curriculum Objective
To use imagination in constructing oral stories.

Anti-Bias Area
Culture

Anti-Bias Skill
To promote awareness of and respect for diversity in culture.

Materials
Fabric samples with distinctive cultural patterns, shoes, cooking utensils, boxes, jewelry, sports or leisure equipment, all of which are representative of many cultures; cloth bags from different cultures.

Approach
Incorporation

Facilitation
Divide the class into small groups of five. Each group should receive a bag that contains a minimum of five objects from a variety of cultures. The task is to create a story based on these items. You may have to review the objects to ensure that the children understand the function, country of origin, and, if appropriate, the correct name. Bring the class together and have each group present its story.

Community Resources
Family donations or research stores that carry items representative of different cultures (UNICEF, Oxfam, Trade Aid, etc.).

Modem Pal

Age

8–11 years

Curriculum Area

Language Arts

Curriculum Objectives

To compose narratives for regular correspondence; to learn to use e-mail technology

Anti-Bias Area

Ability

Anti-Bias Skill

To interact comfortably with people who are differently abled.

Materials

Computer with modem; visiting physical or occupational therapist; and a center serving young people with physical challenges.

Approach

Personalization

Facilitation

Students of this age need practice expressing themselves and learning about others through writing. Invite a physical or occupational therapist to talk about specific children. Have the therapist describe a number of physical challenges (spina bifida, cerebral palsy or Down's syndrome, etc.) and what it is these children have difficulty doing. At the same time the therapist should provide important personal information about the children: their participation in organizations/clubs such as Girl Scouts; favorite hobbies; favorite school activities, etc. Make sure the therapist also brings photographs of the children so the students can attach a visual image to their future pen pals.

Arrange for a weekly electronic correspondence session to occur between your class and a class at a center that serves young people with physical challenges. Children can work in pairs or individually. Have the students share their pen pals' letters so the entire class can benefit from this exchange.

Community Resource

List of centers serving young people with physical challenges in your community.

Nursery Rhymes Biases

Age
8–11 years

Curriculum Area
Language Arts

Curriculum Objectives
To practice analysis and critical thinking.

Anti-Bias Areas
Gender, Age

Anti-Bias Skill
To challenge stereotypes.

Materials
Selected nursery rhymes.

Approach
Incorporation

Facilitation

Read a few nursery rhymes. Ask the children to listen critically to them and to identify aspects of attitude or characterization that feel biased in any way. Have them discuss how they could modify the rhymes to reflect a more bias-free form of literature. List their suggestions on chart paper and then assign the class to rewrite those nursery rhymes they find particularly disrespectful. These can be illustrated and posted, or compiled into a book and displayed in the school's library.

Examples include: "Three Blind Mice" has the farmer's wife being excessively cruel; "What are little boys made of? and what are little girls made of?" depict stereotypical masculine and feminine values; "Ding Dong Bell" has little Tommy drowning a cat for fun; "Little Miss Muffet" is portrayed as a weak, frightened female; "Eaper Weaper, chimney sweeper" is violent toward his wives; "Little Polly Flinders" gets whipped because she sits near a fire to warm up and dirties her dress.

Follow up this activity by reading *Father Gander Nursery Rhymes* by Dr. Douglas Larche. The class can compare their versions with the author's. Have the class discuss how the illustrations reflect a more inclusionary approach.

Selected Nursery Rhymes

◎ There was an old woman who
  lived in a shoe
she had so many children
  she didn't know what to do
She gave them some broth
  without any bread
She whipped them all soundly
  and put them to bed.

(*continued*)

- When Jack's a very good boy
  He shall have cakes and custard
  When he does nothing but cry
  He shall have nothing but mustard.
- Curly locks, curly locks wilt thou be mine?
  Thou shalt not wash dishes, nor yet feed the swine;
  But sit on a cushion and sew a fine seam,
  And feed upon strawberries, sugar, and cream.
- Elsie Marley is grown so fine
  She won't get up to serve the swine
  But lies in bed till 8 or 9
  Lazy Elsie Marley.
- Will you marry me, my pretty maid?
  What is your father—a farmer
  What is your fortune—my face
  Then I can't marry you.
- There was an old woman sat spinning
  And that's the first beginning;
  She had a calf,
  And that's half,
  She took it by the tail,
  And threw it over the wall,
  And that's all.
- Needles and pins,
  Needles and pins,
  When a man marries
  His troubles begin.

Witches Get Bad Press

Age
8–11 years

Curriculum Area
Language Arts

Curriculum Objective
To practice literary analysis.

Anti-Bias Areas
Appearance, Race

Anti-Bias Skills
To challenge stereotypes; to be proactive against discriminatory behaviors.

Materials
Illustrations of witches; Halloween cards; and picture book stories about witches.

Approach
Incorporation

Facilitation

Begin this activity by involving students in a free association of words and images in response to the word *witch.* Write their answers on the board and have them put a *P*(ositive) or *N*(egative) next to each word. Tally and analyze the results. If the amount of negatives outnumber the positives, ask the class to consider what might be the contributing factors.

As a follow-up to this discussion bring out a sample of Halloween cards, illustrations, and picture books. In small groups, ask the students to describe the prominent physical characteristics of witches that appear in these media. Have them think about the associations that arise in their minds as a result. Discuss the implications of always associating a woman in black with something negative, bad, or fearful. Help them make the connection to society's predisposition toward any people of color.

Mistaken Perceptions

Age
8–11 years

Curriculum Area
Language Arts

Curriculum Objectives
To improve comprehension and critical thinking skills; to develop creative writing skills.

Anti-Bias Areas
All Areas

Anti-Bias Skill
To gather information and draw conclusions based on facts.

Materials
True Story of the Three Little Pigs, by Jon Sciezka.

Approach
Incorporation

Facilitation
Read the *True Story of the Three Little Pigs.* Engage the class in a discussion in which they can identify how erroneous perceptions can lead to mistaken assumptions about one's motives and behaviors.

Have the class select another fairy tale and rewrite it. They should create a version that demonstrates how a character makes an assumption about how people will behave based on their appearance. For example, in the story of Cinderella, children could select either the stepmother's or stepsister's perspective:

> My mother remarried and suddenly I had a brand new sister. Everybody thought she was so nice just because she was thin and pretty. Whenever I asked her to help me do my hair the way she did, she would start whining and complaining.

Use the regular narrative editing and revision process for skills practice. Bind the stories and have the children read them aloud to one another over the week.

Killer Statements and Gestures

Age
8–11 years

Curriculum Area
Language Arts

Curriculum Objectives
To listen, interpret, and understand feelings and motives in social situations.

Anti-Bias Areas
Gender, Ability, Age

Anti-Bias Skill
To be proactive against discriminatory behaviors.

Materials
Sample killer statements: "That's a stupid idea. You know you are too young."; "You're really weird!"; "Are you crazy or retarded?"; "Only boys/girls do that!"; "That's for sissies."

Approach
Modified Personalization

Facilitation
Engage the students in a discussion that asks them to remember a time when they worked very hard at something and felt that their effort was neither understood nor appreciated. Get the children to identify specific situations and retell what was said or done in response that made them feel badly.

Ask the group to consider the following: "Have you ever wanted to share an idea, a feeling, or something you made, but were afraid to because of the fear that someone might put you down? What kinds of things do people say or do that puts us down, or puts down our ideas and achievements?"

Discuss the experiences shared by students and help them to make the connection that all of us at sometime have had thoughts or feelings that were "killed" off by another's negative comments or physical gestures. Review the killer statements. Encourage the students to identify how the negative statements are actually biased against one's gender, ability, or age.

Inform the class they are going to become researchers for the day. They must keep a record of all the killer statements or gestures they hear or see in the classroom, in the school yard, at lunch, and at home. The next day the class will share their findings and discuss strategies that will enable them to cope when such behaviors are directed against them or someone else.

Individual Coat of Arms

Age
9–11 years

Curriculum Area
Language Arts

Curriculum Objectives
To practice analysis and visual and oral descriptions.

Anti-Bias Areas
Culture, Gender, Race, Belief

Anti-Bias Skill
To value uniqueness of self, others, and families.

Materials
Large bristol board; scissors; markers; and magazines.

Approach
Modified Personalization

Facilitation
Explain to the group that in the Middle Ages members of noble families who went into battle and were heavily armed were hard to recognize. To solve this problem, their heraldic emblems were displayed on a shield. These images symbolized the family name.

Have the children create their own coat of arms. They can draw, write, or design a collage from magazine pictures to depict the following:

- Happy or good things that have happened in life.
- Goals or plans for future career.
- Fears or secret dreams.
- People important to you. A person you would like to meet.

Have the children present their creations to the class so that the group can learn about and appreciate everyone's individuality.

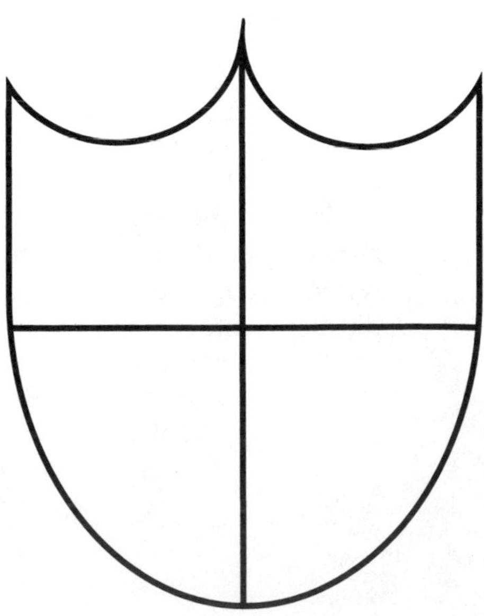

Creating an individual coat of arms.

Name Anagrams

Age
9–11 years

Curriculum Area
Language Arts

Curriculum Objective
To develop vocabulary.

Anti-Bias Area
Culture

Anti-Bias Skills
To strengthen self-identity and increase self-esteem.

Materials
Lists of different names.

Approaches
Incorporation and Modified Personalization.

Facilitation
This activity can be done as a morning brainteaser. Design a list with a number of names appropriate to the class level and ability. As a bonus, let those children whose names do not appear create their own personalized anagram. The following list is not exhaustive; more suggestions can be found in *The Guinness Book of Names,* by Leslie Dunkling.

Alex—axel	Carol—coral	Daniel—nailed	Dennis—sinned
Edgar—raged	Eric—rice	Ezra—raze	Gerald—glared
Glenda—dangle	Gustave—vaguest	Ingrid—riding	Kate—teak
Laura—aural	Lewis—wiles	Lydia—daily	Nancy—canny
Olga—goal	Rosa—soar	Ruth—hurt	Seamus—amuses
Selina—aliens	Tabitha—habitat	Tessa—seats	Thelma—hamlet
Theresa—heaters		Vera—rave	

Being Differently Abled

Age

9–11 years

Curriculum Area

Language Arts

Curriculum Objectives

To practice critical thinking and expressive writing skills.

Anti-Bias Areas

Ability, Family Composition

Anti-Bias Skill

To demonstrate empathy.

Materials

Knots on a Counting Rope, by Bill Martin Jr. and John Archambault.

Approach

Incorporation

Facilitation

Read *Knots on a Counting Rope* to the class. Have the children think about and discuss all the possible effects of either being blind or deaf. What things can one do? What things are difficult or impossible? What kind of attitude and support are required?

Ask each child to write a response to the following question: "If you had a choice between not being able to see and not being able to hear, which would you choose?" They must give reasons for their decisions. Share these ideas with the whole group.

Expansion

Have the children research stories about their birth or special family events to share with the class.

Following Instructions

Age

9–11 years

Curriculum Area

Language Arts

Curriculum Objective

To decode words that have letters facing different directions.

Anti-Bias Area

Ability

Anti-Bias Skill

To demonstrate empathy.

Materials

Prepared sheets.

Approach

Modified Personalization

Facilitation

Distribute the following activity sheet. Tell the students that some children with learning difficulties have trouble reading because their brains often mix up the way letters look. Give the students 5 minutes to complete the sheet. After the time limit is called, ask the students to discuss what they found confusing and how they felt. Have them think about the kinds of emotions children with learning problems face on a daily basis in school. If you want to prepare similar sheets, the letters have to be written backwards, upside down, and scrambled.

This activity is designed as a sensitivity training exercise. Teachers need to use discretion in view of the number of children with learning difficulties in the school system today. Stress the empathy perspective.

1. WɿiɈɘ youɿ ɴamɘ iɴ cabital ƨɿɘɈɈɘl ta tyɘ woɈɈod fo tyɘ bagɘ.
2. Bɘlom ti bɿam a ciɿɔlɘ tyat si Ɛ .ɴi ɴi biawɘɈɘɿ.
3. In tyɘ mibblɘ fo tyɘ bagɘ bɿam a ɿɘctaɴglɘ tyat mɘaƨuɿɘƨ Ƨ .ɴi ɴo ɘaɔy ƨibɘ.
4. Raise youɿ yanb wyɘɴ you aɿɘ ɿɘaby.

Dogs Who Work

Age
9–11 years

Curriculum Area
Language Arts

Curriculum Objective
To apply knowledge in a creative writing experience.

Anti-Bias Area
Ability

Anti-Bias Skill
To demonstrate empathy.

Materials
Visitor and Seeing Eye™ guide dog.

Approach
Personalization

Facilitation
Invite a trainer of Seeing Eye™ dogs to talk to the class. The discussion should include demonstrations of how the dog learns to guide people who are blind, and all the tasks and commands the dog must perform.

The follow-up activity focuses on a creative writing interpretation of what the children just experienced. Have them write an imaginary conversation taking place between a Seeing Eye™ dog and an ordinary nonworking dog. After the task is completed, pairs of students can act out their dialogues to the whole class.

Community Resource
Local branches of the American Foundation for the Blind and the Canadian National Institute for the Blind.

An Aesop Fable

Age
9–11 years

Curriculum Area
Language Arts

Curriculum Objectives
To increase critical thinking and listening comprehension; to analyze a fable for its moral.

Anti-Bias Area
Appearance

Anti-Bias Skills
To challenge stereotypes; to promote awareness of and respect for diversity in appearance.

Materials
"The Lion and the Mouse"; paper and pens.

Approach
Incorporation

Facilitation
Read Aesop's fable "The Lion and the Mouse" to the class. In the follow-up discussion have the students consider the importance of size and how that relates to the moral of the fable. Focus the discussion on how people of different sizes are viewed. Get the children's perceptions and discuss the implications of their assumptions. To conclude this activity conduct a brainstorming session during which the students come up with 10 reasons why it is advantageous to be small.

Television Advertising

Age
10–11 years

Curriculum Area
Language Arts (Media Literacy)

Curriculum Objectives
To use critical thinking and analytic skills.

Anti-Bias Areas
Gender, Race, Culture, Age, Ability

Anti-Bias Skills
To make inferences; to challenge stereotypes.

Materials
Three advertising analysis charts for each child; pencils.

Approach
Incorporation

Facilitation
Assign the class to watch television advertising for several days. Make sure they screen ads at different times: weekday afternoon, weekday evening, and Saturday morning. Get them to fill out the following chart for each product they saw advertised. The form can be used either as a checklist or students can write in missing information. Each child should bring three charts to class for a group analysis.

The assignment should be preceded with a review and discussion of things to look for: does the ad stereotype, exaggerate, or make fun of some physical aspect of a person?; is the tone humorous or serious?; who is being represented, according to gender, race, culture, age, or ability?

The group analysis should focus on:

- Who is the target market for the products?
- Can anyone else use these products?
- Who is predominantly represented in television ads?
- Did anyone in the class feel left out? Why?

Television Advertisement

	Gender	Race	Culture	Age	Physical Ability
	F ☐	White ☐	Hispanic ☐	Child ☐	Walking ☐
Product________________	M ☐	Black ☐	Greek ☐	Teen ☐	In a wheelchair ☐
		Asian ☐	Chinese ☐	Adult ☐	Signing ☐
People Represented:			Native ☐	Senior ☐	Blind ☐

Comment:

Stereotypes:

Made fun of?

Humorous?

Serious?

Assessing television advertisements for stereotyping or unfair representation.

Helpful Communication

Age

10–11 years

Curriculum Area

Language Arts

Curriculum Objectives

To strengthen ability to give precise instructions; to listen effectively in order to follow directions.

Anti-Bias Area

Ability

Anti-Bias Skill

To promote awareness of and respect for diversity in ability.

Materials

Paper and pencil; blindfolds for half of the class.

Approach

Modified Personalization

Facilitation

Divide the class up into pairs. Each individual in the pair should have an opportunity to give directions and follow directions. Ask one member of the pair to put on a blindfold while the other member draws four dots randomly on the paper. The task requires the seeing person to verbally direct the blindfolded person's pencil from dot to dot in one uninterrupted line.

After each member has had a turn guiding and following, bring the class back together to discuss the following questions:

- What did they find more difficult, directing or following instructions? Why?
- What strategies worked/did not work? Why?
- What emotions did they feel during the experience?
- What did they do to cope with their emotions?
- What did they learn from this exercise?

Creating Legends

Age

9–11 years

Curriculum Area

Language Arts

Curriculum Objectives

To become familiar with the Native peoples' (American, Australian, New Zealand) tradition of transmitting culture orally; to write individual creation legends.

Anti-Bias Area

Culture

Anti-Bias Skill

To promote awareness of and respect for diversity in culture.

Materials

Legends from a variety of Native cultures; see resources such as *From the Dreamtime: Australian Aboriginal Legends; Land of the Long White Cloud: Maori Myths, Tales and Legends; The Legend of the Indian Paintbrush.*

Approaches

Incorporation and Personalization

Facilitation

Select three legends from among three distinctive Native cultures. Explain the nature of legends that were meant to be handed down from generation to generation through oral transmission. The Australian, Maori, and North American Native legends are primarily creationist in that they explain: how distinctive geological formations and geographic areas were created; how certain animals derived particular characteristics; the lives of people and how key rituals and customs were derived. It is important to emphasize that each Native group has evolved its own set of legends, with totems and art forms that visually illustrate them.

Read the three legends and have the children identify the common structural aspects: some kind of conflict; intervention of a spirit that lends guidance or prophecy; the explanation of how something/one/place originated, etc. The focus of this activity is for the children to create their own legends. When completed, let the children take turns presenting their legends to the class.

Follow up this activity with oral storytelling by family members or representatives from Native community or cultural groups.

Community Resources

Local Native cultural center. Contact national organizations that might have listings of Native associations in different areas such as the American Indian Curricula Development Program and the Native Council of Canada.

Drama Improvisation

Age
10–11 years

Curriculum Area
Language Arts

Curriculum Objectives
To use critical thinking and expression in dramatic improvisation.

Anti-Bias Areas
All Areas

Anti-Bias Skills
To challenge stereotypes; to be proactive against discriminatory behaviors.

Materials
Masks from different countries; starters for drama scenarios.

Approach
Incorporation

Facilitation
This activity can tackle any area of bias and takes its direction from the starter scenarios. The improvisation can involve two or three children at one time who assume a persona behind the mask. The persona's character is determined by the teacher's scenario, however, the teacher should be prepared for a wide range of responses. The entire class participates by observing the improvisation, then discussing the issues they have heard. The class should analyze issues of discrimination and address alternative strategies to challenge the biases. Masks help ease the children's shyness in front of a large group and assume another persona. Sample improvisation starters include:

- A person walks into a small grocery store and asks for curry powder. The storekeeper answers, "We don't carry that kind of stuff here. You have to go into one of *those* stores."
- Parents are looking for a babysitter and interview a male teenager. The 16-year-old enters wearing a baseball cap backwards. The mother says, "I have a 6-month-old baby. You know babies are very fragile. Have you actually ever done any babysitting? Don't you only have time for hockey and baseball?"
- Two 10-year-olds are playing a board game and realize they need a third player. One child says, "Let's ask my grandmother. She loves board games." The second child answers, "How's an old lady like that going to be able to remember anything? Old people are too forgetful to play."

Comic Strip Authors

Age
10–11 years

Curriculum Area
Language Arts

Curriculum Objective
To invent dialogue and characterization for a comic strip.

Anti-Bias Areas
Gender, Culture, Race

Anti-Bias Skill
To promote awareness of and respect for diversity in race, culture, and gender.

Materials
Comic strips with speech balloons blanked out, enlarged and laminated.

Approach
Incorporation

Facilitation
Begin the activity with a brief discussion on the nature of comic strips. Have the students consider: who is usually depicted; whether there is generalization or stereotyping; and what, if any, are some of the gender-related issues.

Distribute a selection of enlarged comic strips with blank dialogue balloons. Challenge students to invent their own story lines, characters, and dialogue that better reflects the anti-bias approach.

Expansion
Another variation of this idea is to find an interesting action photo with several persona. Make speech balloons for each and have the students create dialogue for the scenario.

Dreams for a Better Future

Age
10–11 years

Curriculum Area
Language Arts

Curriculum Objectives
To practice conflict resolution and problem solving.

Anti-Bias Areas
All Areas

Anti-Bias Skills
To listen to and value other points of view; to examine alternatives.

Materials
Paper and pencils; skit props, as needed.

Approach
Incorporation

Facilitation
Divide the class into small groups of five and have each group prepare a presentation on any issue of its choice. Tell the children that the skits must:

1. present a problem dealing with conflict or discrimination;
2. identify possible solutions; and
3. depict what the world will be like once this problem is resolved.

The skits only need to be five minutes in length, but each child must have a role in the presentation. Allow the groups at least 30–40 minutes per day over the course of a week to brainstorm, work out the script, and rehearse speeches. Depending on the class's abilities, a large group brainstorming of possible topics might be helpful to focus ideas prior to the small group work.

Tool Sort

Age
6–8 years

Curriculum Area
Mathematics

Curriculum Objectives
To practice criteria selection and classification skills; to stimulate divergent thinking.

Anti-Bias Area
Culture

Anti-Bias Skills
To appreciate how people use objects differently; to examine alternatives.

Materials
Collection of tools: sea sponge, binoculars, tuning fork, large stick, hour glass, trowel, glasses, garlic press, masking tape, rope, pencil, hearing aid, bucket, chopsticks, bamboo brush, wooden pestle, degchi, and metal drinking straw; *Tools,* by Ann Morris; chart paper and markers.

Approaches
Incorporation and Personalization

Facilitation
Read *Tools* to get the children thinking about how people all around the world use tools differently. Pull out the stick from your collection and ask the children to think about all the possible different purposes for and ways to use a stick. List these on chart paper. Help them assign functions to the tools: cooking, planting, measuring, counting, walking, and writing, etc.

Bring out your collection; have the children identify each tool and all of its possible uses. Encourage them to sort the tools according to criteria they choose, and allow them to re-sort as often as they wish.

Offer information about the culture in which the tool is used. Discuss how different cultures use similar tools for different purposes.

Expansion
Have the children create new and unusual uses for a hammer, a telescope, a stethoscope, and a fishing rod.

Community Resource
List locations where a diversity of tools and the necessary research on their country of origin and function can be obtained.

Hardware Handiness

Age
6–8 years

Curriculum Area
Mathematics

Curriculum Objectives
To refine visual and tactile discrimination; to create and reproduce patterns.

Anti-Bias Area
Ability

Anti-Bias Skill
To promote awareness of and respect for diversity in ability.

Materials
Several clipboards with magnetic strips glued in rows; assortment of hardware nuts and bolts in varying shapes, sizes, and thicknesses.

Approach
Modified Personalization

Facilitation
The children need to explore the materials thoroughly before attempting this activity, which focuses on creating and re-creating a pattern without the use of their sight.

As the children create patterns according to shape, size, thickness, and equivalent numbers, elicit verbal descriptions from them about the individual pieces of hardware. Instruct them to pay particular attention to corners, number of edges, roundness, length, and degree of thickness. Have the children complete the following two tasks:

1. Looking and Copying
   Pair children. Ask one child to create a pattern and the other child to re-create the design through observation.
2. Feeling, Listening, and Doing
   Group children in pairs and blindfold one in the pair. Give each child a turn at creating a pattern; then pass the clipboard to the blindfolded child who must re-create the pattern in a row below. To assist in this exercise, have the child who is to reproduce the design, analyze the pattern first and pick out the requisite hardware before putting on the blindfold. As the children become more comfortable with the challenge, eliminate this preparatory step. Have them feel the pattern, identify what kind and how many of those items they need, and then proceed with the task.

After the children have completed this exercise, have them discuss how they felt before, during, and after the task. Ask them what strategies they began to use to make the task easier. Ask them to think about people who are blind and what daily challenges they may face.

People Sort

Age

6–8 years

Curriculum Area

Mathematics

Curriculum Objectives

To practice attribute, identification, classification, and comparison skills.

Anti-Bias Areas

Appearance, Gender, Race, Culture

Anti-Bias Skills

To recognize, label, and discuss similarities and differences.

Materials

Flip chart and markers.

Approach

Personalization

Facilitation

Prepare some charts ahead of time that illustrate diversity among the class in skin color, height, hair, and eye color. Ask the children to stand when they fit the category, and have another child count and record the number in the appropriate box. Have the children create their own attribute categories and chart the results.

Older children can transform this data into a bar graph for more advanced visual comprehension of quantity and quality.

People Living in My Home

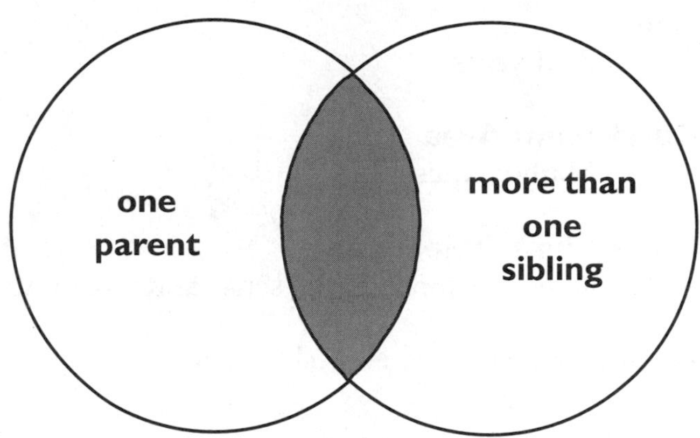

Using sets to recognize similarities and differences.

Age

7–10 years

Curriculum Area

Mathematics

Curriculum Objectives

To create and understand sets and intersection of sets.

Anti-Bias Areas

Age, Family Composition

Anti-Bias Skills

To recognize, label, and discuss similarities and differences; to promote awareness of and respect for diversity in family composition.

Materials

Rope to make circles; flip chart and markers.

Approach

Modified Personalization

Facilitation

Ask the children to stand in the appropriately roped-off circle if they meet the criteria for each question. Have them remain standing even if members of the set change as long as they meet the criteria. Help them try to create intersecting sets if two attributes apply simultaneously.

Have the class record results. Each child should record individual results and examine how many different attributes apply. This will start children thinking about class inclusion.

Some possible criteria include children with:

- one brother, stepbrother, adopted brother
- one sister; stepsister, adopted sister
- more than one sibling
- no siblings
- one parent, two parents, same gender parents, biracial parents (use latter two, if applicable)
- a baby in the family
- one set of grandparents, two sets of grandparents, or a variation
- relatives besides parent(s) living at home
- children who are the oldest/youngest in the family

A Tangram Tale

Age
8–11 years

Curriculum Area
Mathematics

Curriculum Objectives
To understand spatial sense and work with two-dimensional geometric relationships.

Anti-Bias Area
Culture

Anti-Bias Skill
To promote awareness of and respect for diversity in culture.

Materials
Grandfather Tang's Story, by Ann Tompert; class set of tangram puzzle pieces.

Approach
Incorporation

Facilitation
Read *Grandfather Tang's Story* to introduce the cultural significance of this game. It is believed that tangrams originated in China over 2,000 years ago. More than 1,500 images can be made with the seven tan pieces; the only winner is the individual child.

Distribute the seven geometric pieces to each student and use them to design as many different objects, animals, and people as possible using all seven tans. For each successful design, the student must describe the placement of each newly rearranged geometric shape.

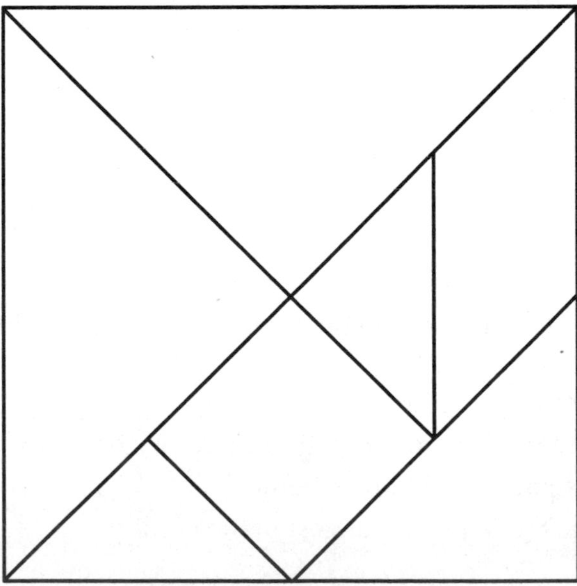

The basic pattern of a tangram.

Coping with Change

Age
9–11 years

Curriculum Area
Mathematics

Curriculum Objective
To practice using new units of measurement in length and capacity.

Anti-Bias Area
Culture

Anti-Bias Skill
To cope effectively with change.

Materials
Metric cards; sheet of measurable objects.

Approach
Incorporation

Facilitation
Discuss with the class how much of our knowledge about units of measurement comes from our cultural background. For example, older civilizations had systems that used units of length based on the body. The Egyptians had a one cubit measurement, based on the distance between the elbow and the fingertip. King Henry I of England measured the distance between his nose and his fingertip, and had it declared to be a yard. In the United States we have one system for measuring length, weight, and volume. In Europe and Canada they have an equivalent system called the Metric System, which was developed in France in the 1790s.

Review the units of measurement for length: inch, foot, and yard; introduce the metric equivalents: centimeter and meter. Do the same for volume: ounce, quart, gallon versus liters. Prepare a sheet of measurable objects and have the class determine whether they should use meters or liters:

- pool filled with water
- wire needed to fix cable
- hair length
- distance between New York and Pennsylvania
- length of a toenail
- liquid in a small medicine bottle
- length of a football field
- the height of a car
- size of one's wrist
- can of pop

Introduce the unit of measurement for mass (gram) in a similar fashion. Help them to remember the units by asking key questions: How long? How full? How heavy?

Expansion
There are special measurements still in use: fathom, knot, degree, light-year, hand. Have the class find out what they are used to measure and how, why, and when they were designed.

Food Pyramid

Age

6–7 years

Curriculum Area

Science

Curriculum Objectives

To practice classification skills and think divergently.

Anti-Bias Area

Culture

Anti-Bias Skill

To promote awareness of and respect for diversity in culture.

Materials

Enough pyramids for small groups, designed with corresponding sections for dairy, meats and fish, grains, fruits, vegetables, and fats and sweets; food magazines; scissors; glue and paddles; and *Eating Fruits and Vegetables from A to Z*, by Lois Ehlert.

Approach

Incorporation

Facilitation

Read *Eating Fruits and Vegetables from A to Z* to introduce children to the wonderful variety of fruits and vegetables that are grown around the world. Bring in samples of the less common food items for children to examine by touch, smell, taste, and sight.

Introduce the concept that all foods can be divided into five basic groups. Show the food pyramid and explain each section. Have the children think about traditional foods prepared at home and consider into which part of the food pyramid they would be placed. In small groups, have the children cut out, sort, and glue food pictures on the appropriate sections of the pyramid. Ensure your materials are broadly representative of different cultural diets.

Expansion

The Nutrition Lotto Game, available from Lakeshore/Wintergreen (LA 673), reinforces the concepts of essential food groups in this multilevel activity.

Community Resource

Public health departments should be able to provide additional resources such as charts, posters, or kits dealing with this topic.

Trees Are Like Us

Age
6–7 years

Curriculum Area
Science

Curriculum Objectives
To observe, make comparisons, and think critically about commonalities among all living things.

Anti-Bias Area
Appearance

Anti-Bias Skill
To recognize, label, and discuss similarities and differences.

Materials
Felt pieces of tree parts; flip chart paper and marker; matching laminated cards made from maple, oak, cedar, balsam, aspen, beech, and chestnut; and *A Tree Is Nice,* by Janice Udry.

Approach
Incorporation

Facilitation
Read *A Tree Is Nice* to prepare the children to think about what trees need to survive. Ask the children to name significant parts of a tree and what function these parts fill. As the children volunteer answers, hand them a felt piece and invite them to place it on the felt board.

List the parts and functions on flip chart paper:

taproots—water
trunk—support, structure
bark—protection
branches—support and structure
leaf—food source

Have the children think about what they need to survive. Emphasize the commonalities among all living things: necessity for food, water, air, and protection. Encourage the children to make the connection that despite differences in external appearances, all animals, humans, and plants share basic similarities.

Expansion
Follow this experience with a set of matching cards with real leaves. Have the children pair the appropriate cards and describe the differences in shape and color. Make the materials accessible for further exploration.

Bandage Science

Age
6–8 years

Curriculum Area
Science

Curriculum Objective
To learn about the reason for different skin colors.

Anti-Bias Area
Race

Anti-Bias Skills
To gather information and draw conclusions based on facts; to promote awareness of and respect for diversity in race.

Materials
Bandages

Approach
Modified Personalization

Facilitation
Distribute bandages to each child in the class. Have them keep a fingertip bandaged for three days. On the fourth day let them remove the bandage and observe the change that occurred in the finger's skin color. Ask them to describe their observations. Encourage them to generate possible reasons for this change.

Explain that human skin has a special substance called melanin. Everybody has different amounts of melanin that we get from our parents. When the melanin is exposed to sunlight, it spreads out and causes the skin to darken. When it is covered, the skin gets lighter.

Ask them to consider the relation of melanin to the various skin tones in the class. Introduce the word *albino* and inform them that albinos have no melanin.

You've Come a Long Way

Age
7–9 years

Curriculum Area
Science

Curriculum Objectives
To sequence and describe changes that happen to the human body during the growth cycle.

Anti-Bias Areas
Gender, Race, Culture, Age

Anti-Bias Skill
To recognize, label, and discuss similarities and differences.

Materials
Photos of each child from infancy to the present; mural paper; and markers.

Approach
Modified Personalization

Facilitation
Hold up several photographs of the children as infants and have the class guess who is the baby in the photo. Elicit from the group some of the physical changes that happen over this 7–9-year period: crawling; walking; learning to talk, catch a ball, ride a bike, etc.

Assign each child to arrange the photos in a time line on a sheet of mural paper. Under each photo in the appropriate space on the time line, the children should describe what physical changes are occurring. Have the children interview their parents to find out at what age they acquired new skills. Have them fill in under the present year what skills they are gaining or hope to master.

Food—Past and Present

Age
8–10 years

Curriculum Area
Science

Curriculum Objective
To discover how change and continuity relate to food technology.

Anti-Bias Area
Culture

Anti-Bias Skill
To listen to and value other points of view.

Materials
Chart paper and pens.

Approach
Personalization

Facilitation
Invite a panel of senior citizens from a variety of cultural backgrounds to chat with the class about the changes in food consumption and technology associated with storage and production. Have the class generate a list of questions to pose to the panel prior to the visit:

- What types of fruits/vegetables were available?
- Where did one shop for meats? dairy products? vegetables?
- How were foods kept fresh? How was food storage different?
- What is new technology in food preparation for them? What has remained the same?
- How often did they eat certain foods?
- What foods were served on special occasions?
- What foods are canned/processed now that were not before?

After the guests have gone, have the class construct a chart that illustrates these generational differences.

Food Stories Created by Sound

Age

8–11 years

Curriculum Area

Science

Curriculum Objective

To collect and present information in narrative form with sounds.

Anti-Bias Area

Culture

Anti-Bias Skill

To recognize, label, and discuss similarities and differences.

Materials

Reference books on food production (*Food and Farming; Rice; Sugaring Time,* etc.); paper and pencils; and sound makers: cellophane, cans, rulers, water in a jar, metallic tray, etc.

Approach

Incorporation

Facilitation

Assign the task of creating a story by sound. Have groups of six children review a method of food gathering or production illustrated in the reference books. To facilitate this task have the children first write a brief sequence of actions that depicts the story line. They can then decide on the types of sounds required and devise ideas for their production. Many of the animal and motor noises, or even sounds of thumping, creaking, etc., can be made by the children themselves. They will need to use their creativity in selecting objects that will simulate the appropriate sounds.

As each group presents their story, suggest to the class that they shut their eyes in order to visualize the actions more successfully.

Possible topics for the sound stories include: a sugar cane harvest, shrimp fishing expedition, cattle/sheep ranch, dairy farm, chicken farm, rice paddy. (Adapted from Joan Miller's *Sharing Ideas. An Oral Language Programme.*)

Somewhere in Africa

Age

7–10 years

Curriculum Area

Art

Curriculum Objectives

To practice measurement and problem-solving skills by designing and constructing a three-dimensional art project.

Anti-Bias Area

Culture

Anti-Bias Skill

To promote awareness of and respect for diversity in culture.

Materials

Small- and medium-sized cardboard boxes (cereal, shoe, cake mix, shortening, etc.); scissors; light aluminum cans; glue; string; cardboard scraps; pencils; aluminum foil; wooden scraps; nails and hammers; and *Somewhere in Africa,* by Ingrid Mennen and Nikki Daly.

Approach

Incorporation

Facilitation

Start this activity by asking the class to hypothesize what life in Africa is like. What kinds of homes do children live in? What kinds of sounds might they hear? What kind of clothing would they see people wearing? What kinds of activities do children like to engage in? What kinds of vegetation and animals might they encounter? The purpose of this probe is to see if the group has stereotypical perceptions and assumptions about life and people in Africa.

Read *Somewhere in Africa;* follow up the reading by asking the children to discuss in what ways their predictions were incorrect. Elicit a list of things that are common between the child living in Africa and themselves. Help them to understand that the human needs of shelter, food, and entertainment are universal; though climate and economic ability dictate what form these needs take.

Focus on the types of toys with which children in Africa (and other parts of the world) play. Explain to them that toy vehicles (trucks, cars, vans, buses, planes) are very common and popular with the children. In fact, older children usually make such toys for younger ones. Show them the construction materials and tools available. Offer guidance during both the designing and construction phases.

These creations can later be donated to children living in shelters.

Expansion

This creative activity can be followed with a writing experience. Have the children pretend their vehicle is real and describe where they would travel for their "dream of a lifetime trip."

Community Resource

Foster Parents Canada sponsored an exhibit of over 100 such metal toy vehicles made by children in Africa. Check for catalogs or brochures from Foster Parents for pictures to show the children.

Making an American Quilt

Age

9–11 years

Curriculum Area

Visual Arts

Curriculum Objective

To promote the creative expression of feelings and ideas through the visual arts.

Anti-Bias Areas

Culture, Gender, Class

Anti-Bias Skill

To promote awareness of and respect for diversity in culture.

Materials

Tar Beach, by Faith Ringgold; material scraps; felt pieces, batik pieces, etc.; thread and needles; and collage materials.

Approach

Modified Personalization

Facilitation

Read *Tar Beach* to the class. Conduct a follow-up discussion that explores the children's understanding of racism and what life means to an economically disadvantaged family. Explore the metaphor of Cassie's "flying to freedom," and encourage divergent responses among the children.

Ask the class to design individual patches that will then be sewn together to create a class quilt. The patch design should reflect something of importance to them and/or their families, or a dream for their family. Once the quilt is completed, mount it outside the classroom door for others in the school to experience.

Art Forms of Aboriginal Peoples

Age

9–11 years

Curriculum Area

Visual Arts

Curriculum Objectives

To learn about visual art techniques from a different culture; to experiment with symbols and colors.

Anti-Bias Area

Culture

Anti-Bias Skill

To encourage openness to new experiences; to promote awareness of and respect for diversity in culture.

Materials

Pictures of Australian Aboriginal bark and dream map paintings, Northwest Coast Indian art, Inuit sculptures and paintings from Baker Lane and Cape Dorset, and paintings from American Plains Indians.

For bark paintings: recycled brown paper bags; brown, yellow, black, white, and red pencils.

For dream maps: white paper; chopsticks, blunt bamboo skewers, or sticks; and various earth-toned tempera paints.

Approach

Incorporation

Facilitation

After the children have experienced the *Creating Legends* activity, focus their attention on the artwork that usually accompanies these stories. Show the variety of indigenous art forms and have the children guess what the artwork is depicting. Point out how Aboriginal artists use certain symbols to depict the story and leave much to the viewer's imagination. In particular, the Australian Aborigines do not have a written language so that each line and dot has a critical meaning.

Hold up a sample/photo of Aboriginal bark and sand paintings. Explain briefly the origin of each art form. Bark painting originates from Arnhem Land in Australia's Northern Territory. Artists use bark from the eucalyptus tree, heated by fire and flattened by stones. Paint colors are derived from different stones and pigments. Dream map painting was originally done in the sand to convey sacred images. Now dream maps are acrylic paintings that depict stories of certain places, hunting, and landscapes related to mythological events.

Have the children analyze the primary stylistic difference in technique. The bark paintings use an X-ray technique that shows internal organs and skeletons of animals and humans, while the dream maps are composed of circles, ovals, arcs, straight and curved lines, and hundreds of dots that fill in the spaces.

(*continued*)

Offer the children a choice to illustrate their own legends in either art form or create dream maps of real or imaginary places. Children will be required to dip the blunt end of a chopstick or skewer into the paint and then press it onto paper to create the dots. Display a sheet with a few symbols to assist those trying this art form: kangaroo tracks, boomerangs, water hole, and walking straight (the appendix has an Aboriginal Art Symbol guide). Have the children share their stories or dream maps with the class.

Expansion

Visit a cultural center, local art gallery, or museum to view Native paintings and sculptures.

Community Resources

This activity requires advance research into Native art forms in order to collect samples and information. Contact Native associations and the Australian High Commission for possible photographs. Contact local Native American Cultural/Community centers to arrange for speakers to visit and share information with the class.

Lakeshore/Wintergreen's Arts and Crafts Catalog offers kits dedicated to Mexican Bark painting (SC7-GP618) and Southwestern Indian Sand Painting (SC7-GP197). These kits give the children an opportunity to reproduce designs, images, and patterns typical of the art forms of these two distinctive cultures. It is the author's preference that children first learn about art forms, and then apply the information using their own creativity and imagination.

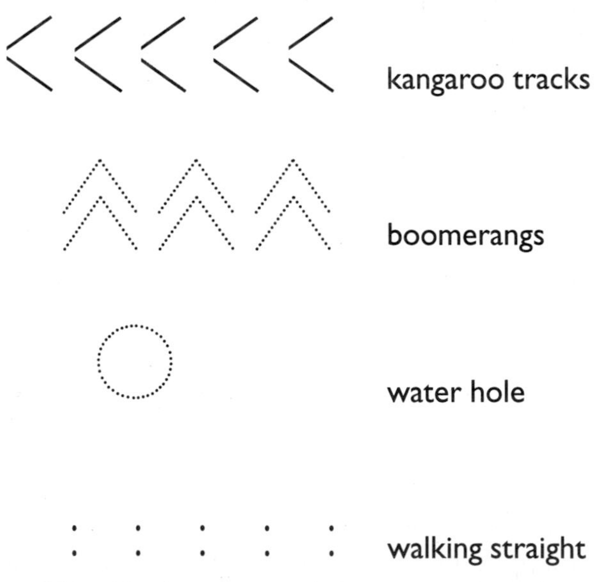

Using Aboriginal art symbols to create a legend.

Ma Liang and the Magic Brush

Age

10–11 years

Curriculum Area

Visual Arts

Curriculum Objective

To use the medium of painting to illustrate a situation that requires a proactive approach.

Anti-Bias Areas

Culture, Class

Anti-Bias Skill

To be proactive in helping others.

Materials

Watercolors and paper; variety of paintbrushes; and *Ma Liang and the Magic Brush* (Chinese folktale).

Approach

Incorporation

Facilitation

Read *Ma Liang and the Magic Brush*. Have the children focus on two aspects of the story:

1. Why Ma Liang is a hero.
   - Use of creative problem-solving skills to outwit a greedy mandarin.
   - The refusal to misuse his talent to benefit someone's power.
   - The use of his talent to help others less fortunate.
2. The nature of the ethical and social issues in China.
   - Oppression of the poor; greed of the richer classes.
   - The willingness of the mandarin to abuse someone's talent in order to further his wealth and power.

Ask the group if they had the power to make something real, what would they paint and why? Give the watercolors and paintbrushes to the children and remind them to "use them wisely." After the paintings are completed have the children describe the situation they selected and the solution they designed.

Resources for Elementary School Children

The following list of books provides supplementary resources and bibliographic information for the activities included in this chapter. Children and teachers may use the titles to expand interest on a specific topic or for additional background research.

Bruno Brontosaurus

Rubel, N. (1983). *Bruno Brontosaurus.* New York: Avon/Camelot Books.

Dinosaur Sort

Wilson, R. (1986). *100 dinosaurs from A to Z.* New York: Grosset and Dunlap.

Stellaluna

Cannon, J. (1993). *Stellaluna.* San Diego, CA: Harcourt, Brace and Co.

Stewart, F. T., and Charles, P. (1988). *Birds and their environment.* New York: Harper Collins Children's Books, Inc.

Woodward, K. (1991). *How does a bird fly?* London: Usborne Publishing Ltd.

Experiences in Vision

Greenaway, F., and Young, J. (1991). *Amazing bats.* Toronto, Canada: Stoddart Publishing.

Grossman, P. (1991). *The night ones.* San Diego: Harcourt, Brace, Jovanovich.

Fly Away Home

Bunting, E. (1991). *Fly away home.* New York: Clarion Books.

Living out of a Bag

Wolf, B. (1995). *Homeless.* New York: Orchard Books.

Mrs. Katz and Tush

Polacco, P. (1992). *Mrs. Katz and Tush.* New York: Bantam Books.

Cultural Celebrations

Chocolate, D., and Massey, C. (1992). *My first Kwanza book.* New York: Scholastic.

Gold, B. (1993). *The magician's visit: A Passover tale.* New York: Viking.

Heymsfield, C., and Guzner, V. (1996). *The matzah ball fairy.* New York: UAHC Press.

Saccone, V. (1996). *ABC's of Kwanza activities: An easy way to learn about Kwanza—for kids of all ages.* Nashville, TN: J.C. Winston Publishing Co.

Abuela's Weave

Castaneda, O. S. (1993). *Abuela's weave.* New York: Lee and Low Books.

Omens and Signs

Jackson, E. (1994). *Winter solstice.* Brookfield, CT: Millbrook Press.

The Sharing Quilt

Polacco, P. (1988). *The keeping quilt.* New York: Simon and Schuster.

Smucker, B. (1995). *Selina and the bear paw quilt.* Toronto, Canada: Stoddart Publishing.

Weaver's Booth Game

Haskins, J. *Count your way through . . . series. Arab World* (1991). *China* (1987). *Greece* (1996). *India* (1990). *Korea* (1989). Minneapolis, MN: Carolrhoda Books.

Tiktala

Mackinnon, M. S. (1996). *Tiktala.* Toronto, Canada: Stoddart Publishing.

Kusugak, M. (1993). *Northern lights.* Toronto, Canada: Annick Press.

Constructing an Igluvigak

Reynolds, J. (1993). *Frozen land. Vanishing culture.* San Diego, CA: Harcourt, Brace and Co.
Shemie, B. (1989). *Houses of snow, skin, and bones.* Montreal/New York: Tundra Books.

Spirits of the North

Goddesses, heroes, and shamans: A young people's guide to world mythology. (1994). New York: Kingfisher.

Who Belongs Here?

Burns-Knight, M. (1993). *Who belongs here? An American story.* Gardiner, ME: Tillbury Publishers.

Interviewing for Information

Archibald, E. (1997). *A Sudanese family.* Minneapolis, MN: Lerner Publications Co.
Gogol, S. (1996). *A Mien family.* Minneapolis, MN: Lerner Publications Co.
Kuklin, S. (1992). *How my family lives in America.* New York: Bradbury Press.
Malone, M. (1996). *A Guatemalan family.* Minneapolis, MN: Lerner Publications Co.
Murphy, N. (1997). *A Hmong family.* Minneapolis, MN: Lerner Publications Co.
O'Connor, K. (1996). *A Kurdish family.* Minneapolis, MN: Lerner Publications Co.
Silverman, R. L. (1997). *A Bosnian family.* Minneapolis, MN: Lerner Publications Co.

Contributions Made by Immigrants

Shalant, P. (1988). *Look what we've brought you from Vietnam: Crafts, games, recipes, stories, and other cultural activities from new Americans.* New York: Julian Messner.

Political Activists

Goldfarb, M. (1982). *Fighters, refugees, and immigrants: A story of the Hmong.* Minneapolis, MN: Carolrhoda Books.

Recipes for Peace

Uchida, Y. and Yardley, J. (1993). *The bracelet.* New York: Putnam and Grosset Group.

Chair for My Mother

Williams, V. B. (1982). *Chair for my mother.* New York: Greenwillow Books.

What Do Moms Do?

Merriam, E. (1989). *Daddies at work.* New York: Simon and Schuster, Books for Young Readers.
Merriam, E. (1989). *Mommies at work.* New York: Simon and Schuster, Books for Young Readers.

In Other Words

Walker, J. C. (1993). *In other words.* Toronto, Canada: Annick Press.

Augmentative Communication Experience

Mayer-Johnson. (1992). *Picture communication symbols, Books 1–3.* Solana Beach, CA: Mayer-Johnson.

Communication Machine

Lee, J. (1991). *Silent lotus.* New York: Farrar, Straus and Giroux.

Creative Holidays

Dhanjal, B. (1996). *What do we know about Sikhism?* New York: Peter Bedrick Books.
Ganeri, A. (1995). *What do we know about Hinduism?* New York: Peter Bedrick Books.
Fine, D. (1995). *What do we know about Judaism?* New York: Peter Bedrick Books.
Husain, S. (1995). *What do we know about Islam?* New York: Peter Bedrick Books.

Houses and Homes

Morris, A. (1992). *Houses and homes.* New York: Mulberry Paperback Book.
White, S. (1995). *Welcome home.* Chicago: Children's Press.

Houses Around the World

Bowyer, C. (1978). *A children's book on houses and homes.* London: Usborne Publication.
James, B. (1994). *The mud family.* Toronto: Oxford University Press.
Le Sieg, T. (1966). *Come over to my house.* New York: Random House.
Moore, H., and Sorville, C. (1995). *Pyramids to pueblos. 15 pop-up models for students to make.* New York: Scholastic Professional Books.

Mapping a Neighborhood

Hollenbeck, K. (1997). *Exploring our world: Neighborhoods and communities.* New York: Scholastic Professional Books.

Big Is Beautiful

Clements, A. (1988). *Big Al.* New York: Scholastic Books.
Munsch, R. (1983). *David's father.* Toronto, Canada: Annick Press.

Swimmy Felt Board Story

Lionni, L. (1963). *Swimmy.* New York: Random House.

Special Gifts

Bogart, J., and Reid, B. (1994). *Gifts.* Richmond Hill, Ontario: North Winds Press.
Children of the world. (1987). Milwaukee, WI: Gareth Stevens Publishing.

Picture Card Scramble

Beim, J. (1950). *The swimming hole.* New York: Morrow.

Signing In

Arthur, C. (1979). *My sister's silent world.* Chicago: Children's Press.
Collins, H. S. (1992). *Signing at school.* Eugene, OR: Garlic Press.
Collins, H. S. (1995). *Songs in sign.* Eugene, OR: Garlic Press.
Collins, H. S., Kifer, K., and Solar, D. (1994). *Mother Goose in sign.* Eugene, OR: Garlic Press.
Faith, K. (1996). *Handsigns.* Vancouver, Canada: Raincoast Books.
Litchfield, A. (1980). *Words in our hands.* Chicago: Albert Whitman and Co.
Wheeler, C. (1995). *Simple signs.* New York: Puffin Books.

No One Loved Horace

Green, L. (1983). *No one loved Horace.* Peterborough, England: Minimax Books.

Mama Will You Love Me?

Jaosse, B. (1991). *Mama will you love me?* San Francisco: Chronicle Book.

Similes About Myself

Woods, A. (1982). *Quick as a cricket.* Singapore: Child's Play (International) Ltd.

Why Am I So Different?

Simon, N. (1976). *Why am I so different?* Chicago: Albert Whitman.

Fact Sheet on Discrimination

Grunsell, A. (1990). *Let's talk about racism.* London: Aladdin Books, Gloucester Press.
Vigna, J. (1992). *Black like Kyra. White like me.* Morton Grove, IL: Albert Whitman and Co.

Nursery Rhymes Biases

Larche, D. W. (1985). *Father Gander nursery rhymes.* Santa Barbara, CA: Advocacy Press.

Mistaken Perceptions

Sciezka, J. (1989). *True story of the three little pigs.* New York: Viking.

Name Anagrams

Dunkling, L. (1974). *The Guinness book of names.* Enfield, England: Guinness Superlatives.

Being Differently Abled

Martin, B., Jr., and Archambault, J. (1966). *Knots on a counting rope.* New York: Henry Holt and Co.

An Aesop Fable

Aesop's fables. (1985). Selected and illustrated by M. Hague. New York: Holt, Rinehart and Winston.

Creating Legends

Archibald, J., Friesen, V., and Smith, J. (Eds.) (1993). *Courageous spirits. Aboriginal heroes of our children.* Penticton, BC: Mokakit Education Research Association.

de Paola, T. (1988). *Legend of the Indian paintbrush.* New York: Putnam.

Ellis, J. (1991). *From the dreamtime. Australian Aboriginal legends.* Victoria, Australia: Collins Dove.

Land of the long white cloud. Maori myths, tales, and legends. (1989). Retold by K. Te Kanawa. Auckland: Penguin Books.

Taylor, C. J. (1993). *How we saw the world. Nine Native stories of the way things began.* Montreal, Canada: Tundra Books.

Verall, C. (Ed.) (1988). *All my relations. Sharing native values through the arts.* Toronto, Canada: Canadian Alliance in Solidarity with Native Peoples.

Tool Sort

Morris, A. (1992). *Tools.* New York: Lothrop, Lee and Shepard Books.

People Living in My Home

Garza, C. (1990). *Family pictures: Cuadros de familia.* San Francisco: Children's Book Press.

Brynjolson, R. (1996). *Foster baby.* Winnipeg, Canada: Pemmican.

Tompert, A. (1990). *Grandfather Tang's story.* New York: Crown Publishers.

Food Pyramid

Ehlert, L. (1989). *Eating fruits and vegetables from A to Z.* San Diego, CA: Harcourt, Brace and Jovanovich.

Trees Are Like Us

Udry, J. (1956). *A tree is nice.* New York: Harper and Row.

Food Stories Created by Sound

Food and farming. (1994). Australia: Dorling Kindersley Book, Ltd.

Johnson, S. (1985). *Rice.* Minneapolis, MN: Lerner Publication Co.

Lasky, K. (1983). *Sugaring time.* New York: Macmillan Publishing Co.

Miller, J. (1988). *Sharing ideas. An oral language programme.* Melbourne, Australia: Thomas Nelson.

Somewhere in Africa

Mennen, I., and Daly, N. (1992). *Somewhere in Africa.* New York: Dutton's Children's Books.

Making an American Quilt

Ringgold, F. (1991). *Tar beach.* New York: Crown Publishers, Inc.

Ma Liang and the Magic Brush

Wyndham, R. (1971). *Ma Liang and the magic brush.* In *Tales the people tell in China.* New York: Julian Messner.

Other Readings

Badt, K. L. (1994). *Good morning. Let's eat.* Chicago: Children's Press.
Badt, K. L. (1994). *Greetings.* Chicago: Children's Press.
Badt, K. L. (1994). *Hair there and everywhere.* Chicago: Children's Press.
Badt, K. L. (1995). *Let's go.* Chicago: Children's Press.
Bailey, D. (1990). *Where we live series: Australia; Hong Kong; India; and Trinidad.* Madison, NJ: Steck-Vaughn.
Corbett, S. (1995). *Shake, rattle, and strum.* Chicago: Children's Press.
Feder, J. (1995). *Table, chair, bear. A book in many languages.* Boston: Houghton Mifflin Co.
Kelly, K., and Jaeb, E. (1995). *Sleep on it.* Chicago: Children's Press.
Kalman, B. (Ed.) (1993). *The lands, peoples, and cultures series.* New York: Crabtree Publishing Co.
Lodha, M. (1994). *Stories of prejudice, pain, and peace.* Pinawa, Manitoba: Edgemont Enterprises Ltd.

Appendix

ANTI-BIAS AREA ABBREVIATIONS			
AB:	Ability	FC:	Family Composition
AG:	Age	GEN:	Gender
AP:	Appearance	R:	Race
BEL:	Belief	SX:	Sexuality
CLS:	Class	ALL:	All Anti-Bias Areas
CUL:	Culture		

REPRODUCIBLE ANTI-BIAS ENVIRONMENTAL SUPPORT CHART

List materials available to children in each area.

AGE	DRAMATIC PLAY	ENVIRONMENT/ SCIENCE	LANGUAGE ARTS	MATH/ MANIPULATIVE	SENSORY	CREATIVE	LARGE MOTOR EQUIPMENT	ANTI-BIAS SKILL
MONDAY								
Anti-Bias Area								
TUESDAY								
Anti-Bias Area								
WEDNESDAY								
Anti-Bias Area								
THURSDAY								
Anti-Bias Area								
FRIDAY								
Anti-Bias Area								

REPRODUCIBLE COMMUNITY RESOURCES CHART

WHERE I CAN FIND:

COMMUNITY RESOURCES	MATERIALS/ITEMS	COMMENTS

REPRODUCIBLE LITERATURE RESOURCE LIST

Alphabetical Listing by Authors' Surnames

TITLE	AUTHOR	ANTI-BIAS AREAS									
		AB	AG	AP	BEL	CLS	CUL	FC	GEN	R	SX

ANTI-BIAS MATRIX

POSITIVE SELF-CONCEPT	**AGE GROUP** Infant; Toddler; Preschool-Kindergarten; Elementary School	**PHYSICAL ENVIRONMENT** Indoor/Outdoor Furnishing/ Equipment	**CURRICULUM AREAS** E.g.: Lang; Science; Soc-emo; Math; Social Studies	**INTEREST AREAS** E.g.: Sand; Creative; Dramatic Play	**POLICIES** E.g.: Family Involvement; Behavior Management	**ROUTINES** E.g.: Feeding; Toileting; Sleeping
RECOGNIZE INDIVIDUAL CHARACTERISTICS AND THOSE OF OTHERS						
RECOGNIZE SELF IN RELATION TO FAMILY						
RECOGNIZE SELF IN RELATION TO LARGER GROUPS: PEER, ETHNO-RACIAL, AND CLASS						
MUTUAL RESPECT						
AWARENESS AND RESPECT FOR OTHER CULTURES, RACES, BELIEFS						
RESPECT FOR GENDER AND ABILITY EQUITY						
ABILITY TO SEE DIFFERENT POINTS OF VIEW						
ABILITY TO EXAMINE ALTERNATIVES						
ACTIVE OBSERVING AND LISTENING						
ABILITY TO IDENTIFY SIMILARITIES AND DIFFERENCES						
ABILITY TO CONSTRUCT RELATIONSHIPS						
ABILITY TO NOTICE FAIR AND UNFAIR BEHAVIOR						
ABILITY TO GATHER INFORMATION						
AFFECTIVE SKILL BUILDING						
FOSTER POSITIVE SENSE OF SELF						
ABILITY TO TRY NEW EXPERIENCES						
ABILITY TO WORK COOPERATIVELY						
ABILITY TO DEMONSTRATE EMPATHY						
PROACTIVISM						
ABILITY TO MAKE CHOICES						
ABILITY TO CHALLENGE STEREOTYPES						
ABILITY TO PARTICIPATE IN GROUP ACTION						
ABILITY TO TAKE ACTION AGAINST UNFAIR SITUATIONS OR COMMENTS						

DEVELOPMENTAL OVERVIEW ACTIVITY CHART

LEGEND	
Infant	**Preschool**
Toddler	Elementary

POSITIVE SELF-CONCEPT		MUTUAL RESPECT		UNDERSTANDING SIMILARITIES/DIFFERENCES	EMPATHY	PROACTIVISM
Bouncing Balloons ***Family Hide-and-Seek*** ***Family Lullabies*** ***Hand/Foot Water Play*** ***Tin Can Stacking***						
	Textured Snake					
Family Puzzle ***A Book of Me***						
	Basket Nesting ***Hide and Find Box***					
Diving Pool ***Mobile Mania***						
	Feely Smelly Cubes ***Bumpy Feelings*** ***Drum Madness***					
Lids and Tops						
	Tongue Pull ***Textured Nesting Cans*** ***Texured Sound Shakers*** ***Finger Painting Pictures***					
Stickers on You and Me						
	Hidden Hankies ***Ribbons and Bows***					
Scrubbie Play ***Ring Game***						
		Drum March *Baby Dressing*				
Hide and Find the Toddlers *Family Place Mats*			*Rock Around the Clock* *Knobs in a Box*			
	Emotions Peek-a-boo Board			*Mixed-up Suitcase*		
Me Collage			*Bandage Time* *Buried Treasure*			
	Bathtime for Babies					
Family Messages *Are You My Mother?*		*Mirror Reflections* *House Cleaning*				
	Lacing Faces		*Matching Fabrics*			
Family Matchup *Magnet Play*		*Building Spools* *Feeling Fingers*				
	Tall Body Felt Board		*Signing a Name*			
Crying Babies *Book of Routines* *Handprinting*		*Washing and Drying Clothes* *Bumpy Goop* *Noodles and Things* *Brown Dough Sticks* *Beanbag Toss*				
	Stuffed Nylons *Making Music*		*Gluing Faces* *The Obstacle Course*			
		Jars and Lids				
	Opening and Closing Surprises *Laundry Scoops*		*Exploring Mobility Devices* *Scrub Painting*			
		Vermicelli Play				

DEVELOPMENTAL OVERVIEW ACTIVITY CHART

(continued)

LEGEND	
Infant	**Preschool**
Toddler	Elementary

<table>
<tr><th>POSITIVE SELF-CONCEPT</th><th>MUTUAL RESPECT</th><th>UNDERSTANDING SIMILARITIES/DIFFERENCES</th><th>EMPATHY</th><th>PROACTIVISM</th></tr>
<tr><td colspan="2">Silly Putty Silliness</td><td></td><td></td><td></td></tr>
<tr><td></td><td colspan="2">Changeable Faces
Buttons and Beads
Matching Paint Chips
Ivory Snow® Smear
Bunches of Bags
Squishy Water Play
Ramp Fun</td><td></td><td></td></tr>
<tr><td>Emotion Book</td><td></td><td>Fun with Paint Chips</td><td></td><td></td></tr>
<tr><td colspan="2">Face-to-Face Puzzles</td><td></td><td></td><td></td></tr>
<tr><td>Mixed-up Creatures</td><td>Diversity Puzzle</td><td>Who Is Underneath?</td><td></td><td>Shoe Sort Game</td></tr>
<tr><td>Whose Voice Is That?</td><td>Bread Delivery</td><td>Conservation Task Cards</td><td></td><td></td></tr>
<tr><td>Sands of Many Colors</td><td>Painting to Music</td><td></td><td></td><td></td></tr>
<tr><td>Family Flannel Board</td><td colspan="2">Friendship Dominoes</td><td></td><td></td></tr>
<tr><td colspan="2">Body Sounds</td><td></td><td></td><td></td></tr>
<tr><td></td><td colspan="2">Lots of Breads</td><td></td><td></td></tr>
<tr><td>I Can Do Place Mat</td><td>What's in A Name?</td><td></td><td colspan="2">What Belongs Together</td></tr>
<tr><td>The Family House</td><td>Word Picture Puzzles</td><td colspan="2">Puzzle by Number</td><td></td></tr>
<tr><td></td><td></td><td>More Fun with Paint Chips</td><td></td><td></td></tr>
<tr><td></td><td></td><td></td><td>Worm Puzzle</td><td></td></tr>
<tr><td>The Guessing Bag</td><td></td><td></td><td></td><td></td></tr>
<tr><td colspan="2">People Puzzles</td><td></td><td></td><td></td></tr>
<tr><td></td><td colspan="2">Hats, Hats, Hats Lotto Game</td><td></td><td></td></tr>
<tr><td>Group Mural of Likes and Dislikes</td><td>Spice Matchup</td><td colspan="2">Letter Cards</td><td></td></tr>
<tr><td colspan="2">The Body Bingo Game</td><td>Language Cards</td><td>Sounds Are Us</td><td></td></tr>
<tr><td></td><td>Grocery Matching</td><td>Mystery Prop Game</td><td>Books in Braille</td><td></td></tr>
<tr><td colspan="2">Lacing Hands</td><td></td><td></td><td></td></tr>
<tr><td></td><td colspan="2">Grain Play</td><td></td><td></td></tr>
<tr><td></td><td></td><td colspan="2">Playdough in a Glove</td><td></td></tr>
<tr><td></td><td>Papier-mâché Creatures</td><td>Fishing for Cultural Patterns</td><td></td><td></td></tr>
<tr><td></td><td>Fun with Geometric Shapes</td><td>Ways of Carrying Babies</td><td></td><td></td></tr>
<tr><td></td><td></td><td colspan="2">Hair Beading</td><td></td></tr>
<tr><td></td><td></td><td colspan="2">Outside Treasure Hunt</td><td></td></tr>
<tr><td></td><td>Tasting Milk</td><td>Amazing Hair Dramatic Play</td><td colspan="2">What Can You Do to Help?</td></tr>
<tr><td></td><td>Memory Game</td><td>Body Parts</td><td colspan="2">Life Cycle in Sequence</td></tr>
<tr><td></td><td>Let's Talk About . . .</td><td>Classification Board Game</td><td colspan="2">Job Cards</td></tr>
<tr><td></td><td>Cheese Puzzle</td><td>Pattern Match-up Board</td><td>Moving Through Space</td><td></td></tr>
<tr><td></td><td>Stick Puppet Drama</td><td>People Sponge Painting</td><td></td><td></td></tr>
<tr><td colspan="2">Silhouette Guess</td><td colspan="2">Scooter Board Skills</td><td></td></tr>
<tr><td></td><td></td><td>Create Your Own Color</td><td>Barefoot Art</td><td></td></tr>
<tr><td></td><td>Shape Changes</td><td>Missing Parts</td><td>What If . . . ?</td><td></td></tr>
<tr><td></td><td>Changes in Appearance</td><td>Pasta Power</td><td>What Does This Person Need?</td><td></td></tr>
<tr><td></td><td>Holiday Dress</td><td>Don't Judge by Appearances</td><td>The Missing Pic Symbol</td><td></td></tr>
<tr><td></td><td>Seriated Surprise Boxes</td><td></td><td>Helping Hands for All</td><td></td></tr>
<tr><td></td><td colspan="2">Matching Feely Bag</td><td></td><td></td></tr>
<tr><td></td><td>Counting Board Game</td><td>Designer Shade</td><td colspan="2">Whose Job Is It Anyway?</td></tr>
<tr><td colspan="2">Ice Cube Melt</td><td></td><td>The Cooperative Relay Game</td><td></td></tr>
<tr><td></td><td colspan="2">The Friendship Square</td><td></td><td></td></tr>
<tr><td></td><td>Counting Children</td><td></td><td>Ball Toss</td><td></td></tr>
<tr><td></td><td>Brown Is Beautiful</td><td></td><td>Unisex Dress-up for Dolls</td><td></td></tr>
<tr><td></td><td>Musical Scarves</td><td></td><td></td><td></td></tr>
<tr><td></td><td>Dramatic Pulley Play</td><td></td><td></td><td></td></tr>
<tr><td></td><td>Spray Bottle Art</td><td></td><td></td><td></td></tr>
<tr><td></td><td>Go Bake Card Game</td><td></td><td></td><td></td></tr>
<tr><td></td><td>It Looks Like Spilled Cocoa</td><td></td><td></td><td></td></tr>
<tr><td></td><td>Newspaper Collage</td><td></td><td></td><td></td></tr>
</table>

DEVELOPMENTAL OVERVIEW ACTIVITY CHART

(*continued*)

LEGEND	
Infant	**Preschool**
Toddler	Elementary

POSITIVE SELF-CONCEPT	MUTUAL RESPECT	UNDERSTANDING SIMILARITIES/DIFFERENCES	EMPATHY	PROACTIVISM
Who's in My Family		People Sort	Fly Away Home	Nutrition Is . . .
Dinosaur Acrostics	People Living in My Home		Living out of a Bag	Poverty and Families
Dictionary of Family Names	Food Pyramid	Tool Sort	The Value of Money	Fact Sheet on Discrimination
Community Calendar	Picture Story Writing	Bruno Brontosaurus	Hardware Handiness	Political Activists
Poster Ads	Mrs. Katz and Tush	Dinosaur Sort	Signing In	Recipes for Peace
Commemorative Stamps	Dancing Time	Lifestyle Differences	Who Belongs Here? II	The Many Forms of Proactivism
Individual Coat of Arms	Geography Web	Bones and Bodies		
		Sports Logos		
Name Anagrams	Food—Past and Present	Dinosaur Eggs	Who Belongs Here?	Ma Liang and the Magic Brush
Oral Histories	Comic Strip Authors	Trees Are Like Us		Nursery Rhymes Biases
		Interviewing for Information		
Similies about Myself	Creating Legends	Contributions Made by Immigrants	I Can't Understand You	
The Story of a Name	Art Forms of Aboriginal Peoples	Cultural Celebrations I	Pass the Beanbag, Please	
Name Play	No One Loved Horace	Rock Garden	Dreams for a Better Future	
		Cultural Celebrations II		
A Gift for You	Mapping a Neighborhood			
Getting to Know One Another		Mama Will You Love Me?	Access for Everyone?	Community Project
Why Am I So Different?		You've Come a Long Way	The Gossip Sheet	Television Advertising
Special Gifts	Storytelling with Objects	Work and Leisure	Caption It	Ecology Debate
The Importance of a Name	Creative Holidays	Coping with Change	Dogs Who Work	An Aesop Fable
	Houses Around the World			
	Houses on the Move	Food Stories Created by Sound		Witches Get Bad Press
		Who Goes? Who Stays?		
Famous Homes		Homes and Houses	Being Differently Abled	Drama Improvisation
	Houses of the Future	Stellaluna	In Other Words	Swimmy Felt Board Story
	Tangram Tale	Star-Moon	Augmentative Communication Experience	Killer Statements and Gestures
	Can We Be the Same and Different?	Multiple Meanings	Mechanical Busy Board	
	Flying Animal Match Game	The Inuit and Ecology	Riding in Someone Else's Wheelchair	
	Flight Patterns	Spirits of the North	Writing without Hands	
	Money Jars	Arctic Nutrition	Communication Machine	
	Bandage Science	Mayan Math	Experiences in Vision	
	Making an American Quilt		The Bat Sensory Cave	
	Somewhere in Africa		Chair for My Mother	
	Tiktala		What Do Moms Do?	
	Building a Dome		Construction Time	
	Constructing an Igluvigak	Mistaken Perceptions		
	Carving Experience		Picture Card Scramble	
	M is for Mom		Helpful Communication	
	Musical Find-a-Chair		Modem Pal	
	Omens and Signs			
	Abuela's Weave		Oral Motor Practice	
			Following Instructions	
		Patterns All Around		
		Yarn Pictures		
		Weaver's Booth Game	The Sharing Quilt	
			Story Scramble	
			Big Is Beautiful	
			What's Happening in This Picture?	
			Puppet Dreaming	

Annotated Literature Resource List: Anti-Bias Children's Books

1. Avery, M., & Avery, D. (1995). *What is beautiful?* Berkeley, CA: Tricycle Press.
   This book encourages children to recognize different forms of beauty in various individuals and to recognize their own beauty. Includes an attached mirror.
2. Badt, K. (1994). *A world of difference: Greetings.* Chicago: Children's Press.
   Exploration of social, political, religious greetings, and responses all over the world. This is part of a series that looks at the similarities and differences in shoes, food, bags, toys, transportation, places to sleep, musical instruments, etc.
3. Baer, E. (1995). *This is the way we eat our lunch.* New York: Scholastic Press.
   A taster's trip around the world, sampling all kinds of food children have for lunch.
4. Bailey, D. (1993). *Sisters.* Toronto, Canada: Annick Press.
   Board picture book for toddlers that explores the images of sisters together in daily life.
5. Bailey, D. (1994). *Grandpa.* Toronto, Canada: Annick Press.
   One of a series of board books aimed at celebrating different activities shared between infants and grandfathers in different cultures.
6. Bang, M. (1983). *Ten, nine, eight.* New York: Mulberry Books.
   Counting backwards, Black father and daughter share warm "math" times before bed.
7. Bear, G. (1991). *Two little girls lost in the bush.* Ahenaken, F., & Wolfart, H.C. (Ed.). Saskatoon, Canada: Fifth House Publishers.
   A true story told by a Cree grandmother about the time her little sister and she were lost for two days in the densely forested wilderness of northern Saskatchewan. The story is told in both Cree and English, and shows the self-reliance, strength, and wisdom of a little girl.
8. Benjamin, A. (1992). *Young Helen Keller: Woman of courage.* New York: Troll Associates.
   An easy-to-read biography about how, as a young child, Helen struggled to communicate and be understood.
9. Blaine, M. (1975). *The terrible thing that happened at our house.* New York: Scholastic Press.
   Mother goes back to work and rules change in the household.
10. Brynjolson, R. (1996). *Foster baby.* Winnipeg, Canada: Pemmican.
    Easy-to-read story describing what children need from families, plus detailed information for parents/teachers to answer questions about families.
11. Buritzer, E. (1994). *What is God?* Willowdale, Canada: Firefly Books.
    An exploration of different religions and beliefs around the world.
12. Burns-Knight, M. (1993). *Who belongs here? An American story.* Gardiner, ME: Tilbury House.
    Explores the implications of intolerance toward refugees by asking who would remain if all of our ancestors had been asked to leave the country?
13. Bursik, R. (1992). *Amelia's fantastic flight.* New York: Henry Holt and Company.
    Amelia uses her aviation skills and sense of adventure to fly to 14 countries around the world.
14. Caines, J. (1982). *Just us women.* New York: Harper Trophy.
    Aunt and niece plan and enjoy a special car trip all by themselves.
15. Carter, A. R. (1997). *Big brother Dustin.* Morton Grove, IL: Albert Whitman and Co.
    A book about Down's syndrome.
16. Chaikin, M. (1990). *Hanukkah.* New York: Holiday House.
    Available through the Children's Braille Book Club, this dual track braille/English picture book depicts the historical story of the origins of Hanukkah.
17. Clements, A. (1988). *Big Al.* New York: Scholastic Press.
    Big Al is a nice but scary-looking fish who has no friends because of his appearance. The story shows how he deals with discrimination.
18. Collins, B.A. (1992). *Clever sticks.* London: Walker Books.
    Ling Sung feels discouraged at school because he is unable to do the things other children can do. One day he uses his paintbrushes in a special way, evoking admiration from others.
19. Cooke, T. (1994). *So much.* London: Walker Books.
    Baby is visited by extended family members including aunts, uncles, grandparents, and cousins. All hug and play with the baby in an individual manner.
20. Cooper, M. (1995). *I got community.* New York: Henry Holt and Company.
    This book depicts different people and how they help one another within a community.
21. Cowan-Fletcher, J. (1993). *Mama zooms.* New York: Scholastic Books.
    Describes how a mother in a wheelchair takes care of her child.
22. Davol, M. (1993). *Black, white, just right.* Morton Grove, IL: Albert Whitman and Company.
    A girl explains how her parents are different colors, have different tastes in art, food, pets, and how she is different too.

23. De Luise, D. (1990). *Charlie the caterpillar.* New York: Simon and Schuster Books for Young Readers.
Young caterpillar meets animals who continuously refuse to play with him because they think he is ugly.
24. Dijs, C. (1990). *Are you my mommy?* New York: Simon & Schuster.
Explains in a fun way various types of family structures.
25. Dorling Kindersley Limited. (1992). *La hora de la comida.* U.S.: Dutton Children's Books.
Spanish board book about mealtimes for infants and toddlers.
26. Dwight, L. (1991). *Babies all around.* New York: Checkerboard Press.
Board book on typical infant/toddler activities depicting children of various races.
27. Dwight, L. (1992). *We can do it.* New York: Checkerboard Press.
This book tells the story of five children with special abilities and what they are able to do.
28. Ehlert, L. (1992). *Moon rope.* San Diego, CA: Harcourt, Brace, Jovanovich.
A dual text of English and Spanish.
29. Elwin, R., & Paulse, M. (1990). *Asha's mums.* Toronto, Canada: Women's Press.
Asha tries to explain to her classmates that her family comprises two mothers.
30. Eyvindson, P. (1986). *Old enough.* Winnipeg, Canada: Pemmican.
A father dreams about everything he will do with his newborn son only to realize too late that he has missed these opportunities.
31. Fahlman, R., & Graeme, J. (1990). *Hand in hand: Multicultural experiences for young children.* Toronto, Canada: Addison-Wesley.
Includes nine full-color children's books with a multicultural, multiracial mix of young children in contemporary Canadian communities. Books are written in English, French, Spanish, and Chinese.
32. Feder, J. (1995). *Table, chair, bear. A book in many languages.* Boston, MA: Houghton Mifflin Co.
Illustrations of objects found in a child's room and labeled in 13 different languages.
33. Friedman, I. (1984). *How my parents learned to eat.* Boston, MA: Houghton Mifflin Co.
Cultural similarities and differences are explored as a Japanese girl and an American sailor each secretly attempt to learn the other's way of eating.
34. Gilmore, R. (1995). *Lights for Gita.* Toronto, Canada: Second Story Press.
A story about the differences an Indian immigrant family experiences when they celebrate Diwali in a new country.
35. Greenfield, E. (1991). *Big friend, little friend.* New York: Black Butterfly Children's Books.
A child who is Black compares his relationships with his big and little friends.
36. Greenfield, E. (1991). *Daddy and I . . .* New York: Black Butterfly Children's Books.
A child who is Black does housework with his dad.
37. Greenfield, E. (1991). *I make music.* New York: Black Butterfly Children's Books.
A girl who is Black explores various ways to make music.
38. Greenfield, E. (1991). *My doll, Keshia.* New York: Black Butterfly Children's Books.
A girl who is Black talks about her doll.
39. Greenfield, M. (1994). *The baby.* New York: HarperCollins Children's Books.
The illustrations and simple text depict the everyday life of a baby who is Black.
40. Grimes, N. (1978). *Something on my mind.* New York: Dial Books.
Words and pictures reflect the thoughts and feelings of children who are Black.
41. Grobel, R. (1995). *Two eyes, a nose, and a mouth.* New York: Scholastic Books.
Facial features depicting individual uniqueness.
42. Grossnickle-Hines, A. (1986). *Daddy makes the best spaghetti.* New York: Clarion Books.
A look into a family sharing household tasks.
43. Harris, P. (1995). *Hot cold sky bold.* Toronto, Canada: Kids Can Press.
Opposites are explored through children and adult faces.
44. Haskins, F. (1992). *Things I like about grandma.* Emeryville, CA: Children Book Press.
An African-American girl tells of her close relationship with her grandma.
45. Hearn, E. (1992). *Good morning Franny.* Toronto, Canada: Women's Educational Press.
This is the story of Franny's adventures in a wheelchair with her friend Ting.
46. Henry, G. (1994). *Granny and me.* Toronto, Canada: Women's Press.
A child deals with the death of a grandmother with whom she shared many daily activities.
47. Hoya-Goldsmith, D. (1994). *Day of the dead, a Mexican-American celebration.* New York: Holiday House.
Exploration of All Soul's Day and the accompanying social customs and traditions of this celebration.
48. Hudson, W. (1993). *I love my family.* New York: Scholastic Books.
A story describing family members at a family reunion.
49. Igris, T. (1992). *When I was little.* East Orange, NJ: Just Us Books.
Grandpa reminisces about life when he was a boy, by telling grandson how different things were.
50. Ingle, A. (1992). *Rainbow babies.* New York: Random House.
This board book shows toddlers of various racial backgrounds at play.

51. James, B. (1994). *The mud family.* Toronto, Canada: Oxford University Press.
This story describes how Anasazi family life depended on rainfall.

52. Jaosse, B. (1991). *Mama, do you love me?* San Francisco: Chronicle Book.
Inuit children test the limits of independence as mother reassures that love is unconditional. The book explores Inuit culture.

53. Johnson, D. (1991). *What kind of babysitter is this?* New York: Scholastic Books.
Taking time to see what someone is really like helps dismantle stereotypes or assumptions.

54. Jukes, L. (1995). *I'm a girl.* Boca Raton, FL: Cool Kids Press.
Short simple statements describe what one can do as a female.

55. Kissinger, K. (1994). *All the colors we are.* St. Paul, MN: Redleaf Press.
Dual track scientific photo explanation of how children get their skin color.

56. Klassen, D. (1994). *I love to play hockey.* Winnipeg, Canada: Pemmican.
White and Native friends play and dream about playing hockey in the big league.

57. Kreisler, K., & Rotner, S. (1994). *Faces.* New York: Macmillan Publishing.
Different faces of children from all over the world depicted in photographs.

58. Kroll, V. (1995). *Hats off to hair.* Watertown, ME: Charlesbridge Publishing.
Children explore the many ways to style hair.

59. Kusugak, M. (1990). *Baseball bats for Christmas.* Toronto, Canada: Annick Press.
This book describes life in the high Arctic.

60. Kusugak, M. (1992). *Hide and sneak.* Toronto, Canada: Annick Press.
This Inuit story about a figure who hides children and loses them forever contains items and symbols significant to Inuit culture.

61. Lee, J. (1991). *Silent lotus.* New York: Farrar, Straus, Giroux.
Very gentle story about a nonverbal child.

62. Levine, E. (1989). *I hate English.* New York: Scholastic.
A touching story of a young immigrant girl from Hong Kong who learns she can have the best of two worlds by learning to communicate in two languages.

63. Liddell, S. (1994). *Being big.* Toronto, Canada: Second Story Press.
A story exploring being big and not fitting in with the class.

64. Lindsey, J. (1991). *Do I have a daddy?* Buena Park, CA: Morning Glory Press.
A story about a single-parent child. A special section for single mothers and fathers is included.

65. Litchfield, A. (1971). *A button in her ear.* Chicago, IL: Albert Whitman and Company.
A story dealing with hearing loss and hearing aids in a little girl's life.

66. Little, J. (1995). *Jenny and the Hanukkah queen.* New York: Penguin USA.
This book addresses Hanukkah and its traditions.

67. A Little Simon Book. (1988). *Let's eat.* New York: Simon & Schuster.
A dual track English/Spanish board book illustrating foods that toddlers like to eat.

68. Loewen, I. (1986). *My mom is so unusual.* Winnipeg, Canada: Pemmican.
A mother describes the stress and work experienced as a single parent.

69. Loewen, I. (1993). *My kokum called today.* Winnipeg, Canada: Pemmican.
Kokum, an elder, calls a young Native girl home to the reserve to experience the Round Dance. Explores gender roles of women holding community together, and offers glimpses into Native traditions.

70. Mandelbaum, P. (1990). *You be me, I'll be you.* New York: Kane/Miller Book Publishers.
Anna's sad; she wants white skin and straight hair like her dad. With the help of some coffee grinds and flour, Anna and her dad explore what it would be like to be each other.

71. McDermott, G. (1992). *Papagayo the mischief maker.* San Diego, CA: Harcourt, Brace, Jovanovich.
This book describes a South American legend.

72. McDermott, G. (1993). *Raven.* New York: Scholastic Press.
A tale from the Pacific Northwest describing the beginnings of existence.

73. Mendez, P. (1989). *The black snowman.* New York: Scholastic Press.
An African storytelling shawl with magical qualities builds a Black snowman.

74. Mennen, I., & Daly, N. (1990). *Somewhere in Africa.* New York: Dutton Children's Books.
This story debunks the stereotypical vision of Africa as a land only of lions and jungles.

75. Merrifield, M. (1990). *Come sit by me.* Toronto, Canada: Women's Press.
Children explore the significance of playing with a child who has AIDS.

76. Morris, A. (1992). *Bread, bread, bread.* New York: William Morrow and Company.
This book depicts different types of breads eaten throughout the world.

77. Morris, A. (1992). *Houses and homes.* New York: William Morrow and Company.
This book provides a photographic description of varying houses and homes found throughout the world.

78. Morris, A. (1994). *Loving*. New York: William Morrow and Company.
A pictorial account of families and friends throughout the world nurturing one another.

79. Morris, A. (1995). *Shoes, shoes, shoes*. New York: Lothrop, Lee and Shepard.
This book shows many different types of shoes worn by various people.

80. Morris, A. (1995). *Weddings*. New York: Lothrop, Lee and Shepard.
Rituals and ceremonies associated with weddings are described.

81. Munsch, R., & Askar, S. (1995). *From far away*. Toronto, Canada: Annick Press.
A child's perspective on immigration and adjustment to a new country is described.

82. Newman, L. (1989). *Heather has two mommies*. Boston, MA: Alyson Publishing.
This story tells the variety of family forms in children's lives today with a focus on same-sex parenting.

83. Newman, L. (1993). *Saturday is Pattyday*. Toronto, Canada: Women's Press.
Story of a child's life that becomes emotionally affected by her gay parents' divorcing.

84. Nikola-Lisa, W. (1995). *Being with you in this way*. New York: Lee and Low Books.
The book celebrates the differences in people.

85. Oberman, S. (1997). *The always prayer shawl*. New York: Puffin Book.
A prayer shawl is handed down from grandfather to son in the story of Jewish traditions and the passage of generations.

86. Ormerod, J. (1985). *Reading*. London: Walker Books.
This simple board book depicts a special relationship between a father and his baby. Others in series include *Sleeping*, and *Dad's Back*.

87. Owens, M. (1988). *A Caribou alphabet*. Willowdale, Canada: Firefly Books.
This book brings the world of the Caribou and life in the Arctic alive.

88. Oxenbury, H. (1983). *The dancing class*. London: Walker Books.
Children of different races and gender participate in a ballet class.

89. Oxenbury, H. (1987). *Say goodnight*. London: Walker Books.
This board book illustrates babies playing all day and then falling asleep.

90. Payne, L. (1994). *Just because I am. A child's book of affirmation*. MN: Free Spirit Publishing.
A book on self-perception and self-acceptance for young children.

91. Pegram, L. (1994). *Rainbow is our face*. New York: Black Butterfly Children's Books.
This board book illustrates two Black girls having a bath before bed and learning about the beauty of their skin.

92. Pennington, D. (1994). *Itse selu: Cherokee harvest festival*. Watertown, ME: Charlesbridge Publishers.
This book tells about a day in the life of Little Wolf in the ancient Cherokee village on the day of Green Corn Festival. It is written in words easily understood by school-aged children.

93. Pinknay, B. (1995). *Jojo's flying sidekick*. New York: Simon and Schuster Books.
A girl is ready to be tested for her yellow belt promotion.

94. Pinkney, A., & Pinkney, B. (1997). *Pretty brown face*. San Diego, CA: Harcourt Brace & Co.
A book about embracing self-identity for children who are Black.

95. Plain, F. (1994). *Grandfather drum*. Winnipeg, Canada: Pemmican.
A native story that reveals how the great white owl became what it is today.

96. Playskool. (1994). *Mealtime, bathtime, playtime, bedtime*. Canada: Hasbro Canada.

97. Playskool. (1994). *My nose, my toes*. London: Reed Children's Books.
This book shows body parts in large photographic form for babies and toddlers.

98. Polacco, P. (1988). *The keeping quilt*. New York: Simon and Schuster.
A Black boy, Jewish grandmother, and cat without a tail develop a warm, strong bond of friendship.

99. Polacco, P. (1992). *Mrs. Katz and Tush*. New York: Bantam Books.
A homemade quilt ties together the lives of four generations of an immigrant Jewish family, remaining a symbol of enduring love and faith.

100. Quinlan, P. (1987). *My dad takes care of me*. Toronto, Canada: Annick Press.
This book deals with gender role reversal as father stays home and mother goes to work.

101. Reid, S. (1992). *Grandpa Dan's toboggan ride*. Toronto, Canada: Scholastic Press.
A grandpa and grandson spend quality time together as an ordinary day in the park becomes an exciting adventure.

102. Reiser, L. (1993). *Margaret and Margarita*. New York: Greenwillow Books.
Margaret, who speaks English, and Margarita, who speaks only Spanish, meet in the park and have fun playing together despite the language barrier.

103. Ricklen, N. (1988). *Grandma and me*. New York: Simon and Schuster.
This board book illustrates active grandmothers in play with their grandchildren.

104. Ringgold, F. (1996). *Dinner at Aunt Connie's house*. New York: Hyperion Paperbacks for Children.
Two Black girls are introduced to 12 inspiring African-American women who instill a new sense of pride in their heritage.

105. Sadu, I. (1992). *Name calling.* Toronto, Canada: Well Versed Publication.
This story addresses the spread of name calling throughout a school and its final resolution.

106. Sanderson, E. (1990). *Two pairs of shoes.* Winnipeg, Canada: Pemmican.
A girl receives dress shoes and beaded moccasins from her blind grandmother. She must learn when and how to use each pair.

107. Schur, M. (1994). *Day of delight.* New York: Dial Books.
A Jewish Sabbath in Ethiopia is described.

108. Senisi, E. (1993). *Brothers and sisters.* New York: Scholastic Press.
This book explores sibling relationships and family life.

109. Shaw-Mackinnon, M. (1996). *Tiktala.* Toronto, Canada: Stoddard Publishing.
Explores Inuit beliefs, traditions, and the Arctic environment.

110. Shea, P. (1995). *The whispering cloth. A refugee's story.* Honesdale, PA: Boyds Mills Press.
A young girl in a Thai refugee camp in the mid-1970s finds the story within herself to create her own quilt amid discrimination and death.

111. Simon, N. (1976). *All kinds of families.* Chicago, IL: Albert Whitman and Company.
The meaning of families and how each family is different is explored.

112. Slier, D. (1991). *Me and my grandma.* New York: Checkerboard Press.
A board book describing the loving relationships between infants and grandmothers of various racial backgrounds.

113. Slier, D. (1991). *Me and my grandpa.* New York: Checkerboard Press.
A board book describing the loving relationships between infants and grandfathers of various racial backgrounds.

114. Slieszka, J., & Smith, L. (1992). *The stinky cheese man and other fairly stupid tales.* New York: Scholastic Press.
This book provides a spoof on fairy tales and challenges stereotypes.

115. Smith, L. (1991). *Glasses, who needs 'em.* New York: Penguin Books.
This picture book deals with the problem of a reluctant child's first pair of glasses.

116. Teague, K. (1990). *Arms and legs.* Toronto, Canada: Editions Renyi.
A dual language text looks at a variety of children's arms and legs.

117. Teague, K. (1990). *Faces.* Toronto, Canada: Editions Renyi.
A book with Hindi and English text looks at a variety of children's faces. Other books in the series combine English with other languages.

118. Thomas, R., & Stutchbury, J. (1991). *Skin and hair.* Toronto, Canada: Irvin Publishing.
A scientific picture book showing the functions of skin and hair for all people.

119. Torres, L. (1993). *Subway sparrow.* New York: Farrar, Straus and Giroux.
Theme of cooperation is explored as people of different ages, gender, and cultures work together to save a sparrow.

120. Valentine, J. (1994). *One dad, two dad, brown dad, blue dad.* Boston, MA: Alyson Wonderland.
This book explores family composition with a focus on same-sex parenting.

121. Walker, J. (1993). *In other words.* Toronto, Canada: Annick Press.
A story about children who do not communicate verbally.

122. Weiss, G. (1967). *What a wonderful world.* New York: Simon & Schuster.
The song made famous by Louis B. Armstrong is illustrated and retold.

123. Wheeler, B. (1993). *I can't have bannock but the beaver has a dam.* Winnipeg, Canada: Penguin Publishing.
This is a story about the making of bannock and how the beaver delayed it.

124. Williams, V. (1990). *More, more, more said the baby.* New York: Greenwillow Books.
A book about three babies and the adults who love them.

125. Willis-Hudson, C. (1990). *Bright eyes, brown skin.* East Orange, NJ: Just Us Books.
Four young children enjoy activities of a typical day with confidence, happiness, and good self-esteem.

126. Willis-Hudson, C. (1992). *Good night, baby.* East Orange, NJ: Scholastic Press, 1992.
This board book for infants and toddlers uses the image of an African-American baby in its depiction of the beginning of a new day.

127. Wing, N. (1996). *Jalapeno bagels.* New York: Atheneum Books for Young Readers.
A story about a bicultural family.

128. Ziefert, H. (1992). *Where's Mommy's truck?* New York: HarperCollins.
A story about a mother who drives a truck.

LITERATURE RESOURCE LIST: ANTI-BIAS CHILDREN'S BOOKS

Titles correspond to the Annotated Literature Resource List beginning on page 333 and indicate areas of bias represented.

TITLE	AUTHOR	AREAS OF BIAS									
		AB	AG	AP	BEL	CLS	CUL	FC	GEN	R	SX
1. *WHAT IS BEAUTIFUL?*	AVERY M. & D.			X					X		
2. *A WORLD OF DIFFERENCE: GREETINGS*	BADT K.						X		X	X	
3. *THIS IS THE WAY WE EAT OUR LUNCH*	BAER E.						X				
4. *SISTERS*	BAILEY D.								X	X	
5. *GRANDPA*	BAILEY D.		X				X			X	
6. *TEN, NINE, EIGHT*	BANG M.								X	X	
7. *TWO LITTLE GIRLS LOST IN THE BUSH*	BEAR G.						X		X		
8. *YOUNG HELEN KELLER: WOMAN OF COURAGE*	BENJAMIN A.	X							X		
9. *THE TERRIBLE THING THAT HAPPENED AT OUR HOUSE*	BLAINE M.								X		
10. *FOSTER BABY*	BRYNJOLSON R.						X	X			
11. *WHAT IS GOD?*	BURITZER E.				X						
12. *WHO BELONGS HERE? AN AMERICAN STORY*	BURNS-KNIGHT M.						X	X			
13. *AMELIA'S FANTASTIC FLIGHT*	BURSIK R.								X		
14. *JUST US WOMEN*	CAINES J.								X		
15. *BIG BROTHER DUSTIN*	CARTER A.	X									
16. *HANUKKAH*	CHAIKIN M.	X			X		X				
17. *BIG AL*	CLEMENTS A.			X							
18. *CLEVER STICKS*	COLLINS B.A.						X			X	
19. *SO MUCH*	COOKE T.							X		X	
20. *I GOT COMMUNITY*	COOPER M.								X	X	
21. *MAMA ZOOMS*	COWAN-FLETCHER J.	X						X			
22. *BLACK, WHITE, JUST RIGHT*	DAVOL M.									X	
23. *CHARLIE THE CATERPILLAR*	DE LUISE D.			X							
24. *ARE YOU MY MOMMY?*	DIJS C.							X			
25. *LA HORA DE LA COMIDA*	DORLING KINDERSLEY LIMITED						X			X	
26. *BABIES ALL AROUND*	DWIGHT L.									X	
27. *WE CAN DO IT*	DWIGHT L.	X						X			
28. *MOON ROPE*	EHLERT L.						X			X	
29. *ASHA'S MUMS*	ELWIN R. and PAULSE M.							X			X
30. *OLD ENOUGH*	EYVINDSON P.		X						X		
31. *HAND IN HAND: MULTICULTURAL EXPERIENCES FOR YOUNG CHILDREN*	FAHLMAN R. & GRAEME J.			X	X		X		X	X	
32. *TABLE, CHAIR, BEAR. A BOOK IN MANY LANGUAGES*	FEDER J.						X				
33. *HOW MY PARENTS LEARNED TO EAT*	FRIEDMAN I.						X	X			

LITERATURE RESOURCE LIST: ANTI-BIAS CHILDREN'S BOOKS *(continued)*

TITLE	AUTHOR	AREAS OF BIAS									
		AB	AG	AP	BEL	CLS	CUL	FC	GEN	R	SX
34. *LIGHTS FOR GITA*	GILMORE R.				X		X				
35. *BIG FRIEND, LITTLE FRIEND*	GREENFIELD E.								X	X	
36. *DADDY AND I . . .*	GREENFIELD E.							X	X	X	
37. *I MAKE MUSIC*	GREENFIELD E.						X		X	X	
38. *MY DOLL, KESHIA*	GREENFIELD, E.								X	X	
39. *THE BABY*	GREENFIELD E.								X	X	
40. *SOMETHING ON MY MIND*	GRIMES N.									X	
41. *TWO EYES, A NOSE, AND A MOUTH*	GROBEL R.									X	
42. *DADDY MAKES THE BEST SPAGHETTI*	GROSSNICKLE-HINES A.								X		
43. *HOT COLD SKY BOLD*	HARRIS P.									X	
44. *THINGS I LIKE ABOUT GRANDMA*	HASKINS F.		X			X		X		X	
45. *GOOD MORNING FRANNY*	HEARN E.	X					X				
46. *GRANNY AND ME*	HENRY G.	X					X		X		
47. *DAY OF THE DEAD, A MEXICAN-AMERICAN CELEBRATION*	HOYA-GOLDSMITH D.				X						
48. *I LOVE MY FAMILY*	HUDSON W.							X		X	
49. *WHEN I WAS LITTLE*	IGRIS T.		X							X	
50. *RAINBOW BABIES*	INGLE A.									X	
51. *THE MUD FAMILY*	JAMES B.						X				
52. *MAMA, DO YOU LOVE ME?*	JAOSSE B.						X				
53. *WHAT KIND OF BABYSITTER IS THIS?*	JOHNSON D.		X						X	X	
54. *I'M A GIRL*	JUKES L.								X		
55. *ALL THE COLORS WE ARE*	KISSINGER K.									X	
56. *I LOVE TO PLAY HOCKEY*	KLASSEN D.									X	
57. *FACES*	KREISLER K. & ROTNER S.									X	
58. *HATS OFF TO HAIR*	KROLL V.						X		X	X	
59. *BASEBALL BATS FOR CHRISTMAS*	KUSUGAK M.A.				X		X			X	
60. *HIDE AND SNEAK*	KUSUGAK M.A.						X		X		
61. *SILENT LOTUS*	LEE J.	X									
62. *I HATE ENGLISH*	LEVINE E.						X			X	
63. *BEING BIG*	LIDDELL S.			X							
64. *DO I HAVE A DADDY?*	LINDSEY J.						X				
65. *A BUTTON IN HER EAR*	LITCHFIELD A.	X							X		
66. *JENNY AND THE HANUKKAH QUEEN*	LITTLE J.				X		X				
67. *LET'S EAT*	A LITTLE SIMON BOOK						X				

LITERATURE RESOURCE LIST: ANTI-BIAS CHILDREN'S BOOKS *(continued)*

TITLE	AUTHOR	AREAS OF BIAS									
		AB	AG	AP	BEL	CLS	CUL	FC	GEN	R	SX
68. *MY MOM IS SO UNUSUAL*	LOEWEN I.							X		X	
69. *MY KOKUM CALLED TODAY*	LOEWEN I.		X				X				
70. *YOU BE ME, I'LL BE YOU*	MANDELBAUM P.						X	X		X	
71. *PAPAGAYO THE MISCHIEF MAKER*	MCDERMOTT G.						X				
72. *RAVEN*	MCDERMOTT G.				X		X	X			
73. *THE BLACK SNOWMAN*	MENDEZ P.									X	
74. *SOMEWHERE IN AFRICA*	MENNEN I. & DALY N.						X			X	
75. *COME SIT BY ME*	MERRIFIELD M.	X									
76. *BREAD, BREAD, BREAD*	MORRIS A.					X	X				
77. *HOUSES AND HOMES*	MORRIS A.						X				
78. *LOVING*	MORRIS A.						X		X	X	
79. *SHOES, SHOES, SHOES*	MORRIS A.						X				
80. *WEDDINGS*	MORRIS A.				X		X				
81. *FROM FAR AWAY*	MUNSCH R. & ASKAR S.						X				
82. *HEATHER HAS TWO MOMMIES*	NEWMAN L.							X			X
83. *SATURDAY IS PATTYDAY*	NEWMAN L.							X			X
84. *BEING WITH YOU IN THIS WAY*	NIKOLA-LISA W.			X					X	X	
85. *THE ALWAYS PRAYER SHAWL*	OBERMAN S.				X		X	X			
86. *READING*	ORMEROD J.								X		
87. *A CARIBOU ALPHABET*	OWENS M.						X				
88. *THE DANCING CLASS*	OXENBURY H.								X	X	
89. *SAY GOODNIGHT*	OXENBURY H.									X	
90. *JUST BECAUSE I AM. A CHILD'S BOOK OF AFFIRMATION*	PAYNE L.			X			X			X	
91. *RAINBOW IS OUR FACE*	PEGRAM L.									X	
92. *ITSE SELU: CHEROKEE HARVEST FESTIVAL*	PENNINGTON D.				X		X				
93. *JOJO'S FLYING SIDEKICK*	PINKNAY B.								X		
94. *PRETTY BROWN FACE*	PINKNEY A. & B.						X			X	
95. *GRANDFATHER DRUM*	PLAIN F.		X				X				
96. *MEALTIME, BATHTIME, PLAYTIME, BEDTIME*	PLAYSKOOL						X				
97. *MY NOSE, MY TOES*	PLAYSKOOL									X	
98. *THE KEEPING QUILT*	POLACCO P.		X				X	X		X	
99. *MRS. KATZ AND TUSH*	POLACCO P.	X	X		X	X	X	X		X	
100. *MY DAD TAKES CARE OF ME*	QUINLAN P.								X		
101. *GRANDPA DAN'S TOBOGGAN RIDE*	REID S.		X								

LITERATURE RESOURCE LIST: ANTI-BIAS CHILDREN'S BOOKS *(continued)*

TITLE	AUTHOR	AREAS OF BIAS									
		AB	AG	AP	BEL	CLS	CUL	FC	GEN	R	SX
102. *MARGARET AND MARGARITA*	REISER L.						X			X	
103. *GRANDMA AND ME*	RICKLEN N.		X							X	
104. *DINNER AT AUNT CONNIE'S HOUSE*	RINGGOLD F.						X			X	
105. *NAME CALLING*	SADU I.						X			X	
106. *TWO PAIRS OF SHOES*	SANDERSON E.	X	X				X				
107. *DAY OF DELIGHT*	SCHUR M.R.				X		X				
108. *BROTHERS AND SISTERS*	SENISI E.B.	X	X					X	X	X	
109. *TIKTALA*	SHAW-MACKINNON M.						X				
110. *THE WHISPERING CLOTH: A REFUGEE'S STORY*	SHEA P.						X			X	
111. *ALL KINDS OF FAMILIES*	SIMON N.						X	X		X	
112. *ME AND MY GRANDMA*	SLIER D.		X							X	
113. *ME AND MY GRANDPA*	SLIER D.		X							X	
114. *THE STINKY CHEESE MAN AND OTHER FAIRLY STUPID TALES*	SLIESZKA J. & SMITH L.			X							
115. *GLASSES WHO NEEDS EM*	SMITH L.	X									
116. *ARMS AND LEGS*	TEAGUE K.						X			X	
117. *FACES*	TEAGUE K.						X			X	
118. *SKIN AND HAIR*	THOMAS R. and STUTCHBURY J.									X	
119. *SUBWAY SPARROW*	TORRES L.		X				X		X		
120. *ONE DAD, TWO DADS, BROWN DAD, BLUE DAD*	VALENTINE J.							X			X
121. *IN OTHER WORDS*	WALKER J.	X									
122. *WHAT A WONDERFUL WORLD*	WEISS G.		X				X			X	
123. *I CAN'T HAVE BANNOCK BUT THE BEAVER HAS A DAM*	WHEELER B.						X	X		X	
124. *MORE, MORE, MORE SAID THE BABY*	WILLIAMS V.						X			X	
125. *BRIGHT EYES, BROWN SKIN*	WILLIS-HUDSON C.									X	
126. *GOOD NIGHT, BABY*	WILLIS-HUDSON C.									X	
127. *JALAPENO BAGELS*	WING N.				X		X				
128. *WHERE'S MOMMY'S TRUCK?*	ZIEFERT H.								X		

BRAILLE GUIDE

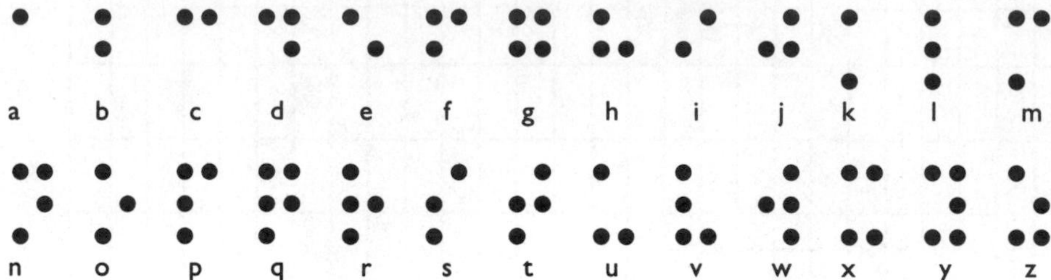

When the number sign appears before the symbols for *a* through *j* that means that the character after it is a number and not a letter.

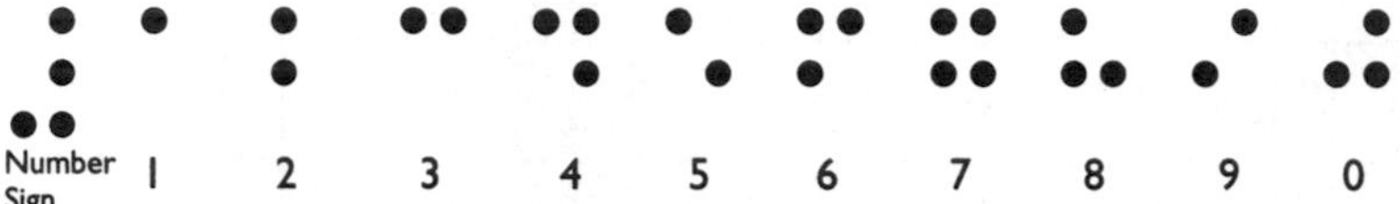

AMERICAN MANUAL ALPHABET

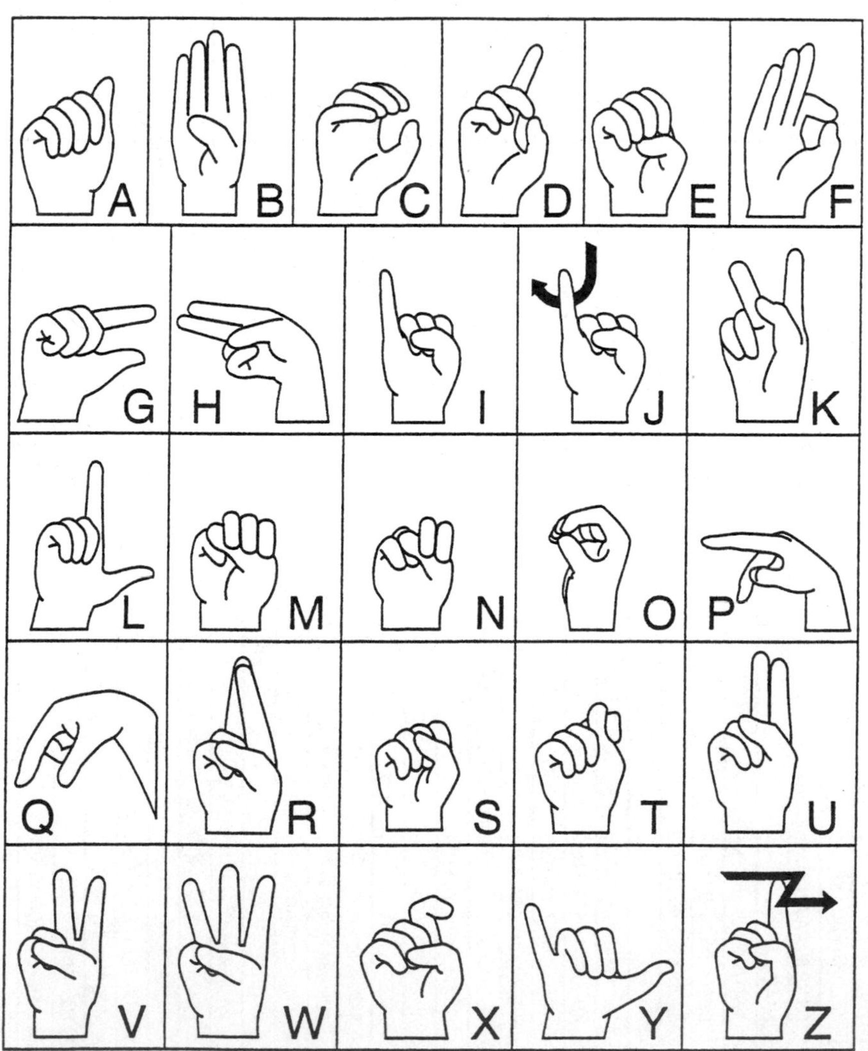

NUMBERS—AMERICAN MANUAL ALPHABET

1	2	3	4	5
6	7	8	9	10
11	12	13	14	15
20	21	30	40	50
60	70	80	90	100

EXAMPLES OF SIGNED ENGLISH

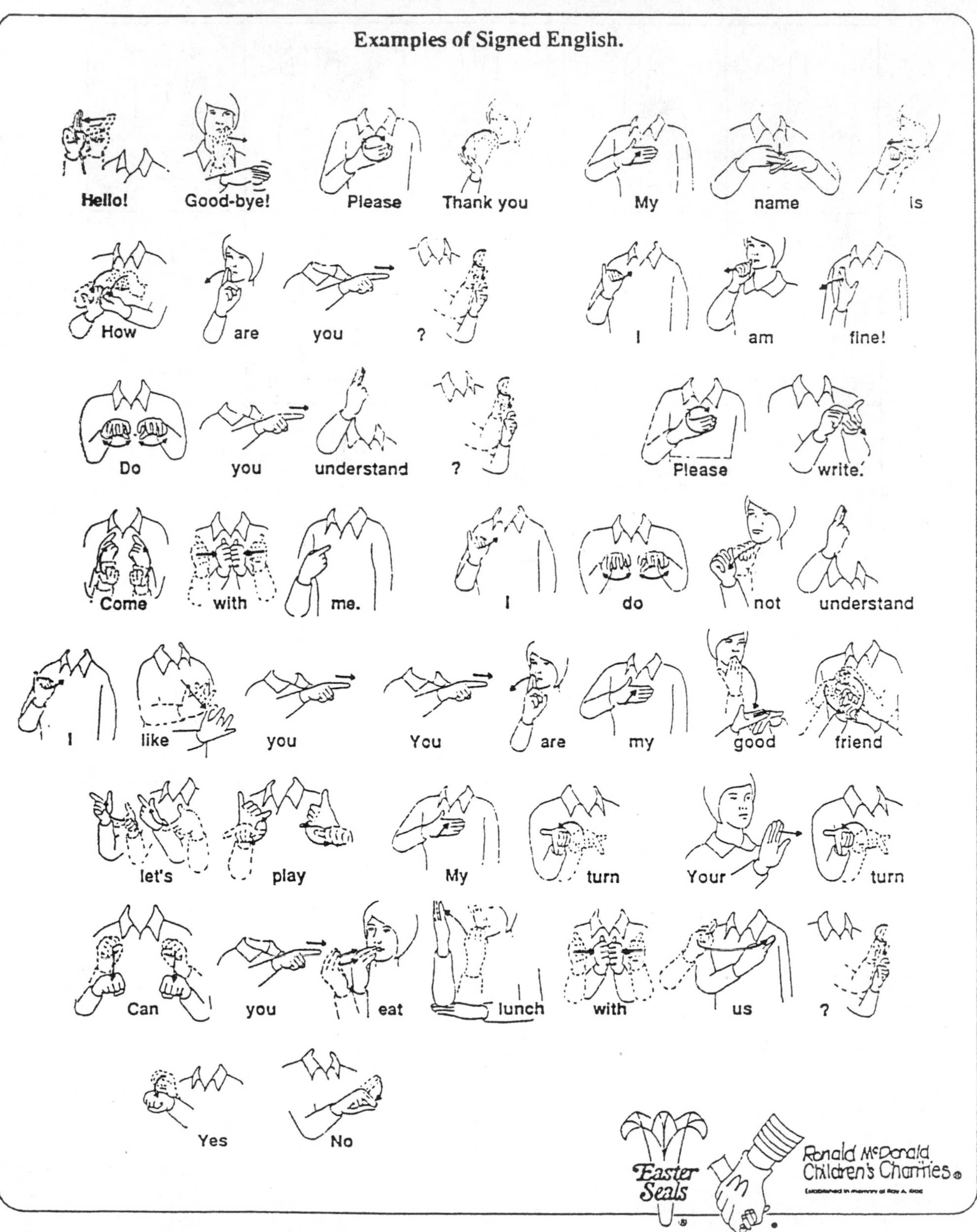

ABORIGINAL ART SYMBOLS

Campsite, Hill, Digging hole, Waterhole

Person sitting, Windbreak

Boomerang, Clouds, Rainbow

Spear, Digging Stick

Snake, Smoke, Water flow, Lightning

River, Bushfire

Rain, Ants, Eggs

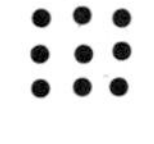

Rain

Path, Track, Bodypaint

Footprints

Coolamon (carrying dish), Shield

Spear thrower

PIC SYMBOLS

bathtub
beanbag chair
bunk beds
carpet
chair
cupboard
drawer
fireplace
lounge chair
recliner
toilet

Teacher Resources

Teacher Resources fall into three primary categories:

1. equipment, toys, materials;
2. books (theoretical and practical); and
3. organizations and publications.

This appendix provides information on equipment and organizations. Bibliographies of anti-bias/diversity education materials have been collected by numerous other authors:

Neugebauer, B. (Ed.). (1992). *Alike and different. Exploring our humanity with young children.* (rev. ed.). Washington, DC: National Association for the Education of Young Children.

Saderman Hall, N., and Rhomberg, V. (1995). *The affective curriculum: Teaching the anti-bias approach to young children.* Toronto, Canada: Nelson Canada.

Chud, G. and Fahlman, R. (1995). *Honouring diversity within child care and early education.* 2 Vols. British Columbia, Canada: Ministry of Skills, Training, and Labour and the Centre for Curriculum and Professional Development.

Teaching Materials

Most of the following early childhood educational supply companies offer multicultural, multiracial, nonsexist, and special needs equipment and resources. The author does not endorse specific materials available for purchase from these catalog companies. Use discretion when evaluating the materials. Some items might be accurate in representing racial features but stereotypical in depicting gender roles. Be vigilant and alert for newer, smaller companies that often will respond to educators' needs in this area. This listing includes a number of such specialty resources.

Afro-American Publishing Company
819 Wabash Avenue, South
Chicago, IL 60605
(312) 922-1147

American Indian Resource Center
6518 Miles Avenue
Huntington Park, CA 90255
(213) 583-1461

ARTS Inc. (also known as Arts Resources for Teachers and Students)
134 Henry Street
New York, NY 10002
(212) 962-8231

Childcraft
2920 Old Tree Drive
Lancaster, PA 17603
1-800-631-5652

Childscope
91 Armstrong Avenue
Georgetown, ON L7G 4S1
1-800-668-4302

Childswork/Childsplay
Center for Applied Psychology, Inc.
P.O. Box 1586
King of Prussia, PA 19406
1-800-962-1141

Community Playthings and Rifton Equipment for the Handicapped
Box 901
Rifton, NY 12471-0901
1-800-777-4244

Communication/Therapy Skill Builders
Early Intervention Materials
Psychological Corporation
Box 839954
San Antonio, TX 78283-3954
(210) 299-1061

Constructive Playthings
1227 East 119th Street
Grandview, MO 64030-1117
1-800-448-4115

Creative Educational Surplus
9801 James Circle, Suite C
Bloomington, MN 55431
1-800-886-6428

Early Childhood Multicultural Services
#201-1675 West 4th Avenue
Vancouver, BC V6J 1L8
(604) 739-9456

Faces: The Magazine About People
Cobblestone Publishing
7 School Street
Peterborough, NH 03458-14101
(603) 924-7209

Gryphon House
Box 275
Mt. Rainer, MD 20712
1-800-638-0928

Kaplan
P.O. Box 609
1310 Lewisville-Clemmons Road
Lewisville, NC 27023-0609
1-800-334-2014

Kimbo's Educational Records and Cassettes
10 North Third Avenue
Long Branch, NJ 07740
1-800-631-2187

Lakeshore Learning Materials
P.O. Box 6261
2695 E. Dominguez Street
Carson, CA 90749
1-800-421-5354

Music for Little People
P.O. Box 1460
Redway, CA 95560
1-800-346-4445

People of Every Stripe
P.O. Box 12505
Portland, OR 97212
(503) 282-0612

Pueblo to People
P.O. Box 2545
Houston, TX 77252-2545

Redleaf Press
450 North Syndicate
Suite 5
St. Paul, MN 55104-4125
(612) 641-6629

Roylco
30 Northland Road
Waterloo, ON N2V 1Y1
(519) 885-0451

Sandy and Son Educational Supplies
1360 Cambridge Street
Cambridge, MA 02139
1-800-841-7529

Snailbrush
7668 Settler's Way
North Gower, ON K0A 2T0
(613) 258-7491

Tree Huggers
501 Palmerston Boulevard
Toronto, ON M6G 2P2
(416) 516-8444

Weston Woods Press
389 New Town Turnpike
Weston, CT 06883-1199
1-800-243-5020

Wintergreen
14 Connie Crescent, Unit 10
Concord, ON L4K 2W8
1-800-268-1268

Organizations and Publications

Resources Promoting Awareness of Native Americans and Canadians

American Indian Curricula Development Program
c/o United Tribes Technical College
3315 University Drive
Bismarck, ND 58501

Anishinabe Reading Materials
Duluth Indian Education Advisory Committee
Independent School District
709 Lake Avenue and Second Street
Duluth, MN 55802

Department of Education
Offices of Indian Education
Washington, DC

Department of Indian Affairs
and Northern Development
10 Wellington Street
Hull, Quebec K1A OH4
(819) 997-0811

Grand Council of the Crees of Quebec
24 Baywater Avenue
Ottawa, ON K1Y 2E4
(613) 761-1655

Inuit Tapirisat of Canada
170 Laurier Avenue West
Suite 510
Ottawa, ON K1P 5V5
(613) 238-8181

Native American Center for the Living Arts, Inc.
25 Rainbow Mall
Niagara Falls, NY 14303

Native American Materials
Development Center
407 Rio Grande Boulevard NW
Albuquerque, NM 87104

Native American Research Information Service
University of Oklahoma
555 Constitution Street, Room 237
Norman, OK 73037

Native Council of Canada
2-384 Bank Street
Ottawa, ON K2P 1Y4
(613) 238-3511

Native Women's Association of Canada
9 Melrose Avenue
Ottawa, ON K1Y 1T8
(613) 722-3033

Navajo Curriculum Development and Production Center
Box 587, Chinle Unified School
District No 24
Chinle, AZ 86503

United Indians of All Tribes Foundation
Community Educational Services
Discovery Park, P.O. Box 99100
Seattle, WA 98199 (206) 285-4425

Resources for Children with Special Needs

Clearinghouse on Handicapped and Gifted Children
The Council for Exceptional Children
1920 Association Drive
Reston, VA 22901-1589

National Center for Infants, Toddlers and Families
734 15th Street NW
Washington, DC 20005
(202) 638-1144

The Braille Book Club
National Braille Press
88 St. Stephen Street
Boston, MA 02115
(617) 266-6160

National Info Center on Deafness
Gallaudet University
800 Florida Avenue NE
Washington, DC 20002-3695

Resources for Multiracial, Multicultural, and Gender Education

American Association of University Women
1111 16th Street NW
Washington, DC 20036-4873
1-800-225-9998

Association for Multicultural Counseling and Development
5999 Stevenson Avenue
Alexandria, VA 22304
(703) 823-9800

Association of Multiethnic Americans
1060 Tennessee Street
San Francisco, CA 94107
(415) 548-9300

Bias-Free Early Childhood Services
3495 Lawrence Avenue East, Suite 202
Scarborough, ON M1H 1B3
(416) 439-6392

Canadian International Development Agency (CIDA)
200 Promenade du Portage
Hull, Quebec K1A 0G4
(613) 997-5456

Center for Interracial Unity
3208 South State Road
Davison, MI 48423
(313) 653-5033

Council on Interracial Books for Children
1841 Broadway
New York, NY 10023
(212) 757-5339

Congress of Black Women
590 Gerrard Street E
Toronto, ON M4M 1Y3
(416) 961-2427

Cross Cultural Communication Centre
2909 Dundas Street W
Toronto, ON M6P 1Z1
(416) 760-7855

Cultural Links: A Multicultural Resource Guide
Multicultural Project for Communication and Education
186 Lincoln Street
Boston, MA 02111
(617) 492-1063

Early Childhood Diversity Network Canada
229 Hillcrest Avenue
Willowdale, ON M2N 3P3
(416) 221-6434

Education Equity Concepts
114 East 32nd Street
New York, NY 10016
(212) 725-1803

Information Center on Children's Cultures
United States Committee for UNICEF
331 East 38th Street
New York, NY 10016
(212) 686-5522

Institute for Peace and Justice
4144 Lindell, Room 122
St. Louis, MO 63108
(314) 533-4445

Interracial Family Alliance, National Headquarters
P.O. Box 16248
Houston, TX 77222
(713) 586-8949

National Black Child Development Institute
11023 15th Street NW, Suite 600
Washington, DC 20005
(202) 387-1281

National Council for Research on Women
530 Broadway, 10th Floor
New York, NY 10012
(212) 274-0730

Ontario Women's Directorate
2 Carlton Avenue, 12th Floor
Toronto, ON M5B 1J3
(416) 979-5000 Ext. 7647

UN High Commissioner for Refugees
280 Albert Street, Suite 401
Ottawa, ON K1P 5G8
(613) 232-8691

Urban Alliance on Race Relations
675 King Street, Suite 202
Toronto, ON M5V 1M9
(416) 703-6607

Women's Action Alliance
370 Lexington Avenue
New York, NY 10017
(212) 532-8330

Women's Educational Equity Act Publishing Center
Education Development Center
55 Chapel Street, Suite 222
Newton, MA 02158-1060
1-800-225-3088

Bibliography

Beck, B. (1965). *The first book of the ancient Maya.* New York: Franklin Watts, Inc.

Bosak, S. (1991). *Science is . . .* (2nd ed.). Richmond Hill and Markham, ON: Scholastic Canada and the Communication Project.

Bowman, B. T., & Stott, F. M. (1994). Understanding development in a cultural context. In B. Mallory and R. New (Eds.), *Diversity and developmentally appropriate practices* (pp. 119–133). New York: Teachers College Press.

Bowyer, C. (1978). *A children's book on houses and homes.* London: Usborne Publication.

Bright ideas. Teacher handbooks. Language resources. (1987). Warwickshire, England: Scholastic Press.

Cech, M. (1990). *The global child: Multicultural resources for young children.* Ottawa, Canada: Heath and Welfare Canada.

Cech, M. (1996). *Global sense.* Menlo Park, CA: Innovative Learning Publications.

Children of the world series. Milwaukee, WI: Gareth Stevens Publishing.

Chud, G. (1993). Anti-bias education: An approach for today and tomorrow. *Interaction, 7* (2), pp. 18–20.

Clark, L., DeWolf, S., & Clark, C. (1992). Teaching teachers to avoid having culturally assaultive classrooms. *Young Children, 47* (5), 4–9.

Clements, D., Gilliland, C., & Holko, P. (1992). *Thinking in themes.* Melbourne, Australia: Oxford University Press.

The common curriculum. Policies and outcomes grades 1–9. New foundations for Ontario education. (1995). Toronto, Canada: Ministry of Education and Training.

The complexities of childhood. (1982). Chart prepared by M. Taylor, C. McIntyre, & M. Wood. Ontario, Canada: Ministry of Education.

Dalton, J. (1985). *Adventures in thinking: Creative thinking and cooperative talk in small groups.* Melbourne, Australia: Nelson.

de Cou-Landberg, M. (1994). *The global classroom* (Vol. 1). Reading, MA: Addison-Wesley Publishing.

Derman-Sparks, L. (1992). Reaching potentials through anti-bias, multicultural curriculum. In S. Bredekamp and T. Rosegrant (Eds.), *Reaching potentials: Appropriate curriculum and assessment for young children* (Vol. 1). Washington, DC: National Association for the Education of Young Children.

Derman-Sparks, L., and the A.B.C. Task Force (1989). *The Anti-bias curriculum: Tools for empowering young children.* Washington, DC: National Association for the Education of Young Children.

Derman-Sparks, L., et al. (1980). "Children, race and racism: How race awareness develops," *Interracial Books for Children Bulletin, 11,* (3 & 4), 3–9.

Dowton, K. (1983). *Working with themes: Ideas across the curriculum.* Melbourne, Australia: Primary Education/Nelson.

Dunkling, L. (1974). *The Guinness book of names.* Enfield, England: Guinness Superlatives.

The early years portfolio guide. (1993–1994). Toronto, Canada: Board of Education.

Ellis, J. (1991). *From the dreamtime. Australian Aboriginal legends.* Victoria, Australia: Collins Dove.

Friends with care. Disabilities worksheets. Toronto, Canada.

Gallaudet College Press. (1983). *Signed English. The comprehensive dictionary.* Washington, DC: Kendall Green Publications.

Gestwicki, C. (1995). *Developmentally appropriate practice: curriculum and development in early education.* Albany, NY: Delmar.

Goddesses, heroes and shamans. A young people's guide to world mythology. (1994). New York: Kingfisher.

Goleman, D. (1995). *Emotional intelligence.* New York: Bantam Books.

Gomez, A. (1992). *Crafts of many cultures.* New York: Scholastic Professional Books.

Gonzalez-Mena, J. (1993). *Multicultural issues in child care.* Mountain View, CA: Mayfield Publishing Company.

Hayes, L. (1991). *A fountain of language development for E.C.E. and the special child, too.* New York: Vantage Press.

Kindersley, B., & Kindersley, A. (1995). *Children just like me: A unique celebration of children around the world.* Australia: UNICEF and Moondrake and London: Dorling Kindersley Ltd.

Land of the long white cloud. Maori myths, tales, and legends. (1989). Retold by K. Te Kanawa. Auckland, New Zealand: Penguin Books.

Maslow, A. (1954). *Motivation and personality.* New York: Harper and Row.

Matterson, E. (Ed.). (1969). *This little puffin . . . Finger plays and nursery games.* Harmondsworth, England: Kestrel Books.

Mayer-Johnson. (1992). *The picture communication symbols.* Books 1, 2, 3. Solana Beach, CA: Mayer-Johnson Company.

Miller, J. (1988). *Sharing ideas. An oral language programme.* Melbourne, Australia: Nelson.

Neaman, E. (Ed.). (1992). *Folk rhymes from around the world.* Vancouver, Canada: Pacific Educational Press.

New, R. S. (1994). Culture, child development, and developmentally appropriate practices: Teachers as collaborative researchers. In B. Mallory and R. New (Eds.), *Diversity and developmentally appropriate practices* (pp. 65–83). New York: Teachers College Press.

Ramsey, P. (1987). *Teaching and learning in a diverse world: Multicultural education for young children.* New York: Teachers College Press.

Reynolds, J. (1993). *Frozen land. Vanishing culture.* San Diego, CA: Harcourt, Brace and Co.

Robinson, M. (1992). Parenting a child with special needs. In B. Neugebauer (Ed.), *Alike and different.* (pp. 108–114). Washington, DC: National Association for the Education of Young Children.

Shemie, B. (1989). *Houses of snow, skin and bones. Native dwellings: The far north.* Montreal, Canada: Tundra Books.

Siska, H. (1980). *People of the ice: How the Inuit lived.* Vancouver, Canada: Douglas & McIntyre.

Stonehouse, A. (1991). *Opening the doors: Child care in multicultural society.* Watson, Australia: Australian Early Childhood Association Inc.

Tell me about your family. Learning and study guide. (1994). Canada Committee for the International Year of the Family. Ottawa, Canada: Vanier Institute of the Family.

Te whariki. Draft guidelines for developmentally appropriate programmes in early childhood services. (1993). Wellington, New Zealand: Ministry of Education. Learning Media Ltd.

Thornburg, P., & Thornburg, D. (1989). *The thinker's tool box: A practical and easy approach to creative thinking.* Palo Alto, CA: Dale Seymour Publications.

Warren, R. (1977). *Caring.* Washington, DC: National Association for the Education of Young Children.

Wattle Park Teacher's Centre. (July 1978). *Lively learning centres.* Wattle Park, New Zealand.

Williams, S. (1983). *Round and round the garden.* Oxford, England: Oxford University Press.

Wilson, R. (1986). *100 dinosaurs from A to Z.* New York: Grosset and Dunlap.

Wood, B. (1991). *When cultures meet.* Auckland, New Zealand: Longman Paul Ltd.

Yolen, J. (Ed.). (1994). *Sleep rhymes around the world.* Honesdale, PA: Boyds Mills Press.

York, S. (1992). *Developing roots and wings. A trainer's guide to affirming culture in early childhood programs.* St. Paul, MN: Redleaf Press.

Index

Activities listed by subject area and by age group as indicated.